MW00462678

COWBOY CONSERVATISM

NEW DIRECTIONS IN SOUTHERN HISTORY

SERIES EDITORS
Peter S. Carmichael, *West Virginia University*
Michele Gillespie, *Wake Forest University*
William A. Link, *University of Florida*

The Lost State of Franklin: America's First Secession
Kevin T. Barksdale

Bluecoats and Tar Heels:
Soldiers and Civilians in Reconstruction North Carolina
Mark L. Bradley

Becoming Bourgeois: Merchant Culture in the South, 1820–1865
Frank J. Byrne

Lum and Abner: Rural America and the Golden Age of Radio
Randal L. Hall

Entangled by White Supremacy:
Reform in World War I–era South Carolina
Janet G. Hudson

The View from the Ground: Experiences of Civil War Soldiers
edited by Aaron Sheehan-Dean

Reconstructing Appalachia: The Civil War's Aftermath
edited by Andrew L. Slap

Southern Farmers and Their Stories:
Memory and Meaning in Oral History
Melissa Walker

Law and Society in the South:
A History of North Carolina Court Cases
John W. Wertheimer

COWBOY CONSERVATISM

Texas and the Rise of the Modern Right

Sean P. Cunningham

THE UNIVERSITY PRESS OF KENTUCKY

Copyright © 2010 by The University Press of Kentucky

Scholarly publisher for the Commonwealth,
serving Bellarmine University, Berea College, Centre
College of Kentucky, Eastern Kentucky University,
The Filson Historical Society, Georgetown College,
Kentucky Historical Society, Kentucky State University,
Morehead State University, Murray State University,
Northern Kentucky University, Transylvania University,
University of Kentucky, University of Louisville,
and Western Kentucky University.
All rights reserved.

Editorial and Sales Offices: The University Press of Kentucky
663 South Limestone Street, Lexington, Kentucky 40508-4008
www.kentuckypress.com

Maps by Dick Gilbreath and Jeff Levy,
University of Kentucky Cartography Lab

14 13 12 11 10   1 2 3 4 5

Library of Congress Cataloging-in-Publication Data
Cunningham, Sean P.
    Cowboy conservatism : Texas and the rise of the modern right / Sean P.
Cunningham.
        p.   cm. — (New directions in Southern history)
    Includes bibliographical references and index.
    ISBN 978-0-8131-2576-3 (hardcover : alk. paper)
    1. Texas—Politics and government—1951–   2. Conservatism—
Texas—History—20th century. I. Title.
    F391.2.C86 2010
    976.4'063—dc22   2010003210

This book is printed on acid-free recycled paper meeting
the requirements of the American National Standard
for Permanence in Paper for Printed Library Materials.

Manufactured in the United States of America.

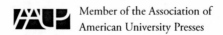
Member of the Association of
American University Presses

For Laura

Contents

Maps and Illustrations

Maps

Illustrations

Preface

I began the preliminary research for this book in the fall of 1988, while a sixth grader at Waters Elementary School in Lubbock, Texas. Of course, "research" might not be the right word, but my love of and interest in postwar American political history—and even my fascination with political imagery, ideology, and iconography—can, in many ways, be traced back to a series of memories rooted in the political culture of the late 1980s.

I remember my sixth grade social studies teacher, Mrs. Stephens, dividing our class into four groups. Each group was assigned one of the four candidates who were represented that year on the two major party tickets for president and vice president of the United States. One group was assigned George Bush, another Dan Quayle, and yet another Michael Dukakis. My group got Lloyd Bentsen. I recall being disgruntled. The groups were charged with the task of presenting a "campaign advertisement" on behalf of our assigned candidate. I remember thinking, "How can I, a Texan, honestly say anything nice about a Democrat?" My parents were conservative Republicans, which, of course, meant that I was a conservative Republican. I recall a conversation I had with my father over dinner one evening at about the same time period. Having no memory of any president other than President Reagan, I remember asking, almost fearfully, "Dad, what would happen if a Democrat was actually elected president?" My father replied with several scenarios up to but not including Armageddon, but I specifically recall him saying that inflation would go "through the roof." I don't think I knew what inflation was, but I was certain that it wasn't a good thing.

Sometimes popular culture also has a way of shaping our youth. Few television shows in the late 1980s provided me with more laughs and memories than did *Saturday Night Live*. The classic sketch comedy show, long known for its political parodies, was in rare form in the fall of 1988. Each week, it seemed, a different skit portrayed Dan Quayle as either less than intelligent or childishly naive, George Bush as "wimpy," or Michael Dukakis as boring. I recall more about *SNL*'s re-creation of campaign commercials and debates in 1988 than I do about the actual campaign commercials or debates of that year. One mock commercial suggested that all great presidents throughout American history had been tall and pointed out that George Bush was tall—and that Michael Dukakis was clearly too short to be an effective president. Another suggested that because Bush's parents were "Americans" while Dukakis's parents were Greek immigrants, the choice as to which would be the best leader was obvious.

On November 5, 1988, three days before the GOP's third straight presidential election landslide victory, *Saturday Night Live* ran a skit called "Dukakis After Dark." The premise was simple. Dukakis, portrayed brilliantly by Jon Lovitz, began the skit by announcing to the television audience at home that the following thirty-minute block of airtime, which he had purchased months earlier in hopes of giving a last-minute boost to his campaign, would, in light of the futility of his campaign, be used instead to throw a lavish party—one that, he said, would be paid for in part by "your" tax dollars. He then traded his suit jacket for a velvet one and proceeded to mingle with the guests at the party. These represented a "who's who" of American liberalism—or at least American liberalism as it had come to be popularly perceived in the late 1980s. Ted Kennedy, portrayed by Phil Hartman, was in attendance—inebriated and sexually harassing Dukakis's wife, Kitty. Lloyd Bentsen, portrayed by the episode's host, Matthew Modine, persuaded Dukakis to admit that he had secretly been planning to raise taxes "through the roof." Leroy Neiman, portrayed by Kevin Nealon, presented Dukakis with a painting of what the nuclear aircraft carrier *Nimitz* would look like if it were transformed into a floating homeless shelter. Even Willie Horton, the man whose name became synonymous in 1988 with Dukakis's record on crime and white fears of black sexual assault, was in attendance. At one point in the skit, Horton thanked Dukakis for the furlough that allowed him to attend the party, where he could enjoy "dirty dancing" with Donna Rice, the woman who had become notorious for her sexual dalliances with the one-time Democratic presidential frontrunner, Gary Hart. Dukakis then made his way over to Jimmy Carter, portrayed by Dana Carvey. After Carter described himself to Dukakis as a "free-spending, malaise-ridden liberal downer," the two were distracted as Joan Baez, portrayed by Nora Dunn, began to sing a folk song she'd composed in honor of the gathering.

> Unilateral disarmament, abortion on demand
> Take everybody's guns away, and toss them in the sand
> Free needles for the addicts, free condoms for the kids
> We'll not blame the criminals for anything he did
> For who can say what's right or wrong?

Is there such a thing as sin?
And does it really matter, if wars we lose or win?

The skit closed with Dukakis thanking the guests for their attendance and participation, but not before admitting that "Reaganomics works. It really does. I mean, aren't you better off than you were eight years ago? I know I am. How about the rest of you? I wish you weren't, but you are. You are better off. And there's no denying it."

The skit was obviously laced with satire. As a sixth grader, I thought the skit was funny but also that it was largely true. Liberalism was a failed philosophy, it seemed. Liberals did want to raise my taxes, even though, as an eleven-year-old, I did not yet pay any taxes. Liberals were also immoral. Beyond anything, liberals were losers. I could not recall, in my lifetime, a liberal winning an election.

These images stuck with me for years and, sadly, shaped many of my young perceptions of political ideologies and party politics. Images have the power to do that—to shape perceptions and, therefore, to shape behavior. This was certainly true of me as an impressionable youth, though I think it was also true for many Americans during the last decades of the twentieth century—an era in which television advertising, public relations, product marketing, and image formulation grew increasingly paramount. Even into the twenty-first century, political campaigns often seem more focused on image than issues.

As memorable and influential as my limited participation in the 1988 presidential campaign was to my developing political consciousness, even more memorable and probably more influential was my newfound fascination with the assassination of John F. Kennedy. More than anything else, the national attention paid to the twenty-fifth anniversary of that tragic event sparked my interest in American history. JFK was everywhere in November 1988. Each major network (and several cable channels) ran specials on the assassination. Topics ranged from firsthand accounts of the tragedy to explorations into the various conspiracy theories surrounding the event to examinations of Kennedy's legacy. The JFK assassination fascinated me then; it continues to fascinate me now.

That the assassination had taken place in Dallas was crucial to my interest. I had been born in Dallas eleven years earlier, at a time when the city was just beginning to overcome the stigma of being the venue of the assassination. I was a die-hard fan of "America's Team," the Dallas Cowboys, and my parents loyally followed the exploits of Jock, J. R., and Bobby Ewing each Friday night. For me, the Kennedy assassination did not seem to be something distant or historical; it seemed to have taken place in my own backyard.

In various ways, this book reflects each of these memories from the fall of 1988. To understand modern Texas politics is to understand that when John F. Kennedy died in the streets of the state's most famous city, everything changed. A Texan became president of the United States and did so on a tarmac at Love Field in Dallas. The then governor of Texas, who later became one of the first and most famous conservative Democrats to abandon the party of secession, eventually ran for president even as the scars he carried from a bullet that had also struck JFK probably remained his most famous characteristic. At the same time, as the nation moved into arguably its most tumultuous period in a century, Texans increasingly wrestled with their own political loyalties, especially as the Democratic Party to which most were affiliated began to unravel due to factional tensions—state and national, conservative and liberal—and occasionally radical. Over the next several years, the relative stability of a liberal consensus that had long defined state and national politics while undergirding a powerful but tenuously balanced "New Deal coalition" gave way to challenged loyalties and redefined relationships between political parties and ideologies. The world in which Michael Dukakis's liberalism was vilified and ridiculed in 1988 was not the same world in which Kennedy took his last breath.

My own political sensibilities have moderated and matured since 1988, though my parents might tell you that I've "gone lib." (Graduate education in the humanities tends to do that to a person.) More than anything, though, my awareness of the power of image and perception in shaping political behavior has led me to look at politics differently and, more important, to question the relationship between image creation, public perception, and political behavior. I selected Texas as the setting for this research for several reasons, not the least of which is that, as most visitors to Texas will confirm, the Lone Star State has a personality all its own—one rooted in legends. It seems to me that legends need powerful and emotionally charged images, a simple story of good versus bad, and heroic, larger-than-life icons. Is there a state in more abundant supply of these things than Texas?

Acknowledgments

No project of this magnitude can be completed alone. I would like to begin by thanking Stephen Wrinn, Anne Dean Watkins, Ashley Runyon, Ila McEntire, Robin DuBlanc, and everyone associated with the University Press of Kentucky. Their passionate courtship of me and this project is what convinced me that publishing with UPK would be a good decision. They have not disappointed. I would also like to thank my dissertation advisers Brian Ward (now at the University of Manchester, UK) and William A. Link, Richard J. Milbauer Professor of History at the University of Florida. Any graduate student would be lucky to work with either one of these mentors; I was fortunate to work closely with both. My doctoral experience at UF was far better than I ever could have hoped for and this, I believe, is a credit to the scholarly wisdom, patience, communication skills, and dedication of these two men. I have also had the pleasure of working with several other professors at both the University of Florida and Texas Tech University, where I received my MA in 2002. Among those professors are Robert McMahon (now at Ohio State University), Joseph Spillane, George Esenwein, Donald Walker, Alywn Barr, Randy McBee, Paul Deslandes (now at the University of Vermont), Lynda Kaid, and Spiro Kiousis. I would also like to thank Kevin Kruse for reading and offering his thoughts on an early version of chapter 5, as well as my faculty colleagues at Texas Tech for their encouragement, support, and professional guidance.

Numerous historians, archivists, and librarians across the country also contributed to this effort. Specifically, I would like to thank the archivists and staff at the Southwest Collections at Texas Tech University; Robert Bohanan at the Jimmy Carter Presidential Library in Atlanta, Georgia; William McNitt at the Gerald R. Ford Presidential Library in Ann Arbor, Michigan; the entire staff at the Lyndon B. Johnson Presidential Library in Austin, Texas; Brenda Gunn, Stephanie Malmros, and the entire staff at the Center for American History at the University of Texas at Austin; Jennifer Mandel of the Ronald Reagan Presidential Library in Simi Valley, California; Dan Santamaria of the Seeley G. Mudd Manuscript Library at Princeton University; George Schultz at the Cushing Library at Texas A&M

University; Kathryn Stallard and the staff of the John G. Tower Library and Archives at Southwestern University in Georgetown, Texas; and Carol Leadenham as well as the entire staff at the Hoover Institution on War, Revolution, and Peace, Stanford University.

While professional and academic support was obviously necessary for a project such as this one, just as necessary was the encouragement, love, and support I received from friends and family. First, I would like to thank my grandfather, J. Pat Cunningham, who in 1980 became the first Republican county commissioner elected in Potter County, Texas, and who gave me my first taste of just how powerful the Reagan tidal wave of the 1980s was. My grandfather passed away in 2007 and I regret that he never had the chance to review this finished product. I would also like to thank my parents, Kirk and Kay, who taught me about life, love, service, and sacrifice—and are in large part responsible for the man I am today. Each of these people, along with my brother Eric and sister-in-law Averi, grandmothers, friends, church family, in-laws, and colleagues, uniquely contributed to my ability to complete this project. I would also like to thank Mike and Sally Shelton, Frank and Jenelle Allen, Mitch and Natalie Gumpl, and Scott Campbell—all friends or family who generously provided room and board to me on at least one of the many research trips I conducted as part of putting this book together. I thank you all very much.

Last, but certainly not least, I would like to thank my wonderful wife, Laura. Laura has been with me through the duration of this project and sacrificed her own academic and career ambitions to serve mine as I progressed through my graduate career at the University of Florida. She gave of herself willingly and always joyfully, and supported and endured my numerous research trips, many of which took me out of town for weeks at a time. Simply put, I could not have done this without Laura and will be forever grateful. She is the love of my life and I thank God for bringing the two of us together during my time in Gainesville, and I am even more thankful that she was willing to relocate with me to Lubbock, Texas, where we now have the joy of raising our daughter, Caitlin.

Introduction

In May 1968, less than two months after announcing to the world that he would not run for reelection, Lyndon Johnson remained desperate to understand the convergence of political events that had so decisively unraveled his presidency. Surprisingly, no state puzzled Johnson more than his home state of Texas. In seeking to understand the changing political climate of the state that had sent him to Washington first as a representative, then as a senator, Lyndon Johnson charged George Reedy, his former press secretary and recently rehired special counsel, to prepare an analysis of Texas politics that could be used to benefit the Democratic Party in the upcoming general election. Reedy titled his report "Forces at Work in Texas."

"The political problems of Texas are complicated by the vast amount of territory that is covered," Reedy wrote. "The state ranges over so much of the nation that it comprises areas which differ in their geography, economy, history, and social outlook. The treaty of annexation authorizes Texas to divide itself into five states and the problems of Texas political leaders would be greatly simplified if this should happen as they could then deal with relatively homogenous populations." Reedy went on to detail the demographic, social, and economic nuances across the various regions of the state. He also discussed the impact of urbanization as well as the growing disconnect between Texas liberalism—which he said was actually populism confused with liberalism—and the evolving national liberal establishment. Among his many conclusions, Reedy warned that Texas, affected by numerous circumstances unique to most other southern states, could potentially become a bastion of conservative Republicanism in the coming decades.[1]

Fast-forward almost four decades to 2004. That year, the platform of the Texas Republican Party reaffirmed the United States of America as a "Christian nation," denounced the "myth of the separation of church and state," demanded the inclusion of abstinence-only sex education for public schools, and called for the elimination of, among other things, the Department of Energy, the Environmental Protection Agency, the Internal Revenue Service, the income tax, the gift tax, the inheritance tax, the capital gains tax, the payroll tax, and various state and local property taxes.[2] That same year, as Texas Republicans held all twenty-seven statewide elected offices, the Republican and former Texas governor George W. Bush won his second term as president of the United States, carrying more than 61 percent of his home state's vote—the seventh straight GOP presidential nominee to carry Texas.[3] At the dawn of the twenty-first century, it seemed that George Reedy had been correct; Texas—once among the most yellow of "yellow-dog Democratic" states—was a bastion of conservative Republicanism.

This book is about political change as it evolved in one of the nation's largest and most important states during the tumultuous seventeen-year period between John F. Kennedy's assassination in Dallas and Ronald Reagan's ascension to the presidency in 1980. Certainly, partisan realignment is the most obvious aspect of that change. Texas was once as solidly Democratic as any state in the nation. By the end of the twentieth century, it was among the most solidly Republican. A simplistic analysis of this transformation, based in large part on the perception that Texas has always been a conservative place, might suggest that—as Ronald Reagan, the preeminent icon of modern conservatism, once similarly quipped—Texas didn't leave the Democratic Party; the Democratic Party left Texas. Yet the political changes that gripped Texas during the last decades of the twentieth century resulted from a far more complex mélange.

To be sure, more than mere partisan affiliation changed in Texas during the 1960s and 1970s. The state's economy changed. Cities grew larger and more industrial. Farms became larger and more consolidated. Suburban populations exploded. The oil and natural gas industries grew wealthier and more powerful. State demographics changed, as a flood of men and women from all parts of the country—Rust Belt to Sun Belt and all parts in between—converged in places like Dallas, Houston, Austin, and San Antonio, hoping that the Lone Star State's surging economic tide would carry them to a safer and more secure life. Most of these changes did not originate in the 1960s and 1970s, but they matured during this period and contributed to an evolving political context. All the while, growing national discord perpetuated fears, hostility, distrust, and disillusionment, forcing Texans—as all other Americans were forced—to reconcile their vision of what America was supposed to be with what America had actually become.[4]

In Texas, the reconciliations of this discord were primarily debated and constructed in the political arena, broadly defined. As a result, the Democratic Party changed at both the state and national levels. The Republican Party changed as well. As the issues upon which America's postwar liberal consensus had been built grew increasingly complicated, both parties struggled to adjust. Both parties experienced periods of factional discord and ideological readjustment, even as they attracted new voters while alienating longtime party loyalists along the way. Both parties struggled to define themselves in the tumultuous context of war, domestic unrest, race riots, a sagging national economy, and the debate over government's role in each issue. America's liberal consensus collapsed in the 1960s, taking the New Deal coalition with it. This collapse profoundly undermined Texas's traditional party structure, even as the genesis of a new political culture was found in the rubble.

Yet, in a related—and perhaps more important—development, Texans' fundamental concept of party politics—their impressions, interpretations, and attitudes—changed in dramatic ways during the 1960s and 1970s. This change, more than any other, hastened the collapse of the traditional political order in Texas. As older issues were seen in new contexts, new issues emerged to threaten tradition, and party leaders warred with one another, the perceived meanings that Texans had of what it meant to be a liberal and what it meant to be a conservative also changed. In fact, the change in the perceived meaning of these two terms, and especially the possible consequences that Texans associated with each of these ideologies, explains—as much as does anything else—the transformations that ultimately led to the ascendancy of a new conservative coalition, born in the wake of a sinking New Deal coalition undermined by wars both foreign and domestic, hot and cold, real and unreal.

To study the political transformations that shaped Texas during the last decades of the twentieth century is to see that the issues, events, and personalities that defined Texas politics coalesced in the 1960s and 1970s into a new political culture, the interpretive battle over which ultimately explains the state's partisan realignment. In other words, the battle to redefine Texas political culture through either a conservative or a liberal worldview, rather than through partisan loyalties, explains why it was not until the 1960s and 1970s that the Republican Party was successful in asserting itself in ways never before seen in the state's history.

At the root of this shift in Texans' perceptions of partisanship and political ideology were the construction of, magnification of, and capitaliza-

tion upon certain images and icons. What and whom Texans associated
with liberalism in 1980 was different than what and whom they had associated with liberalism twenty years earlier. The same can be said of conservatism. More important was that Texans associated their reconstituted
images of liberalism with the Democratic Party, and their reconstituted
images of conservatism with the Republican Party. This change was born
out of a new era in American political history, one dominated by target
marketing, public relations, advertising, and the projection of emotion-
evoking images and messages mass-communicated for political purposes.
More simply, Texas politics in the 1960s and 1970s was defined by public
perceptions that were shaped by the purposeful use of specific images and
icons that, collectively, transformed the state's political culture and led to
partisan realignment. The formation of a significant Republican Party in
Texas coincided with and was informed by these transformations in public
perceptions.

One such icon was Barry Goldwater, who failed in his bid for the
presidency in 1964 in large part because his brand of conservatism was
perceived by a majority of Americans to be dangerous and extreme, even in
Texas.[5] Yet within a decade the political philosophy most commonly identified as dangerous and extreme, especially in Texas, was not conservatism
but liberalism. As the national Democratic Party unraveled during the
1960s due to political assassinations, rising crime rates, civil disobedience,
racial militancy, and intensified factionalism, the state Democratic establishment tried but failed to insulate itself against the national onslaught,
using a banner of conservatism as its shield. Instead, beset by its own warring factions of conservatives and liberals, the Texas Democratic Party
slowly crumbled while the national Republican Party assumed the mantle
of a redefined conservatism strengthened by a revived coalition of fiscal
libertarians and social moralists tied together by an evolving but never
wholly new brand of anticommunism.

Within this context, conservatives in the Republican Party convinced a
majority of Texans by the close of the 1970s that liberalism was the philosophy of "acid, amnesty, and abortion" and that the Democratic Party
was the party of liberalism. The argument proceeded in that order. The
reconstitution of political ideologies (as publicly perceived) preceded partisan realignment. Complicating matters, conservative state Democrats did
not always fight against these reconstituted perceptions and, in many cases,
unintentionally contributed to partisan realignment even as they fought to
protect the established monopolistic power structure from which they benefited. Even more complex was the common practice of Texas liberals vot-

ing for conservative Republicans as a protest against the conservative hegemony within their own party, but also with the hope of forcing realignment. In this sense, the story of modern Texas conservatism cannot and should not be told strictly as a story of Texas Republicanism, for without the actions of Texas Democrats, the conservative Republican ascendancy in Texas might have had a very different look. And it was indeed the "look"— the image of a conservative philosophy, personified in Ronald Reagan, championing "law and order," "plain folks Americanism," and "God-fearing patriotism"—that both state and national conservatives benefited from and used to build a viable and ultimately dominant Texas Republican Party. This was "cowboy conservatism."

The Democratic Party dominated Texas politics until the 1960s and 1970s in large part because it was seen as the party of populist cowboy conservatism. In contrast to the perception of a Republican Party dominated by a wealthy and elitist establishment whose power was based in the country clubs of the northeast, most Texans had long believed that the Democratic Party best represented the values of hard-working, patriotic, Christian Americans. For decades, most Texans had viewed the Democratic Party as the party of states' rights, the party of limited and responsible government, and the party that had won two world wars and overcome a great depression. This perception fomented loyalty and loyalty evolved into tradition; Texans trusted the Democratic Party. Yet even beyond the overwhelmingly important matters of trust, tradition, and loyalty—and to be certain Texans had been loyally trusting the Democratic Party since before the first Confederate shots were fired at Fort Sumter in 1861—the vast majority of white Texans supported the Democratic Party simply because they believed the Democratic Party supported them.[6]

Those perceptions unraveled in the 1960s and 1970s under the weight of national issues that seemed to reflect a decline in family values, an impotent military, and an incompetent and untrustworthy federal government. The prevalence of broadcast media in the 1960s and 1970s brought national images into Texans' homes. National problems became local problems, and local problems created local fears that demanded new solutions.[7] As Texas became more industrialized, more suburban, more middle class, and more influential in shaping national political discourse, a majority of Texans began to lose confidence in the Democratic Party and increasingly questioned their partisan loyalties. Which party would fight the hardest to protect states' rights? Which party would be toughest on crime? Which party wanted to protect the traditions and values to which families and Texans had long subscribed? Which party best represented the families whose sons had sacrificed their lives to fight a war that so many scorned and some had even dodged? Which party understood what it would take to make America great once again? That the answers to these questions were necessarily vague and ambiguous mattered little, for simplicity of message was also at the heart of image formation and the conservative worldview.

Interestingly, the Republican Party did not easily or quickly emerge as the automatic answer to these and similar questions, at least not in Texas. The GOP was not predestined to assume dominance in Texas. Throughout the 1960s and 1970s, as liberal Texas Democrats fought for their party by voting for another, conservative Texas Democrats increasingly campaigned by promoting not their partisan identification but their philosophical convictions. Because of the widening disconnect between the state and national party, however, those campaigns were increasingly difficult to sustain. By the end of the 1970s, most white Texans—and a good many Mexican American Texans—began to find solace in a national Republican Party that, philosophically if not practically, seemed better prepared to handle the series of national crises that combined to paint a portrait of national decline.[8] By the time of Reagan's election in 1980, most Texans (no longer a "Silent Majority") supported the Republican Party—at least in national campaigns—because they believed the Republican Party supported them. As Democrats were increasingly associated with a liberalism perceived as elitist, weak, and unpatriotic, it was clear that public perceptions were driving partisan realignment in Texas.

Beyond the importance of understanding the political transformations within Texas as a gateway to a fuller understanding of that state's history, it is equally or more important to recognize Texas's significance in the history of postwar American politics more broadly. Put another way, the story of modern American politics, and in particular the rise of modern American conservatism and the crisis of modern American liberalism, cannot be told without understanding the central role played by Texas. There are two key reasons why the exploration of Texas is vital to moving historians closer to a more complete understanding of postwar politics and modern conservatism. First, Texas, through its sheer size and presence, has commanded a national stage and exerted national influence for decades. Yet, this influence has dramatically increased since the early 1960s. Its most visible manifestation has been the persistence of Texas political leaders operating with national power. From Lyndon Johnson to John Connally and Lloyd Bentsen, from John Tower to James Baker and Tom DeLay, from George

Bush to Dick Cheney to George W. Bush, few states, if any, have contributed as heavily to postwar American politics as has Texas.

Second, situated centrally in what the former conservative political strategist Kevin Phillips called in the late 1960s the new American "Sun Belt," Texas has not only stood at the heart of postwar America's ideological, economic, demographic, and social development, but has also existed as a bridge connecting the political traditions of the South with the rugged frontierism and individualistic ethos of the American West.[9] Texas has been at the forefront of national urbanization, suburbanization, and even exurbanization. During the last decades of the twentieth century, Texas was home to four of the nation's top-ten largest and fastest-growing cities, embraced and benefited from the Rust Belt to Sun Belt migration of industrial workers, and established itself as the nation's energy nucleus—particularly through the emergence of the ever-expanding and influential 1970s oil industry. Texas was also central to the rise of the military-industrial complex, boasted the most vibrant economy in the country for much of the 1970s, and became an operations hub for the emerging evangelical Christian Right.[10]

Furthermore, Texas offers a multifaceted setting that mirrors yet simultaneously contradicts traditional interpretations of race in the 1960s. Texas was, generally, a less heated front for the African American civil rights movement and yet fierce racism and segregation was palpable in several sections of the state. At the same time, however, Texas's demographics reflect a racial dynamic far more complicated than most areas of the South, where racism was focused more directly on blacks seeking integration and a political voice. In Texas, a significant Mexican American population—one that was larger than the black population of the state—altered political sensibilities pertinent to broader notions of white supremacy and even definitions of whiteness itself.[11]

This book will frequently distinguish between Texas's various regions. Most typically, references will be made to four regions: East Texas, South Texas, Central Texas, and West Texas. Several basic assumptions can be gleaned simply from these geographic distinctions, but much more can still be said about the unique characteristics, demographics, and socioeconomics of each section. Such an understanding is necessary for any study of the state's political culture. For instance, only in East Texas—the region bordering Louisiana and extending not quite to present-day Interstate 45—did the presence of a large concentration of African Americans contribute to a political climate similar to that in much of the Deep South. Yet, as V. O.

Texas's major cities and county boundaries.

Key's classic work, *Southern Politics in State and Nation,* illustrates, East Texas did not mirror the "black belt" voting blocs of other southern states, where race was a far more salient issue in elections. At the same time, racial diversity was by no means limited to East Texas. In fact, far greater racial diversity existed in South Texas, where high concentrations of Mexican Americans (and Mexican migrants) created a very different sociopolitical dynamic. Class tensions ran high in these regions, particularly in South Texas, where a small but powerful number of conservative landowners typically controlled the economy in which large numbers of Spanish-speaking peoples attempted to forge a living. In this economic context, the political culture of South Texas has been most aptly compared to the system of "bossism" and ward politics that characterized northeastern politics for much of the late nineteenth and early twentieth century.[12] Central Texas, on the other hand, was settled predominantly by German immigrants and was an early bastion of western frontierism and rugged individualism. Much of Central Texas arguably still embraces the state's heritage of independence and tradition more tenaciously than does any other section, as historically evidenced by the region's Union loyalties preceding the Civil

War as well as by a consistent willingness to do what virtually no other region of the state was willing to do, at least until the 1960s and 1970s: vote Republican. West Texas has long provided a base for the state's energy industry, with much of the state's wealth pumped out from the oil fields of the Permian Basin and the natural gas deposits of the Texas Panhandle. This region, which has a rich history of ranching and, therefore, a strong western regional identification, is also the largest cotton-producing area of the state—and one of the largest in the nation. The abundance of West Texas counties boasting little to no politically significant African American population long offset the political significance of East Texas counties concerned with race and also mirrors, demographically, the American Southwest far more than it does the American South.[13] Variations also existed within each of these regions. Major urban metropolises like Dallas and Houston complicated the political culture of North and East Texas, while San Antonio and Austin became eclectic hubs for sources of political conservatism, moderation, and liberalism in South and Central Texas. Austin, in particular, forged an identity as one of the nation's fastest-growing and most dynamic cities, welcoming the relocation of numerous industrial, technological, and even entertainment enterprises. As the state capital, Austin has also obviously been the seat of state political power while simultaneously being home to the state's flagship (and probably most liberal) public university, the University of Texas. The religious makeup of the state also varies by region. The state's heavy Baptist influence and traditional anti-Catholic impulses have, for instance, necessitated a political reckoning with the overwhelmingly Catholic and Hispanic population of South and far West Texas. Beyond that, white dispensational Protestantism in Texas has long reinforced notions of independence, self-determination, free will, and a resistance to change and reform.[14]

To understand the political and social culture of Texas is to see that demographic, economic, cultural, racial, and religious distinctions combined with the vast expanse of its land to create a state that defies easy regional identification. Many historians have long debated the question of whether Texas is a southern state, a western state, or something else—something unique. As much as anything else, Texas has long fashioned itself, to one degree or another, as a populist state. Having been the birthplace of the Farmers' Alliance that eventually evolved into the short-lived Populist Party of the 1890s, Texas was at the epicenter of a political movement that fused economic interests and political worldviews common in both the South and the West in the late nineteenth century. At a fundamental level, populism reflected, as historian Richard White puts it, "a political challenge to the dominant Northeast."[15] While the enemy populists blamed for the country's problems changed over time, the impulse to fight against an established elite has persisted throughout Texas's history and helps to explain both the state's political culture and its regional identity. As Donald Critchlow has argued, conservatism by the end of the twentieth century mirrored the tenets of the populist tradition by implying "opposition to the status quo, rebellion against the establishment, a democratic faith in the people, and a deep suspicion of the wisdom of the liberal elites in government, the media, and academia."[16] The answer, then, to the question of whether Texas is a southern state or a western state may very well be that Texas—like the populist philosophy that has informed so much of its political culture—was and is concurrently southern, western, and altogether unique—and is therefore as complicatedly American as it is anything else.[17]

In addition to the historical literature that addresses the question of Texas's regional identity, this book has also been heavily influenced by a growing list of recent studies on modern conservatism and postwar American politics. Historians such as Dan Carter, Joseph Crespino, Donald Critchlow, Matthew Dallek, Michael Flamm, Kevin Kruse, Matthew Lassiter, William Link, Lisa McGirr, and Jonathan Schoenwald have influenced and inspired the explorations and arguments advanced in this book. These historians have individually and collectively pursued answers to the question of why electoral politics in the United States took the course that it did during the last half of the twentieth century.[18]

Certainly, nuances and complications exist. Historians have debated the regional genesis of modern conservatism, some proposing that it was born in the South, others proposing the West. Some historians have emphasized modern conservatism's origins in the suburbs, the farms, or even the working-class enclaves of the Rust Belt. Various personalities have been identified—Ronald Reagan, Barry Goldwater, George Wallace, Jesse Helms, Phyllis Schlafly. Different issues have been explored—crime and the emergence of "law and order" as a political issue, civil rights and the role of race, a slumping national economy, the war in Vietnam, the rise of a politically active Christian Right. These and other answers proposed by the aforementioned historians and others have each added to our understanding of national political transformations in the postwar era.

Yet as the popular saying goes, everything is bigger in Texas. Certainly the story of modern conservatism's ascendancy is no different. As such, the overall picture of political change described in the following pages can be grasped only via a limited selection of carefully chosen historical fragments.

Therefore, this book merely reflects a portrait of the exhaustive body of records that serves to further our understanding of the political transformations that shaped Texas during this critical period. Perhaps Texas, as complicated as it is, might be the perfect setting in which to build the bridge that connects each of these perspectives.

Chapter 1

The Eyes of Texas
Political Culture and Tradition

In his seminal 1949 study of southern politics, the esteemed political scientist V. O. Key offered a detailed analysis of the Texas political culture and tradition at midcentury. Assessing the state's regional identity, he argued that the "changes of nine decades have weakened the heritage of southern traditionalism, revolutionized the economy, and made Texas more western than southern." On the relationship between politics and economics, Key asserted that Texas was primarily "concerned about money and how to make it, about oil and sulfur and gas, about cattle and dust storms and irrigation, about cotton and banking and Mexicans." In this context, Key argued that trumping virtually all other issues in Texas was the persistent debate over the extent, scope, and role of government in shaping the economy. Finally, on the issue of electoral politics, Key argued that Texas, more than any other southern state, and in "as sharp a form as is possible under a one-party system," operated within a strained political culture rooted in the discourse of political ideology. According to Key, factions of conservatives and liberals, exemplified by colorful and powerful personalities, dominated the state's midcentury political culture, while most Texans based their own political behaviors upon the publicly constructed definitions ascribed to each personality, faction, and ideology.[1]

For these and other reasons, the Texas political culture and tradition was—and is—complicated and unique. That complexity is largely rooted in the pride Texans have in their state's distinctive and colorful history—a history that is the stuff of legend. Schoolchildren in Texas grow up with those legends; they are compelled to do so by law. From the honor and courage exemplified by the 183 men who held off as many as 6,000 Mexican soldiers for thirteen days at the Alamo before sacrificing their lives for the dream of independence to the state's brief period as an independent republic to secession and rebellion to cattle drives, cowboys, Indian wars, and the Old West, Texans have long prided themselves on the legends that buttress their state's unique history.[2] When mixing these with other, more stereotypically southern and western traditions, Texans have constructed a history and a political culture that defy simple regional categorization. This amalgam of legends, traditions, and cultures has contributed to the formation of a unique political heritage notable for its colorful personalities, its conservative commitment to tradition and loyalty, and its somewhat paradoxical positioning as a state often at the forefront of change, radical factionalism, and political disunion. Understanding the modern Texas political culture and tradition, the origins of which are arguably more than two centuries old, is fundamental to understanding the transformational paths taken by conservatives and liberals, Democrats and Republicans in the 1960s and 1970s.

Revolution, Republic, Rebellion, Reconstruction, and Radicalism

Texas history is peppered with stories of conflict. Following a period of exploration that began in the late sixteenth century, which inaugurated centuries of conflict between the Native Americans already well established in Texas and encroaching Europeans, much of late seventeenth- and eighteenth-century Texas was shaped by competition between Spain and France. Spain eventually established dominance in Texas, but between 1810 and 1821 a war for independence was fought and finally won, pushing Spain permanently out of Texas while creating the independent nation of Mexico. By 1835, Mexico was struggling against a war of rebellion in Texas. Mexico fought to maintain control over the largely Anglo population it had enticed to move into the region in hopes of creating a geographical buffer zone between its new nation and the ever-expanding United States. Most new migrants to Mexican Texas had come from the American South in search of opportunities that were either inaccessible in the United States or had been denied them. Slaves came, too, though obviously not by choice. The Anglo-American settlers rebelled against Mexican authority, in part because they wanted to protect their "property" against the antislavery laws being advanced by the newly dictatorial Mexican regime of Antonio López de Santa Anna. They rebelled for other reasons as well, including a patriotically American belief in representative democracy and local autonomy couched in the stereotypical frontier mentality of the American West. After legendary battles at the Alamo and San Jacinto, Texans won their independence from Mexico in 1836.

Yet independence did not end the conflicts. Between 1836 and 1845, Texas existed as an independent republic, plagued by debt, military instability, and diplomatic ambiguity. Annexation to the United States was finalized in 1845, though not formally completed until February 1846. The annexation debates were essential to the development of Democratic dominance in Texas. Though once relatively popular in the South, the Whig Party forfeited most of its support in the region due to its stance on slavery and, in Texas, its stance on annexation. Nationally, Whigs led the opposition to Texas annexation; Democrats, increasingly the party of the South, led the fight for it. In 1848, a war between the United States and Mexico, fought in part over Texas's disputed status, ended with the Treaty of Guadalupe Hidalgo, which, among other things, established the Rio Grande River as Texas's southern boundary. By 1860, Texas Democrats—Sam Houston's vociferous unionism notwithstanding—were working closely with other southern Democrats to ensure that proslavery planks were included in their national party's platform. As prospects for resolution faded and the sectional conflict deepened, secession became a reality for South Carolina, Mississippi, Florida, Alabama, Georgia, and Louisiana. Secession became reality for the Lone Star State on March 2, 1861—exactly twenty-five years, to the day, since Texas had declared independence from Mexico. Even in 1861, Texans had a flair for the dramatic.

Like all other southern states joining the Confederacy, Texas seceded from the Union because of slavery, not states' rights. In fact, the most "southern" aspects of the state's complicated regional identity are rooted in the politics of slavery, annexation, secession, war, and reconstruction. In its "Declaration of the Causes," Texas political leaders made clear that their decision to join the United States had been dependent upon the protection of "negro slavery." The formation of the Republican Party, the secession document explained, posed a grave threat to the "beneficent and patriarchal system of African slavery." Nonetheless, over time—and in large part because of the state's Reconstruction experience—Texans, as did most other southerners, constructed a memory of secession and war rooted in the notion of rugged individualism and states' rights, not merely the protection of slavery.[3]

As recently as the 1990s, it was common for Texas politicians, and even some newspaper editorialists, to analogize the images of Reconstruction to contemporary federal expansion, while using those same images to communicate fear and provoke generations-old hostilities. These images have included unwelcome "Yankee" carpetbaggers who came "in the dark of night, looted the liberties of Texans," and left state citizens "broke and bitter." Despite the fact that much of this popular memory was constructed out of fallacious material (carpetbaggers held no more than 25 percent of all offices during Reconstruction, for instance), the memory that Texans retained of the post–Civil War period profoundly reinforced preexisting attitudes about the role of government. These attitudes also shaped an evolving hostility toward all sources of control and dominance based outside the state. As Randolph Campbell put it, "Reconstruction alone did not shape the future of political life in Texas, but the era contributed heavily to the popular opposition to taxing and spending for public purposes and to the general lack of civil rights that characterized the state's politics after the 1870s."[4]

As Texas struggled against and within the framework of Reconstruction, the state also continued to evolve in ways that made it unique and increasingly different from the rest of the South. The emergence of the cattle industry coincided with growing tensions between Native American tribes in the northwest and western portions of the state, while remembered tales of cowboys, gunfighters, and the stereotypically "Wild West" are rooted in the abbreviated but no less significant reality of those personalities and activities.

Among the best examples of the fusion of southern and western traditions in Texas was the radicalization of the countryside that eventually formed the Populist Party, arguably the most successful third-party movement in American history. The late nineteenth century was a period of adjustment and frustration for farmers across the country. In Texas, a growing population and convenient access to railroads contributed to the general shift from subsistence to commercial agriculture. Increasingly tied to the national market, Texas farmers put more land under plow, despite (and even causing) lower prices for their less diversified harvests. Former slaves competed with Mexican Americans and Mexican immigrants in an economic structure in which landowning became increasingly unrealistic and manual labor, tenancy, and sharecropping were the norm. More monopolized landholdings, competition between the races, lower prices at market, and the general sense that Americans were moving toward an industrial society and away from the Jeffersonian vision of a nation connected by small, independent farmers, challenged the status and prestige of men and women whose families had inherited the yeoman dream.[5]

Farmers responded to these hardships in different ways. Organizations like the Grange educated farmers and fostered social interaction and cooperation but did not address economic grievances. During the final days of Reconstruction, however, farmers began to focus on these grievances and increasingly blamed their problems on outside forces. The populist tendency to blame "foreign agents of control" both reinforced and intensified the state's tradition of valuing independence and localism while distrusting non-Texan corporations or governments. Monopolistic railroads were blamed for gouging farmers with exorbitant shipping rates. Northeastern banks were blamed for saddling farmers with unrealistic interest rates, making the repayment of loans a virtual impossibility. Northeastern investors were blamed for profiting off the system and exacerbating conditions. By the late 1870s, farmers had grown angrier, more hostile, and more political, and in September 1877, many of them met in Lampasas, Texas, where they organized the National Farmers' Alliance and Industrial Union. Over the next decade, this organization, more commonly known as the Southern Farmers' Alliance, agitated against the distant entities it perceived to be at the heart of local problems.[6]

In 1890, Texans, thanks in large part to the support of populist farmers, elected James Stephen Hogg their new governor. Though a loyal Democrat, as the state's attorney general, Hogg had made a name for himself among populists, prosecuting monopolistic railroads and introducing antitrust legislation to Texas a year before Congress passed the Sherman Anti-Trust Act. Hogg was among the first to embrace populism by absorbing the movement into the Democratic Party. Still, the push for a third party continued. In 1892, the Farmers' Alliance, along with several other competing alliances, met in Omaha to nominate national third-party candidates and adopt a platform under the banner of the People's Party. The People's—or "Populist"—Party enjoyed widespread success in the South and West, carrying four states in the 1892 presidential election, sending nearly fifty men to Congress over the course of the decade, and electing governors in several western states. Populism proved so powerful that by the mid-1890s, electoral necessity forced the Democratic Party to do what some Democrats, like Texas's Hogg, had already done—adopt much of the movement's agenda.[7]

Though populism quickly became a Texas Democratic tenet, the movement, broadly speaking, nevertheless reflected many Texans' willingness to break from tradition and challenge the political status quo. Texas farmers viewed their worsening conditions in the context of national economic changes. In response, they quickly identified a set of enemies upon which they could shower blame. Throughout the twentieth century, Texans continued to lead charges against various incarnations of "the establishment" even as they consistently elected conservative Democrats who rhetorically nodded to the people while actually advocating policies that maintained and even consolidated power in the hands of landowners and corporations. This homegrown establishment—defined by George Green as a conglomeration of conservative politicians and oil, banking, insurance, and other corporate interests intent on maintaining power—perfected the practice of blame shifting while projecting itself as an agent of the people.[8]

At the end of the nineteenth century, the Texas political culture reflected a blending of the patriotic and independence-minded individualism memorialized by the state's revolution and rebellion, a historical pattern of organizing against established and distant authorities, and the one-party dominance that gave voice to it all. In the coming decades, that culture of populist conservatism persisted even as it adjusted to much unexpected and transformative change.

Progressivism, Backlash, and Depression

The twentieth century began for Texans in a glorious, oil-drenched bonanza. As the reincorporation of Populists into the Democratic Party became increasingly certain, a massive oil strike was made near Beaumont on a small hill known as Spindletop. Production from this well alone reached 17.5 million barrels in 1902 and inspired a boom in drilling across the state that would eventually lead to the establishment of Texas as the nation's energy-producing giant. As oil boomed, cities grew; as cities grew, the nation evolved, and Texans joined other Americans in a collective search for order, efficiency, and reform.[9]

Texas progressivism was fueled, in part, by a populist impulse toward reform that had never fully disintegrated, despite partisan fusion. Texas progressivism was also hastened by the Galveston hurricane of 1900, the most devastating natural disaster in American history, in which some six thousand people had perished, along with nearly half of the city's edifices. To rebuild Galveston, local leaders developed a new system of city government designed to maximize efficiency through appointments and commissions. Within two decades Galveston's progressive form of city government was adopted by several Texas cities and, eventually, by more than five hundred other cities across the nation.[10]

Reforms in city government aside, Texas progressivism was primarily driven by the politics of prohibition. In 1917, Senator Morris Sheppard (D-TX) authored a prohibition amendment that, when ratified two years later, became the Eighteenth Amendment to the U.S. Constitution. Sheppard, whom Texans had elected to the Senate in 1912, was popular because of his orations on the "Lost Cause," lower tariff rates, antitrust issues, and the need to solve the credit problems still plaguing farmers. He played a powerful role in the Senate until his death in 1941, consistently balancing the state's conservative traditions with its impulse for populist agitation and change.[11]

By 1920, new personalities, issues, and organizations emerged to usher in an astounding decade of political change. The most powerful independent organization in Texas during the early 1920s was the Ku Klux Klan. The Klan first organized in Texas in 1920 in Houston. Soon, Klan chapters were dotted around much of the state. Advertising itself as a protector of Christianity, the Klan attracted a largely middle-class membership on the basis of its call for "100 percent Americanism." The Texas Klan of the early 1920s rallied supporters by demagoguery on issues other than just race, identifying numerous agents of unwelcome and "foreign" influence. Most influential was the Klan's grand call for "law and order," morality, and specifically prohibition. By 1923, the Texas Klan boasted more than 150,000 members, all of whom were male. On the momentum of Klansman Earle Mayfield's surprising election to the U.S. Senate in 1922, the Texas Klan ran and won seats in the state legislature and local offices in 1924.[12]

The Klan's momentum, however, slowed considerably later in 1924, thanks largely to a statewide backlash against organized terror and vigilantism. The Klan's candidate for governor that year lost his bid to Miriam Ferguson, better known as "Ma," largely because the hooded society failed to replicate its alliance with the now anti-Klan prohibitionists who had helped carry Mayfield to the Senate two years earlier. Instead, aided by growing public outcries against the Klan, Ferguson became the first female governor in Texas history, though all who voted for her knew very well that her husband, Jim—better known as "Pa"—would actually be the one in charge. Jim Ferguson had served as governor from 1915 to 1917 when, despite being reelected to a second term, he was impeached for a series of scandals and other conflicts, most notably one involving academic freedom at the University of Texas. This dramatic publicity, melded with an effective populist (and wet) political style, enabled the Fergusons to dominate Texas politics during the 1920s, not by consistently winning elections, but by consistently being an issue in and of themselves. "Fergusonism" carried the banner of populism into the state's modern age, though in actual practice it reoriented and even distracted Texas politics away from specific issues and toward more dramatic national issues.[13]

The decade's most significant elections came in 1928. Earle Mayfield, the incumbent senator and Klan representative, lost his bid for reelection to Tom Connally, who used his opponent's connections to the hooded society as a prime campaign weapon. Even more significant was the national Democratic Party's presidential nomination of New York governor Al

Smith. Wet, urban, and Irish Catholic, Smith had been close to the Democratic presidential nomination in 1924, but was denied the honor because of intraparty squabbling between rural southern conservatives, most of whom were dry, and urban, immigrant-backed northerners, most of whom were wet. In 1928, many Texas Democrats objected to Smith's stance on prohibition, though many more opposed his religion. Thus intraparty factionalism, mixed with widespread distaste for the nomination of a northern, wet Catholic, led Texas to abandon the party of secession in a presidential election for the first time in state history. Though not yet a portent of partisan realignment, Texans' support for the Republican Herbert Hoover suggested a continued willingness to buck partisan tradition and loyalty in favor of a stronger commitment to both ideology and image.[14]

Despite momentary and isolated flirtations with the Klan and the Republican Party during the 1920s, the Great Depression resolidified Texas as a Democratic bedrock in the 1930s. As was true of other states' economies, the Texas economy experienced both boom and bust in the 1920s. New oil discoveries, expanded drilling, and related growth in banking, insurance, manufacturing, and office and highway construction gave Texas the appearance of a rapidly urbanizing and economically thriving state. By 1928 Texas had assumed its position as the nation's leader in oil production, while young cities like Lubbock, awarded the new Texas Technological College (later Texas Tech University) in 1923, became a state leader in cotton production thanks to new technologies that made the massive Ogallala Aquifer a major underground irrigation source. Agricultural expansion— much of which had arisen as a result of global demand during World War I—did not, however, lead to economic benefit or even security for Texas farmers. Cotton prices fluctuated dramatically throughout the decade, contributing to farm instability. When the stock market crashed in October 1929, most Texans, along with editorialists in the *Dallas Morning News,* dismissed the crisis as a problem only for the vilified Northeast. New oil discoveries continued to encourage Texans in the belief that their state was immune to the financial crisis of the Northeast, though that perception was shattered quickly as overproduction and industrial underconsumption wreaked havoc on oil prices, which fell from $1.30 per barrel in 1930 to 10¢ in 1931 and 4¢ in 1933. Unemployment reached 23 percent in Houston by 1931, while nature's great irony, the Dust Bowl, scattered topsoil to the wind and pounded Texas farmers into submission, contributing to a billion-dollar decrease in the state's aggregate farm value between 1930 and 1940.[15]

Texans looking for change and security in 1932 went to the polls and elected Ma Ferguson to be their governor and Franklin Delano Roosevelt to be their president. Ferguson ran on a platform of lower taxes, but won primarily because she and Pa were somehow simultaneously familiar *and* representative of change. Roosevelt carried 89 percent of the state's vote, thanks in large part to two Texas congressmen—John Nance Garner, Speaker of the House and FDR's running mate in 1932, and Sam Rayburn, a future Speaker of the House who would also earn fame as Lyndon Johnson's political mentor. As was true in other states, Roosevelt's New Deal had a profound impact in Texas. Agencies like the Civilian Conservation Corps, the Public Works Administration, the Works Progress Administration, and the National Youth Administration—supervised in Texas by a young and ambitious Lyndon Johnson—brought the state thousands of jobs, while the Agricultural Adjustment Act, the Rural Electrification Act, and the Home Owners Loan Corporation brought some relief to Texas farmers and families.[16]

Roosevelt was popular in Texas because he was a Democrat committed to helping solve the nation's worst economic crisis in history. That it took a New Deal and the federal expansion that came with it was not an insignificant price to pay for many Texans. A delegate to the 1932 Democratic National Convention, George Mahon, a future congressman from Lubbock, spoke for many conservative Texas Democrats when he commented that he and his fellow delegates were "Democrats first and New Dealers second." Despite conservative rumblings, the depression overpowered ideological commitments and, in 1936, Roosevelt and Garner carried 87 percent of the Texas vote on their way to a second term.[17]

From progressivism to the Klan, and from Hoover to FDR, consistent in Texas's political culture during the first four decades of the twentieth century—as had been the case during the late nineteenth century—was a tendency to blame "foreign" influences for social and economic hardships. However, as Texas matured, it struggled to balance these impulses with its historical inclinations toward independence, rebellion, and reform. Many Texans reveled in the state's maverick persona and elected officials whom they perceived to be carrying on that tradition, even as the consistent election of those officials reinforced the hegemony of one-party rule. On the eve of the greatest conflagration in human history, Texas remained a state deeply connected to its past, with a political culture and tradition that reflected the tenuous balance of that past.

World War, Cold War, and Modernization

World War II ushered in a new phase in the history of Texas. The war caused unprecedented economic changes that would inform both social and political transitions. V. O. Key's midcentury assessment of Texas politics as portending heightened ideological factionalism and even bipartisanship was, in part, based on observations of the first four decades of the century. However, Key's assessment was also heavily influenced by wartime and early postwar economic and demographic changes. Those changes included the maturation and growth of a powerful oil industry as well as population growth, urbanization, suburbanization, and in-migration patterns fueled by workers abandoning the Rust Belt factories of the North in favor of higher-paying and more abundant jobs in the new Sun Belt–based military industrial complex. As more people moved into Texas, more Texans moved into the middle class, relying on either the defense or extractive industries for their paychecks. Simply put, the demands of World War II forced a mobilization of the home front that began the process of modernization in Texas. The cold war furthered and solidified that process. All the while, the national Republican Party—the chief beneficiary of postwar Democratic factionalism—slowly began making inroads with conservative Texas voters hoping to protect their new jobs, their new homes, their new families, and their nation's new role as a global superpower embroiled in a fierce ideological struggle, many believed, against atheism, oppression, and tyranny.[18]

The Japanese attack on Pearl Harbor forced the United States to reassess many of its military operations and strategies. Among these reconsiderations was the geographic stationing of military and naval bases. Fearing that heavily concentrated and accessible coastal bases were a national security risk, government officials began the process of rebuilding and relocating America's national defense operations to the American West, where isolation and more clement weather meant greater security and stability. Texas benefited from this shift in strategy as much or more than did any other state, with the possible exception of California. In 1941, the United States contributed more than $500 million to the Texas economy through the purchase of military hardware and supplies. San Antonio became home to three of the nation's most important air force bases, in Kelly, Brooks, and Lackland, while also boasting the "West Point of the Air"—Randolph Field. Fort Worth's Carswell Field headquartered the Army Air Corps. Home by the early 1950s to aviation giant Bell Helicopter, Fort Worth—along with growing Dallas–Fort Worth-area suburbs Garland and Grand Prairie—also became a hub for wartime aviation construction. Texas, additionally, played a major role in the development and harnessing of nuclear energy. In 1942, the isolation of the panhandle city of Amarillo was attractive enough to warrant the construction of Pantex, a nuclear bomb production plant which, within a few years, thanks in large part to its connection with the Manhattan Project based in nearby Los Alamos, New Mexico, became the nation's predominant nuclear weapons assembly and disassembly plant, a position it held for the duration of the cold war. Pantex continued its nuclear disassembly work into the twenty-first century.[19]

The expansion of the military-industrial complex in Texas wholly invested the state in the war effort. Texas also contributed heavily to the national celebration of heroism emanating from both the home front and the battlefields. Though Dwight Eisenhower was also claimed by Kansas, Texans publicized the fact that he had been born in the North Texas town of Denison. Chester Nimitz, the chief naval commander in the Pacific theater, was a native Texan of German descent, calling the Central Texas town of Fredericksburg home. Another Texan, Audie Murphy, became the most decorated soldier of the war before embarking on a very successful career in Hollywood, where he gained fame playing war heroes and frontier "cowboys." Oveta Culp Hobby, wife of former Texas governor William P. Hobby, served as director of the Women's Army Corps and eventually became the first secretary of the Department of Health, Education, and Welfare. Astoundingly, Texas A&M University produced more officers during World War II than did West Point. Though Texans accounted for only 5 percent of the nation's total population, they comprised 7 percent of the total number of active war participants—some 750,000. More than 22,000 Texans lost their lives in World War II.[20]

Texans produced for the war effort in other ways as well. In addition to a boom in agricultural production, caused most notably by increased global demands for cotton and cattle, the state's extractive industries also fueled the national war effort and set the stage for Texas's significant role in the emerging cold war. Oil pipelines were constructed that connected Texas to major industrial factories all across the country, including the 1,254-mile "Big Inch" pipeline that, by 1944, connected East Texas oil fields to factories in Philadelphia and surrounding areas in New Jersey. The Rubber Reserve Corporation made synthetic rubber production a $325-million wartime boon to Houston's economy. That corporation's profitability was due in large part to thriving petrochemical industries based in Beaumont, Port Arthur, and Corpus Christi. The nation's largest tin-smelting plant was located in Texas City, near the Gulf Coast between Galveston and Houston. Postwar economic growth in Texas further attracted new industries and new corporations, including offices for Dow Chemical, Sinclair Oil, Shell Oil, Texaco, and Texas Instruments, which created the integrated silicon microchip used in calculators and computers. Between 1940 and

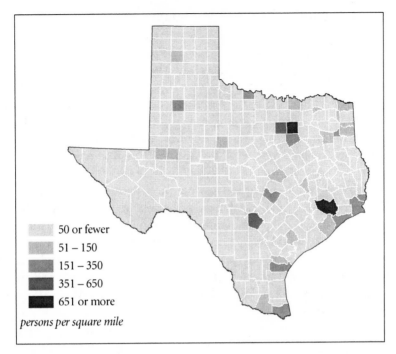

The state's population density in 1960.

	50 or fewer
	51 – 150
	151 – 350
	351 – 650
	651 or more

persons per square mile

1950, the number of Texans employed in some sector of manufacturing doubled.[21]

Industrial growth also contributed to urbanization and suburbanization. During World War II, more than half a million Texans relocated within the state from rural to urban areas. This shift made Texas, for the first time, predominantly urban. Between 1940 and 1950, the population of Houston grew by 55 percent. Corpus Christi's population grew by 90 percent. Dallas, Fort Worth, and San Antonio also experienced significant population growth. Between 1950 and 1960, the Dallas suburb of Irving grew from a population of 2,621 to more than 45,000. During the same time, Houston, Dallas, Fort Worth, and El Paso each annexed more than ninety square miles into their city domains. The Dallas–Fort Worth metroplex saw a rapid increase in suburbanization, with ninety-six area municipalities born by 1960. The number of suburban Houston municipalities reached sixty-eight during the same time. As cities and suburbs grew, the state poured millions of dollars into highway construction, thus easing transportation headaches and enabling further development, not to mention inner-city decline and de facto racial segregation.[22]

Wartime and postwar industrial job opportunities in these urbanizing areas were so abundant that an agricultural labor shortage emerged during the early years of World War II. This shortage led to the creation of the Bracero Program, a controversial agreement between the United States and Mexico in which Mexican migrant workers were recruited for agricultural jobs no longer being filled by the state's population, white or black. Between 1942 and 1947, approximately 219,000 legal (and more than 300,000 illegal) Mexican migrants came to the United States to provide agricultural labor for the growing economy. Thousands of these workers came to Texas, where they were so notoriously ill treated that, by the program's close in the early 1960s, Mexico was refusing to send more workers to the state. Nonetheless, agricultural labor was becoming increasingly the domain of the "nonwhite," while Anglo Texans more commonly moved to urban, and then suburban, areas, taking the better-paying industrial jobs. Texas's complicated definitions of "whiteness," with roots that were, by midcentury, many decades old, conflated with the state's more diverse racial and ethnic demographics to create a unique culture of race relations different from that in most other southern states.[23]

In the midst of complicating race relations and a thriving new economy, Texas politics was increasingly defined by Democratic factionalism—divisions cut more fervently along conservative-liberal lines than at any point in history. State and local issues continued to inform the public's perceptions of what it meant to be conservative, what it meant to be liberal, and which candidates best represented the philosophies of most Texans. The emergence of mass broadcast media simultaneously heightened the importance of national issues to this process. The Texas political culture that evolved in the postwar era, though often couched in simple terms of being either pro– or anti–New Deal, was also affected by unprecedented economic growth, the fear that that growth would be undermined by unnecessary government regulations, and the paranoia that behind every corner lurked a potential agent of subversion. This political climate intensified preexisting divisions within the Texas Democratic Party and gave isolated and momentary beacons of hope to the state's fledgling GOP.[24]

The emerging cold war provided a national context for these competing factions. Importantly, this national context tended to supersede local concerns when ideological definitions were being publicly constructed. When Texans defined candidates or parties as "conservative" or "liberal," they typically used national issues for their contextualization. The most conspicuous element of this national context was the emerging red scare. The specter of communism emerged as a major force shaping conservative politics in Texas during the 1940s. It also contributed to the rise of several small but vocal extremist groups. At the same time, the growing discord between state conservatives and national party leaders erupted into full-scale political rebellion for four straight presidential elections between 1944 and 1956. In each instance, many conservative Texas Democrats either threatened to or actually did abandon tradition when voting at the national level, choosing ideological commitment ahead of partisan loyalty. Each instance represented a step toward the formation of a legitimate two-party system in Texas, though each case was momentary and eventually followed by a recommitment to the tradition of Democratic loyalty.[25]

The first of these episodes came in 1944 when a group of conservative Democrats, angry over the state party's commitment to the national renomination of Roosevelt for a fourth term, organized a revolt at the state party convention. Dubbed the Texas Regulars, these conservatives formed a short-lived third-party movement dedicated solely to FDR's defeat in the general election. The Texas Regulars—many of whom continued to hold a grudge against FDR for his decision to dump John Nance Garner from the ticket in 1940 and instead run alongside the left-wing friend of organized labor, Henry Wallace—adamantly and vocally opposed the New Deal as well as the wartime economic restrictions (such as rationing) that, they argued, were impeding free enterprise.[26]

The Regulars' defection did not affect many local races, where most conservative Democrats continued to run and win offices under the party name and with the backing of those in the Regular movement. Furthermore, the defection had only a limited effect on the presidential race, though the 12 percent it received in statewide vote totals was hardly insignificant. Much of the Regulars' failure in 1944 can be attributed to an inability to cooperate with state Republicans who sympathized with the movement's anti–New Deal conservatism but demanded that the Democratic rebels support the GOP presidential nominee, Thomas Dewey, rather than the Regulars' uncommitted slate of electors. Nonetheless, the revolt was a significant moment in the history of Texas politics. Though impeded by bickering similar to that which had destroyed Al Smith's chances in 1928, the Texas Regular movement of 1944—in the context of a drastically different state economic structure—proved more indicative of long-term political change than did the defections of 1928. Ultimately, the precedent established by conservative Texas Democrats, unhappy with the direction of the national party and willing to abandon that party out of ideological conviction, was as significant as anything else born of the revolt.[27]

Though secondary as an issue when compared to the animosity evoked

by the New Deal, the Supreme Court's 1944 decision in *Smith v. Allwright*—
a Texas case in which the state's all-white primary was ruled unconstitu-
tional—also roused the ire of conservative Texas Democrats, many of
whom used the decision as another rationale for the Regulars' defection. In
addition to eight other planks, which dealt primarily with issues of economic regulation, labor unions, and government bureaucracy, the Texas
Regulars' 1944 platform called for the return "of state rights which have
been destroyed by the Communist-controlled New Deal" and the "restora-
tion of the supremacy of the white race."[28] As was true in most southern
states, such associations between race and communism were common in
Texas in the early postwar years. In Texas, however, most conservative
Democrats stressed privately, and sometimes publicly, that race relations
were only a secondary concern. The racist vote was not big enough to warrant being a candidate's sole focus. The bigger and more dangerous enemy,
according to conservatives in the state Democratic establishment, was the
expansion of New Deal liberalism and all it allegedly entailed, including
support for radical labor, Marxist doctrine being taught in the college class-
room, acceptance of homosexuality and other forms of sexual perversion, a
regulated economy that smacked of totalitarianism, and the push for racial
equality that underscored a dangerous brand of socialism and class
consciousness.[29]

In 1948, four years after the revolt of the Texas Regulars, a rebellion
fueled by similar sentiment emerged in the Deep South and then expanded
into peripheral southern states like Texas, where the connections between
liberalism, communism, and race continued to grow. Motivated primarily
by Harry Truman's public support for antilynching legislation, abolition of
the poll tax, the Fair Employment Practices Committee, the desegregation
of the federal government and armed forces, and civil rights for African
Americans more generally, conservative Deep South Democrats organized
the States' Rights Democratic Party in 1948, a third party whose members
were soon dubbed "Dixiecrats." Several former delegates from Texas, some
of whom had participated in the Regulars' revolt of 1944, pushed to support the Dixiecrat movement. However, most conservative Texans were less
inclined to abandon their partisan loyalties in 1948 than they had been in
1944, when race had been only a secondary concern. The uncommitted
slate of electors running under the banner of the Texas Regulars in 1944
had earned 12 percent of the state's vote. Strom Thurmond, the Dixiecrat
nominee for president in 1948, garnered only 9 percent in Texas, though he
carried Louisiana, South Carolina, Alabama, and Mississippi, in which he
received a whopping 87 percent of the vote. Only in North Carolina did the

Dixiecrat ticket fare worse than it did in Texas. In fact, Truman's 66 percent of the 1948 vote in Texas was the highest plurality he received from any state in the nation.[30]

Truman's overwhelming victory in Texas belied serious and manifest tensions between state conservatives and state liberals in the late 1940s. Yet it also illustrated the tenacity of partisan loyalties and traditions. The revolts of 1944 and 1948 shared much in common, but their constituencies were actually quite different. The Dixiecrat vote of 1948 drew support almost exclusively out of East Texas, the only section of the state with a concentrated black population. The Dixiecrat revolt was almost entirely the manifestation of a racial backlash. The Regular movement of 1944, on the other hand, had drawn voters from across the state. Those voters had more in mind than simply issues of race when they temporarily defected from the Democratic Party.[31]

The emerging red scare, hastened in the late 1940s by espionage scandals, Soviet expansion into Eastern Europe, and the "fall of China," made conservative anticommunists paranoid, defensive, and occasionally aggressive in their zeal to rid Texas of subversion. In postwar Texas, a countersubversive brand of anticommunism gave rise to several grassroots political action groups. In this climate of fear and paranoia, the conservative Democratic establishment was forced not only to fight off the liberal minority within its own party but also to meet the challenge of an emerging anticommunist far-right wing.[32]

The postwar red scare blossomed quickly in Texas because its elements had been brewing in the state for decades. Anticommunism was certainly a significant element of the Ku Klux Klan's appeal in the early 1920s, and among the nation's first elected and most notable red-baiters was Congressman Martin Dies, representing a district from Southeast Texas. Dies became the first chairman of the House Committee on Un-American Activities, serving in that capacity from 1938 to 1944. He pioneered many of the red-baiting techniques later perfected by Joseph McCarthy, including the practice of making public accusations without evidentiary support and the use of broadcast media as a mobilization tool. Dies, however, was by no means the only Texas red-baiter serving in an elected capacity during the period. Among the state's most famous and charismatic public officials was W. Lee O'Daniel, better known as "Pass the Biscuits Pappy," a nickname he carried as a result of his very popular radio show, which featured country and western music and advertisements for his Fort Worth–based flour business. More important, O'Daniel's radio program served as a base for his successful gubernatorial bid in 1938. Reelected in 1940 and then elected senator in 1941, O'Daniel masterfully reflected many of the elements that would make future politicians in Texas successful. He personified the image of the "nonpolitician" outsider, populist, and "good ole boy." He also made palatable a brand of right-wing anticommunism not noted for its subtlety. Having won his first election on a platform of "the Ten Commandments" and a motto of "the Golden Rule," O'Daniel used red-baiting tactics in subsequent campaigns to rally conservative support. In one instance, O'Daniel publicly charged that wartime rationing was "a Communistic, totalitarian measure designed to beat the people of the US into submitting to the edicts of an autocratic, bureaucratic dictatorship."[33]

In 1946, a controversy over academic freedom and allegations of "Marxist subversion" at the University of Texas so magnified the profile of fired university president Homer Rainey as to allow him a platform upon which to run for governor. Lambasted in the campaign as a friend of radical labor and an adherent of radical left-wing ideology, Rainey was soundly defeated in a multicandidate Democratic primary and subsequent runoff against the ultimate victor, Beauford Jester. All things considered, Jester served as a relatively moderate governor. He was vociferously antiunion but was willing to negotiate with black leaders and even supported various civil rights measures, the passage of which, he argued, would take the wind out of many liberal and northern Republican sails. In July 1949, however, Jester suffered a sudden heart attack and died. He was succeeded by the state's lieutenant governor, Allan Shivers, who served the remainder of Jester's term before winning election in his own right in 1950.[34]

As governor from 1949 to 1957, Shivers ruled Texas during a time of intense anticommunist activity. During the early 1950s, several notable grassroots organizations, such as the Minute Women of Houston, began to exert greater pressure and enjoy wider influence at the local level, affecting school board elections, textbook adoptions, curriculum development, and even the firing of one superintendent deemed too "liberal" to serve the city's schoolchildren and their property-tax-paying parents. Organizations like the Minute Women were reacting to the red scare hysteria that had gripped Texas and the nation. In this context, most challenges to the traditional order were seen as subversive and suspect.[35]

The Shivers administration was further confronted with several monumental changes in race relations—changes that threatened to make race a greater issue in Texas than ever before. One of these changes occurred in 1950, when the Supreme Court ruled in *Sweatt v. Painter* that the University of Texas could not exclude an African American from admission to its law school. This case helped pave the way for other NAACP cases to more effectively challenge the doctrine of "separate but equal," most notably *Brown v. Board of Education* (1954). The Supreme Court's actions also, however, added fuel to the countersubversive fire by making the Court another in the growing litany of federal institutions threatening to undermine Texans' desire for local control. Sensing the climate of right-wing hysteria, Shivers challenged these court decisions and mitigated the cries of the far-right wing by more seamlessly incorporating the fears and concerns of white, anticommunist Texans into the agenda and rhetoric of the state's conservative Democratic establishment.[36]

In the 1950s, Allan Shivers exerted as much or more influence on the earliest stages of partisan realignment and modern conservatism in Texas than anyone else. In 1952, he emerged as a major player on the national political scene by spearheading another defection of conservative Texas Democrats opposed to their party's presidential nominee. Yet the defection of 1952 was, at least among state party leaders, far more universal and influential than had been the previous intraparty revolts of 1928, 1944, and 1948. The overriding issue of the 1952 presidential election, at least as it played out in Texas, was whether or not the state would be allowed to maintain ownership of its offshore tidelands. Despite Truman having won a landslide victory in 1948, his popularity in Texas suffered a precipitous decline beginning in 1949. Several reasons account for this, including opposition to New Deal expansionism, fears of communism and subversion, disagreements over race relations and civil rights, and a culture of corruption that seemed to plague Washington and the administration. Yet, despite the fact that several of Truman's closest advisers hailed from Texas, Truman's popularity in the state suffered primarily because of the president's decision to instruct his attorney general to file suit against Texas, claiming federal ownership of the tidelands and, more important, the revenue generated from oil discoveries in those lands. Needless to say, a vast majority of Texans opposed relinquishing ownership rights to these tidelands, especially to the federal government, and claimed that the state maintained rights to the tidelands—defined as offshore lands extending three marine leagues (or about 10.5 miles) into the Gulf of Mexico—as a result of the annexation agreement that had officially brought Texas into the Union in 1845.[37]

Shivers used the tidelands controversy as justification for his leadership in another state Democratic revolt, this one targeting the national party's presidential candidate, Adlai Stevenson. Unlike in 1944 or 1948, Eisenhower, rather than enjoying the support of only an isolated faction of conservative Democrats, became the first Republican presidential candidate to receive an official endorsement from the Texas Democratic Party. Shivers then joined every other candidate for statewide office in 1952 by cross-filing as a Republican, thus appearing on ballots as the gubernatorial nominee of both parties. When the votes were counted in November, Shivers the Democrat had defeated Shivers the Republican by more than nine hundred thousand votes and Eisenhower had carried the state with a 53 percent majority. Shivers's actions in 1952 contributed to the popular image of the Republican Party as an emerging alternative for state conservatives whose footing with the national Democratic Party seemed increasingly less certain.[38]

In 1953, Eisenhower, who had openly supported Texas's claims of tidelands ownership during his campaign a year earlier, signed a law coauthored by the newly elected senator from Texas, Price Daniel. This law guaranteed the state ownership of its tidelands and the revenue generated as a result. Having successfully used the tidelands controversy to demonstrate a tangible and immediate threat posed by the federal government to the people of Texas, Shivers expanded his power and influence. For the next several years, he continued to lead the conservative Democratic opposition to all things liberal, once again organizing a successful "Texas Democrats for Eisenhower" movement in 1956.

His popularity and influence within the Democratic establishment, however, began to dip slightly in 1956, in large part, ironically, because of his partisan disloyalty. Hoping to avoid the defections that had given the state to Eisenhower in 1952, loyalist influencers in the Texas Democratic Party, such as Sam Rayburn, Lyndon Johnson, and Price Daniel, worked to deny Shivers a position of leadership within the 1956 state convention. As a result, the state Democratic Party did not officially endorse Eisenhower in 1956 as it had four years earlier. At the same time, when Daniel vacated his Senate seat in 1956 in order to run for (and win) the governorship, the intraparty divisions that had emerged between Democratic loyalists, "Shivercrats," and moderate liberals opened the door for Texas liberals' favorite son, Ralph Yarborough, to win a 1957 special election to the U.S. Senate. Twice beaten in races for the governorship by intense race- and red-baiting, Yarborough capitalized on the intraparty splits and won a multicandidate race that, because of state laws governing special elections, did not require a runoff.[39]

Despite factional polarization within the Texas Democratic Party, Shivers still enjoyed the national spotlight and relished being seen as an independent and rebellious maverick. The question of whether or not Shivers would support the Democratic Party's presidential ticket garnered significant attention, which is one reason why he again bucked party tradition in 1960 to endorse Richard Nixon over John F. Kennedy. Though Democrats continued to dominate state and local elections, Republican presidential candidates clearly began to attract healthier followings in Texas during the 1950s, thanks largely to Shivers's stand that ideological conviction trumped partisan loyalty.[40]

It would be a mistake, however, to simplify the broader narrative by saying that Texas Republicans became viable or that a legitimate two-party system emerged in Texas during the 1950s. As conservative Texas Democrats brought unprecedented popularity to the Republican Party, the state GOP nonetheless struggled with its own factionalism throughout the decade. The party took a major step toward legitimacy in 1952 when it purged itself of the patronage-obsessed leaders whose utility for the party had long been based solely in receiving scraps from the national party's table. With new but still relatively powerless leadership, the Texas GOP—for the first time—began to focus on electoral success and real growth, not simply the favor of the national party. This purge, however, came at the price of increased discord. This discord manifested in 1952 over the GOP's presidential nomination, with many longtime party loyalists favoring the candidacy of the isolationist Senator Robert Taft of Ohio. For many Texas GOP loyalists, Taft represented a purer and more conservative brand of Republicanism than did the moderate Eisenhower. Also contributing to Taft's popularity in Texas was the fact that many state Republicans resented the fact that Eisenhower's popularity in the state was primarily the result of "Ike Democrats." For the few but committed and loyal Texas Republicans, attracting conservative Democrats was one thing, but relinquishing control to conservative Democrats was another—and many saw it as a devil's bargain they did not wish to make. Indeed, in office Eisenhower largely ignored the state's still embryonic Republican Party, choosing instead to cooperate with Shivers and the conservative Democratic establishment. In this political context, the growth enjoyed by the Texas Republican Party during the 1950s was largely the result of actions taken by state Democrats, not Republicans. Put another way, political power in Texas remained firmly entrenched within the Democratic Party even as national Republicanism became slightly more popular.[41]

All the while, the actions of conservative Democrats, liberals, and Republicans publicly reflected the maverick spirit of an independent Texas so deeply rooted in the state's political culture and tradition. An important example of this independence, as well as a critical aspect of the immediate political developments of the decade, was the tendency of Texas liberals no longer to support conservative Democrats during general elections, a tactic both spiteful and strategic—and one that became more common in the 1950s. Texas liberals rued the relative powerlessness they had been relegated to by the conservative majority within their own party, particularly since FDR's death in 1944. Yet for years, these liberals had still consistently supported the Democratic nominee for virtually every office in Texas, despite their ideological misgivings. Shivers's ability to organize a consistent mass defection among party conservatives in national campaigns—something that twice destroyed the liberal Stevenson's Democratic presidential candidacy in the state—angered and alienated Texas liberals and encouraged many to consider more actively ways to foment a permanent conservative migration to the GOP. That migration, liberals hoped, would free the Texas Democratic Party to support liberal candidacies at all levels of government: local, state, and national. As state conservatives increasingly refused to support liberal national candidates, state liberals began more commonly to withhold their support for establishment Democrats. In both cases, the long-term beneficiary was the Texas Republican Party, though again it is clear that Republican success in Texas depended upon receiving either the spiteful and strategic support of state liberals or the antiliberal support of conservative Democrats. Without these endorsements or contributions, Texas Republican campaigns usually languished and typically failed.[42]

In this climate of factionalism and confusion—and despite the occasional anomalous win in a local or state election of a liberal Democrat or a Republican—conservative Democrats maintained a firm grip on the state's top prize, the governor's mansion, and controlled Texas throughout the 1950s and into the 1960s. Still, the more precedents that were established for partisan realignment and Republican growth, the easier Republican efforts to communicate respectability and viability became. At the dawn of a new decade, the Texas political culture, rooted in traditions of independence, Democratic loyalty, and populist conservatism, struggled to hold back the tide of ideological conviction and polarization.[43]

The Fluke

Democrats finally broke the Shivercrats' power in 1960 when John F. Kennedy and his running mate, Lyndon Johnson, squeaked out a narrow, two-point win in Texas on their way to one of the closest and more controversial presidential elections of the twentieth century. Overcoming issues of religion (Kennedy was the first Catholic nominee since Al Smith's infamous campaign in 1928) and a well-organized, though almost exclusively urban, Republican effort spearheaded by Dallas County GOP chairman Peter O'Donnell, a young and increasingly influential conservative power-broker, the Kennedy-Johnson ticket reestablished Texas as a Democratic state. Still, the fact that Richard Nixon lost Texas only by 46,000 votes out of the almost 2.3 million cast, despite the presence of a Texan on the Democratic ticket, the relatively minor ideological differences between the two parties evident at the time, and the efforts of the popular incumbent Democratic governor Price Daniel working on behalf of his party, indicates how strongly the action of voting Republican at the presidential level—particularly in the evolving and thriving postwar economic and urbanizing climate—had become favored by conservatives in the state over the course of the previous decade.[44]

After Kennedy's narrow win in 1960, it was clear that for the Texas GOP to free itself from the grip of the conservative Democratic establishment it needed to maintain viability in future presidential elections. More important, it also needed a legitimate and viable presence in nonpresidential election years. This meant running legitimate and viable campaigns in state and local races and, eventually, doing something it had never done—winning a statewide contest in the post-Reconstruction era. Such a victory had always seemed out of reach—that is, until 1961.

Lost in the excitement over the presidential campaign was the fact that Lyndon Johnson actually won two elections in Texas in 1960. He and the head of his party's ticket carried the state's electoral votes for the first time in a presidential election since 1948. He also, however, won reelection to the U.S. Senate. Not willing to risk his status as majority leader, Johnson refused to bow out of his bid for reelection to the Senate despite being selected as his party's vice presidential nominee. Running for two offices simultaneously, Johnson angered many in the state Democratic establishment who wished to avoid the necessity of a special, off-year election in 1961. The state Democratic establishment's fear of the special election was not without precedent. Four years earlier, similar circumstances involving Price Daniel's election as governor had required a special, off-year election in order to fill Daniel's vacated Senate seat. That election had resulted in a victory for the liberal Ralph Yarborough, who won despite capturing only 38 percent of the vote. In a race that did not provide for a runoff and featured two legitimate conservative options in Martin Dies and the Republican, Thad Hutcheson, 38 percent proved a victorious plurality. Following Yarborough's election, conservatives in the Texas Democratic establishment feared that future special elections mixed with unusual circumstances could lead to more strange electoral consequences. Still firmly in control of the state legislature, these conservative Democrats altered the rules governing future special elections so that, by 1961, those elections would require a runoff between the leading two vote-getters, thus minimizing the probability that a candidate representing either the liberal Democratic faction or the GOP could win.[45]

Many of these conservative Texas Democrats were also responding to what they feared was an evaporating cushion of power. In 1954, Johnson, who had won in 1948 by running, essentially, as a conservative, easily won his first Senate reelection bid, defeating his Republican opponent, Carlos Watson (though it mattered little then or now what his opponent's name was) by earning an overwhelming, but not unexpected, 85 percent of the vote. In 1960, Johnson's opponent was John Tower, a relatively unknown professor of political science at Midwestern University in Wichita Falls. Running an aggressive campaign that made significant use of Nixon's appeal in urban areas across the state, the Republican Tower won an unprecedented 41 percent of the vote against the Democrat Johnson in the general election. Though Johnson had not publicly dignified the legitimacy of his opponent's campaign by campaigning himself, Tower's showing was an impressive feat and unquestionably made him the leading Republican contender for the Senate seat that Johnson vacated upon winning the vice presidency.[46]

When Johnson officially vacated his Senate seat in January 1961, Daniel appointed William A. Blakely as the state's interim senator. A conservative business leader from Dallas, Blakely seemed a perfect fit for the Democratic establishment and ran a reasonably successful special-election campaign, winning a plurality of Democratic votes thanks, ironically, to liberals' inability to unify behind a single candidate. Instead, three liberal candidates, each buoyed by Kennedy's victory in the state and Yarborough's success in 1957, vied with Blakely for Democratic loyalties. Blakely won the conservative vote, liberals split their vote three ways, and Tower carried the GOP vote. The newly legislated rules governing special elections set the stage for a runoff between Blakely and Tower—a contest that precedent suggested, because it pitted two conservatives against each other, would end in another Democratic victory.[47]

Blakely, however, underestimated the influence, alienation, and anger of liberal Texas Democrats. Texas liberals, though a minority within their own party, certainly carried enough clout that, when unified, they could make the difference in a close election. Unwilling to court liberal voters or to recognize the seriousness of Tower's emerging popularity in GOP and nonpartisan conservative circles, Blakely ran an uninspired and flat campaign. Tower, on the other hand, benefited from the hard work and ceaseless efforts of an aggressive campaign team as well as the ambivalence of liberal Democrats, many of whom began to talk of sitting the runoff election out entirely—a practice that became known as "going fishing on election day."[48]

For both disgruntled liberals and Tower's conservative Republican supporters, the idea of developing a legitimate two-party system in which conservatives controlled the GOP and liberals controlled the Democratic Party evolved as a powerful bridge uniting two seemingly incompatible factions. Tower grew fond of comparing the state's one-party system to "Communist Russia" and stressed to Republicans and prospective conservative Democratic converts that the two-party system was necessary in order to promote open debate and systematic democracy. Tower actively sought to prioritize the establishment of a two-party system despite conservative Democrats' perception that the seat of dominance in the national GOP rested in the Northeast among despised moderates like Nelson Rockefeller. "As a conservative I often wish that my own party were free of some of its liberal elements and that its policies were more resolutely conservative," Tower told an audience in Brownwood during the campaign. "But I would much rather be a constituent of a large, moderately conservative party that could reasonably expect to always influence public policy and periodically control the government, than a small, more conservative, but politically impotent group."[49]

Tower succeeded in making the two-party system and "ending the power of the political bosses" the two most salient issues of the 1961 runoff campaign. He also managed to undermine Blakely's conservative credentials by noting that the Dallas businessman had publicly supported both Kennedy and the "New Frontier" during the presidential campaign a year earlier. Kennedy's popularity in Texas began to fade almost immediately after he assumed office, making the charge an effective one. Though Blakely countered that he was "just being a good Democrat" and that Tower was the candidate of "modern Republicanism" and Eisenhower internationalism, the Republican seemed to maintain an edge in momentum and public buzz for most of the runoff.[50]

Tower also enjoyed the efforts of grassroots organizations like those participated in by Betty Andujar of Fort Worth. Andujar, who in 1972 won election as a Republican to the Texas State Senate, recalled the Tower campaign of 1961 as a "backyard" campaign. "People would have meetings in their homes and we would get our friends—we could get our church circle friends—to come, and John Tower would occasionally come, and they would hear him, and he was acceptable to them," she remembered more than three decades later. "That was the way we built it. People would have coffees in their homes or the backyard, and you would get your neighbors or anybody you could get to come. Once they were there, I think they got a good impression of the party and what it stood for." Andujar also noted that Tower's grassroots efforts were "almost entirely [made up of] women because, after all, the men were working."[51]

Throughout the campaign, sensing the momentum coming from such backyard rallies, Blakely persistently tried to undermine Tower's appeal to conservatives. This was, in fact, the only significant agenda of his runoff campaign. Blakely and other establishment Democrats argued that if Tower were a real conservative he would not welcome the support of disgruntled liberals. When the state's preeminent liberal periodical, the *Texas Observer,* endorsed Tower on the grounds that a Republican victory would hasten realignment, conservative Democrats countered that Tower should have repudiated the endorsement. In speeches by Blakely and his supporters, Tower's name was routinely mentioned alongside the names of Rockefeller and New York senator Jacob Javitz, both icons of the so-called northeastern establishment. One Democratic Party form letter asserted that Tower was "quite ready to play ball not only with the liberal faction of his own party but with the liberals in the Democratic Party."[52]

Establishment Democrats also tried to use Tower's education as evidence against his conservatism. Upon finishing graduate work at Southern Methodist University in Dallas, where conservative critics charged he had been "moderate so far as civil rights" were concerned, Tower briefly enrolled for postgraduate study at the London School of Economics and Political Science, a school Tower admitted was "widely known as the seat of 'socialist intellectual' disciplines of the notorious Harold Laski and Lord Keynes." The charge seemed so potentially damaging that Tower mailed voters a form letter in which he said he was "proud" to have "paid his own way" to the school, and that he had chosen the school "deliberately to study the socialist intellectual mind" in order to "understand the socialist" as his "enemy."[53]

The Tower-Blakely runoff further illustrated how anticommunism and red scare politics continued to play an important role in Texas in 1961. Asked in Houston whether or not he favored eliminating the House Committee on Un-American Activities, Tower responded that he believed it should be expanded, not eliminated.[54] Another national issue that seemed to play a significant role in the campaign was the debate that emerged over the so-called Connally Amendment. Named after the former senator from

Texas Tom Connally, the Connally Amendment was a declaration that the United States reserved the right to determine for itself whether issues fell under the jurisdiction of the World Court or of domestic courts. By the early 1960s, some thirty nations had agreed to accept the compulsory jurisdiction of the World Court, with the United States being the only country to include a caveat such as the Connally Amendment. When Lyndon Johnson began to advocate for the repeal of this amendment, Tower objected and rallied conservatives who feared that being subjected to the compulsory jurisdiction of the World Court was tantamount to "subjecting ourselves to the whims of communist and non-American courts."[55]

Tower used this controversy, along with a campaign designed to present himself as a "family man" and a "church man from a church family," to project an overall image as the candidate most in tune with Texans' basic attitudes, morals, and values. He opposed measures that would cost local schools control over their own operations should they accept government grants. He routinely waxed poetic about the virtues of the "free enterprise system" and charged that the liberalism of the national Democratic Party was kin to forms of socialism. He supported the limitation of foreign aid, even to countries whose interests were aligned with those of the United States. He also, very importantly, courted one of the key ingredients of the Democratic establishment's longevity, the support of oil companies. Tower strongly pushed for the protection of the oil depletion allowance, a measure that allowed oil producers to deduct 27.5 percent of their oil supply's annual value from their taxes each year for ten years—a tax benefit that paid, many times over, for the cost of initial investment while significantly reducing liabilities.[56]

For many Texans, supporting Tower became almost chic in 1961. Words and phrases like "new" and "different" and "a rare moment" peppered editorials, campaign contribution letters, and public speeches. The notion of electing a Republican to the Senate seemed to grip many Texans as an opportunity to reassert the state's tradition of maverick independence. Tower capitalized on this momentum and "rare" opportunity, rallied disaffected conservative Democrats whose loyalty to the establishment was weakening, benefited from the support of liberals, many of whom aided the Republican by simply not participating in the election, and reoriented the campaign discussion along the lines of national issues like taxes, foreign policy, and the role of the federal government. In doing this, Tower succeeded in making the election a referendum on the perceived liberalism of the national Democratic Party, while also convincing a growing contingent of conservatives that Texas desperately needed a two-party system.

Despite the best efforts of the well-funded Democratic establishment, Tower succeeded in becoming the first Republican senator from Texas since the Reconstruction era. He won by only 10,343 votes out of the more than 886,000 cast; his election was publicly dismissed as a "fluke" by many conservative Democrats, though they also privately acknowledged the reality that the days of the establishment's relatively uncontested domination in state and local elections were probably behind them. Even more important, conservatives from across the country viewed Tower's election as a seminal event. Thousands of congratulatory telegrams, letters, and phone calls from all corners of the nation showered Tower's campaign headquarters in the days following the election. Most expressed hope that Tower's victory would signal the beginning of a conservative revival and that the Republican Party could overcome its subjugation to the liberal northeastern establishment. Though Tower's election did not result in an immediate movement toward a two-party system in Texas, it was a remarkable opening salvo in a decade that would witness tougher challenges, increased factionalism in both parties, and a national conversation that began to more earnestly emphasize ideology ahead of partisan loyalty and tradition.[57]

Characterized by a tenuous balance among independence, rebellion, tradition, and loyalty, the roots of Texas's political culture extend into the state's history as far back as the early nineteenth century. Proud, with a penchant for nostalgia, Texans have long valued in their candidates the same basic characteristics they ascribe to their state and like to believe about themselves. Texans pride themselves on a patriotism rooted in their state's unique war for independence. They distrust and spew hostility toward most agents of "foreign" control, especially the vilified northeastern establishment that contributed to, in popular memory, the horrors of Reconstruction, the impoverishment of farmers, and the emergence of the federal welfare state. For decades they were convinced that the Democratic Party was the only party that represented their values, though the occasional rebellion against that tradition made the state's role in the Solid South less than solid.

As Texans tried to balance their maverick independence with their partisan loyalties, the world around them changed in profound ways. Their country became embroiled in two world wars and then a cold war. The relationship between the federal government and the people was revolutionized, as were the state's economy, geography, and demography. Oil fueled industrialization, urbanization, modernization, and the influx of thousands of opportunity-seeking neo-Texans. Each of these changes complicated the way that Texans applied their historic political culture to contemporary issues. In the process, Texans reassessed the meanings of conservatism, liberalism, and loyalty and struggled to maintain their historic balance among these impulses.

The rise of modern conservatism and the subsequent emergence of a strong and even dominant Texas Republican Party were delayed, however, by a decade-long struggle against extremism and perceptions of extremism. The Texas Democratic establishment maintained power through the 1960s and into the 1970s, despite obstacles that had manifested and matured as early as the 1940s. Democrats maintained power in large part because the nascent Republican Party was unable to fend off charges of extremism in the 1950s and early 1960s. This public relations war polarized factions within both parties and inhibited many state conservatives' impulse to abandon the fractured Democratic ship in favor of Republican waters. Understanding the most powerful national instance of perceived extremism necessitates, at least regarding Texas, a brief flashback to the world of Bruce Alger.

Chapter 2

Growing Pains
The Politics of Extremism

John Tower's stunning victory in 1961 can and should be seen as a seminal moment in the process of constructing a legitimate two-party Texas. Tower, however, was not the first Republican in the postwar era to make electoral waves in Texas. Coinciding with Dwight Eisenhower's popularity and a national trend toward fervent anticommunism was the rather anomalous success of Bruce Alger. In 1954, as the credibility of Joseph McCarthy began to crumble nationally, Alger became the first Republican since Reconstruction to win a congressional seat from Texas's fifth district.

Alger's victory must be understood in the context of early 1950s political culture. As Eisenhower made voting Republican at the presidential level more acceptable in Texas, and red scare anticommunism spoke to conservatives' postwar fears and paranoia, Alger's tenure in Congress reflects a complicated period in the history of the Texas GOP and, more important, the growing pains of modern conservatism. Between 1954 and 1964, as Eisenhower again carried Texas in 1956 and Nixon nearly did the same in 1960, a handful of local politicians like Alger waged a far more divisive and ideological war designed to separate conservatives from the Democratic Party. In doing so more effectively than any other local Republican of the period, Alger voiced many of the themes that conservatives would employ in the coming decades. At the same time, Alger also contributed to the most common critique levied against conservative Republicans during the era—that they belonged to a party that coddled a fringe, extremist minority and that sensible, mainstream Texans could and should continue to look to the Democratic Party for their peace and security.

In large part because of this critique, what Bruce Alger began in 1954 was lost by 1964, when both he and his party's nominee for president, Barry Goldwater, were soundly rejected by Texans who, against the backdrop of national, state, and local tragedy, reiterated their commitment to tradition, loyalty, and the perception of mainstream and moderate Democratic doctrines. The politics of extremism acted as an albatross around the

Dallas congressman Bruce Alger, c. 1960. The inscription reads, "To John [Tower], Texas and the Nation's 'Little Giant' —my colleague of the 'Other' Body—with admiration and respect. Sincerely, Bruce Alger, Texas 5th." (Courtesy of the John G. Tower Library and Archives, Georgetown, TX)

necks of Texas Republicans, who saw the gains of the Eisenhower years squelched by 1964.

The Career of Bruce Alger

In 1954 the Texas state legislature passed the Communist Control Act. Similar to laws passed in other state legislatures, this act outlawed the Communist Party in Texas. A handful of liberals aggressively opposed the measure as a violation of First Amendment rights, but could do nothing to thwart its momentum. The legislation passed easily. Under this act, persons convicted of involvement with the Communist Party in Texas faced a maximum sentence of twenty years in prison and up to a $20,000 fine. Allan Shivers, the state's popular governor, known nationally as the renegade who spearheaded the well-known Texas Democrats for Eisenhower movement, advocated making the maximum sentence not prison, but death.[1]

It was in a political culture conducive to this act that Dallas's Bruce Alger came to be the congressman representing Texas's fifth district. Alger was the first Republican elected to Congress from any district in Texas since Harry Wurzbach, the lonely Republican who represented San Antonio from 1920 until his death in office in 1931. Born in Dallas in 1918, Alger graduated from Princeton University in 1940 before serving as a B-29 commander in the Pacific during World War II. Following the war, he returned to Dallas where he enjoyed success in the city's postwar real estate and construction boom. In 1954, Alger won election to Congress, defeating his Democratic opponent, Wallace Savage, by a margin of 53–47 percent. Savage's 1954 campaign struggled for several reasons. A bitter primary fight between Savage and another, more liberal candidate had cost Democrats far more money than was typically spent for such a race. As a result, campaign contributions were less available for the general election. Business leaders were also hesitant to provide further financial backing to Savage. The acrimonious primary fight further forced each Democratic candidate to wage a more aggressive, offensive campaign, which resulted in the alienation, in this case, of the losing liberal constituency. One local area newspaper went so far as to attribute Alger's victory to the support he received from "liberal Democrats and labor union members" who either passive-aggressively opposed Savage by not voting, or opposed him outright by voting for Alger.[2]

Alger, on the other hand, enjoyed surprisingly widespread support. He benefited from a well-organized corps of grassroots door-to-door and neighborhood organizations, most of which were led by cadres of Republican women. He received the *Dallas Morning News*'s de facto endorsement when the paper refused to endorse the conservative Democratic candidate, as was typical. He also enjoyed the support of Edward Marcus, cofounder of the Neiman Marcus department store chain, as well as that of sympathetic local television station WFAA, which allowed him several guest appearances on a popular morning show directed toward women called *Coffee Time*. During the final week of the campaign, Alger appeared on the show five times. On four of those occasions, Alger was accompanied by either Dwight Eisenhower or Richard Nixon. In fact, Eisenhower's participation in Alger's 1954 campaign was an unusual break from the norm for the president, who typically supported conservative Texas Democrats as a nod to the critical support those Democrats had provided him in 1952. As Savage struggled to maintain the support that would traditionally have been his, Alger used Eisenhower's popularity and the budding support of local businesses, grassroots women volunteers, and the media to score an impressive and surprising victory.[3]

As Tower would do in 1961, Alger in 1954 ran as a conservative dedicated to building a viable state Republican Party. He argued that his campaign was a necessary step toward the construction of a legitimate two-party system. His campaign brochures, newsletters, and advertisements featured two headlines: "Dedicated to Building a Two-Party System" and "An Eisenhower Republican." Alger included on the cover of his campaign brochure a photograph of him and Eisenhower shaking hands. At virtually every public appearance, Alger delivered some variation of a standard stump speech that he entitled "Why Republican Majority Is Essential." "We must decide whether we wish to stick with the job of restoring our country to solvency, of keeping our economic and moral integrity, of making the United States a bulwark against World Communism . . . or whether we want to swing back—leftward—along the easy downhill stretch that leads to bankruptcy, bungling, and further bending to the global Red threat," Alger would say. According to Alger in 1954, a Republican majority was essential to fighting communism abroad and protecting against communist infiltration at home, promoting efficiency in government, lowering taxes, stopping inflation, and ensuring peace, security, and a strong national defense.[4]

Over the next several years, Alger's rhetoric grew more conservative as he began to focus more tightly on national issues. Throughout 1955, Alger focused on drawing connections between what he called "liberal" or "New Deal" economics and socialism. He often criticized liberals' "something-for-nothing philosophy," as he saw it, and called advocates of that philosophy "avowed socialists" who were "undermining the country's economic strength as a friend—not an avowed enemy such as the communist we have come to recognize as antithetical to all we believe—and now is dedicated to the overthrow of our country." Alger warned that Americans "recognize communism as an enemy, yet communism is economically a socialistic form of government, and there is the great danger. Too many of our well-meaning socialistic friends of the last two decades are playing right into the communistic hands. The godless materialism of this philosophy must not be for this great country of ours." For Alger and many of his conservative constituents, the line between New Deal liberalism and socialism was thin, if it even existed at all, while the line between socialism and communism was only one of gradation. All such political philosophies, he argued, worked together against the common good of the nation.[5]

In addition to intensified and broadened opposition to "liberal" economics, race also played a far more important role in Alger's first reelection campaign than it had two years earlier. In 1954, even against the backdrop of *Brown v. Board of Education*, Alger largely minimized race as an issue. By 1956, the swelling discomfort over school desegregation created an atmosphere in which conservatives in both parties were able to use race as a weapon, most often couched synonymously with the growing communist threat, big government, and socialism. Alger used race as a wedge designed to separate conservatives from the Democratic Party. On September 24 he released a statement in which he denounced "forced integration," said that *Plessy v. Ferguson* was "right" and *Brown v. Board* was "wrong," noted that the *Plessy* court had consisted of six Republicans, while the *Brown* court consisted of seven Democrats, and vowed not to change his "convictions, merely because a Democrat Supreme Court rejected the correct doctrine announced by a Republican Supreme Court sixty years ago." Despite these frequent injections, race was still not yet something that a Texas Republican could safely overexploit in a campaign. Acknowledging that his Democratic opponent in 1956 was also an avowed segregationist, Alger was careful not to make race the sole issue of the campaign, knowing that to do so would risk making a traditional Democratic candidate more appealing. Instead, Alger said that "segregation should not be an issue in this campaign," citing his and his opponent's agreement on the issue, while applauding his opponent for adopting "the Republican view." This aversion to discussing race, at least explicitly, would become a mainstay in Texas Republican campaign strategy in the coming decades.[6]

As important as race was in 1956, it comprised only a fraction of Alger's larger message about conservatism, partisan loyalty, and his own qualifications to best represent the people of Dallas. As he had in 1954, Alger again used WFAA-TV as a stage for his reelection campaign, though this time he had his own program—*Coffee with Your Congressman, Bruce Alger*. On October 26, 1956, Alger was introduced to local television audiences as "a family man" who "knows the problems of feeding and raising a family." Alger was then welcomed onto the set, accompanied by his family, each member of which was then individually introduced. During those introductions Alger mentioned the local schools that his children attended as well as the Sunday school class in which they were currently participating.[7]

In addition to local television exposure, Alger also benefited from evolving, effective, and diversified grassroots efforts such as Operation Yard Sign, Operation Car Sign, Operation Telephone Poll, Operation Doorbell, and Operation Victory Drive, the last-named of which was specifically designed to provide transportation to prospective voters who otherwise might not make it to the polls on election day. These grassroots organizations further distributed a flyer rejecting what it called the "lies" of the Democratic opposition, including charges that Alger had courted the "Negro Vote," was a tool of "wealthy Republicans," and that the Democratic Party was the "future." Alger's campaign volunteers worked tirelessly to tell Dallas voters that the Republican candidate was a "Jeffersonian in thinking" and that he "accurately represents the viewpoint of the people." "Have Southern Democrats held the line against Socialism and encroachment on States Rights?" these volunteers questioned in flyers and brochures designed to depict Alger as a conservative populist. Alger clearly benefited from such grassroots efforts, which worked to undermine conservatives' loyalty to the Democratic Party by associating that party with socialism and "Northern radicals." For Alger loyalists, Republicanism was the wave of the future, the voice of the middle class, and the best defense against encroaching communism, socialism, and liberalism.[8]

The political mastermind behind Alger's campaigns in Dallas in the late 1950s and early 1960s was a wealthy young investor from the area named Peter O'Donnell. O'Donnell's success in coordinating Alger's campaigns and sustaining the Republican's career would eventually carry him into ever-higher levels of power within the state and national Republican Party. In 1960, O'Donnell engineered Richard Nixon's relatively successful, though ultimately losing, Texas campaign against John F. Kennedy. Nevertheless, he made Dallas the most pro-Nixon city in the nation that year. In 1961, O'Donnell engineered Tower's shocking election to the U.S. Senate and, in 1964, would get yet another opportunity to lead a conservative charge—this time running Barry Goldwater's campaign.[9]

With O'Donnell at the helm, Alger's reelection campaigns were noted for their emphasis on national, not local, issues. More precisely, Alger's campaigns communicated national issues—what he often called the battle of "Conservative versus Liberal control of Congress"—as fundamentally local. Alger once called Eisenhower a "native son" of Texas and "the most prominent Texan who ever lived." (Eisenhower was born seventy miles north of Dallas in Denison, Texas, though he always claimed Kansas as his home state.) In 1956, Alger commented on the tidelands controversy by saying that the "New Deal Supreme Court" had tried to take away "your tidelands."[10] This tactic of personalizing national issues along partisan lines was used with great effect by other conservatives and many Republicans in Texas for decades to come as a means of making the party's message more consistent and GOP candidates more appealing. National animosities were highlighted in order to undermine local Democratic loyalties. By emphasizing family, church, free-enterprise economics, and anticommunism, Alger was able to do what future Republican conservatives would also do— attract a sizable following among a growing white, Protestant, and suburban middle class.

By 1959, Alger's conservative rhetoric seemed, to some national observers, more radical than it had seemed just a few years earlier, particularly in the context of the growing national liberal consensus and corresponding fatigue of red scare anticommunism. In Dallas, though, he continued to attract a sizable following as a voice of practical and reasonable conservatism. That Bruce Alger was its congressional representative furthered the widely held belief that Dallas, by the early 1960s, was the capital of right-wing American conservatism. In advance of Nikita Khrushchev's famous visit to the United States that fall, Alger denounced the Soviet leader and warned that Stalin's prediction of a United States that would "spend itself into bankruptcy" was on the brink of becoming true thanks to New Deal liberalism, something conservatives feared had infiltrated and moderated Eisenhower's administration.[11]

In 1960, the same year that he very famously led a raucous protest against Lyndon Johnson outside the luxurious Adolphus Hotel on the streets of downtown Dallas, Alger called a proposed civil rights bill a "masquerade" to promote "forced integration and massive federal aid to education." He then warned that the bill's provision for a $10,000 fine or two years of imprisonment as punishment for interfering with or obstructing school desegregation would "land you in jail" for simply disagreeing with racial integration. He also charged that the bill's efforts to eliminate racial discrimination in job hiring destroyed citizens' "right" to hire and fire whom they wished. Alger was at the forefront of the GOP in pioneering the use of race as a segue to broader, more "color-blind" criticisms of federal intervention and inappropriate government intrusions. Whether the issue was race or national security, Alger's rhetoric grew more dogmatic and strident in the late 1950s and early 1960s.[12]

Alger's opposition to school desegregation, or even civil rights more generally, did not place him outside of the conservative mainstream. His growing affiliation with General Edwin A. Walker and the John Birch Society, however, did. Edwin A. Walker was a Texas-born career military man, probably most famous for a failed assassination attempt made against him by Lee Harvey Oswald in February 1963. While serving in Germany in 1961, General Walker initiated an anticommunist indoctrination program he called "Pro-Blue"—alluding to the practice of some global mapmakers to recognize the expansion of communism with the color red and "free" areas with the color blue. Walker was subsequently charged with distributing to his troops literature published by the militantly anticommunist grassroots organization the John Birch Society. He resigned under pressure in November 1961, moved to Dallas, and immediately became a cult hero among anticommunist conservatives, particularly in Texas and other parts of the South.[13]

Just a few months later, Walker entered the race for the governorship of Texas. He did so as a Democrat, despite the pleadings of Bruce Alger, who was convinced that the patriotic Walker, ill treated by what he saw as a disturbingly liberal military, was perfectly suited for a career in the Texas Republican Party. Walker's resistance to switching parties was rooted in his segregationist convictions. Though he had helped lead Eisenhower's determined effort to integrate Little Rock's Central High School in 1957, Walker had also participated in segregationist protests in Mississippi and other parts of the Deep South, where conservative Democrats, who ruled in a one-party system dominated by issues of race, vigorously resisted the integrationist changes mandated by the Supreme Court and federal government. Though his action was not a significant display of bipartisanship, Alger nonetheless supported Walker's bid for the governorship, which ended in an embarrassing sixth-place finish out of six candidates running in the Democratic primary.[14]

Alger's support for Walker reflected his movement over time into increasingly right-wing waters. At the very least, Alger's conservatism came to be seen as more extreme as his career progressed. Alger, who once lost a vote in Congress 378–1 (the issue was whether or not to provide free milk for elementary school children) never passed or even significantly influenced a single piece of legislation during his decade in Washington.[15] What he did accomplish, however, was the acquisition of a wide following of both admirers and detractors, attracted to the Dallasite's proclivity for national attention on national issues. While Alger was courting Walker, he also found his name increasingly connected with the actions of the John Birch Society, which enjoyed a relatively sizeable following of loyalists in Dallas. Though Alger's critics often associated him with the extremism of both Walker and the Birchers, in truth Alger's relationship with the far-right anticommunist organization was less than warm. On numerous occasions, Alger publicly criticized Birch founder Robert Welch for "militaristic and dogmatic" tactics, though Alger always tempered his remarks by reminding audiences that he agreed with the society's basic principles and vision. When, in the spring of 1961, Alger suggested on local television that the John Birch Society's tactics caused more harm than good to the conservative cause, so many letters of dissatisfaction poured in from Dallas-area citizens that Alger was forced to respond with a form letter to his own supporters in which he defended his anticommunist credentials.[16]

Alger's last successful reelection campaign came in 1962. That year, for the first time in any of his campaigns, the issue of religion was front and center in Alger's construction of a conservative vision for Dallas. Though he had alluded to religion in earlier campaigns, those allusions had always come in the context of his critiques on liberalism, socialism, and communism. Until 1962, however, Alger was a relatively consistent proponent of the separation of church and state, particularly on the issue of whether or not churches should receive federal dollars. The Supreme Court's famous decision in *Engel v. Vitale* changed Alger's stance on the role of religion in shaping conservative worldviews. The court's decision to essentially ban school-sponsored prayer riled Alger and many of his followers. For the final two years of his tenure in office, Alger grew far more committed to preserving the Protestant Christian traditions he believed were reflected in his Dallas constituency.[17]

Alger's campaign in 1962 did not, however, abandon other aspects of the conservative worldview for a critique solely focused on the nation's spiritual drifting. Alger latched onto numerous hot-button issues in the early 1960s, each of which was designed to pit voters who were protective of vaguely defined local control and free enterprise against the encroachments of "Kennedy-liberalism" and the federal government. For instance, Alger aggressively used the issue of public housing to his advantage in 1962. In a brochure widely distributed across his congressional district, a pro-Alger grassroots organization called Dallas Voters against Public Housing told voters that "Public Housing is wrong because those who work for a living and pay their rightful share of taxes are forced against their will to subsidize others." "Public Housing," the brochure warned, "is the greatest step toward socialism." In cooperation with such grassroots organizations, Alger denounced the federal program and, more important, the Democratic Party that supported it. This denunciation included harsh words for Dallas's mayor, Democrat Earle Cabell, whose support for the program and for his party was used by Alger as evidence of the mayor's unfitness for office.[18]

For most of his career, Alger was committed to building a two-party system in which conservatives belonged to the Republican Party. Yet in the early 1960s, Alger's attacks against Democratic liberalism were not often accompanied with much Republican fanfare. Alger, like many local conservatives, yearned for a national GOP that embraced rather than marginalized the right wing.[19] Disgruntled by the prominent leadership of northeastern moderates like Nelson Rockefeller, Alger largely avoided the word "Republican" in 1962, favoring instead the word "conservative." Always insistent on prioritizing national issues in local campaigns, Alger and O'Donnell both chose to emphasize Democratic liberalism as the campaign's chief target. "No matter how conservative a Democrat may be personally," Alger argued in one campaign brochure, "unless he abstains from voting on the organization of Congress, he votes to put leadership of Congress in the hands of radical liberals."[20] Even after helping Alger win reelection in 1962, O'Donnell took every possible opportunity to scare Texas voters away from the Democratic Party. Noting in December that area Congressman Joe Pool, elected as a conservative Democrat, "flip-flopped" on Kennedy's Medicare bill, O'Donnell said, "There is a lesson for Texas conservatives in this sorry spectacle. Once elected, new Democrat congressmen will not act or vote as conservatives. They are conservatives of convenience who take off their conservative campaign clothing once the election is over in order to get along with the liberals who control the national Democratic Party."[21]

Alger's Democratic opponent in 1962 was Bill Jones. Jones, more than any previous Democrat running against Alger, tried to paint the Republican incumbent as an extremist—as dangerous and out of step with average Texans. He called Alger "individually irresponsible" and charged that the Republican was using emotional scare tactics to win reelection.[22] Jones lost, but in 1963, Alger's rhetoric intensified, growing more noticeably defiant and extreme—particularly in its criticism of President Kennedy—and eventually landed him in hot water. [23]

Alger's vitriolic attacks against Kennedy placed him in an awkward position on November 22, 1963, when the President was murdered on the streets of Alger's congressional district in downtown Dallas. In following weeks, Alger was clearly shaken and unclear as to how to respond. In his first weekly newsletter following the assassination, he expressed much grief and sorrow, defending his previous newsletters as "opposition, not hate." The national media's rush to blame Dallas, in part, for Kennedy's death— citing the city's proclivity for right-wing hostility, the John Birch Society's popularity, Alger's confrontation with Johnson in 1960, and another famous incident earlier in the year in which U.N. ambassador Adlai Stevenson was physically confronted by a female protester—placed Alger and other local conservatives on the defensive against charges of extremism.[24]

Just over five months later, in May 1964, Alger, preparing for another reelection bid, told his campaign staff that the upcoming campaign would be his toughest fight yet. The Democrat opposing Alger was Dallas's mayor, Earle Cabell. Cabell, Alger warned, had received more consistently positive exposure in Dallas than he had. Though this assertion is debatable, considering Alger's previous use of television and his always-entertaining rhetoric, the Republican's campaign determined to use television to its advantage in 1964, knowing that image would be the determining factor in the election. Throughout his career Alger always tried to fashion himself as a populist and an underdog. He based this image on his being consistently outmatched in campaign funds by his Democratic opponents. Yet Alger's image had grown more divisive, more extreme, and less mainstream since the late 1950s. Dallas's volatile atmosphere only enhanced this perception. In 1964, Alger acknowledged that the presence of a Texan in the White House coupled with Kennedy's assassination in Dallas would create a very inhospitable climate for his reelection. He worried that the less conservative of Dallas's two newspapers, the *Dallas Times Herald,* would "stage a far more vicious campaign . . . than it [had] ever done before." "The assassination will be a factor," Alger told his campaign staff. "There are a sizable number of voters who will tie together the Johnson demonstration, the Adlai Stevenson incident, and the assassination and will react against our candidacy." [25]

Alger knew that his reelection bid depended on maintaining the image that he was a mainstream, patriotic Texas conservative rather than an extremist. His campaign strategy was rooted in an effort to label Cabell a "phony conservative" who was "committed to the ultra-liberal Johnson program." Alger warned that Cabell would be a "rubber-stamp for Johnson" and even tried to connect Cabell, through Johnson, to "Adam Clayton Powell, the lawlessness of the civil rights demonstrators, [and] the whole sorry Democratic mess in Washington." "Our whole approach has got to be less scholarly, more dramatic," one campaign staffer told a group of pro-Alger volunteers. "Scareheads and dramatic headlines and questions in our literature will be more effective than long discussions of past history and comparisons of voting records." [26]

Many of Alger's constituents disapproved of this tactic and worried about their congressman's image as an extremist. Quite simply, the feeling in Dallas in 1964 was one of defensive caution. With a Democratic Texan in the White House and the very fresh memory of Kennedy's murder, locals retreated from the divisive and ideological conservatism that had made Alger popular for ten years. Some expressed a fear that reelecting Alger would send the wrong message to a nation still grieving over the death of its president. Many warned Alger to wage a campaign based on positives, not negatives. Reflecting later on his 1964 defeat of Alger, Earle Cabell believed his opponent had become imbued with an "obstructionary" rather than conservative philosophy. "It made Welch and his Birch Society look like communists," Cabell said in an interview in 1974. When asked why he was able to defeat Alger, Cabell cited Alger's "negativism" and the fact that, in the wake of Kennedy's death, Democrats enjoyed "pretty good cohesion." Running as a conservative Democrat, Cabell held backyard barbeques, gave away plenty of cold beer, and effectively courted the area's precinct chairmen, district commissioners, and all the state legislative candidates on his way to ousting the "obstructionary" Alger from his congressional seat.[27]

A Republican consistently dismissed by his Democratic opponents as part of the extreme right wing, Bruce Alger had, nonetheless, defied the political odds to win five elections in Dallas before finally losing in 1964. It is important to note in hindsight, however, that Alger seemed far less extreme when he was first elected in 1954 than he did in 1964, when he finally lost. Part of this was due to the fact that Alger's rhetoric grew more militant during his ten years in office. More of it, however, was due to the fact that the national political culture grew less militant during that same period, the result of a series of episodes that spotlighted the perceived dangers that came with the conservatism of a man like Bruce Alger.[28]

Alger was not the only conservative to go down to defeat in Texas in 1964. Though not running for office himself, conservative campaign strategist Peter O'Donnell lost two campaigns in 1964. Not only did his favorite congressman from Dallas fail to win reelection, but the presidential candidate whose campaign he had helped to construct also went down to a decisive defeat, thanks in large part to the same climate of political contrition, moderation, and antiextremism that doomed Alger.[29]

Icons and Voices

Bruce Alger lost in 1964, but the transition of modern Texas conservatism into its future Republican home had only just begun. Despite agitation, growth, and significant factional tensions within both parties during the preceding decades, the concurrent rise of modern Texas conservatism alongside a viable Texas GOP actually began in earnest in 1964, ironically, with the landslide national election of a liberal Texas Democrat.

Texans' understanding of the relationship between political ideology and partisan politics, and especially their understanding of what it meant to be conservative and what it meant to be liberal, was redefined during the 1960s and 1970s. This redefinition was shaped, in large part, by those influential enough to warrant the most media coverage, as well as those influencing the media's agenda from within. Throughout the 1960s, as social changes collided with political traditions in a state where power had long depended on loyalty and tradition, the established status quo came under fire, questioned by both the Right and the Left, while a Texan in Washington worked feverishly, against the odds, to maintain it. Within this context, and rather quickly, ideological definitions and popularities came increasingly under the influence of an image-conscious political culture. As a result, as Bruce Alger's career had highlighted, political parties become more inextricably linked to national issues, redefined ideological perceptions, and icons.

Lyndon Johnson was one such icon. As an icon against which conservatives would define their own political beliefs throughout the 1960s and 1970s, LBJ stands as a central figure in the rise of modern conservatism, both nationally and in Texas. As the first president to call Texas home, Johnson had been in office less than a year when an overwhelming majority of Texans went to the polls in November 1964 to support their native son's bid to win his own full term in the Oval Office. That Texans would rally behind a native son, even a liberal one, is not terribly surprising. For most Texans, the issue at hand in 1964 was not liberalism but rather loyalty, contrition, and moderation.

Johnson's shadow hovered over national politics in the 1960s much as it had in Texas throughout his early career. Johnson emerged as a major political presence in Texas as a New Deal liberal, but was perfectly willing throughout his career to adjust his ideological leanings to the context of his times. In 1937, he ran as a New Dealer. In 1948, he won as a cold warrior, opposing civil rights and supporting the antilabor Taft-Hartley bill. By 1964, no longer bound to the constituency of just one district or state, he was imagining the Great Society. These inconsistencies reflected Johnson's true love and passion—himself and his desire to win elections. Yet Johnson, though ideologically more a liberal than anything else, was also a pragmatist. LBJ always boasted that his agenda was Texas's agenda. Johnson's support in Texas bears this out, despite the fact that most Texans identified themselves as conservative or moderate—certainly not liberal. Thanks to forces spiraling out of his control, however, Johnson, by the end of his presidency, had come to personify the failures of 1960s liberalism in much the same way that Ronald Reagan eventually came to personify the perceived successes of modern conservatism.[30]

Johnson's inability to manage his own image, painfully obvious by the end of his presidency, while others so clearly used him as a negative icon, speaks loudly to the force of perception. One of Johnson's greatest adversaries, and among the most influential emerging voices of the Texas liberal minority of the early 1960s, was Ronnie Dugger. Dugger was a Texas liberal-populist who, in 1954, became the first editor of the new and ultimately very influential liberal periodical the *Texas Observer*. Dugger used the *Observer*, despite a circulation of only ten thousand, to promote what he called "a spirit of independence." He sought to expose the graft, corruption, and privilege he and other liberals believed characterized the conservative Democratic establishment, which worked to keep liberals on the outside looking in at the corridors of power and influence in Austin.[31]

Dugger also helped to promote the liberal practice of supporting Republicans as a means of fomenting realignment and two-party politics. In doing this, Dugger employed a language similar to that used by emerging conservative populists as a weapon against national liberalism. A Texas liberal whose strongest and most hated enemy had traditionally been the conservative domination within his own party, Dugger was an outspoken critic of "elitist establishments." Though sharing many progressive goals with Johnson, Dugger nonetheless saw Johnson's pragmatic balancing act between liberal and conservative values as akin to the voter fraud, sweetheart construction deals, and other instances of alleged corruption that dogged LBJ's entire career. Yet Dugger's liberal aggression against the establishment of his own party, Johnson included, also lent credence to Republican claims that their party was the authentic and uncorrupted voice for honest, hardworking, conservative Texans. Liberals like Ronnie Dugger undermined the established Democratic power from within while, at the same time, enhancing the Republican image and even supporting Republican candidates as a form of protest.[32]

While Dugger emerged as an influential voice for Texas liberals and Johnson struggled to make everyone happy, the dominant voice of Texas Republican conservatism was John Tower. Tower's strategy was less pragmatic and more ideological than either Johnson's or Dugger's. After gaining national prominence in 1961 by becoming the first Republican to win a Senate seat in Texas since Reconstruction, Tower used his elevated status to redefine conservatism, vilify liberalism, and reshape the public's assumptions about the relationship between those philosophies and party politics. "Modern American conservatism," Tower wrote in January 1963, "is the antithesis of authoritarianism." According to Tower, liberalism was the new gateway to authoritarianism and meant more bureaucracy and less control for Texans. "The conservative would leave as much to popular control in the area of public decision as possible," Tower wrote. "He is essentially 'liberal' in the more classical definition of the term." The key to Tower's success was his moderate style. Though firmly committed to the conservative cause, Tower, unlike other conservatives, understood the importance of mainstream acceptance. Ideologically committed, Tower nonetheless never lost sight of his ultimate goal, Republican growth.[33]

Others were not as cautious. As Johnson and Dugger feuded, and Tower eloquently extolled the virtues of classical liberalism in the modern conservative mind, more brazen and seemingly extreme voices continued to wage a public relations war for the hearts and minds of Texas. The impact of those voices, however, cannot be properly understood outside of the sudden, shocking, and interrupted context of gunshots fired from the Texas School Book Depository on November 22, 1963. The assassination of John F. Kennedy elevated charges of radical extremism to a much more powerful, pertinent, and damaging level and temporarily made prioritizations of ideology less acceptable.

Dallas's Shame

The Kennedy assassination was a tremendously important event in the history of Texas and one that embarrassed many across the state, particularly in Dallas. To be sure, Bruce Alger and Edwin Walker's home city had been stigmatized as a bastion of extremism prior to November 22, 1963. Yet, regardless of the fact that Lee Harvey Oswald was quickly identified as a left- rather than a right-wing assassin, the perception of Dallas as inviting such radicalism permeated characterizations of the city before and especially after November 22. Oswald's murder just two days later, carried live on national television, only added to the image of Dallas as a throwback to the vigilante Wild West. With Oswald dead, much of the nation's ire was quickly redirected toward Dallas. In 1971, John Tower described the nation's attitude toward Texas and Dallas in the wake of Kennedy's death as laced with "hostility and even hatred." Tower always recalled the tragic events of November and December 1963 as the "grimmest experience" of his life.[34]

Kennedy's assassination presented Texas with a massive public relations problem, particularly with Johnson's assumption of the presidency. Still, Texas could not purge itself of political ideology, nor could it erase the tragedy from the nation's memory. It could however, try to soften its image. This became the most popular strategy for Texans of influence. For instance, Earle Cabell's decision to run against Bruce Alger in 1964—a campaign he won by highlighting Alger's perceived extremism—opened the door for Eric Jonsson, cofounder of the electronics giant Texas Instruments and future inductee into *Fortune Magazine*'s "Business Hall of Fame," to run for mayor of Dallas in 1964 in part to implement a national public relations campaign to get people's minds off of the gruesome tragedy that had

Right to left: President John F. Kennedy with Lyndon Johnson, John Connally, and Ralph Yarborough at a rally in Fort Worth on the morning of November 22, 1963. (Courtesy of the *Dallas Morning News*)

taken place in Dealey Plaza. Eventually elected three times, Jonsson prioritized the rebuilding of Dallas's self-esteem and did so by refashioning the city into one of the nation's most flourishing, pushing projects for downtown revitalization, the construction of a convention center, city hall, public library system, and airport—eventually Dallas–Fort Worth (DFW) International Airport.[35]

Many other Texans saw Johnson's presidency as their best chance for rebuilding the state's image. Johnson's early popularity grew in proportion to his ability to appear stable and moderate, even as he used Kennedy's martyrdom as a powerful political weapon designed to pass long-stalled progressive legislation under the banner of the slain president's posthumous legacy. No piece of legislation relied on the assassination more than the Civil Rights Act of 1964. Though some Texans recoiled at the thought of Johnson pushing through such a transformative piece of legislation, a majority of white Texans, unlike whites in much of the Deep South, were, especially in view of the assassination, either resigned to the new social realities or relatively ambivalent. To be sure, Johnson's championing of the Kennedy agenda on race was not without opposition in his home state, but unlike southerners elsewhere, most Texans were less inclined to resist, in large part because of the shame of JFK's death as well as LBJ's hand in the bill. Johnson's push for civil rights temporarily gave Republicans a boost in the South, but the GOP received little such boost in Texas, where Democrats received, temporarily, a pass.[36]

Kennedy's death, Texans' embarrassment, and Johnson's presidency collectively explain why, in 1964, Texas Republicans were so dejected by the prospect of running a presidential campaign against Johnson rather than Kennedy. Texas Republicans had long believed that Kennedy would dump Johnson from his ticket in 1964. Without Johnson's name on the Democratic ticket, Texas Republicans hoped to carry their state for the GOP by attracting conservative party jumpers, as they had in 1952 and 1956. Instead, like a battalion rallying to the rescue of a wounded comrade, establishment Texas Democrats, with Kennedy's death shadowing the entire political atmosphere, began to embrace Johnson and solidify the party's base. Former Texas governor and conservative Democrat Allan Shivers, who gained national fame for his repeated endorsements of Eisenhower and Nixon, was among the first of many Texas conservatives to endorse LBJ for president in 1964. Kennedy's assassination in Dallas made charges of extremism more damaging, less negotiable, and the prospects for Republican successes less likely.[37]

The Vise of Extremism

In 1964, Johnson wanted Americans, and especially those in his home state, to see him as stable, moderate, and presidential. Though he worked to project this image of himself, Johnson more directly accomplished this by characterizing his Republican opponent as radical and dangerous. Johnson ultimately succeeded at both goals and, at the same time, fashioned the image of extremism—that quality that his Republican opponent, Barry Goldwater, famously said was "no vice"—into a vise that squeezed every drop of momentum out of the Arizona senator's campaign.

Goldwater emerged as the GOP nominee after an intraparty struggle that virtually destroyed his campaign before it even started. These warring factions, conservatives on one side and moderates on the other, severely undermined the Republican Party's credibility, particularly in the antiextremist context of 1964. Conservatives like Phyllis Schlafly, the influential grassroots organizer and author of the best seller *A Choice, Not an Echo,* referred to moderate Republicans like Nelson Rockefeller as "liberals" and viewed those "liberals" as conservatives' chief rival for national influence

Lyndon B. Johnson takes the Oath of Office aboard *Air Force One* at Dallas Love Field, November 22, 1963. (Courtesy of the Lyndon B. Johnson Presidential Library, Austin, TX)

and power. At the same time, moderate Republicans viewed conservative "extremism" as their chief rival for national respectability.[38] Though less crucial in Texas than in other states, this division manifested in Texas in important ways, paralleled liberals' struggle to find a voice within the state Democratic Party, and ultimately undermined Goldwater's popularity in the state.[39]

To be an extremist in 1964 was almost as bad as being a communist in 1952. The charge of extremism seems even more damaging in hindsight. Prior to the fall of 1964, for instance, Goldwater enjoyed much support in Texas. During John Tower's 1961 senate campaign, local Republican strategists courted Goldwater as a potential "difference-maker." An endorsement from and public appearance with Goldwater, Tower campaign strategists argued, would go a long way toward assuring victory.[40] The quest to gain

Goldwater's endorsement is particularly telling when viewed against the backdrop of Tower's persistent warnings to his campaign staff to avoid, at all costs, being labeled as extremist or part of the "against everything crowd" of conservatives. Prior to 1964, Goldwater was not viewed in Texas as an extremist.[41]

That Goldwater was not perceived as an extremist, and in fact enjoyed significant popularity in Texas, is further revealed in polling data collected by Peter O'Donnell just one month prior to Kennedy's death. The data, collected exclusively from Texans, concluded that, in Texas, "neither Republicans nor Democrats identify Goldwater as part of the radical right, but both would like to see him repudiate it in so many words." The study further quoted one sympathetic Democratic survey participant who said that Goldwater would "be out of his mind if he had anything to do with [an organization like the John Birch Society]." According to the polls, most Texans viewed Goldwater as a responsible conservative and found "strong appeal in Goldwater's desire to reduce heavy government spending."[42]

Even after Kennedy's death and Texans' subsequent quest for national reconciliation, Goldwater remained relatively popular in Texas. One study conducted in the summer of 1964 concluded that most Texans "actually like Goldwater as a man better than they like LBJ. But, they are afraid of Goldwater to varying degrees because of the bad, frightening things they have heard about him from the Demos and because of the lack of constructive statements he himself has made." The report concluded that many Texans were "just waiting for reasons to vote for Goldwater." In that scenario, most Texans would "vote for LBJ as the lesser of two evils (if they are afraid of BG) OR as the man they already know something about."[43]

Despite his relative popularity, however, no semblance of any significant movement on Goldwater's behalf ever emerged in Texas. This can largely be explained by the reality that no significant Republican Party yet existed in Texas, at least not one that could survive without the cross-voting of disgruntled Democratic conservatives or protesting liberals. Republican success stories, like Tower's in 1961 or Bruce Alger's from 1954 to 1962, were dismissed as flukes or isolated and extremist flirtations. With a Texan atop the Democratic ticket, Kennedy's assassination fresh in everyone's mind, and the fear of extremism or even the perception of extremism looming over the entire political landscape, Republicans simply had no chance in 1964.[44]

What little vocal and public support Goldwater did have in Texas only contributed to the perception that his campaign was the arm of the Republican Party's lunatic fringe. One of the Texas conservatives most vocally opposed to Johnson, and correspondingly supportive of Goldwater, was J. Evetts Haley. Among Texas's most outspoken ideologues, Haley was a rancher, historian, proud member of the John Birch Society, and longtime thorn in liberal Democrats' sides. Haley was a vociferously anticommunist Democrat with Allan Shivers's penchant for courting conservative Republicans. His antipathy toward the liberalism within his own party manifested clearly for the first time in 1936 when his leadership of a small, short-lived, and relatively impotent third-party movement called Jeffersonian Democrats of Texas gave organizational birth to his nascent conservatism. He is perhaps most famous for his scathing indictment of Lyndon Johnson in a book entitled *A Texan Looks at Lyndon: A Study in Illegitimate Power,* published in 1964. Despite a wide audience for his views on Johnson, Haley was typically marginalized by the Texas press and dismissed as a fringe player of the Far Right.[45]

Dallas-based oil baron H. L. Hunt was also among Goldwater's earliest and most faithful supporters. Like Haley, though, Hunt never became a major political power broker in Dallas because, as *Texas Monthly* magazine put it years later, he was considered an "arch-conservative" on the "lunatic fringe of the Right." Hunt was also hounded by unfounded rumors of his participation in assassination conspiracies against Kennedy, part of a larger trend in the American Left to dismiss Oswald's guilt in favor of a more sinister and extremist plot calculated and administered against JFK by the Far Right—a trait that in later years reflected a fundamental shift to, as Richard Hofstadter put it, the "paranoid style" of American politics, characteristic of the Right and the Left. Though Hunt was largely devoid of tact and lacking in political charm, his conservatism was similar to Bruce Alger's, whose career in Dallas helped organize small coalitions of grassroots conservatives, but, alone, was not enough to make any major impact on the state's political establishment.[46]

Also associated with Hunt, and closely aligned with the John Birch Society in Texas, was Dan Smoot. Smoot served in the FBI until 1951, when he resigned and relocated his family to Dallas, where he began working with Hunt on the production and distribution of a conservative newsletter called *Facts Forum.* By 1964, Smoot was producing his own weekly conservative newsletter, *The Dan Smoot Report,* in which the conservative activist communicated his opposition to such things as nationalized health care, liberalism in the State Department, and LBJ's proposal to relinquish sovereignty of the Panama Canal. These three individuals—Haley, Hunt, and Smoot—were among the most prominent Texas conservatives to oppose Lyndon Johnson in 1964, though each failed to attract an influential, credible, or sizable following, in large part because the political climate was especially sensitive to the appearance of radicalism.[47]

AuH$_2$O in '64

The only credible efforts on behalf of Goldwater's losing battle were waged by John Tower and Peter O'Donnell. Campaigning for Goldwater, Tower continued his efforts to convince Texans that Republican conservatism, unlike modern Democratic liberalism, was rooted in ideals of individual liberty, limited government, and what he called a "diffusion of power." He also tried, ineffectively, to counter the increasing perception of conservatism as synonymous with extremism. While campaigning for Goldwater, Tower often spoke of "government with a heart," noting that Republicans "recognize and support the concept of equality of opportunity under the law." Though Tower actively supported Goldwater, he was far more interested in growing a viable Texas Republican Party. Hoping to nationalize local politics, he asserted in speeches and through literature distributed across Texas that the national Democratic Party was the real "establishment"—home to "liberal elites" who could not be trusted to protect the popular conservative majority in his state. This rhetoric would eventually succeed, but still could not overcome the antiextremist fears that shadowed Texas in 1964.[48]

Still, Tower's efforts earned him the seconding speech at the 1964 Republican National Convention in San Francisco. Knowing that he had the attention of Texans whom he would ask to reelect him in two years, Tower spoke with force. As was consistent with his strategy for encouraging realignment, his message was not why Goldwater should be president, but why Republican conservatism was the solution for a nation plagued by lawlessness, amoral cities, and Democratic weakness. "We are faced with a growing menace to our security and sovereignty as a free nation, in the form of a Godless ideology, based in the Kremlin, and possessed by men determined to wreak their will on the whole world," Tower said. He continued:

> We are faced with a new foible in our society, caused in part by moral decay, which effective political leadership could overcome. Consider . . . for a moment . . . this terrible tragedy: We've come to the point when people can be mauled and beaten and even killed on the streets of a great city with hundreds of people looking on, and doing nothing about it. We have come to the point where, in many cases, the lawbreakers are treated with loving care . . . while those who uphold and

champion the rule of law and order are looked upon in some quarters as suspect. I submit that this is the direct result of the gradual reduction of our people to a status of dependency on government, to an erosion of our sense of individual responsibility, and a departure from the biblical admonition that we are our brothers' keepers.[49]

In addition to the usual call for law and order, which would become a conservative mantra by 1966, Tower's speech also clearly foreshadowed the powerful infusion of social conservatism into Republican politics. It also, no doubt, affirmed the intellectual affinity that many Christians had with anticommunism and antiliberalism. Tower's speech did not necessarily cause Texans to reevaluate the links between liberalism and communism, or to reconsider Goldwater, but it did reflect the feeling among many Christian conservatives that liberals did not fully appreciate the ramifications of big government in the context of the cold war.[50]

Goldwater himself never made much of an effort to court evangelicals. A major reason for this was that in 1964 no organized religious conservative movement yet existed, at least not in Texas. Moreover, even among poorly organized portions of the religious community, Goldwater's campaign not only failed to rally support but was actually rejected and denounced. In Dallas, which was home to the largest Southern Baptist, Methodist, and Southern Presbyterian congregations in the nation as well as more than eight hundred churches within the city limits alone, Goldwater's appeal was lukewarm at best.[51] Texas clergy were typically just as loyally Democratic as anyone, while many pastors publicly criticized Goldwater's conceptions of economic justice and world peace.[52] Though Goldwater tried to portray his campaign as a crusade, saying that "the real war liberals fear is a holy war—a war of the faithful for their long-lost self respect and dignity—a war for individuality waged on the spiritual plane of ideas and principles, the reawakening of hope and faith," his efforts were largely ineffective.[53]

If John Tower was the public face of populist conservatism in Texas, Peter O'Donnell was its lifeblood. O'Donnell's list of impressive success stories—Alger, Nixon, and Tower—was rooted in his prioritization of ideology ahead of partisan loyalty, though in later years his priorities would shift. Whether in public or in private, O'Donnell was adamant in his support for "true conservatism" and threatened to bolt the GOP if Nelson Rockefeller or Michigan governor George Romney received the 1964 nomination. Privately, O'Donnell dreamed of turning the Republican Party into the only suitable and reliable home for conservatives.[54]

Whether it was articulated by Tower, O'Donnell, or Goldwater himself, the nascent conservatism in Texas, among true believers, was almost synonymous with an emboldened antiliberalism. "Liberals have taken us too far to the left for the good of the nation, particularly when we find ourselves in a worldwide struggle with the forces of the extreme left," Goldwater wrote Tower in 1963. "They have deserted the lessons of history and perverted the real meaning of the word liberal."[55] Liberals, not communists, were to blame for the nation's weakness, he argued.[56] Texas Republicans, though small in number and lacking significant influence, used Goldwater's 1964 campaign to highlight what the Republican National Committee (RNC) called the "Big Lie of Big Government." In the coming decades, such assertions would carry much more weight and liberalism would replace conservatism as the more extreme political philosophy, at least according to most Texans.[57]

By the fall of 1964, Goldwater's biggest problem in Texas—besides the fact that his opponent was a Texan—was the perception that he was an extremist. Had Goldwater simply been perceived as a conservative, it seems likely that more Texans would have supported him, as polls conducted less than a year earlier indicated they might. The perception of Goldwater as extreme, though certainly enhanced by his own rhetoric and the activities of supporters like Haley, Hunt, Smoot, and Alger, was largely the product of a concerted effort to frame Goldwater this way, first by his opponents in the GOP primary and then by Johnson.

Goldwater's campaign organizers in Texas should have paid closer attention to studies conducted in 1963 that warned of the dangers that would befall their candidate in the state should he be perceived as an extremist. When Allan Shivers surprised many by endorsing Johnson over Goldwater, he did so in large part because of the growing perception by the fall of 1964 that Goldwater's views were too extreme.[58] As the fall campaign progressed, the DNC provided Texas Democrats with pamphlets called "A Goldwater Primer in Five Parts." One section said that "Barry the Bomber wants to Go to war with China, Go to war with Cuba, Go to war in Eastern Europe, Go to war in Germany, Provoke the Soviet Union, [and] Go to war in Vietnam." Texas Democrats used the pamphlet along with more subtle approaches to position Goldwater as an enemy of the farmer, citing his opposition to a farm subsidy bill, and as an enemy of the working class, mainly because of his Republicanism.[59]

Goldwater was also attacked as an extremist by the moderate wing of his own party. Throughout their primary battles, Rockefeller had painted Goldwater's conservatism as radicalism. During the Republican National Convention in San Francisco, as the nation saw what appeared to be a hostile takeover of the GOP initiated by Goldwater conservatives, Rockefeller Republicans used the media to disparage their political brethren as dangerous, further polarizing the party's already estranged wings. Goldwater was aware that his opponents were prepared to fight the campaign on these grounds when he addressed the convention floor with his famous line, "Extremism in the defense of liberty is no vice." In alienating the GOP's moderate wing, Goldwater cut his base of support in half and opened the door for a series of Democratic attack ads that highlighted Republican factionalism.[60]

Attacks subsequently came from almost everywhere. The *New Republic* published a special magazine entitled *1189 Psychiatrists Say Goldwater Is Psychologically Unfit to Be President!* The AFL-CIO published literature trying to link Goldwater to radicalism by charging that the Republican nominee was a "provocateur of hate." These and similar charges were made reasonably by linking Goldwater to the John Birch Society, and outrageously by asserting that Kennedy had been murdered by the same hate virtually endorsed by the Republican candidate, a charge particularly effective in Texas.[61] Even oil and business leaders in Texas, who had initially provided Goldwater with his strongest base of support, began to shy away from the GOP nominee in the wake of reports outlining Goldwater's hardline position on nuclear weapons and foreign affairs.[62]

Goldwater did as poor a job of repudiating the charges of extremism as he did in marketing his own brand of conservatism. Whereas conservatives in the coming years defined their philosophy against the backdrop of specific national issues, Goldwater largely avoided specific issues—and was criticized heavily for doing so. In Houston, for instance, Goldwater championed his campaign theme of "peace through strength, progress through freedom; purpose through Constitutional order"—yet spoke of a vague philosophy without mention of any practical application. His campaign strategists feared charges of extremism, yet Goldwater himself insisted on sticking to his ideological guns, with the result that the Republican message in 1964 struck an uneasy and ineffective balance between cautious uncertainty and brazen recklessness.[63]

Not only did Johnson work hard to attach the extremist stigma to his Republican opponent, he also wisely took advantage of the media's fascination with the nation's first Texan President to initiate a public relations campaign designed to negate the potential appeal of Goldwater's frontierism and cowboy persona.[64] Johnson dictated the when, where, and how of virtually all his photo ops in Texas and was often pictured on his ranch riding his horses, boots shining and cowboy hat doffed. He was privately obsessed with his desire to be seen as a "cowboy" and "local hero."[65] Though both candidates tried to wear the image of rugged frontiersman, only Johnson was successful in Texas.[66]

Despite all his advantages in Texas, Johnson took little for granted. Throughout the fall campaign, Johnson's team continued to carefully craft and assert its message of Democratic moderation contrasted with Republican extremism. The campaign rarely disparaged conservatives or Republicans without qualifying the remark as a reference to the "extremist varieties."[67] Meanwhile, the Texas Democratic Committee distributed pamphlets across the state with the slogan "For a Decent Home in a Decent Neighborhood—Johnson/Humphrey for the USA." Another such brochure was emblazoned with the slogan "Johnson/Humphrey must be elected— The alternative is frightening"—with an arrow connecting the word "frightening" to a menacing photo of Goldwater. Yet another brochure featured a picture of an unsmiling Goldwater, with arms stretched out, and the slogan "In these hands—the hope of America's Children and Youth. The stakes are Too High for you to Stay at Home."[68]

The Johnson campaign's fears of a late Goldwater charge did not take into consideration the ineptitude of Goldwater's strategists. Barry Goldwater made five separate visits to Texas during his bid for the White House. During those trips, he managed to rally sizable crowds hostile to four more years of what he called, "Kennedy-Johnson liberalism." One rally in Wichita Falls, Tower's hometown, drew more than twelve thousand supporters.[69] Yet, his campaign did such a poor job of providing local and state media with advance schedules that his rallies in Texas were rarely captured on film. Goldwater also avoided Dallas and West Texas, areas arguably the most tightly connected to the western populist-conservative ideals he championed.[70]

Whether Goldwater's campaign underestimated its level of support in these regions or overestimated its supporters' loyalty is unclear. What is clear is that during each visit, the Texas media consistently pushed Goldwater onto the defensive. His speeches failed to deflect charges of extremism. When Goldwater had chances to attack Johnson, he shifted attention to Hubert Humphrey instead. Almost fearful of attacking a Texan in Texas, Goldwater deferred to Johnson and tried to convince apathetic audiences to support such proposals as Social Security privatization. It was not so much that Goldwater advocated such change that made him dangerous and ineffective, though many Texans did see Social Security privatization as a benefit to elitist northeastern Republicans. The larger problem was the fact that, when given a small window of opportunity, Goldwater consistently failed to make news, let alone sound bites—nor did he rebuke the charges of radicalism. Like Johnson, Goldwater did not like the media. Unlike Johnson, however, Goldwater did not understand their power and blamed the media for their role in making him appear dangerous and extreme.[71]

The most successful aspect of Barry Goldwater's miserable showing in 1964 was a speech delivered on his behalf by Ronald Reagan. Before a national TV audience on October 27, 1964, Reagan delivered what came to be remembered as "the Speech"—a blistering attack on Johnson, liberals, and the Washington establishment. It was a "thoughtful address" (as it was introduced) about the Goldwater campaign, but really benefited Reagan far more than the man whose credentials he was trumpeting. Shortly after Reagan's speech, Texas Republicans became increasingly enamored with the former Hollywood actor, who quickly became one of the most anticipated and frequently courted guests for statewide GOP fund-raisers throughout the 1960s and 1970s. Reagan's speech helped make him an icon of the conservative movement and began a long-standing and successful relationship between him and Texas conservatives.[72]

Reagan's popularity appears to validate early campaign literature and polling data, which showed support for many of Goldwater's ideas throughout Texas. Most Texans favored limited government and even distrusted Washington as an establishment in the same populist vein as they had traditionally distrusted big business (and big labor). It also indicates the paramount importance of personal image in campaigning. Reagan's smile and affinity with the camera softened the framing of the conservative message, while avoiding a softening of the message itself. Texans who wanted to connect with the energy of the conservative movement were reluctant to do so with Goldwater at its head. Furthermore, Reagan could criticize Lyndon Johnson and liberalism in Texas without running the risk of forcing Texans to vote against their native son in an actual election. Reagan's appeal also shows the importance of timing. The fact that Kennedy had been killed in Texas in 1963 helped Johnson win Texas in 1964. Loyalty and a Democratic tradition also helped Johnson in Texas. However, over the next several years, these obstacles to conservative GOP progress were minimized or eliminated.

The emergence of Ronald Reagan notwithstanding, the 1964 elections were not kind to Republicans in Texas. Ralph Yarborough won re-election against his Republican challenger from Houston, George Bush. Massachusetts-born, Connecticut-raised, battle-tested by World War II, and Yale-educated, Bush, by the early 1950s, had relocated his family first to Midland, Texas, then to Houston, where by 1964 he had emerged not only as a successful oilman but also as chairman of the Harris County

Republican Party. Bush was no extremist. Yet, during his 1964 campaign, Goldwater extremism functioned as a noose around Bush's neck. Like Johnson, Yarborough rarely described himself as "liberal" but enthusiastically talked about his populist agenda for the working class. When he was not trying to link his campaign to Johnson's, Yarborough did all he could to disparage Bush as the worst of both Republican worlds—a privileged northeastern Connecticut Republican and an extremist. Yarborough lambasted Bush as a "darling of the John Birch society"—which was wholly inaccurate, but in the context of Goldwater's campaign seemed believable. Yarborough's strategy put Bush on the defensive and prevented him, like the head of the GOP ticket, from mounting an effective campaign.[73]

In November, Lyndon Johnson crushed Barry Goldwater in Texas, winning in a 63–37 percent landslide. Yarborough similarly crushed Bush, though Bush—whose campaign was modeled after John Tower's successful effort just three years earlier—won one hundred thousand more votes in Texas than did Goldwater, indicating that many Johnson supporters opposed Yarborough. Regardless, Republicans all across the state fell by the wayside. Bruce Alger lost in Dallas, as did the only other GOP congressman in Texas, Ed Foreman of Odessa. Johnson's 26 percent margin of victory was the largest pro-LBJ margin in the South. Comparatively, Johnson barely carried Florida, by just over 2 percent, won by 13 percent in North Carolina, and succeeded by only 6 percent in Virginia. The Deep South, in contrast, overwhelmingly sided with the Republican. Goldwater carried Georgia by 8 percent, Louisiana by 13 percent, South Carolina by 18 percent, Alabama by 29 percent, and Mississippi by an eye-popping 74 percent. As political pundits, Johnson included, were already seeing the impact of civil rights on the transformation of the Solid South, no such transformation appeared to be on the horizon in Texas. It was a very calm period before the impending storm.[74]

The political atmosphere in Texas during 1964 provided Lyndon Johnson with an almost perfect set of conditions in which to campaign. Texas was still overwhelmingly Democratic and loyal to its native son. It was also a state seeking redemption in the wake of tragedy. Texans were especially fearful of extremism—or of being perceived as extreme—and Johnson's campaign solidified the importance of stability and moderation, while convincing the public that Goldwater was dangerous. The Republican nominee had his followers in Texas but could not rally them in the face of such obstacles. He failed to mount an effective media campaign and could not protect himself against the barrage of extremist darts aimed in his direction. Charges of extremism doomed Goldwater and conservatives like him, including Bruce Alger.

As these conditions favorable to Democrats dissipated in the coming months and years, a repackaged vision of populist conservatism—of smaller government, anticommunism, and Judeo-Christian morality—emerged in Texas that coincided with an attack on the meaning of liberalism, publicly reconstructed within the contexts of lawlessness, war, and weakness.

Chapter 3

Reconstructing Conservatism

Antiliberalism and the Limits of
"Law and Order"

On March 26, 1968, Ben Carpenter, then president of the conservative Texas and Southwestern Cattle Raisers Association, delivered a speech at the organization's annual membership convention. Carpenter used the occasion to describe what he considered the slippery slope of American moral decline. He delivered a fourteen-page address on the dangers of "liberal moral relativism," which had "permeated and threatened to destroy society." "We pussyfoot among a lot of high-sounding names," Carpenter told his audience. "We call drunkards 'alcoholics,' . . . homosexuals 'deviates,' slackers 'pacifists,' . . . and criminals 'victims of society.' . . . I think the time has come when we should and must draw a line separating compassion from softheadedness, permissiveness and timidity." Citing Edward Gibbon's study on the rise and fall of the Roman Empire, Carpenter compared America's decline with the dissolution of "the great political force which had held the civilized world together for more than 500 years." Where did the Roman Empire go wrong? Its decline resulted from excessive government spending, an unwillingness of the young men to bear arms in defense of their country, widespread sexual immorality, the spread of effeminacy, and a social and cultural disregard for religion. Carpenter warned of rising crime rates, particularly rampant rape, and said that regardless of the "liberal" perspective, America had not always been "that way."[1]

Carpenter's speech reflected both the evolution of the conservative worldview since 1964 and numerous themes that would continue to pepper conservative political rhetoric in the coming decades. The hypermasculine posturing of men like Carpenter also grew out of notions of white southern honor and the impulse to protect family, home, and tradition against "invasion." In the context of the mid-1960s, perceiving liberalism as not only a threat to family and to individual liberties, but also as the political embodiment of weakness, affected Texans' relationship between party and philosophy.

Between 1965 and 1968, the fear of rising crime rates intermixed with images of riots and violence to fuel the potency of a reinvigorated conservative rhetoric. The momentum generated by these images emerged as a tool far more useful to conservative Republicans than had been the case just a few years earlier. Very quickly after Goldwater's rejection as an extremist in 1964, Republican conservatives succeeded in putting the extremist shoe on the other foot, using images of frequent violence, disruptive civil disobedience, antiwar and civil rights protests, and urban chaos to vilify national Democrats and liberals. During that same time, as "law and order" emerged as the standard mantra of conservatives in both parties looking to rally electoral support across Texas, intraparty factionalism continued to plague candidates who aggressively fought to label and vilify their opponents' weaknesses before themselves being labeled and vilified. The struggle to avoid being perceived as extreme persisted, but it also quickly became bipartisan.[2]

Repackaging Republicanism

For many Texans, the fear that America was slipping into a violent abyss during the mid-1960s seemed very real. These fears were intensified by the routine coverage incidents such as race riots and protests received from national and local media. Each night, Texans with access to television could, before sitting down to their dinner, be reminded that not only was the world still the dark and foreboding place it had been throughout the cold war, but that all across America, challenges to the social order were becoming more common while crime seemed to be on the rise. Rising crime rates may not have been caused by such challenges to stability, but there is little doubt that the tumultuous landscape of the mid-1960s coalesced, for many, into a singular image of chaos and disorder.[3]

These images affected public perceptions, causing disillusionment and fear, and, in powerful ways, extended into a political culture that was rapidly polarizing along ideological grounds. Conservative Republicans hoped that by associating such images with liberalism, they could shift Texans' critical focus onto the perceived dangers of liberalism and the Democratic Party connected to that philosophy. At the same time, conservative Texas Republicans argued that government's failure to deal with the growing climate of lawlessness, disorder, and violence was evidence of Democratic liberalism's failure—and Lyndon Johnson's.[4]

Johnson's response to rising crime rates, which largely embraced new research associating structural poverty with urban decay and crime, gave Texas conservatives ammunition in the battle to equate liberalism with weakness. It also helped Republican efforts to undermine Texans' loyalty to Johnson and to the Democratic Party. Johnson eventually addressed crime as a local problem through the Omnibus Crime Act of 1968. Yet, between 1965 and 1968, conservatives made great strides toward rehabilitating their public image by arguing that liberals' attitude toward crime was irresponsible. Liberals arguing that federal programs could reduce crime rates, rather than prioritizing stronger law enforcement at the local level, appeared unsympathetic and even naive to many Texas conservatives, who viewed crime as a problem of permissiveness and moral laxity. In scoffing at the argument that poverty was directly responsible for crime, Republicans also made the smooth transition from criticizing a local problem to blaming a national philosophy. Johnson's Great Society and War on Poverty made calls for smaller government more pertinent than they had been in previous years. At the same time, Republican criticisms against the liberal approach to crime prevention made conservatism appear, to many Texans, much less extreme and far more responsible.[5]

Undoubtedly, the association of lawlessness with permissiveness, moral laxity, and the weakness of federal responses also contributed to linkages between race and crime. Johnson typically avoided direct correspondences between race and crime, other than to argue that racial discrimination had contributed to poverty and therefore to crime. Crime, Johnson argued, was a national problem requiring a national solution. Publicly, Johnson dismissed the law and order rhetoric of men like Ben Carpenter as a "scare tactic." Most Texans, however, joined the color-blind chorus in blaming liberals, rather than any particular race, for rising crime rates. Calling for a conservative approach to law and order, many white Texans were appealed to not on overtly racial or partisan grounds, but on philosophical and ideological ones.[6]

Much of what Ben Carpenter referred to in his speech to the Texas and Southwestern Cattle Raisers Association—rising crime rates and rampant rape, for instance—was somewhat less true in Texas than it was in other parts of the nation. National figures indicate that between 1960 and 1968, the number of reported violent crimes per 100,000 people nearly doubled, from 161 to 298. Nationally, the number of rapes per 100,000 people increased from 10 to 16. Similar increases were reported on the number of burglaries and other forms of property crime. In Texas, such increases were slightly less, though certainly still significant.[7] Regardless, the fear that without vigilant protection, such chaos could be on the horizon rallied many Texans around the law and order issue and gave conservatives an opportunity to reestablish credibility in the post-Goldwater political culture.[8]

Race riots and antiwar protests were relatively rare in Texas, though the images of such chaos were broadcast into Texans' homes daily. Sadly though, isolated but dramatic instances of public violence in Texas also heightened insecurities. Less than three years after Kennedy's assassination in Dallas, Charles Whitman forced Texans to once again witness public carnage—this time in Austin. On August 1, 1966, Whitman, a student at the University of Texas, committed what was at the time the largest mass murder in American history. Early that morning, after stabbing his mother with a bayonet before fatally shooting her in the head, Whitman returned to his Austin apartment, where he stabbed his wife repeatedly as she slept. Within a few hours, Whitman, carrying a Marine Corps footlocker loaded with seven hundred rounds of ammunition, a .30 caliber carbine, a 6 mm Magnum, a .35 caliber Remington pump, a .357 caliber Magnum pistol, two 9 mm Luger pistols, one sawed-off shotgun, and water, toilet paper, and several cans of Spam, obtained a parking permit by posing as an employee of the State Highway Department and made his way to the top of the Main Building—a 307-foot tower that stood as the signature building on the University of Texas campus.[9]

Dressed in overalls and hauling his footlocker, Whitman took an elevator to the twenty-seventh floor before climbing the stairs to the remaining floor to reach the observation deck. There, Whitman immediately killed the receptionist before fatally shooting two tourists. At 11:45 A.M. Whitman began taking aim at students, faculty, and other individuals passing by some three hundred feet below. Poor communication between the University Police Department (UTPD) and the Austin Police Department (APD), along with several ill-advised retaliations by students and faculty who happened to be carrying guns on campus, allowed Whitman's shooting spree to last ninety-nine minutes. Whitman was finally killed by two APD patrolmen, but not before sixteen people had been killed and another thirty-one wounded. As they had in November 1963, Texans once again faced national shame over an outburst of violence.[10]

The Whitman murders contributed to many Texans' feelings of fear, paranoia, and victimization. Just days after the shootings, an editorial in the *Daily Texan,* the student newspaper at the University of Texas, compared Whitman to a "Viet Cong terrorist, killing without mercy and without discrimination." Such viewpoints were common across the state. As Austin joined Dallas as another unenviable host to one of the century's most famous shooting sprees, Texans were afraid, ashamed, and sensitive to what they perceived to be the declining safety, morality, and traditional lifestyle that they had taken for granted. Unlike the Kennedy assassination, however, the Whitman murders intensified the call for stronger defense and law enforcement.[11]

Rising crime rates, images of race riots and protests broadcast from distant places into local homes, and violence in their own backyard made law and order a powerful issue in Texas. Yet, even though it eventually became their most effective political weapon, emphasizing law and order was not Republicans' initial or sole post-Goldwater answer to its public relations problems. Republicans strategized not only to use images of lawlessness and disorder to vilify liberalism, but also simultaneously tried to find ways to shed its own extremist image.[12]

To address this concern, national Republican leaders launched a concerted effort in early 1965 to do to Democratic liberalism what Johnson and the Democratic Party had done to conservative Republicanism in 1964—label it as extreme and out of step with mainstream American values. Shortly after Goldwater's defeat and a purging of its most ideologically committed right-wing leadership, the RNC—led primarily by moderates hoping to build the party while unifying responsible conservative and moderate factions—began to refine a new standard operating procedure for Republican campaigns across the nation. The crux of this new strategy was uniformity. Republicans sought to recast their party in a more reasonable and populist light, while simultaneously attacking liberalism as the philosophy most antithetical to mainstream America. Though it would take years before the majority of Republicans across the country would get in step with this plan, the construction of a successful ideological combat strategy had begun.[13]

In 1965, the Republican National Committee also began efforts—not always successfully—to more actively direct local GOP operations across states like Texas, emphasizing a more uniform marketing strategy that relied upon the incorporation of state and local issues into four broader themes: welfare reform, big government, loss of local power, and responsible and modern (rather than outdated, extremist, or countersubversive) anticommunism. The selection of these themes provided the party with uniformity of message and, in theory, allowed both conservative and moderate Republican factions to unite under a redefined and common philosophy.[14]

Many Texas Republicans, including Houston's George Bush, embraced aspects of the RNC's new strategy, relishing the opportunity to shed the extremist label while contributing to the GOP's growth. After losing his 1964 Senate election bid in large part because he was inaccurately vilified as a "Bircher," Bush worked closely with the RNC throughout 1965 and 1966 in an effort to repackage himself as a responsible conservative. At the same time, however, Bush's desire to shed the extremist label led him to embrace several aspects of the nation's ongoing social debate that other conservatives had been reluctant to engage with. He began to more vocally support civil rights for African Americans and Mexican Americans as well as to champion controversial and relatively unpopular federal initiatives on open housing. Having been successfully vilified as an extremist in 1964, Bush believed, unlike the RNC leadership, that the future of the Texas Republican Party did not lie in fighting an ideological struggle. He consistently downplayed "liberal versus conservative" debates, claiming that those terms were outdated and their meanings relative, depending on where you lived and how old you were. By 1966, Bush had successfully repackaged himself as a moderate, as a supporter of both antipoverty efforts and free enterprise, and as a leader relatively confident that government could solve the problems of urban decay, while also vaguely warning against too much intrusive government. Despite its inherent contradictions, the strategy worked. In 1966, running as a responsible moderate, Bush was elected to Congress, the first Republican ever elected from Houston's seventh district.[15]

Other Texas Republicans used different strategies to advance the party and, surprisingly, win elections. One of those surprises came with the 1966 campaign for the Senate between John Tower and Waggoner Carr. This campaign revealed much about the nature of a reinvigorated antiliberalism in Texas, the success of the GOP's new marketing strategy, and the destructive power of intra–Democratic Party factionalism.

The Fluke, Take Two

As had been the case in 1961, Tower was once again an underdog in 1966. Most Texas Democrats viewed Tower's election to the U.S. Senate in 1961 as a fluke. Democratic insiders were confident they would regain the seat when Tower came up for reelection. His opponent in 1966 was Waggoner Carr, an establishment Democrat with a conservative record, who had served as the state's attorney general and gained some notoriety for a small-scale independent investigation into the Kennedy assassination.

Assumptions about the strength of Carr's conservative appeal and the state's partisan loyalties triggered several early predictions of a Democratic landslide. Carr, however, suffered from several emerging image problems. On September 7, he opened his campaign with a rally in Lubbock, his hometown. It proved to be an inauspicious beginning. Overconfident and unprepared, Carr attracted fewer than two thousand supporters. Earlier in the week, Carr's campaign had made public its expectation that more than ten thousand supporters would attend. Adding to the embarrassment were statewide television and newspaper reports that those in attendance were unenthusiastic and had to be repeatedly prompted to cheer by Carr campaign staffers holding up "cheer" signs.[16]

Carr also evoked much discord within his own party. Viewing Carr as a tool of the establishment, liberals opposed Carr's candidacy, as they had done with Blakely's candidacy against Tower five years earlier. Bumper stickers reading "Sometimes Party Loyalty Asks Too Much" became popular among liberals vocal in their opposition to Carr. Many liberals cited Allan Shivers's "Democrats for Eisenhower" in inciting the need for "revenge" against the establishment of their own party.[17] Even as the political culture had evolved in important ways since 1961, both nationally and in Texas, the joint interest in fomenting a legitimate two-party system once again made strange bedfellows between conservative Republicans and liberal Democrats. Capitalizing on Democratic factionalism, therefore, became a necessary strategy and a powerful weapon for conservative Republicans in 1966.[18]

Tower contributed to the Democratic infighting by proactively courting several traditionally Democratic constituencies, including Mexican Americans. Led in large part by El Paso County GOP chairman Hilary Sandoval Jr., the Texas Republican Party began to more successfully market conservatism to Mexican Americans during the mid-1960s. Marketing conservatism as uniformly "American" and color-blind, the Tower campaign attracted support among Mexican American organizations in South and Central Texas, including the influential and pro-business League of United Latin American Citizens (LULAC), and emphasized the Texas Democratic establishment's poor record on race relations.[19] Corpus Christi City councilman and LULAC associate M. P. Maldonado, for instance, chaired the ultimately influential "Amigocrats for Tower Committee," saying that his support for Tower was based on the "need for a two-party Texas."[20]

Throughout the first six decades of the twentieth century, Mexican Americans in Texas had been segregated by the same customs, traditions, and laws that generally oppressed African Americans in the state. The customs and traditions that allowed for de facto segregation and discrimination, however, began to break down in the 1960s.[21] As the Mexican American population in Texas grew, expectations of political inclusion also grew. Tejanos were a noticeable force in John F. Kennedy's 1960 presidential campaign and even organized "Viva Kennedy" clubs as a means to greater political organization and participation.[22] Yet, three years after Kennedy's death, Mexican American leaders, particularly in South Texas, shifted their focus away from garnering inclusion—a demand often met by white politicians with token appointments or superficial declarations of equality—to a demand for greater influence in the party's agenda-setting process. In 1960, Kennedy's efforts, however nominal, had been seen as a step in the right direction. In 1966, when Waggoner Carr tried to model his appeal to the Mexican American community after Kennedy's strategy from 1960, many viewed the Democrat's efforts as minimal, insufficient, and insincere.[23]

Part of the Mexican American resistance to Carr was rooted in a rather ugly incident in the late summer of 1966 involving Carr and a South Texas contingent of protesting farm workers. When those farm workers in the Rio Grande Valley staged a march to Austin in an effort to rally support for unionization, Texas governor John Connally, openly supporting Carr's campaign, refused requests to mediate with the workers. After Carr also refused to intervene as attorney general, Connally ordered the marchers dispersed. Connally justified this order by saying that the marchers were interrupting traffic along State Highway 10. When the resistant farm workers were met by members of the Texas Highway Patrol and the Texas Rangers, whose relationship with the Mexican American community of South Texas had been historically frigid, a violent confrontation quickly erupted. Rejected by the highest levels of Austin's Democratic establishment, the Mexican American workers were eventually forced to retreat. Connally's response to the marching farm workers cost him considerable support among Mexican Americans in Texas—support he had enjoyed on the basis of his administration's distribution of more than $25 million in education grants designed to help the state's seventy-one thousand Hispanic schoolchildren enrolled in public schools, and despite the fact that more than thirty-three hundred Mexican Americans were employed in state government positions. The goodwill engendered by these actions vanished after the incident with the marching farm workers and Carr, too closely aligned with Connally's decision, saw his already negligible support among Mexican Americans evaporate. Two months later, when the *Texas Observer* ran photographs of Carr attending a 1957 White Citizens' Council meeting with other segregationists, the Democrat's support among minorities was dealt an almost fatal blow.[24]

Tower, on the other hand, avoided labels of extremism by doing something Goldwater had refused to do two years earlier; he denounced the John Birch Society, saying that the organization was too divisive and too dangerous. In late 1965, Tower told both the *Houston Chronicle* and the *Amarillo*

John Tower filming a television documentary about his life for the 1966 campaign. (Courtesy of the John G. Tower Library and Archives, Georgetown, TX)

Daily News that the Birch Society was "a liability to the conservative cause" and "too exclusive."[25] Despite Democratic efforts to vilify Tower as part of the "Goldwater-Birch-Alger-Foreman-Tower-Extremist branch of the Republican Party"—as San Antonio's Henry Gonzalez put it—the incumbent Republican senator avoided such labels. As the campaign progressed, polls indicated that Tower's biggest problem was no longer the image of extremism, but simply the fact that he was a Republican in a Democratic state. "If Tower were running under the Democratic symbol," national pollster

Louis Harris said, "he would have little difficulty winning a second term." Harris cited Tower's ability to shed the "Bircher" label as "the major accomplishment of his campaign."[26]

Tower's campaign provided several lessons for future campaigns in Texas and indicated an important shift in the way conservatives marketed themselves in the state. Tower, as he had done in previous campaigns, emphasized the importance of having a viable second party in the state. In doing so, he once again made the existence of a competitive Texas Republican Party an important issue to conservatives fearful of losing influence at the state and national level as well as to liberals hoping for greater influence in the Democratic Party. Tower also emphasized the principles of small government, repeatedly invoking the name of Thomas Jefferson throughout his campaign. Conservatism, according to Tower, embraced and redefined populism in Texas and could even be linked to the vision of the Founding Fathers. For many, Tower's campaign seemed patriotic and traditional, not radical or extreme. A further lesson learned was the effect that prioritizing national issues could have on a statewide campaign. Tower focused his sharpest critiques of the campaign not on Carr but on "Washington liberals." In doing this, he reinforced national issues as more paramount for Texans than local ones. Tower also co-opted the conservative Democratic attitude on "local and state control." Though his promises were vague and not altogether new, Tower contributed to his popularity by skillfully articulating an image of Republican conservatism as the conservatism of "states' rights" without necessarily (or at least overtly) invoking racialized language. Skillfully separating the issue of states' rights from overt issues of race, Tower also addressed race in a way that few other southerners could; he called for "a moderate and sensible civil rights program for Texas." Critical to Tower's construction of color-blind conservatism and moderation toward civil rights was his infusion of antinorthern animus. In supporting the retention of Texas's right-to-work law, Tower warned that Texas did not have room for "Big Labor" or other "Yankee" obstructions to free enterprise. Simply put, Tower successfully fanned the flames of antinortheasternism and antiliberalism while still running, by Texas standards, a positive and seemingly moderate campaign.[27]

Tower also did an impressive job of communicating his message through the media and via targeted advertising. His advertising largely avoided direct attacks against Carr and was generally viewed as upbeat, optimistic, and creative. Tower was also among the first to take advantage of target marketing strategies, placing advertisements in *Texas Football* magazine—a widely distributed and very popular periodical that provided readers with in-depth coverage of Texas high school, college, and professional football. The ad displayed a list of endorsements from such Texas football heroes as Donny Anderson (Texas Tech University, Green Bay Packers), Tom Landry (head coach, Dallas Cowboys), and Bob Lilly (Texas Christian University)—among dozens of others. The ad also ran in *Game Day* programs at college football venues across the state throughout the fall. Carr was furious that Tower had monopolized advertising to the "football crowd" and was disappointed in his staff for missing such "an obvious opportunity."[28]

Not ignoring the power of television, Tower also one-upped his opponent by airing a thirty-minute documentary called *The John Tower Story.* The film was broadcast across the state and then redistributed to local neighborhoods, where watch-parties were organized for additional screenings. Tower's campaign was so effective that Carr, oddly, charged that it was being run by Ronald Reagan's California team—certainly an indication of the early respect given to Reagan's public appeal and campaign skill. Tower denied the charges and records strongly indicate that Reagan was not involved.[29]

In the end, Tower won reelection with an overwhelming 56.7 percent of a relatively low voter turnout. Carr, a conservative Democrat with the support of a popular governor and a Texan in the White House, failed to hold enough support among minorities, who were voting in heavier numbers in 1966 than they had in a century, failed to vilify his Republican opponent as extreme, seemed shaken by Republicans' effective use of media, and lost support due to the widespread hostility toward the national Democratic Party's inability to deal effectively with crime, violence, and the expansion of government.[30]

The development most responsible for Tower's success, however, was the factionalism within the Texas Democratic Party, which intensified following the 1966 elections. After his surprising defeat, Carr, like other conservative Democrats, quickly began to position himself for future campaigns. Most notably, he began to speak much more passionately about law and order. He stressed the need for harsher sentences for criminals, ending street violence, and the general chaos of protest movements, race riots, and challenges to the social order. He repudiated Johnson's Great Society and randomly attacked Ralph Yarborough's liberal record in the Senate. Connally joined in the sporadic anti-Yarborough fray, publicly linking the liberal to radicalism, revolution, lawlessness, and dangerous extremism. By targeting the state's preeminent liberal icons, these establishment Democrats intensified factionalism within their own party, gave credibility to Republican criticisms of the national Democratic Party, and unintentionally made voting for GOP candidates more acceptable among conservative Texans. Conservative Democrats pursued this strategy because they believed that liberals' disloyalty was costing them elections. These Democrats wanted to put liberals in their place. Conversely, liberals wanted conservatives out of the Democratic Party. Republicans wanted all conservatives in their party. Eventually, each faction would get its wish.[31]

Vietnam

The Vietnam War contributed mightily to the disillusionment and disgust many conservative Texans felt when responding to images of national chaos, lawlessness, and disorder.[32] Generally speaking, attitudes toward the Vietnam War were overwhelmingly hawkish in Texas. Most conservative Texas Democrats supported Johnson's position on the war, though many also believed that a much more vigorous and aggressive exertion of military power would achieve the quick and decisive victory that most wanted. In contextualizing their own images in relation to the war, many conservative politicians used antiwar demonstrations as a contrasting backdrop to their own vision of patriotism, anticommunism, and law and order. Ultimately, the Vietnam War contributed a great deal to Texas conservatives' ability to vilify liberals and, for Republican conservatives, to argue that partisan realignment was Texans' only appropriate long-term political response.[33]

Among the most significant applications of the Vietnam War to a Texas political context was the depiction of the antiwar Left as "liberal" and "cowardly." Texas conservatives in both parties worked, not always in tandem but typically with a common purpose, to redefine liberalism as the ideological cousin of moral relativism and subsequent national decline. Some conservatives argued, as had been tradition since the New Deal, that liberalism had pushed America dangerously close to collectivist socialism and accused the antiwar crowd of having communist sympathies. For Texas Democrats, the vilification of the antiwar Left was necessary in order to solidify credibility and support among disgruntled conservative voters. For Texas Republicans, connecting national Democrats with the antiwar Left, which itself was often associated with out-of-state college campuses and liberal intellectualism, allowed the GOP to more credibly depict the Democratic Party as the party of un-American elitism. Simultaneously, this strategy helped the Republican Party appear more mainstream and populist.[34]

Ideological conservatism and well-strategized antiliberalism only partially explain Texas's hawkish political culture. Also critical was the economic boom in the American Sun Belt that resulted from the rapid expansion of the post–World War II military-industrial complex. With the possible exception of Southern California, nowhere was that economic and population explosion more significant than in Texas.[35] The development of the Sun Belt's military-industrial complex fueled urban growth in Texas and encouraged northerners (many of whom carried with them a Republican family tradition still foreign to most native Texans) to migrate to the Lone Star State for employment. In 1962, Texas firms had military contracts totaling $1 billion. In 1963, that number increased to $1.2 billion. Each subsequent year witnessed even greater surges in military contracts for Texas defense manufacturers, and in 1966 the state enjoyed $2.3 billion in defense business—7.2 percent of all American military contracts. Cities such as San Antonio, which was already home to a thriving military community, certainly benefited, but not to the extent experienced in the Dallas–Fort Worth metroplex. By 1967, eight of the ten largest prime contractors in Texas were based in the greater DFW area. Between 1950 and 1970, 1.2 million men, women, and children moved into Texas from other parts of the nation. Among southern states, only Florida experienced a similar upsurge in raw migration totals. Critics of the war often noted cynically that while continuing involvement in Southeast Asia cost American lives, ending the war would cost Texas defense manufacturers billions of dollars.[36]

The construction of a vast military-industrial complex in Texas contributed not only to the state's economic prosperity, its growing political significance, and its booming population, but also made it a relatively safe haven for pro-war rhetoric. Such a culture attracted conservatives of all stripes, including intellectuals, who during the 1960s began to bridge gaps between high-minded conservative philosophy and grassroots antiliberalism. Few conservative intellectuals had as far-reaching an impact on shaping the ideological convictions of both politicians and the grass roots as William F. Buckley Jr. In March 1967, Buckley, the founder of the influential conservative political magazine *National Review* and descendant of a family with deep roots in Texas, spoke to an audience of Houston conservatives on a subject he dubbed the "dilemmas of liberalism." Gracefully dismissing charges that the conflict in Vietnam was a neocolonial or imperialistic effort, Buckley defended the war to his Texas audience as inherently conservative, defined as both a moral and a pragmatic crusade against global communism.[37]

Buckley also dismissed charges that the war in Vietnam was being sustained for the economic benefit of those with defense manufacturing contracts or other financial stakes in the war, a message unmistakably written for his audience in Texas. Many Texans benefited financially from the war in Vietnam, but few, if any, were willing to cite that benefit as a legitimate reason to support the war. Rather, supporting American soldiers in a fight against communist totalitarianism was characterized as a matter of patriotism, a quality which many conservatives argued was antithetical to the ideology of the antiwar Left. The good financial fortune brought to Texas by the Vietnam War was welcomed, but it was the state's anticommunist, antiliberal, conservative heritage that drove the public's stated support for the war effort. By shifting criticism away from those capitalizing financially on the war and toward those whose activity undermined the war effort, Buckley's speech affirmed in many Texans' minds the connections between liberalism, weakness, antiwar activism, and the national Democratic Party.[38]

Pro-war rhetoric was heard in abundance in Texas during the late 1960s. Many conservatives vocalized hawkish sentiments similar to Buckley's, but not always with Buckley's style. For instance, Joe Pool, a conservative Democrat from Dallas, drew noticeable public support by advocating for a formal congressional declaration of war in Vietnam. Pool admitted that his support for such a declaration was based on the hope that it would allow for the prosecution of antiwar "peaceniks" under various loyalty, sedition, and treason statutes. Also highly influential in the Dallas area was Dr. W. A. Criswell, pastor of the city's First Baptist Church—the world's largest Southern Baptist congregation. Criswell routinely denounced, both from the pulpit and through local media, antiwar activists as "half-brains," "left-wingers," and "liberals."[39]

Conversely, antiwar sentiment in Texas was rarely homegrown. Antiwar protests originating in Texas were few and far between; the few that were organized were generally not well attended or successful. A handful of antiwar protests were held on the outskirts of LBJ's ranch, though, according to even liberal commentators, these were organized not by Texans but by so-called outside agitators. Only a few protests took place on the state's college campuses. Military installations across Texas were the sites of more active and well-attended protest rallies, but even these were smaller in scale and impact than similar demonstrations held in other parts of the nation.[40]

That most Texans were hard-liners on Vietnam, communism, and liberalism was no surprise. Yet the war in Vietnam nonetheless exacerbated factional tensions in the Texas Democratic Party and heightened points of stress that already existed between the state and national leadership. For Lyndon Johnson, maintaining popularity in his home state, which had become increasingly difficult as the onslaught of Great Society legislation, to

John Tower after his return from Vietnam, c. 1966. The trip convinced
him that the American forces needed better weapons and equipment.
(Courtesy of the John G. Tower Library and Archives, Georgetown, TX)

many Texans, smacked of federal expansionism and socialism, was a prioritized goal and a political necessity. Ultimately and ironically, Vietnam, and
specifically Johnson's support for the war, actually stabilized the president's
stature in Texas when it otherwise might have been severely diminished.
Still, while many conservative Texas Democrats supported Johnson because
of Vietnam, many Texas Republicans argued that neither Johnson nor the
national Democratic leadership was capable of achieving military success in
Southeast Asia.[41]

By 1968, conservative Texans' loyalties, their prioritization of both local and national issues, their interpretation of partisan agendas, and their fear that the nation was slipping into a violent and chaotic abyss exacerbated preexisting intraparty factional tensions and threatened to permanently splinter the state Democratic Party. These Texans were relatively pleased with the response of their locally elected leaders, most of whom were conservative Democrats who campaigned for stronger law enforcement and expressed vague but strongly worded opposition to riots, disorder, and street chaos. For conservative Texans, many of whom began to identify themselves as independent at the national level while remaining committed and loyal Democrats at the local level, the elections of 1968 tested the strength of traditional Texas Democratic dominance.[42]

Intraparty Factionalism

Four months after delivering his speech to the Texas and Southwestern Cattle Raisers Association, Ben Carpenter—a multimillionaire cattle rancher, insurance executive, and the man almost single-handedly responsible for the development of the Las Colinas suburban magnet for corporate relocation into the DFW metroplex—was tapped to head the Texas Democrats for Nixon campaign. Shortly after the appointment, Nixon publicly praised Carpenter as a "good Connally-Democrat," noting that he had always been "an admirer" of the Texas governor. Given the antiliberal venom he had been publicly spewing throughout the year, Carpenter's decision to back Nixon was not a surprise. According to business leaders like Carpenter, liberalism had poisoned the nation's social and cultural climate, making the blending of civic responsibility and political activism crucial to the moral and economic survival of city, state, and nation. In other words, Carpenter's actions—and the actions of many Texas conservatives—indicated the primacy of ideological conviction ahead of partisan loyalty. Upon accepting leadership of the Shivers-like organization, Carpenter distributed a letter to conservative Democratic leaders across the state, explaining simply that he had "no confidence that a national administration under Hubert Humphrey would restore fiscal responsibility in Government and law and order in the country."[43]

Texas Republicans welcomed disgruntled conservatives like Carpenter who used antiliberalism, couched in a worldview that emphasized law and order and hawkish patriotism, to lend public respectability to the GOP while encouraging partisan realignment. In June 1966, a *New York Times* investigation into the nature of Texas politics estimated the number of likely voters in Texas to be at around 3 million, with about 300,000 participating as committed Republicans, 300,000 as liberals, and the remaining vast majority as moderate and conservative Democrats.[44] With Republicans and liberals both working toward realignment, the elections of 1968, and the events preceding those elections, accelerated GOP growth in Texas, though somewhat surprisingly, that growth was not yet enough to result in significant electoral change. In 1968, the Texas-styled New Deal coalition that had dominated state politics since the 1930s survived, though only by the slimmest of margins.[45]

Factionalism within the Texas Democratic Party threatened this success and centered on two individuals—Ralph Yarborough and John Connally. Liberals generally detested Connally, though their affinity for Johnson—Connally's mentor—had softened since Johnson's ascension to the Oval Office. No conservative Texas Democrat possessed a more loyal following than John Connally. In 1966, then in his second of three terms as governor, Connally was among several conservatives who, at the Texas State Democratic Party Convention, attempted to strike a preventive blow against any potential liberal insurgency that seemed to threaten the conservative stronghold in the state. Connally's weapon of choice had been a rhetorical call to ideological arms, couched as a patriotic duty to the independence and frontier spirit of his state, under assault from encroaching federalism. "Greatness is not an attribute of government, but of the people who create them and are their masters," Connally reminded those in attendance. "If this era is to be remembered as a time of greatness, it must be because the people stood taller, rather than because their government grew larger." Despite having been schooled in the LBJ system of politics, Connally—by the mid-1960s—appeared increasingly willing to distance himself from his mentor's philosophy of government.[46]

Johnson, even before assuming the presidency, detested the conservative-liberal factionalism within his home state's Democratic Party and routinely strategized ways to heal that division. Softening the specific but representative rivalry between Connally and Yarborough had, in fact, been a large part of John Kennedy's motivation for visiting Texas in November 1963. Despite the tragic outcome of that visit, factional tensions between the two men had only grown more intense in the subsequent years. Understanding the nature of this division is vital to making broader observations about the relationship between Republican growth in Texas and the appeal of modern conservatism. Without the instability of the traditionally dominant Texas Democratic Party, GOP growth in the state would have continued to be slow going and limited.[47]

Democratic infighting only grew worse over the next two years. In June 1968, with Johnson publicly out of the race and Robert Kennedy assassinated, Texas Democrats convened to nominate a presidential candidate. Competing liberal factions, one representing the candidacy of Minnesota senator and lion of the antiwar crowd, Eugene McCarthy, and the other representing Johnson's vice president, Hubert Humphrey, warred with one another rather than presenting the united front that had aided national liberal aims in previous years. As two factions of Texas liberals competed with one another, most conservatives refused to embrace either candidate and instead backed Connally. The heralding of Connally as a presidential candidate reflected the sincere desires of many grassroots conservatives in Texas, in addition to much of the Democratic establishment. However, promoting Connally, who was not yet a viable national candidate, was primarily a strategy designed to earn the Texas governor a vice presidential nomination.[48]

Connally unquestionably enjoyed widespread popularity in Texas. He had gained a certain aura in the aftermath of the JFK assassination, during which he sustained and survived potentially life-threatening wounds. To a small degree, but one that grew more evident in the coming years, Connally embodied the redemption of Texas in the period after Kennedy's death in Dallas. During the summer of 1968, as the Democratic National Convention in Chicago approached, numerous Texas conservatives began to reinterpret recent electoral history, citing Connally's popularity and coattails as the main reason for Johnson's overwhelming victory in Texas in 1964. Some pundits even speculated that Johnson's decision not to seek reelection was the result of Connally's decision not to pursue another term as governor. Without Connally's coattails to benefit him, Johnson feared he would suffer the embarrassment of losing his home state to what he knew would be a number of conservative alternatives.[49]

In August, conservative Texas Democrats experienced the national convention in Chicago with a sense that they were under siege. On consecutive nights during the convention, members of the Texas delegation found themselves under direct "attack" from antiwar protesters who gathered outside their hotel rooms. Inside the convention hall, tensions were equally high. While promoting Connally's inclusion on the national ticket, conservative Texas Democrats also struggled to repel a liberal advance within their own party led by Ralph Yarborough. Yarborough actively campaigned against Connally's efforts to gain national influence and went through channels in an effort to have the Texas delegation loyal to Connally declared illegitimate. Connally forces responded by blasting Yarborough as a tool of the "liberal left" and initiated a full-scale public relations campaign, blanketing grassroots and local party offices in Texas with material designed to induce fears that without Connally's presence on the national ticket, the Democratic Party would succumb to the designs of northeastern liberals.[50]

In part due to Yarborough's efforts, and in part due to Johnson's lack of active support, Connally achieved neither of his goals during the Chicago convention. Convinced by Johnson that supporting Humphrey would result in a vice presidential nomination, Connally eventually led his conservative Texas delegation into Humphrey's corner. No vice presidential nomination followed. Connally's experience in Chicago left him permanently embittered toward the liberal wing of his party. He believed Johnson had betrayed him by floating the possibility of the vice presidency in exchange for his support of Humphrey. The forces of loyalty and tradition kept Connally in check for the general campaign, but the long-term damage had been done.[51]

Nominated in the midst of a tumultuous convention held by a divided party, Hubert Humphrey lost his bid for the presidency in 1968. Many political observers then and later viewed the 1968 elections as a referendum on the Johnson presidency. This is not, however, how the story played out in Texas. Though defeated by Richard Nixon in a very narrow three-way national race that included Alabama's George Wallace, Humphrey still managed to carry Texas—the only Sun Belt state carried by the Democratic candidate that year. Humphrey's victory in Texas raises a number of interesting questions as to the nature of Texas political culture in the late 1960s.[52]

John Connally's position atop the Democratic Party's campaign efforts in Texas was arguably the biggest factor in Humphrey's success there. Connally's commitment to the Humphrey campaign, despite his being snubbed at the nominating convention in Chicago, was indicative of just how binding the culture of tradition and loyalty was in Texas throughout the 1960s. Connally supported Humphrey for several reasons. Through August, he maintained hope of being added to the Democratic ticket as the party's vice presidential nominee. At the same time, Connally actively opposed the other Democratic contenders, whom he considered far too liberal. When the vice presidential nomination went to Edmund Muskie instead, it was after Connally's loyalty to the party had already been publicly tested at the convention. Connally remained loyal and was, in fact, among a handful of Texas Democrats who endorsed and organized Humphrey's campaign efforts—the only serious efforts organized by any Democrats on behalf of

Humphrey in any southern state. In the early months of the campaign, the trust and popularity Connally enjoyed among Texans were strong enough to keep Humphrey afloat, though unenthusiastic campaigning resulted in a miniscule $150,000 in campaign donations—less than one-tenth of what had been raised for Johnson in Texas four years earlier.[53]

Ironically, Connally's most effective strategy on behalf of Humphrey in Texas was to avoid mentioning Humphrey as much as possible. Rather, Connally focused the Texas campaign on LBJ, the war in Vietnam, and the state's tradition of loyalty to the Democratic Party. Most Texas Democrats choosing to support Humphrey did so because of tradition, loyalty, and anti-Republicanism rooted in their quest to maintain establishment dominance.[54]

These efforts notwithstanding, Humphrey had several problems in Texas. Connally was the recognized leader of the Texas Democratic Party, and his support for Humphrey encouraged others to do the same. Connally, however, could not hide his tepid enthusiasm. As the fall campaign progressed, the united Democratic front began to weaken. When Humphrey gained national momentum by "going dove" and publicly criticizing Johnson's handling of Vietnam, Connally's support wavered—as did Johnson's. During a campaign trip to Houston, Humphrey focused on his proposed "de-Americanization" of the war in Vietnam. Letters to the editor flooded Houston-area newspapers, linking Humphrey with northeastern liberalism, the antiwar crowd, and inherent weakness. Humphrey's liberalism was increasingly difficult to hide from the Texas public as the campaign wore on. The Democratic nominee openly rejected the law and order rhetoric that most conservative Texas Democrats had adopted and refused to establish an official party headquarters in the state, instead milking the funds and energy of the state party. Republicans charged that Humphrey was taking Texas for granted; conservative Democrats, in large part, agreed.[55]

In late September, Humphrey again visited Houston, this time for a Democratic fund-raiser. Here he eagerly joined Ralph Yarborough in multiple photo-ops, referring to himself and Yarborough as a pair of "bona fide liberals." Humphrey's association with Yarborough at the dinner prompted Connally to reject an invitation to introduce Humphrey at the same event. Humphrey's cozy relationship with Yarborough irked Connally and further chilled the Texas governor's already lukewarm support.[56]

For the same reason, Texas gubernatorial candidate Preston Smith also declined an invitation to appear alongside Humphrey at the Houston fund-raiser. Though he shared Humphrey's partisan identification, it was clear from his campaign strategy that Smith shared little else with the Democratic presidential nominee. Smith, who had served as Connally's lieutenant governor since 1962, told advisers to at all costs avoid having his campaign associated with anything "liberal." In the fall of 1968, this meant repudiating Yarborough and avoiding Humphrey. In public, Smith simply dismissed Humphrey's campaign by saying he was "too busy" to help.[57]

Preston Smith's 1968 campaign for the governorship of Texas would have made any Texas conservative proud. Though not especially media savvy, Smith was smart enough to consult numerous public relations and advertising firms in a concerted effort to construct a conservative image tailored to the Texas heartland. At the epicenter of these efforts was a blunt antiliberalism used to distance Smith from the chaos of the national party. Smith addressed mass-mailed form letters to "Dear Property Owners" and spoke eloquently about the Jeffersonian tradition of landowning and of the rights of taxpayers. He supported the retention of right-to-work laws by disparaging "big unions," adding that he believed Texas had been built "on the initiative and hard work of individuals in the free enterprise system." Smith's advertising campaign also reflected these efforts. During the fall of 1968, he ran sixty-second television commercials in which he derided liberals as "defeatist and negative." He labeled himself a traditionalist, a loyalist, and a conservative. Alluding to intensified racial fears, his commercials promised that he would never "leave any of you alone to face riots in the streets of Texas." He vilified special interest groups and big government, and equated liberals to both. Smith, who by 1970 found himself under the tutelage of former Goldwater and Reagan campaign adviser F. Clifton White, even championed his "heritage of individualism" and claimed a populist high ground—one that affirmed him as truly "of the people." The conservative Texas press trumpeted Smith's candidacy as right for Texas on the issues of crime and taxation, but Smith's success was about more than just issues; it was also about not letting a liberalized national party drown a conservative Democrat running for governor in Texas.[58]

Smith's Republican opponent in 1968 was Paul Eggers, a tax attorney from Wichita Falls and a friend of John Tower. Somewhat surprisingly, in light of Tower's popularity, conservative reactions to Eggers were lukewarm at best. Distracted by the presidential campaign, Texas Republicans failed to give their gubernatorial nominee adequate financial support.[59] Eggers also failed to rally conservative Democrats, most whom were more than satisfied with what they had seen from Smith. Texas liberals' support of Eggers, unlike in previous elections involving Tower, also worked against the Republican candidate. When Texas liberals endorsed Eggers, as had been their strategy for promoting a two-party Texas in previous races, con-

Preston Smith visits with Lyndon Johnson in the Oval Office, 1968.
(Courtesy of the Southwest Collection, Lubbock, TX)

servative Democrats, much more effectively than they had in previous years, used that liberal support as a weapon wielded to discourage conservative voters from jumping the party ship. Conservative Democrats dismissed Eggers as a Republican representing the party's moderate wing and, worse, the dreaded northeastern establishment. The Eggers campaign caused many Texas Republicans to question whether the backhanded support they received from liberal Democrats was still a positive.[60]

Eggers's use of media was also ineffective. He largely ceded the mass media to Smith and instead took to the highways, where he spent much of the campaign feebly trying to court not only conservative Democrats, but also minorities, labor leaders, and liberals—to all of whom, he argued, a viable second party was critical. Among liberals and minorities, Eggers was successful and, as Tower had done in 1966, even earned the endorsement of the notably liberal political periodical the *Texas Observer,* though such support cost the Republican more credibility in conservative circles. Eggers's strategy mirrored Tower's successful campaigns of 1961 and 1966, but by 1968 that strategy was much more difficult to maintain in the context of growing antiliberal sentiment and the related need to be uncompromisingly conservative. In the end, Eggers struggled to find conservative supporters and utterly failed to mobilize conservative Democrats against Smith.[61]

Among Texas conservatives, Ronald Reagan was far more popular than Eggers. His election to the governorship of California in 1966 had been met by Texas conservatives with great enthusiasm and excitement—exceeded in cheers on election night only by Tower's defeat of Carr.[62] Though largely overshadowed by later, more successful campaigns for the presidency, Reagan's 1968 bid for the White House, his first, enjoyed widespread support in Texas. Many perceived Reagan very differently in 1968 than they had viewed Goldwater four years earlier. Nearly 50 percent of Texans had found Goldwater too "radical" to risk a vote on in 1964, but only 10 percent of Texans felt the same way about Reagan in 1968. Much of this was due to the national context. Unlike Goldwater, Reagan also maintained support among the state's business community while simultaneously appearing to be a rank-and-file populist conservative without an extremist agenda and with media savvy. Reagan also benefited from George Wallace's campaign in 1968, which absorbed the brunt of Texans' hostility to radical extremism and gave Reagan breathing room against similar attacks. In a sense, Wallace absorbed the extremist labels that Reagan, as a Goldwater disciple, might have been expected to bear in Texas.[63]

Reagan was invited to speak at multiple Republican fund-raisers across Texas in 1967 and 1968, and he quickly became the state GOP's top attraction. Twice in 1967, Reagan headlined a conservative all-star cast at fundraisers in Dallas. The former Hollywood actor did not disappoint. Reagan's speeches in Dallas combined hard-hitting assaults on Robert F. Kennedy, Ted Kennedy, and LBJ with sporadic comedic breaks and a charm that forced the liberal *Texas Observer* to lament, "This man is no Goldwater." While building the prestige of the state GOP, Reagan also avoided alienating conservative Texas Democrats and actually befriended many of them. Referring to conservative Texas Democrats as "God-fearing and patriotic," Reagan excused his bipartisan admirers as victims of the leftward tilt of their national party. He related to Texas Democrats by freely reminding his audiences that he too had once called himself a Democrat. He never left that party, he told them; the party left him. Reagan's popularity in both Republican and conservative Democratic circles created a dilemma for some GOP leaders, who feared that tying their fortunes to Reagan's popularity would eventually lead to a repeat of the Goldwater disaster. However, Reagan's public appeal and ability to drive party growth and respectability in Texas made repudiating the California governor politically untenable and strategically unthinkable.[64]

By perfecting a balance of antiliberal attacks focused on both national and state liberals, Reagan also succeeded in Texas where many other conservatives had failed. In comparing Johnson's Great Society to a second-rate "rehash of the dark, dismal days of the past," Reagan set a standard for LBJ-bashing in Texas. While tactically avoiding any criticism or mention of the popular Johnson ally John Connally, Reagan directly attacked LBJ as an enemy of populist conservatism. In doing so, Reagan contributed to the process of dismantling the dominance of tradition and loyalty among Texas conservatives. Most of Reagan's anti-LBJ critiques targeted the Great Society. He attacked big government as having been set up in opposition to the vast majority of Americans' interests, linked this to Johnson's widening credibility gap, and even blamed LBJ's social policies for the formation of radical leftist splinter groups. He criticized Johnson for not doing enough to win the war in Vietnam, thereby aligning himself with Texas hawks. LBJ-bashing in Texas was a fine art and one that could succeed only by prioritizing Johnson's liberalism while calling upon LBJ to do more, not less, to win the war in Vietnam. In 1967 and 1968, nobody was better at this balancing act than Reagan.[65]

Reagan's speeches in Texas charmed his conservative audiences. He deftly used humor and told appealing stories, but transitioned sharply to measured diatribes against big government, "the planned economy," and "moral laxity and crime in the streets"—all while characterizing the Republican Party as the more populist, future-oriented, and modern of the two major national parties. Reagan's rhetoric was simple, to the point, and had a populist tinge and appeal. He proclaimed himself to be on a "Crusade for the people" and skillfully set conservative Republicanism in Texas apart from liberal, intellectual, and collectivist elitism.[66]

In 1967, Reagan unofficially launched his campaign for the 1968 GOP presidential nomination with a summer barbecue fund-raiser in Amarillo, Texas.[67] Over the next several months, Reagan was consistently the only Republican candidate to outperform LBJ in public opinion polls across Texas and the rest of the South.[68] Such polls underscore the notion that, though the 1968 campaign is generally remembered in Texas as a three-way contest between Nixon, Humphrey, and Wallace, the emergence of Ronald Reagan as a presidential candidate was equally significant and perhaps more so, particularly if analyzed through a long-term lens.[69]

John Tower meets with the Republican candidate for governor of California, Ronald Reagan, c. 1966. (Courtesy of the John G. Tower Library and Archives, Georgetown, TX)

Though Reagan's grassroots popularity was a boon to party respectability and growth in Texas, it also forced the state GOP leadership into an uncomfortable dilemma. Despite the isolated successes of candidates like George Bush and John Tower, the state GOP was still relatively impotent and certainly still dependent on the national party. Moderates and responsible conservatives, primarily focused on avoiding a replay of 1964, feared Reagan's candidacy, despite evidence that Reagan's persona was much different than Goldwater's. This fear cornered state Republican leaders into officially supporting Nixon, not Reagan, for the GOP presidential nomination of 1968. The result was a small-scale eruption of factional division within the state GOP—factions less severe than those endured within the state Democratic Party, but factions that just eight years later evolved into a much more bitter and significant struggle.

These divisions clearly manifested at the Texas GOP Convention in June 1968 when more than three hundred Reagan supporters filed into the Corpus Christi convention hall waving placards in support of a Reagan White House bid. Though largely failing to sway enough party regulars to give Reagan a real chance at the nomination, Reagan's Texas supporters persisted up to and through the national convention in Miami. Their efforts to generate support for the California governor included the sponsorship of an all-night Reagan movie marathon on the evening prior to the convention's first day. The attention Reagan received from his Lone Star State supporters grabbed the majority of print space in Texas newspapers' coverage of the Republican meeting. The *Dallas Morning News* consistently ran three to four stories on Reagan, his wife, and his supporters for every one they ran on Nixon or any other candidate. One reporter noted, "The enthusiasm of the Reagan followers has been perhaps the most spectacular feature of an otherwise lackluster pre-convention period."[70]

On the convention's first day, Reagan met with the California delegation, formally announced his candidacy, and attempted (via a team of strategists and campaign workers) to sway Texas delegates' votes. Many delegates believed the argument that a vote for Reagan would increase the likelihood of his being asked to join the Nixon ticket and fifteen delegates did, for that reason, switch their vote. When approached by reporters in the coming days, each of the remaining Nixon delegates openly supported Reagan's candidacy in the press, but deferred their vote to Nixon, solely, they said, on the basis of his substantial advantage in foreign affairs experience.[71]

Though Reagan's supporters were ultimately unsuccessful, their exuberance in Texas intrigued Nixon and had a clear impact on the development of the GOP nominee's campaign rhetoric. Literally hours after accepting the Republican nomination, Nixon insisted on a private meeting with the Texas leadership—many of whom had backed Reagan at the convention. Trying to convince the Texans of his populist, western bona fides, Nixon referred to the Lone Star State as unique and "not southern" while embracing, by name, Ronald Reagan as an icon of western populism.[72] Still, many Texas conservatives distrusted Nixon, perceiving him, despite his California roots, as the choice of the party's northeastern establishment. Nixon's frustration over his inability to secure the loyalty of Texas conservatives eventually contributed to his selection of Connally as a cabinet member. However, as his general election fight with Hubert Humphrey loomed, Nixon's need to win those conservative loyalties became an ever-pressing problem.[73]

Yellow Dogs

The Republican Party's chief strategy against Hubert Humphrey in the fight to claim Texas's electoral votes was to first associate the national Democratic Party with liberalism, and then to associate liberalism with chaos, weakness, incompetence, untrustworthiness, and divisiveness. Law and order rhetoric was the centerpiece of this strategy. Nixon blamed federal liberalism for failing to address the nation's rising crime rates and for obstructing law enforcement. In reciting crime statistics and using images of lawlessness, Nixon claimed Humphrey was not strong enough to be president and portrayed the Democratic nominee as more concerned with the "rights of the guilty" than with the "rights of the victim."[74]

Nixon also attracted supporters in Texas through emotional appeals that reflected a variety of preconceived prejudices and ideological convictions, ranging from libertarian antistatism to overt racism. Nixon's message, clearly an evolution of the RNC's 1965 strategic dictates for local campaigns, was designed to be universally applicable. Middle-class suburban whites—the "forgotten Americans" that Nixon courted and eventually relabeled as the "Silent Majority"—did not necessarily have to be racist in order to find common ground with Nixon's call for safer neighborhoods. Rural whites, particularly those in East Texas, where racial fears had traditionally been the strongest and the population was most diverse, did not have to live in a suburban neighborhood to see race riots as evidence of social and racial instability, brought on by outside agitators, liberals, and the federal government. By using the power of broadcast media to manipulate images of crime and violence for political effect, Nixon touched on issues that conservative Texas Democrats were also using to great effect, thus advancing his own credibility in the state as a populist conservative.[75]

Nixon's successful use of law and order rhetoric in Texas was also predicated on the state's strong opposition to gun control. Gun-ownership lobbies made public their belief that gun control advocates had more in common with communists than with Americans, compared liberal calls for mandatory gun registration to the Nazis' disarming of Holland and France in World War II, and even warned that liberal gun control measures would be akin to the totalitarian impulse to disarm populations as a means of quelling resistance.[76]

As the fall campaign progressed, it was clear that Nixon enjoyed several advantages over Humphrey in Texas. Between the state's anticommunist hawks who feared liberal passivity in Vietnam and a growing suburban middle class for which the mantra of law and order offered hope that future political leaders might protect them against rising crime rates and violence, the Nixon campaign succeeded in Texas in many places where Goldwater's had fallen flat. Nixon was particularly effective in linking failures in Vietnam to antiwar protests and unchecked crime in the streets, government interference with the rights of private citizens, and bureaucratic inefficiency.[77]

Early polling in Texas indicated numerous other advantages as well. Nixon supporters showed greater enthusiasm and party loyalty than did Humphrey backers, though neither figure indicated significant loyalty; 60 percent of Texas Republicans were committed to voting for Nixon, whereas only 40 percent of Texas Democrats said the same of their candidate. Of course, such statistics are misleading if not balanced with an understanding of the overwhelming advantage Democrats still enjoyed in Texas when it came to partisan identification. Yet, the source of Democratic disillusionment remained important and could be traced to the national convention in Chicago where, among other things, many Texas Democrats reacted with stunned horror to Humphrey's selection of Muskie over Connally as his running mate. Additionally, most Texans saw Nixon as more "presidential" than Humphrey. Lastly, and in contrast to the commonly accepted analysis, polls showed that the independent candidacy of George Wallace cut more deeply into the Democratic base than the Republican one. In other words, polls showed that, in Texas, Wallace actually took more votes away from Humphrey than he did from Nixon, a significant aspect to the larger story surrounding Wallace's campaign in Texas.[78]

Nixon eventually won the general election, but despite all of his advantages in Texas, he still narrowly lost to Humphrey in Texas and to Wallace in the South. Humphrey's narrow victory illustrates the resilience of Democratic loyalties, the extent of anti-Republicanism, and the limits of antiliberalism and "law and order." Texas Republicans made significant gains between 1964 and 1968, but they were still a minority power whose future depended, in large part, on the behavior and strategy of establishment Democrats and the appeal of national conservatism. Quite simply, Hubert Humphrey won Texas in 1968 because Democratic loyalties remained strong enough to overcome the series of advantages enjoyed by a much-strengthened but still vastly outnumbered and outfinanced Texas Republican Party. Such disadvantages would be overcome in the next decade.

By 1968, constructing the proper ideological image, and doing so in a national context, had become a prerequisite to political success. Johnson's national credibility gap, his inability to bring a successful end to the war in Vietnam, and his failure to address crime as most Texans felt it should be addressed undermined Democratic loyalties and opened an important door for Texas Republicans seeking to attract conservative Democrats. Buoyed by the increasing association of liberalism with Johnson's failures, Republicans further linked the president's credibility gap to issues of honesty, integrity, trust, and morality. Over the course of the next decade, the linkage between morality, trust, anticommunism, and antiliberalism became an even more successful bread-and-butter strategy for conservative Republicans.

Just as critical, however, were Texans' fears that their nation was sinking into an abyss. When Texans watched their nightly news broadcasts, they saw images of a nation being torn apart. They saw a nation in which chaos and lawlessness triumphed over order, stability, and tradition. They saw rising crime rates, a seemingly impotent American military, and a growing base of disaffected youth and other constituents challenging the status quo of American cultural tradition. They also saw race.[79]

For many Texans, the words of men like Ben Carpenter were filtered through a social and cultural tradition of racial segregation, discrimination, and fear. The dynamic of race relations in Texas did not define partisan realignment, nor did it singularly shape the political culture of the mid- to late 1960s. It was, however, central to a broader climate of disillusionment, fear, and backlash.

Chapter 4

"I am a Sick American"

Race, Fear, and the Limits of Backlash Politics

On April 15, 1971, the *Lubbock Avalanche-Journal* published an anonymous, full-page advertisement consisting only of text. At the top of the page, in big, bold letters, was a declaration: "I am a Sick American." The text of the ad, credited to "Author Unknown," read as follows:

There are those that claim ours is a "sick" society; that our country is sick; our government is sick; that we are sick. Well, maybe they're right. I submit that I'm sick . . . and maybe you are, too.

I am sick of having policemen ridiculed and called "pigs" while cop killers are hailed as some kind of folk hero.

I am sick of being told that religion is the opiate of the people, but marijuana should be legalized.

I am sick of commentators and columnists canonizing anarchists, revolutionaries and criminal rapists, but condemning law enforcement when such criminals are brought to justice.

I am sick of being told that pornography is the right of a free press, but freedom of the press does not include being able to read the Bible on school grounds.

I am sick of paying more and more taxes to build schools while I see some faculty members encouraging students either to tear them down or burn them.

I am sick of Supreme Court decisions which turn criminals loose on society—while other decisions try to take away my means of protecting my home and family.

I am sick of pot-smoking entertainers deluging me with their condemnation of my moral standards on late-night television.

I am sick of being told it is wrong to use napalm to end a war overseas—but if it's a Molotov cocktail or a bomb at home, I must understand the provocations.

I am sick of not being able to take my family to a movie unless I want to have them exposed to nudity, homosexuality, and the glorification of narcotics.

I am sick of riots, marches, protests, demonstrations, confrontations, and the other mob temper tantrums of people intellectually incapable of working within the system.

I am sick of hearing the same phrases, the same slick slogans, the cries of people who must chant the same thing like zombies because they haven't the capacity for verbalizing thought.

I am sick of those who say I owe them this or that because of the sins of my forefathers—when I have looked down both ends of a gun barrel to defend their rights, their liberties and their families.

I am sick of cynical attitudes toward patriotism.

I am sick of politicians with no backbone.

I am sick of permissiveness.

I am sick of the dirty, the foul-mouthed, the un-washed.

I am sick of the decline of personal honesty, personal integrity and human sincerity.

Most of all, though, I am sick of being told I'm sick. I'm sick of being told my country is sick—when we have the greatest nation that man has ever brought forth on the face of the earth. Fully fifty per cent of the people on earth would willingly trade places with the most deprived, the most underprivileged among us. Yes, I may be sick, but if I am only sick, I can get well. I can also help my society get well—and help my country get well.

Take note, all of you . . . you will not find me throwing a rock or a bomb; you will not find me under a placard; you will not see me take to the streets; you will not find me ranting to wild-eyed mobs. But you will find me at work, paying taxes, serving in the community where I live. You will also find me expressing my anger and indignation to elected officials. You will find me speaking out in support of those officials, institutions and personalities who contribute to the elevation of society and not its destruction. You will find me contributing my time, money and personal influence to helping churches, hospitals, charities and other establishments which have shown the true spirit of this Country's determination to ease pain, suffering, eliminate hunger and generate brotherhood.

But, most of all, you'll find me at the polling place. There—if you listen—you can hear the thunder of the common man. There, all of us can cast our vote—for an America where people can walk the streets without fear.[1]

As the tumultuous 1960s came to a close, more Americans grew less patient with the pace, procedure, and style of social, economic, and cultural change. Disillusionment and, eventually, malaise resulted from a sense that America was "sick." Yet not all citizens responded passively. Dallas civic leader Ben Carpenter, for instance, made remarks in 1968 similar to those of this anonymous "Sick American" a few months before organizing a coalition of conservative Democrats campaigning for Richard Nixon. A year later, dubbed by Nixon as part of a "Silent Majority," many more white, middle-class, and increasingly suburban Texans began to more vocally express themselves, both socially and politically, by challenging the status quo of state and national politics and by adding fuel to the fire that burned hot enough to eventually inspire diatribes similar to the one from this "Sick American."

This fear, frustration, and outrage may simply be recalled as a "backlash" against the perceived leftward drift of the 1960s. Backlash politics, most clearly embodied by the politics of George Wallace, gripped segments of the population from all across the country, Texas certainly included. Yet, the politics of backlash functioned differently in different regions of the country, primarily because the intensity of issues being addressed in those regions varied, as did the cultural and social contexts in which those issues were debated.[2]

Race, integration, and associated white anxieties are the most commonly accepted diagnosis for the political backlash that gripped the South during the late 1960s. Yet, in Texas, backlash politics was more complicated, multifaceted, and dynamic than in most of the South—specifically because race functioned differently in Texas than it did elsewhere. While an important factor in understanding the rise of modern conservatism, race in Texas should be contextually understood as only part of a broader trend toward white fears and frustrations that just as importantly made antiliberalism more credible, varied, and mainstream.

Texas Race Relations, 1945–1967

In 1962, the author John Bainbridge spoke of Texans' attitudes toward race in the context of reactions to the landmark 1954 *Brown v. Board of Education* decision. According to Bainbridge, Texans' response to desegregation

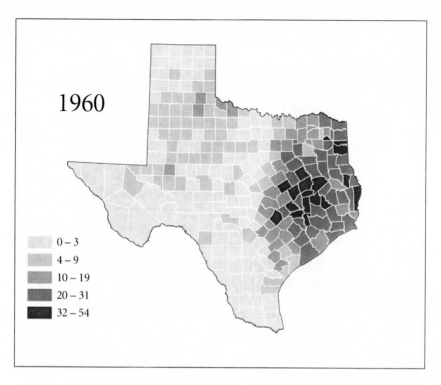

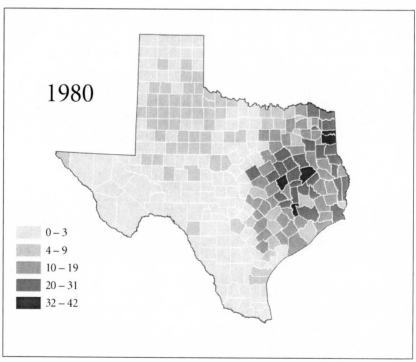

Percentage of black Texans per county in 1960 (top) and 1980 (bottom).

had been "typically American, and then some," even acknowledging that some white Texans had even responded with "genuine endorsement." "In contrast to other Southern states, where the decree was everywhere met with open defiance," Bainbridge noted, "sixty-five school districts in Texas voluntarily ended segregation within a year after it became illegal, and sixty-nine more did the same in 1957."[3]

Even in hindsight, Bainbridge's assessment seems accurate. Since the end of World War II, most Texans had grown more moderate on issues of race than had most of their white southern neighbors.[4] In 1946, nearly half of Texans polled said that they supported the Supreme Court's decision in *Smith v. Allwright* to outlaw the state Democratic Party's practice of restricting primary voting to whites only. When Heman Sweatt attempted to desegregate the University of Texas School of Law, resistance was momentarily strong, but his eventual admittance, thanks to the 1950 landmark Supreme Court decision, *Sweatt v. Painter,* did not lead to significant backlash in Texas. Historian George Green has gone so far as to suggest that after World War II and throughout the 1950s, "there was a movement in Texas toward gradual acceptance of integration." Even the Texas League, one of the nation's most prominent minor league baseball organizations, took steps in the late 1940s and early 1950s to advance the cause of integration in professional sports.[5]

Of course, such incidents do not necessarily mean that race was not an important political issue or a potent campaign weapon in Texas. In 1954, then running for another term as governor, Allan Shivers found that using race as a campaign issue could shore up his vote among rural East Texas whites, many of whom, Shivers feared, found his opponent Ralph Yarborough's folksy populism appealing. As related in one famous story of the 1954 gubernatorial campaign, a black man was hired by the Shivers campaign to drive across East Texas in a brand-new Cadillac covered in "Yarborough for Governor" stickers. The black man would stop at gas stations, as per his orders from the Shivers campaign, and rudely request a fill-up before proclaiming to all within hearing distance that he was "in a hurry to help Mr. Yarborough."[6]

Despite such occurrences, neither massive resistance nor backlash was a common response to race and civil rights in Texas during the 1950s. Only in 1956 did this pattern of benign but reluctant accommodation seem to temporarily break. In August, Shivers used state police to defy court-ordered school integration in Mansfield, a community in southern Tarrant County, part of the growing Dallas–Fort Worth metroplex. A less famous precursor to Orval Faubus's similar stand in Little Rock a year later, Shivers's defiance was not representative of elected officials' views in Texas. Only five of twenty-two congressmen from Texas signed the famed Southern Manifesto of 1956, which called for outright defiance of *Brown* and subsequent court decisions on enforcement. In fact, Texas had more nonsigners of the manifesto than any other southern state, including Lyndon Johnson, Ralph Yarborough, and the very powerful and influential Speaker of the House, Sam Rayburn.[7]

By 1957 it was clear, therefore, that so far as race was concerned, Texas was moving beyond its "southern moorings." In addition to not signing the Southern Manifesto, Johnson and Yarborough provided 40 percent of the southern vote in favor of the 1957 voting rights bill. Shivers's replacement, Governor Price Daniel, refused to address the issue of school integration as several of his fellow southern governors demanded, instead looking for ways to stress greater cooperation and less hostility between races. Commenting on the post-1956 period of Texas race relations, George Green later said that "no state Establishment leader waged a racist campaign, stood in a schoolhouse door, or attempted to do much of anything to prevent the inevitable crumbling of segregation." Quite simply, race relations in Texas through the late 1950s were more moderate than was the norm across much of the South.[8]

Though organized massive resistance did not, for the most part, come to Texas after the *Brown* decision, many white Texans allowed the national ramifications of that decision to shape the way in which they perceived race and government. Those perceptions changed in important ways after 1957, in no small part because of the growing momentum of the civil rights movement outside Texas as well as related legislative debates. In the late 1950s, most white Texans who opposed integration articulated that opposition on fundamentally simple racial grounds. The most common political response was the one that had been in practice for years—to advocate for states' rights while suggesting that segregation was a positive good. For instance, in August 1959, George Mahon, the veteran New Deal congressman from the nineteenth congressional, assured his voters that, "generally speaking . . . the question is one which should be left to the states and local communities." "I do not believe that social intermingling between the white and colored people is good for either race," he added. Despite a qualitative intensification of public rhetoric, socially conservative Democrats like Mahon did not receive a quantitatively significant number of letters in the late 1950s dealing with the issue of race. Among most white Texans, the issue remained relatively calm.[9]

Things began to change in 1963 and 1964, however, as Johnson's push for civil rights gained steam, particularly in the wake of Kennedy's assassi-

Congressman George Mahon of
Lubbock. (Courtesy of the Southwest Collection, Lubbock, TX)

nation. Not surprisingly, many white Texans also reacted with greater
concern. Yet, the stridency of racialized rhetoric also grew less radical during the same time, at least as far as the public's communication with area
officials was concerned. While fear and radicalism still peppered the language of those most hostile to civil rights reform, many more Texans
couched their opposition to racial progress in the more sterile and palatable
terms of constitutionality, or as a fear not of race but of a growing liberal
government. One Texan, identifying himself as a "Christian loyal American," wrote in May 1964 that "our federal government has far too much
power now. . . . This bill will destroy our individual liberty and freedom of
choice, and is directly contrary to the spirit and intent of our Bill of Rights."
Another Texan wrote in August 1964 of his belief that "social or business
equality can never be legislated and nothing but turmoil and strife can ever
result from the effort." He further opined that "equality must be earned
and I believe there is ample opportunity in this country for those who sincerely want to work their way to the top. When it becomes a function of
government to tell private business who it must serve, I believe government
is overextended." For many white Texans, "color-blind" opposition to civil
rights and integration predated the co-optation of that strategy by state and
national politicians in the coming decades, and also, importantly, predated
both the Civil Rights Act of 1964 and the Voting Rights Act of 1965.[10]

As was true across the South, Texas housed a small contingent of whites who actively supported the civil rights movement, though most did not. Regardless, Lyndon Johnson was able to easily defeat Barry Goldwater in 1964, despite the fact that Johnson's support for the movement and the bill had cost him much of the South. Most anti–civil rights whites in Texas chose to absolve Johnson for his stand on race as an obligation or debt to the slain Kennedy, rather than as an indication of long-term policy or ideology. Even on this polarizing issue, the shadow of Dallas still lurked and made Texas's response unique.[11]

Also important in 1964 was John Connally's response to race, which not only reflected attitudes in the state but also helped shape them. Connally was publicly critical of the Civil Rights Act for the same reason that Goldwater and other conservatives denounced it—it was an unwelcome expansion of federal authority. At the same time, Connally was dogged in his criticism of several Deep South governors, Ross Barnett of Mississippi and George Wallace of Alabama, most notably, for their handling of black protestors. Connally believed that massive resistance had emboldened the civil rights movement and agitated the federal government to the point that intervention could no longer be justifiably withheld. Furthermore, Connally felt that civil rights was being thrust upon the rest of the nation—Texas included—because states like Alabama and Mississippi had forced Washington's hand. Responsible conservatives, according to Connally, understood the value of compromise and accommodation.[12]

Connally's support for racial progress was motivated less by a concern for equality than by his desire to avoid similar federal interventions in Texas. As governor, he spent a great deal of energy shaping Texas's image as a racially moderate and southwestern, rather than southern, state. He viewed himself as a racial progressive and openly promoted Texas's heritage of racial and ethnic diversity. He often spoke of a "Texas bloodline" comprised of twenty-six distinct ethnic strands—an effort, not uncommon in the fiercely proud Lone Star State, to promote a nationalistic and uniformly "Texas Heritage."[13]

Demographics and geography also played a role in the way race worked as a political issue in Texas. Relative to the Deep South, the African American population in Texas was comparatively small. The black population was mostly concentrated in the eastern fifth of the state, which, in a state as vast as Texas, meant that many white Texans did not have much daily contact with African Americans compared to whites in other southern states. Even in cities like Dallas, Houston, and Beaumont, where the black population was larger than average, suburbanization efforts that aimed to replace de jure with de facto segregation went largely unchallenged and therefore contributed to the public perception that race was not the urgent political issue that it was elsewhere in the South.[14]

Texans' perceived moderation on race was also a reflection of the waning influence and growing hostility toward extremism. In the mid-1960s, radical organizations like the Ku Klux Klan and even the John Birch Society no longer functioned in Texas with the same gusto as they operated in other parts of the South, a reflection, among other things, of the state's post–Kennedy assassination aversion to extremism in all forms. In 1965, when George Mahon received a handful of pamphlets claiming that civil rights marchers in Selma had engaged in sex orgies along the way and that the marchers were plotting to set up Martin Luther King Jr. as a "black dictator," the congressman dismissed the material as nonsense and suggested that such radical material would have no significant reach with Texas audiences.[15] With most candidates in Texas avoiding race as much as possible in favor of other, more ideological or economic issues, the confrontation between massive resistance and middle-class moderation that characterized racial politics in the suburban South was far less influential, necessary, or apparent in Texas—at least through the mid-1960s.[16]

Even though the employment of color-blind rhetoric in opposition to racial progressivism was relatively common even prior to the Voting Rights Act of 1965, the passage of that act did push more Texas whites to cast their criticisms against federal tyranny. When the white public's outrage over proposed federal laws on open and public housing began to boil in 1966 and 1967, oppositional rhetoric was not overtly racial, but instead tended to warn against "liberal ideas" that reflected "another step toward Communism" and the destruction of "basic human rights." "I am very disturbed over the proposed Civil Rights proposal concerning sale or renting of private property," one Texan wrote in 1966. "I was in favor of the last Civil Rights Bill as I believe everyone should have the right to vote, but when it comes to selling your private home or renting a house or apartment, I believe that is what the word intends—private."[17]

Race and civil rights did have an impact on partisan realignment in Texas. John Tower, for instance, used the debate over public housing to suggest that the Democratic Party was out of step with the Texas mainstream and could no longer be counted on to effectively represent the state. Tower often spoke of the need to preserve a "free society" in which individuals were free to choose their own associations. He described federal action on civil rights in the past years as a step toward "totalitarian society" but always reminded his audiences that he "deplored prejudice and bigotry in any form. I am in favor of equality of opportunity in housing for all people." Tower's rhetoric, like the rhetoric of many other hostile white Texans, reflected the degree to which overt racism had become socially unacceptable by the late 1960s, even in a former Confederate state. Nonetheless, Tower led the Texas Republican charge against the Civil Rights Act of 1966 not by drawing on the public's hostility toward racial equality—at least not overtly—but rather on the public's fear that federal expansionism was generally contributing to the downward spiral of national decline.[18]

To dismiss white Texans' widespread antipathy toward and fear of federal expansionism as "code" for racism is inaccurately simplistic. Clearly Texas maintained a healthy climate for racism, but between 1945 and 1967 that climate consistently moderated, making issues of race less potent and less central to the political culture. Regardless of the fact that color-blind opposition couched in antigovernment rhetoric may have been born out of the race issue, it evolved into a life of its own and reinforced preexisting values of meritocracy and privatization. As many Texans viewed national racial discord as part and parcel of other aspects of perceived national decline—the growing antiwar movement, a rising counterculture, drug usage, and crime—they also bought into a rhetoric that was broader and more encompassing of a populist conservative worldview.

Racial Appeals in the Campaigns of 1968

It is worth revisiting the campaigns of 1968 in order to see the complexity of race as a political issue, as well as to compare Texas with the rest of the mythically monolithic and racially motivated "South." The most prominent national figure to have utilized race as a campaign weapon in the development of backlash politics was George Wallace. Certainly, few in 1963 would have categorized Wallace as "color-blind." Few would have categorized him as color-blind in 1968, either, despite the fact that Wallace's campaign for the presidency did attract segments of the population that would soon be absorbed into a growing tide of conservative and Republican realignment. Whereas many working-class and rural conservatives in the South embraced Wallace's fire-eating populist rhetoric, most Texas conservatives were relatively unimpressed. In the presidential campaign of 1968, Wallace—who carried Alabama with 66 percent of the vote, Mississippi with 63 percent, Louisiana with 48 percent, Georgia with 43 percent, and Arkansas with 39 percent—garnered less than 19 percent of the vote in Texas, by far his worst showing in any state of the old Confederacy. Even in other peripheral South states like Florida, North Carolina, Virginia, and

Tennessee, Wallace ran strong enough to garner an average of around 30 percent. In Texas, Wallace managed to carry only 18 of the state's 254 counties, and 14 of those were concentrated in a sparsely populated area of East Texas that bordered Louisiana.[19]

Wallace's isolated and limited support in Texas was partly a function of the state's changing demography. Republican strategists in the mid-1960s optimistically noted that "many Texas communities have little in common with typical southern towns. The tremendous growth of the state of Texas in the past ten years has been due partly to the influx of thousands of people from other states. A great many are Republicans."[20] Most of those incoming Republicans populated Dallas and Houston, while most Wallace voters in East Texas, though loyally Democratic for decades, identified themselves as politically "independent." They were farmers and were, for the most part, Protestant. Only 8 percent of Texas Catholics supported Wallace in 1968, while only 9 percent of Texas college graduates did so—the numbers in each demographic were significantly lower than Ronald Reagan's support in the run-up to the Republican National Convention that year.[21] A national Harris Poll released in September 1968 identified Wallace's support as "southern" with a few solid pockets in the North. Wallace's influence in the West was negligible—by far his weakest region.[22]

Regardless of his minimal support in Texas, Wallace's presence in the 1968 campaign forced Richard Nixon to make decisions that he otherwise might not have made. Most notably, Nixon's decision to tap Spiro Agnew as his running mate in 1968 is still popularly seen as part of a so-called Southern Strategy designed to win racially motivated white southern voters. Yet in Texas, Agnew was an unpopular choice with conservatives. Although Agnew's reputation for being a hard-liner on race drew praise from many southerners, in Texas far more conservatives balked at Agnew's moderation on economic policy. Even more disconcerting to conservative Texans toying with the idea of voting Republican was the ticket's joint push for various moderations to the GOP platform, on issues ranging from corporate regulations to Vietnam. Among Texas Republicans, these actions reignited charges that Nixon was merely masking his commitment to the Rockefeller wing of the party by talking tough on the campaign trail.[23]

Further reflective of the secondary value that conservatives in Texas placed on race during 1968 were Nixon's blatant efforts to paint Wallace as a liberal in conservative clothing, citing the then former Alabama governor's proclivity toward government intervention and higher taxes as well as Alabama's rising crime rates since 1962. Nixon's efforts undermined Wallace's already low popularity in Texas.[24] Nixon also used Texans' fear of extremism as a means of undermining Wallace's support. Nixon charged that Wallace's preaching of "repression and retrogression in race relations" was divisive and antithetical to conservative values of individual and meritocratic achievement, whereas Nixon was for "greater opportunity for all Americans, justice for all, renewed respect for law, and peaceful resolution of conflicts that mar our society."[25] Discussing the effect of Wallace's campaign on Republican politics in Texas, Peter O'Donnell told John Tower in September 1968, "Wallace was tearing the country apart. Not only is he pitting race against race, but lower levels of education, income, [and] jobs against persons having higher standards in these groups."[26] Such was a common view among Texas Republicans.

Nixon's campaigns in 1968 and 1972, both involving George Wallace, entrenched a strategy of coupling Democratic liberalism with a host of pejoratives collectively intended to redefine liberalism as a philosophy of entitlement and weakness. Race played a role in shaping this redefinition, but was not the singular focus, particularly in Texas, where race had a less galvanizing effect on the voting public. During his first term, Nixon campaign officials openly criticized Wallace as an "advocate of dangerous and collectivist welfare state politics."[27] Among volunteers working for Republican candidates in Texas, Wallace, whose name among many Republicans connoted division, extremism, and unprofessionalism, was simply not a name they wanted their campaign to be associated with. Similar but more benign criticisms were also commonly levied against Nixon, whose willingness to maintain high levels of federal spending to support or expand Great Society programs rankled conservatives disgruntled over the disconnect that they claimed existed between Nixon's words and his actions as president. Criticizing Nixon was an unintended outgrowth of concerted efforts on the part of conservatives to aggressively label their opponents for political benefit.[28]

State and local politics also reflected the complex dynamic of race in Texas, particularly when considering the state's Mexican American population. For instance, Preston Smith won the governorship in 1968, running on a classic law and order platform, though he also distanced himself from Wallace, despite collecting voter registration information from American Party mailing lists.[29] At the same time, Smith worried that the Republican Party was growing more effective in its organization and appeal to Mexican Americans. John Tower's showing among Mexican Americans in 1966 prompted Democrats in 1968 to preemptively organize grassroots "Viva Smith" organizations in South Texas, while also striving to eliminate the problem of liberals "going fishing" on election day. Advising the Democratic campaign, Johnny Morales, director of advertising and public relations for the Cen-Tro Advertising and Public Relations firm in Austin, told Smith that "the only way to campaign and get votes in the Mexican-American precincts is to have rallies with beer and tamales." Smith did more than simply offer beer and tamales. He used a Spanish-speaking television show in Austin, which started with a mariachi band playing a "Kennedy Ballad," to monopolize exposure to Mexican American voters in Central Texas. Before an audience of Mexican American voters in Lubbock, Smith also criticized the Department of Labor and the Department of Health, Education, and Welfare for cutting a job-training program that had appealed directly to South Texas minorities.[30]

Yet despite its success, the Smith campaign of 1968 foreshadowed future Texas Democrats' struggle to balance appeals to the law and order crowd with the need to win minority votes. On the stump, Smith vacillated between his call for government assistance to Mexican Americans and his declaration that government had infringed upon most Texans' rights. As the national Democratic Party struggled to maintain a unified front, the fissure among Texas Democrats, and even among liberals, became more pronounced. Still, it was clear in 1968 that race, at least as it was absorbed into the backlash politics that carried Wallace to such national prominence, was not enough to provide Texas conservatives with a clear campaign strategy.[31]

The Divided Minority

One of the most interesting reflections of how Texas politics was affected by both conservative Democratic and Republican appeals to Mexican Americans is found in the career of Congressman Henry Gonzalez. Gonzalez began his political career in the early 1950s as a member of San Antonio's city council. Elected to the Texas state Senate in 1956, Gonzalez quickly made a name for himself in 1957 when he participated in a thirty-six-hour filibuster against a pro-segregation bill that would have given school boards in Texas the power to assign specific pupils to specific schools. Despite the fact that the bill was just as strongly opposed as it was supported in the Texas legislature, Gonzalez was quickly lionized as a "voice of the voiceless" among Texas liberals. Gonzalez was elected to Congress in 1961, where he continued to agitate on behalf of civil rights for both Mexican Americans and African Americans, eloquently arguing against, among other things, the poll tax and physical abuse in the Bracero Program.[32]

Gonzalez was most committed to Texas's Mexican American community, despite the fact that his assessment of what goals that community should strive for eventually placed him at odds with many of the more po-

litically active members of that constituency. "We are fighting against discrimination," he told the Political Association of Spanish-Speaking
Organizations in Houston in 1965, "not for discrimination in reverse." Gonzalez consistently opposed what he called "special rights" for minorities. In
1966, he told those in attendance at a meeting in Laredo of the League of
United Latin American Citizens that he opposed the concept of "racial quo-
tas" in job hiring. In 1967, he stressed assimilation. He opposed "hyphen-
ated appellations" like "Mexican-American" because, in his words, "whites
don't do that." Gonzalez separated his call for civil rights from the anger
and frustration that boiled over into riots in ghettos and inner cities across
America. In response to such riots, he typically advocated ways to give minority populations what white Americans also wanted—self-government
through local political control. Rarely did Gonzalez promote the idea of
federal intervention as a solution to racial problems. As Texas's most well-
known Mexican American politician, Henry Gonzalez, throughout the
1960s, consistently opposed the notion of identity politics and favored assimilation into the white mainstream.[33]

Considering this platform, Gonzalez's heated opposition to the Chicano
movement of the late 1960s and early 1970s, and especially his opposition
to La Raza Unida, should come as no surprise. La Raza Unida Party was a
third-party movement born in Crystal City, Texas, in January 1970. The
party sought to become the largest third party in the state by mobilizing
Hispanics. La Raza's origins dated back to the mid-1960s, though it was not
until after 1968 that the momentum that eventually led to the party's formation gained steam. One of La Raza's founders, and its most outspoken
leader, was José Ángel Gutiérrez, also a leader in MAYO—the Mexican
American Youth Foundation. Gutiérrez's rhetoric frustrated older political
leaders like Henry Gonzalez. In 1969, Gutiérrez told a reporter from San
Antonio that he might eventually solve the "gringo problem" by "killing"
whites who opposed racial progress. "We're tired of talking," Gutiérrez told
fifteen hundred protesters at a MAYO rally in Del Rio, Texas. "We'll fight
the gringo where he wants to fight. MAYO will crush any gringo who gets
in our way, squashing him like a beetle." Many of the older Mexican
Americans in attendance sat in stunned silence. In January 1970, some reports even began to filter through Houston's white community that MAYO
was about to be reorganized as a more radical and revolutionary organization in which gun-wielding militants would enforce changes in racial politics by violence.[34]

Though La Raza targeted the entire American Southwest, its primary
source of membership was in Texas. La Raza first gained attention from the

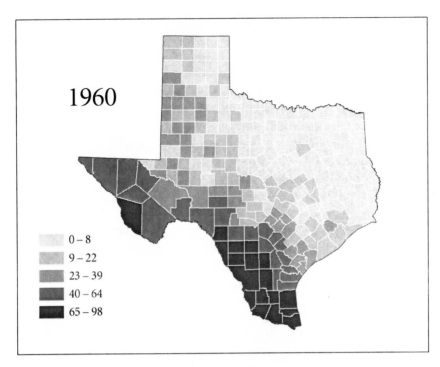

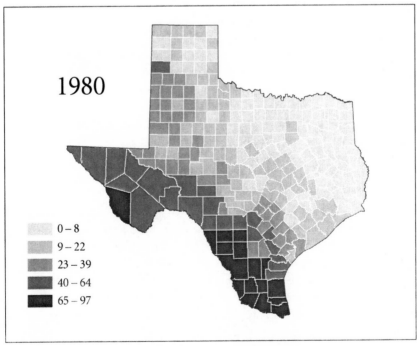

Percentage of Hispanic Texans per county in 1960 (top) and 1980 (bottom).

state's political establishment as a major threat to minority and liberal support for the Texas Democratic Party. According to most conservative whites, La Raza was simply a voice of radicalism. In Texas during the late 1960s and early 1970s, white fears of Hispanic radicalism—especially in South Texas—exceeded fears of black radicalism.[35]

Such fears within the white community were seemingly validated by Mexican American leaders like Henry Gonzalez, who opposed La Raza as fervently as did any politician in the state. Gonzalez warned Mexican American voters in Texas that despite La Raza's stated goal of winning political office, in reality the presence of La Raza candidates on ballots would only divide Democrats and help Republicans. He argued that La Raza was undermining liberal efforts to bring real change to the state and that only in places where Mexican Americans were not the minority would La Raza enjoy any success. Gonzalez even compared La Raza to George Wallace and to the Dixiecrat revolt of 1948, both divisive movements based on race, he argued. Gonzalez also asserted that the growing division between whites and Mexican Americans in Texas was the equivalent of the South's "negro problem," adding that, in Texas, no comparable "negro problem" still existed. Above all, Gonzalez stressed that division within the Democratic Party would only lead to setbacks on the path toward racial progress.[36]

Gonzalez was justified in his fear that division within the Democratic Party over issues of race would help the Texas Republican Party. By strongly opposing the identity politics of La Raza and the Chicano and Black Power movements more broadly, while also advocating on behalf of "Americanism" and "assimilation," Gonzalez undermined such movements and, unintentionally, gave conservatives greater legitimacy on the subject. He also contributed to the evolving perception in Texas that extremism was most dangerous on the political left, not the right. Quite clearly, these results were not his intention. Gonzalez was a loyal Democrat; he enthusiastically campaigned for Hubert Humphrey in 1968 and told audiences of Mexican Americans that Republicans showed up to help only "around election time," and would always forget their promises after the election was over. Yet, in attacking the Republican Party, Gonzalez could not help but reiterate many of the same messages that conservatives were beginning to articulate with greater effect in Mexican American communities during the late 1960s—themes like independence from bureaucracy, intervention, and domination. He was, perhaps, Texas's most effective promoter of the "American Dream" during the late 1960s.[37]

Divisions within the Mexican American community coincided with the political tumult of the early 1970s, and particularly the growing focus on issues with religious overtones such as the Equal Rights Amendment, abortion, school prayer, and gay rights. Such a complicated political culture contributed to the partial realignment and greater activism of Mexican American voters in Texas. Texas Republicans had, since the early 1960s, been just as active in courting Mexican American voters at the local level as had the Democratic Party. A major difference between the GOP's strategy for appealing to Mexican Americans and that of the Democratic Party was that Texas Republicans, following the advice of the RNC, tried to win support among ethnic minorities on the basis of their faith and their sameness—their fundamental Americanism.[38] The Texas GOP also attracted Mexican American voters by openly questioning the state Democratic Party's sincerity when it came to race, thus using intraparty factionalism and the conservative-liberal divide to suggest that the Democratic establishment had no legitimate interest in helping minorities. Texas Republicans further gained Mexican American support by characterizing the state Democratic Party as a "political machine," arguing that until two-party politics became a reality in Texas, Mexican Americans would continue to be denied a political voice.[39]

John Tower deserves much of the credit for attracting more Mexican American and Hispanic voters to the Republican tent during the late 1960s and early 1970s. His campaign against Waggoner Carr in 1966 had illustrated the significance of winning the Hispanic vote in close elections. Tower not only shaped the GOP's appeal to Mexican Americans in Texas during the late 1960s and early 1970s, he also benefited from the very infighting that Henry Gonzalez had both warned of and, in part, contributed to. Many Mexican Americans in South Texas resented the opposition to identity politics that seemed to emanate from the more conservative wing of the state Democratic Party. Within this context of frustration, many of those dissatisfied with traditional liberalism but not willing to commit to La Raza protested against moderate-conservative viewpoints within the Democratic Party by throwing their support behind Republicans like Tower. Texas Republicans were acutely aware in 1970 and 1971 that they had an opportunity to steal Mexican American loyalties from the Democratic Party. Soon, organizations like Mexican American Republicans of Texas (MART) and Tejanos por Tower began to give disgruntled Mexican Americans—both those sharing Henry Gonzalez's vision of assimilation and Americanism and those opposed to traditional Democratic Party intransigence—a new outlet for protest.[40]

Blacks, Busing, and Backlash

John Tower and other Republicans were far less interested or effective in bringing African Americans under the GOP tent than was the case with Mexican Americans. In the early 1970s, although the Republican Party promoted itself both locally and nationally as a party "with its doors open to all people of all races," it became clear to Republicans like Tower that, while winning the Mexican American vote was feasible and would help win elections, winning the black vote in Texas would be too costly and too improbable to warrant significant expenditures in party funds or sweat. Consequently, Republicans could more credibly list things they had done to help Hispanics than blacks. When asked in 1971 what John Tower had actually accomplished on behalf of black Texans, Nola Smith, one of his top strategists, cited the hiring of a black receptionist named Joyce for Tower's Austin office. "She is doing an outstanding job," Smith said of Joyce, "and we have fallen in love with her."[41]

Despite the occasional hiring of a black receptionist, few if any Texas Republicans had any intention of spending the time or money necessary to attract significantly more black voters. Rather, the state GOP worked on appealing to black voters by trying to convince them that drugs, crime, the lack of honesty in government, and general moral decay were all issues of great concern that adversely affected the black community—and that the conservative viewpoint on these issues was actually the viewpoint that most blacks should adopt. In 1971, Marci Sauls, a Republican strategist and an African American, began to encourage the party to at least make some attempt at drawing in more black voters. She suggested organizing Teas for Tower—social gatherings in cities across Texas where blacks could mingle with Republicans. Such teas were typically underfunded and poorly attended by both blacks and whites. Sauls also encouraged the GOP to stress traditional issues of morality and religion in the black community—a strategy she believed would be far more potent and potentially fruitful with blacks than economic or national security arguments. Despite these minimal efforts, the Republican Party remained unpopular and unattractive to most Texas blacks. The negative stigma of supporting a Republican remained so strong in the black community that some black business leaders, when approached by the Texas GOP for various endorsements, refused on the grounds that to do so might lead to economic reprisals from the black community.[42]

As Texas Republican efforts to win more black votes seemed increasingly fruitless and costly, desegregation and busing controversies became more common in Texas in the late 1960s and early 1970s. For instance, in November 1970, just months after the U.S. Supreme Court ruled in *Cisneros v. Corpus Christi Independent School District* to extend *Brown v. Board* (1954) to cover discrimination against Mexican Americans, another case altered the racial and political landscape of Texas—this time primarily for African Americans. In response to litigation initiated in East Texas courts charging that local school districts had been noncompliant in moving to integrate a number of African American schools, U.S. District Court judge William Justice, a liberal appointed to the bench during Lyndon Johnson's final months in the White House, provided a new outline for more rapid public school integration in his decision *United States v. Texas*. The case began after investigations by the Department of Health, Education, and Welfare (HEW) deemed desegregation efforts in some East Texas districts to be deficient. HEW then deferred jurisdiction in the case to the Department of Justice, which named the Texas Education Agency (TEA) and the state as complicit in delaying integration. Justice's decision forced the noncompliant school districts in East Texas to cease their practice of segregated bus routes and consolidate all area school districts without using race as a factor. TEA was charged with the responsibility of conducting annual compliance reviews and imposing sanctions, including the denial of accreditation, to schools in which integration was deemed to have been deliberately delayed or circumvented.[43]

This case received virtually no press coverage until Justice's decision was announced, at which point denunciations poured in from state political leaders and disgruntled area whites. Though the case's impact was felt most dramatically in East Texas communities, particularly in and around the town of Marshall, the decision in *United States v. Texas*, in technically altering the policies of over one thousand school districts with more than 2 million students, further reignited the issue of race and federal encroachment on state and local rights.[44]

It is when studying school integration and busing policies in the late 1960s and early 1970s that Texas seems most "southern." For a brief time in 1970 and 1971, Richard Nixon became more popular in Texas and in the South thanks to a tough stand against busing. John Tower also benefited from the busing issue and capitalized on a preexisting language of taxpayer rights and color-blindness that would evolve as it continued to shape the political discourse of oppositional whites in the coming years. During the height of busing controversies in the early 1970s, Tower editorialized that busing black students had been wrong and immoral prior to 1954 and that doing the same to white students was wrong and immoral in 1971. "Freedom of choice, when it was practiced as the old 'separate-but-equal doctrine,' was an intolerable subterfuge. It was disallowed for that reason. Real freedom of choice in a school system that equalizes opportunity remains the best democratic principle." Tower opposed "forced busing" because, he claimed, it was unfair to treat people differently because of "race, creed, or color." He publicly tried to discredit the notion that students' education could be elevated or hindered simply based on the skin color of the students sitting next to them. Tower even went so far as to cosponsor a constitutional amendment to outlaw forced busing, crediting Nixon with shaping his opinion on the issue. Quite clearly, projecting the image of color-blind conservatism, while certainly not utterly disingenuous, did certainly lend public credibility to Republican opposition to what many believed was a poorly thought-out liberal solution to racial problems.[45]

Both Tower's and Nixon's commitment to the color-blind preservation of white parents' right to send their children to local schools contributed to the emergence of organized grassroots opposition to busing, including the United Concerned Citizens of America (UCCA), organized by a Texan, Mitchell Young. The UCCA was an antibusing league dedicated to maintaining consistent desegregation standards nationwide. Young represented a faction of suburban whites in the South who resented being targeted and reprimanded differently, as they saw it, than other noncompliant school districts in other parts of the nation. At the same time, many more compliant white Texans resented the noncompliance of East Texas districts they believed had forced federal intervention upon the rest of the state. Organizations like the UCCA, therefore, tapped into this resentment and helped unite middle-class white Texans on the grounds that they were being treated unfairly.[46]

Probably the hottest bed of discontent in Texas during the late 1960s and early 1970s, at least as far as the issue of busing is concerned, was Houston. In 1969 the Justice Department cited the Houston Independent School District (HISD) for failing to properly desegregate or achieve a balance in schools on par with population figures, which in Houston meant that at least 30 percent of the student body was supposed to be African American. In February, Robert Eckels, president of the HISD Board of Education, reached out to Bob Eckhardt, a liberal congressman representing most of Harris County. Eckels pleaded with Eckhardt for assistance in mitigating the Justice Department's newfound concern and proposed remedies for HISD, which included the possibility of compulsory busing. Somewhat dumbfounded, Eckels argued that HISD had been operating for years under the impression that it was not only in full compliance with federal standards for desegregation, but had in fact achieved the most non-violent integration in the country, a claim of which the school district was quite proud.[47]

What Eckels and most angry white parents with children in the greater Houston school system feared most was the implementation of a busing plan to achieve racial balance. "These proposals by the Justice Department and the NAACP have caused public concern of such magnitude," Eckels told Eckhardt, "that should we be compelled to follow the suggestions of the motion there is a grave possibility of extreme taxpayer revolt and violence in the communities of a school district that thus far has been the largest district in the nation to achieve integration without violence."[48]

Houston-area parents did not wait for Eckhardt's response. Very quickly, parents began to organize. Signatures were collected on a variety of petitions and protest rolls originating both within the city limits of Houston and, especially, in the surrounding suburbs. "WE DO NOT WANT AND WILL NOT HAVE OUR CHILDREN BUSED TO HOUSTON SCHOOLS," one petition from Baytown, Texas, read—in all capital letters, for added emphasis. "WE STRONGLY URGE YOU TO SUPPORT A CONSTITUTIONAL AMENDMENT TO FORBID SUCH BUSING." Grassroots organization against busing intensified in the Houston area in 1969 and 1970. What then followed in Houston and the surrounding suburbs was, without question, the most massive outpouring of citizen correspondence on any issue of civil rights, segregation, or race in Texas during the postwar era. Bob Eckhardt's office alone received so much correspondence on the issue of busing that it temporarily overwhelmed his staff, creating the need for a new filing system and a more organized system for mailing responses.[49]

The language used by Houstonians to express their dismay was telling. Virtually every letter from an angry white parent emphasized the notion that their "civil rights" were being violated. Most who wrote qualified their hostility with a statement of support for "freedom of choice," not segregation by race. However, almost none would support "forced busing." Beyond race and vaguely defined civil rights, parents raised other concerns. "We are being faced with great property devaluation by this rezoning," one Houston-area citizen complained. Another warned that, when the time came to reelect local leadership, there would "be no Democrats or Republicans in the voting booths, only people who remember those that helped Houston in this desperate time." Many others claimed that busing was a violation of the Constitution and that busing displeased all area residents, including black and Hispanic parents. Almost all letters were peppered with words like "freedom," "Constitutionality," or the rather populist phrase "We the

People." One group of citizens from Baytown, Texas, organized a form letter mailing campaign, in which frustrated parents merely added their signature to the following statement:

> I have been willing and happy to proceed under the fair and sensible
> edict of freedom of choice for integration of public schools. Under the
> new zoning and pairing plan, I feel that the government is striking a
> severe blow at the very system which has traditionally given basic sup-
> port to the American way of education. Please do all within your
> power to protect us and to re-implement freedom of choice in our
> schools.

The general tenor of the correspondence flooding into Eckhardt's office
from scared citizens also indicated that federal intervention in the local
school system, more than simply the issue of race, contributed to the massive uprising of opposition and grassroots political activity. Overt racism
was evident in approximately one out of every one hundred letters the congressman's office received. Though Houston had slowly worked toward
integration for a decade with relatively little opposition, the declaration by
the Justice Department that those efforts had not been good enough riled
area residents and reinforced the growing impression that government was
becoming too large and interfering too much.[50]

In response to this outpouring of concern from his constituents, Bob
Eckhardt responded, in retrospective analysis, a bit insensitively—at least
for a politician up for reelection in the coming months. In 1969, Eckhardt
largely dismissed arguments that the Constitution guaranteed a "freedom
to choose your school." He also blamed the larger problem on HISD, which
he said had a "long history of foot-dragging" that "made integration by
other means more difficult." Rather than assuage fears about busing, re-
serving it as only a last resort, Eckhardt actually endorsed the strategy. In
early 1970, however, Eckhardt, clearly taken aback by the persistence and
depth of concern expressed by area citizens, began sending a slightly more
polished message to his constituents. He stressed that "equal opportunity
for all children to obtain the best possible education is a constitutional
mandate and a constitutional privilege, and nothing short of a constitutional amendment will allow any school district, including HISD, to maintain its present freedom of choice plan." Here, Eckhardt attempted to
straddle the proverbial fence by maintaining his own view that Justice Department intervention was necessary, while also saying that the growing

momentum for a constitutional amendment to outlaw forced busing was, in fact, the only way to save HISD's status quo.[51]

By mid- to late 1970, Eckhardt, approaching reelection, grew far more vague and cautious in his response to local constituents. He had clearly been surprised by the tenacity and longevity of the public's outrage over the busing issue and began to reconsider his own response. He wrote concerned citizens that busing was not an ideal remedy and that it was certainly not the only means by which the goal of integration might be achieved. He also encouraged citizens to stay politically involved and to let their voices be heard, while also promoting the grander vision of freedom and equality in Houston schools, thereby co-opting and mitigating the very language that had defined the opposition's outrage.[52]

As intense as was white Houston's response to the notion of forced busing—perhaps more intense than had characterized any race-related controversy in well over a decade—it ultimately was not enough to pose any significant threat to Eckhardt's reelection. The incumbent congressman won 77 percent of the 1970 Democratic primary vote and ran unopposed in the general election. Busing, by itself, was a hot enough issue to warrant a sizeable backlash, but was not, by itself, hot enough to upset the political status quo.[53]

By 1972, however, some local citizens began to charge Eckhardt with not caring how Houston's parents really felt on the issue and began to pressure their congressman to be more proactive in representing the views of the district. Eckhardt even received a handful of anonymous threats and angry notes, including one that simply read: "This sign is near my house: 'Thank you Congressman Eckhardt; you voted for the Bill of Rights.' I'm going to change it to: 'Fuck you Congressman Eckhardt; you voted for FORCED BUS-SING!'" Few Houstonians familiarized themselves with the complexities of the court decisions or constitutional questions involved; for most people the issue was simple: courts were legislating from the bench an idealistic mandate that involved school collectivism at the expense of decent, hard-working American parents and their children, who would be forced to endure substandard educational conditions in order to benefit minorities, though rarely did Houston citizens overtly mention race in their correspondence or public outcries.[54]

Soon, Eckhardt began to send constituents a much longer and more detailed form letter, in which he outlined the history of segregation in Houston, pointed out that blacks had, for decades, been bused out of their neighborhoods into segregated schools without so much as "a whimper" from the white community, but concluded that "it is NOT TRUE that, just because stupid and cruel acts were committed THEN against blacks, stupid acts should NOW be committed against children who had nothing to do with their forebears' errors." Eckhardt wanted to communicate that he sympathized with local parents' concerns while maintaining his own support for integration. Eckhardt believed that, as long as the issue remained simply busing, as intense as the response to that issue was, he—like other Democratic politicians in Texas—could safely expect to weather the storm and maintain office. Eventually, that strategy would fail him. As other issues began to emerge, many of the same parents most upset with the prospect of seeing their child bused across town to another school became more aware of other issues and began to question whether or not the political status quo in Texas was really the most representative system under which they might live.[55]

As busing fueled many white Houstonians' ire, other issues loosely associated with law and order, crime, and race also infused the growing backlash. Bob Eckhardt received a considerable number of letters from Houstonians concerned with the issue of gun control. In a climate of expanding racial militancy, antiwar protest, and civil disobedience, many Texans began to more proactively seek assurances that their right to bear arms would continue to be protected by state, if not national, law. One Texan compared voting for gun control laws to voting "for communism and socialism. It can only benefit the liberals," he continued, "and inflict greater federal control over the Free Republic States." Eckhardt, a liberal, used his own gun ownership as evidence of his ability to relate to such voters and, in effect, assuage fears that he was too liberal for Houston. At the same time, Eckhardt acknowledged that statistics showing that violent crime rates were reduced in cities with stricter gun laws "impressed" him. Local conservatives feared that Eckhardt might be soft on gun control and, as the controversy surrounding busing continued to swirl, began to more openly criticize the incumbent Democrat, against whom very few had even tried to campaign in recent years.[56]

The fear of tighter restrictions on guns coincided with a growing fear that street chaos and general lawlessness did not appear to be dissipating, even as the turbulent 1960s came to a close. In May 1970, many Texans responded favorably to Nixon's announcement of the Cambodian invasion, not so much because of the impact that invasion might have on the war, but because, as one Texan put it, the nation "needed a stronger policy against riots and lawlessness." Drawing at best a loose connection, these Texans viewed taking the offensive against communism overseas in the same light that they viewed taking the offensive against subversives at home—in which category student radicals, hippies, racial militants, and other "crazy teenagers" were included.[57]

Very few Texans could articulate why such things—lawlessness, disorder, violence, riots, protests—were happening on American streets. Most seemed less than impressed by the fact that such things were not typically happening in Texas; that they were happening anywhere in America meant that the threat to Texas remained real and serious. Clearly, the intensification of backlash politics and calls for law and order was not merely a response to local race issues. Rather, backlash politics in Texas was the result of a far broader impression that America was caught in a downward spiral and that Texas, if it was not careful, could also be gravely threatened.[58]

Like Bob Eckhardt, other Texas Democrats also struggled to respond to the growing momentum of backlash politics. George Mahon, for instance, agreed with his constituents, encouraging them not to sit idly by while "lawlessness" threatened "the whole world." "All thoughtful Americans," he wrote in August 1970, "share a feeling of outrage over the evidences of appeasement of law violators and over the general breakdown of law and order in our country." In another public letter, Mahon theorized as to how the nation had gotten into such a mess and what Texans could do about it: "I feel that many of our troubles today spring from the fact that we have wandered away from the traditions and principles which made our country great. I am a firm believer in the old fashioned virtue of self reliance, and I hold unwaveringly to the view that individual initiative, drive, and discipline need to be more encouraged in our country. People can take terrific strides in improving their standard of living through hard work and self discipline, combined with Christian principles of living." At the same time, Mahon—a New Deal Democrat first elected to Congress in 1934—maintained the highest standards of party loyalty. For him and other Democrats like him, the balancing act of listening to your constituents and supporting your party became ever more precarious in the early 1970s.[59]

Despite opportunities presented by racial discord, busing, gun control, and intraparty factionalism, a confident and increasingly competitive Texas Republican Party still could not overcome—even in the midst of a backlash culture—the tradition of Democratic loyalty that continued to make conservative Democrats the odds-on favorites to win any general election contest. These persistent failures, including George Bush's second failed bid to win a Senate seat in Texas, reflect the limits of backlash in the early 1970s, despite the simultaneous realization that liberalism was becoming an increasingly heavy albatross to carry around one's political neck.

The 1970 Senate Race

In 1970, the rhetoric of antiliberalism finally caught up with Ralph Yarborough. After eighteen years of service as a populist-leaning liberal, Yarborough was defeated in the 1970 Democratic primary by Houston businessman Lloyd Bentsen. Born in 1921, Bentsen flew B-24 combat missions in Italy during World War II before serving for nearly a decade in the U.S. House of Representatives and working his way up the corporate ladder of Houston finance. Bentsen defeated Yarborough in 1970 on the strength of a blatantly antiliberal campaign made far more salient in the context of what many saw as continued national dysfunction—characterized by the politics of race and backlash.

Bentsen's campaign against Yarborough was quintessential and multifaceted antiliberalism. Yarborough was vilified as an "ultraliberal" and a "peacenik." Primarily but not exclusively in East Texas, Bentsen hammered Yarborough as a busing advocate and a radical. He attacked Yarborough's support of Supreme Court decisions outlawing prayer in public schools and ran television advertisements associating Yarborough with Vietcong-flag-waving antiwar protesters. He also stressed Yarborough's connection to the national Democratic Party which, in 1970, was increasingly viewed in Texas as an apologist for mob violence and massive increases in federal spending. In short, Bentsen neutralized Yarborough's record of working on state-level issues and instead made the campaign a referendum on the national Left.[60]

Yarborough, on the other hand, tried to focus on his experience and record while steering clear of the "liberal" label. Yet he also shunned his staff's suggestions that he identify himself in more conservative ways. His platform was based on stereotypically populist and working-class economic initiatives and failed to engage Bentsen on the very subject matter used most effectively against him—namely, national issues surrounding the war in Vietnam, crime, race, and moral relativity. As a result, Yarborough, not surprisingly, did very poorly among middle-class whites.[61]

Yarborough spent far more energy rallying state minorities, advocating bilingual education in South Texas school districts while dismissing arguments that non-English-speaking residents should be encouraged to learn the language of the majority. Broadly speaking, Yarborough's campaign was a mix of antiquated Texas populism and post–Voting Rights Act liberalism—a political style ineffective in much of the urbanizing and subur-

John Tower and George Bush, c. 1970. The photo is inscribed "To my friend, John Tower—with gratitude and respect. 'Happiness is being an elected Texas Republican.' George Bush, M.C., 7th District—Texas." (Courtesy of the John G. Tower Library and Archives, Georgetown, TX)

banizing Sun Belt. The same cannot be said of Bentsen's campaign, which did attract a substantial number of middle-class white conservatives. Bentsen was so overwhelmingly antiliberal that many state liberals, including those in organized labor, refused to endorse or support the Democratic nominee during the general election.[62]

The state GOP's nominee was George Bush, who had lost to Yarborough in 1964. Bush had hoped for a rematch with Yarborough, during which he intended to employ the same antiliberal strategy that Bentsen used in the Democratic primary. Instead, Bush found himself inheriting the support of state liberals and organized labor, which refused to endorse Bentsen. This undermined his palatability among conservative Republicans and only reinforced Bentsen's popularity among moderate and conservative Democrats. Though Bush would eventually get the best of Bentsen, defeating both him and Michael Dukakis in the 1988 presidential election largely on the strength of antiliberalism, in 1970 it was the Republican who seemed a shade too far to the left. With both Bush and Bentsen hoping to wage the general campaign on the grounds of conservatism and antiliberalism, the defaults of tradition and loyalty became paramount deciding factors.[63]

Bentsen's victory over Yarborough confounded Bush's original campaign strategy. Instead of running as the conservative option in a race with the liberal Yarborough, Bush had to repackage himself as an alternative to the conservative Bentsen. Bush's efforts to paint Bentsen as akin to the vilified "northeastern liberal establishment" were futile and, considering Bentsen's record, seemed to be a transparent political ploy. Ironically, however, Bentsen did succeed in reminding voters of Bush's connections to the Northeast and, in effect, turned Bush's strategy against him. Desperate, Bush began to embrace moderate and liberal support by coming out in favor of things like women's rights, including a pro-choice statement on abortion and approval of the Equal Rights Amendment, which in 1970 appeared to be on the brink of passage in the House of Representatives. By November, popular opinion showed Bentsen to be the more conservative of the two candidates, the more "anti-hippie" of the two candidates—which was a particularly important asset in rural Baptist counties in East and Central Texas—and the candidate more likely to remain hawkish in the face of dovish pressures. In the end, Bentsen effectively characterized his opponent as the liberal option and maintained the support of conservative Democrats across the state. In defeating both Yarbrough and Bush, Bentsen effectively demonstrated both the power and the limits of backlash politics and antiliberalism in Texas.[64]

In 1971, when the "Sick American" anonymously published his (or her) diatribe against the evils of modern society, he (or she) tapped into what seemed to be a deeply rooted and powerful sentiment of populist conservatism and backlash politics. Yet, the depth of that backlash was not enough, at least in 1970, to force partisan realignment. Conservative Democrats, in fact, benefited from the backlash even as Republicans became more competitive in the process.

Yet, backlash politics also gave credence to the growing concept of a conservative identity, even if that identity was still bipartisan in Texas. Backlash politics, including the evolution of racialized conservatism into a more mainstream color-blind ethos, tapped into status anxieties and pride issues that, in Texas, functioned in unique ways. Commenting on the formation of a Texas identity, Leigh Clemons has argued that the construction of a unique and prescriptively masculine Texas identity has, over the course of several decades, been consistently communicated and culturally entrenched through public performance. By examining theater, museums, monuments, product marketing, television, and film—among other media—Clemons illustrates how the magnification of a nationalist, white male, brazenly independent, and typically larger-than-life stereotype has defined common perceptions of what it means to be a Texan, who does and does not have access to that identity, and what impact the shadow so widely cast by that identity has on the state's relationship with the rest of the country and among Texas residents.[65]

Certainly critical to this analysis is the role of race. Access to the Texas political culture has long been dependent on one's racial identity, even though the manifestations of racial confrontation have, typically since 1945, been more moderate and sensible than in many other parts of the country. Yet it is apparent that many white Texans adjusted and evolved their views and their rhetoric in regard to race between the late 1950s and the early 1970s. By the late 1960s, radically overt racism had commonly been replaced with protests against federal intervention and the loss of property or parental rights. Rather than being simply "code words," especially when mixed with the law and order rhetoric of the period, such color-blind language reflected both the power of the civil rights movement to make overt racism politically, socially, and culturally unacceptable—quite an achievement—and a genuine if irrational fear of change. Many white and conservative Texans may very well still have been racist, however vaguely defined, but their perceptions and stated views morphed into something broader and, eventually, something sincere.

"Sick Americans" like the one whose diatribe was featured in Texas newspapers in 1971 would soon find more to complain about and fear. In the coming years, corruption and scandal, present at both the state and national levels of government, would create momentum, despite short-term setbacks, for the ousting of all political establishments, thereby fueling the push for partisan realignment. When coupled with the disastrous failure of George McGovern's campaign for the presidency in 1972, the politics of scandal and corruption provided a very necessary component to the construction of a Republican Party that eventually became the new and undisputed home for modern conservatism in Texas.

Chapter 5

Poisons

Establishments in Crisis

Between 1971 and 1974, the political status quo in Texas was challenged from several angles. In these tumultuous years, Texans witnessed widespread scandal and corruption, intraparty factionalism at the national, state, and local levels, intensified challenges to partisan loyalties, and the infusion into the political culture of new and controversial challenges to existing social traditions and moral codes. Contextualized within this political culture was the critically important and simultaneous maturation of antiliberal and antigovernment animus, made more potent by the racial and social revolutions that had gripped American youth and seemingly destabilized American society in the preceding years. These widely held antipathies toward both liberalism and established power manifested not in a refortification of partisan defense, but rather as ideological poisons through which Democratic loyalties were weakened, growing less secure and ultimately less important. If the 1960s witnessed the ignition of America's late twentieth-century social and political upheavals, then the 1970s—and particularly the campaigns of 1972—saw Texans adjust to these new realities.[1]

The Politics of Scandal

Throughout the early 1970s, images of bribery, theft, tax evasion, conspiracy, election fraud, hush money, and an array of other unethical activities undermined Texans' faith in government, politicians, and the civic process in general. At the same time that distrust in government seemed to be on the rise, the ubiquity of scandal and corruption contributed to a statewide reconsideration of partisan loyalties, opened the door for liberal advancement within the state Democratic Party, and lent credence to the most central tenet of populist conservatism—that government had replaced big business as the chief obstacle standing between the American people and honest opportunity. In short, the politics of scandal and corruption hastened ideological reconsiderations in Texas, confused the public's partisan

127

loyalties, and contributed mightily to the breakdown of support for established leadership.

Other than Watergate, the scandals most Americans remember from the early 1970s are former State Department employee Daniel Ellsberg's leaking of the so-called Pentagon Papers to the *New York Times* in 1971 and the resignation of Vice President Spiro T. Agnew in 1973 following his conviction for tax evasion. Nonetheless, national scandals, though highly influential, were only partly responsible for Texans' growing distaste for the political status quo in the early 1970s. There were plenty of scandals deep in the heart of Texas to bring the issue closer to home.

The most infamous example of Texas-grown corruption became known as the Sharpstown Stock-Fraud Scandal. In January 1971, attorneys for the U.S. Securities and Exchange Commission (SEC) filed a lawsuit through federal court in Dallas alleging that former state attorney general Waggoner Carr, former state insurance commissioner John Osorio, and Houston-area banker Frank Sharp had conspired to commit stock fraud. Over the next several months, the scandal dominated the media's coverage of Texas politics and threatened to stain virtually the entire conservative wing of the state Democratic Party. What the Texas public learned throughout the reporting on this scandal in 1971 and 1972 was that Frank Sharp, the chief executive of the Houston-area Sharpstown State Bank, had illegally granted more than $600,000 in loans to state officials, who then used that money to buy stock in another of Sharp's holdings, the National Bankers Life Insurance Corporation. Sharp then managed, through various illegal means, to artificially inflate the value of the stock, allowing investors to reap profits in excess of $250,000. The case's bombshell, however, came when the SEC revealed that Texas governor and state Democratic Party head Preston Smith had actually been bribed by Sharp into manipulating a special session of the Texas legislature in 1969 during which legislation favorable to Sharp and his corporate holdings was passed.[2]

The immediate impact of the Sharpstown scandal appeared to be a boon primarily for state liberals. As the sordid details permeated the state's political culture in the early 1970s, liberals took the opportunity to champion reform legislation, including bills requiring state officials to fully disclose all sources of income. Texas liberals, though reluctant to go so far as to call for federal intervention, did articulate a belief that the "good ole boys" club in Austin had grown far too corrupt to govern effectively and needed dismantling. Many across the state agreed.[3]

With both liberals and Republicans circling the Texas Democratic establishment like sharks in a bloody ocean, it soon became clear that the biggest losers in the scandal were incumbent, conservative Texas Democrats. Sharpstown forced Texans long confident in the efficacy of the conservative Democratic establishment to question the integrity of the party to which they had for so long been loyal. Conservative Democratic candidacies struggled to raise money or rally support in the wake of Sharpstown. In effect, the scandal so undermined the public's faith in the status quo of Texas politics that it allowed liberals to assert far greater influence in the state Democratic Party while, at the same time, it boosted the respectability of antigovernment populist conservative Republicans.[4]

In order to survive, conservative Democrats had to adjust or face consequences. Gus Mutscher, Speaker of the Texas House of Representatives, vilified by liberals and Republicans alike as a "dictator" for both his involvement in the scandal and his obstruction of investigations into the affair, was among those to face the consequences. In September 1971, he was indicted on conspiracy and bribery charges and eventually sentenced to five years probation. Preston Smith's career was also ruined as a result of Sharpstown. Twice elected governor of Texas, Smith failed to win the nomination of his party for reelection in 1972.

The man who defeated Smith was Dolph Briscoe, a businessman and wealthy rancher from Uvalde, a small town in South-Central Texas that proudly proclaimed itself the home of former Speaker of the House and vice president John Nance Garner. Briscoe, a conservative Democrat, succeeded in 1972 in an atmosphere largely inhospitable to the conservative Democratic establishment—or Democrats in general, for that matter. The secret of Briscoe's success was projecting a populist image, complete with blue jeans and cowboy hat. His strategy was simple. In order to survive, conservatives would have to maintain distance from the establishment and rebrand themselves as maverick outsiders. The rancher from Uvalde hammered Smith as an agent of the elite and the corrupt political leadership that needed to be overhauled in Austin. At the same time, he adopted the bulk of Smith's platform and agenda, highlighting tough stands on crime and his support for better training facilities for state law enforcement.[5] Briscoe often spoke about Texans' "value of independence" and reinforced the notion that the government should work for the people, not the other way around. Another of his catch phrases was "Better government, not more."[6] Briscoe routinely infused Frank Sharp's name into speeches on Smith, government corruption, and the need to clean up Austin. He invited the support of state minorities, environmentalist lobbies, and other liberals, not by addressing specific issues of concern to those constituents, but by rallying a collective and shared animosity against established authority.[7] Smith's feeble and ineffective response was to blame his misfortune on the media, often communicating anger over how television in particular had portrayed him unfairly.[8]

Thanks mostly to Sharpstown, scandal permeated the Texas political culture of the early 1970s. Yet, whereas national observers have typically identified this era's backlash against political scandal with Watergate and a temporary setback for the Republican Party, no such strict associations were made in Texas, thanks to Sharpstown. As officials in both parties seemed mired in illegalities, Democrats were, in the public's mind, just as guilty of dishonesty as were Republicans. In fact, Sharpstown offered yet another opportunity for a coalition of convenience between liberal Democrats and conservative Republicans. That coalition became known as the "Dirty Thirty"—a bipartisan collection of representatives vocal in their displeasure over Mutscher's leadership and the corruption still evident in Texas politics. One member of the Dirty Thirty was Fred Agnich, a Republican representative from Dallas County, who called the Sharpstown affair "the greatest abuse of power that I'd ever heard of in politics." Agnich recalled the Dirty Thirty as a coalition of the powerless. "It was easy for the press and the columnists to castigate [anti-Mutscher forces] as the wild-haired, raving, lunatic, liberal fringe," Agnich later remembered. Agnich argued that liberals alone "could not establish credibility" with either the Texas press or the public. Yet in alliance with conservative Republicans and in context of a clear series of legal and ethical violations, both liberals and Republicans enjoyed important degrees of heightened credibility.[9]

That heightened credibility also worked in favor of Betty Andujar, who in 1972 won a seat in the state Senate representing Fort Worth as a Republican. Andujar later credited Fort Worth–area women working on her behalf as a major factor in her election, but also saw the scandal in Austin as a benefit. "Sharpstown was really my friend," Andujar later recalled. "The solid Democrat vote was a habit that had nothing to do, literally, with the candidates themselves," she said of the political culture she experienced prior to Sharpstown. Breaking that habit was critical to her election as a Republican, as it would be for Republicans all across the state. Andujar won election campaigning as an "antiestablishment" outsider—a maverick willing to take on the corruption of the Austin "good ole boys" club.[10]

Thanks in no small part to the politics of scandal, what quickly came to command the loyalties of most Texas voters in the early 1970s was not their tradition of voting Democrat but rather a reinvigorated antigovernment populism that embraced the overthrow of the establishment, sound economics, strong and traditional values on crime and foreign policy: altogether the projection of an image that was completely incompatible with the liberalizing national Democratic Party.[11]

The Trinity River Canal Project

The antigovernment animus rallied out of the politics of scandal also reinforced Texans' proclivity for libertarianism. In Dallas, where antigovernment sentiment had long been popular, the proposed canalization of the Trinity River—which stretched from the Gulf of Mexico just east of Houston all the way to the northernmost suburbs of the Dallas–Fort Worth metroplex (DFW)—not only provided another spark for Republican growth, but also allowed for yet another curious alliance between GOP conservatives and Democratic liberals in the fight to unseat the Texas Democratic establishment.

The proposed canalization of the Trinity River can be traced back to at least 1965, when Lyndon Johnson authorized a $1.6-billion construction project designed to transform the river into a major canal, thus enabling Dallas to compete with Houston for trade and shipping enterprises in and out of the Gulf of Mexico. For years the project had received the wholehearted support of most DFW residents, as they eagerly awaited full federal appropriation. Then, during the spring of 1972, Alan Steelman, a young Dallas Republican aspiring to win a seat in the U.S. House of Representatives, was introduced to a small, household-based organization committed to defeating the Trinity River Canal Project when it was presented to Congress for funding in the upcoming legislative session. The name of the grassroots organization was Citizens Organization for a Sound Treaty (COST). COST organizers, primarily opposed to the idea of higher taxes, had been unsuccessfully trying to rally opposition to the bill for years, but with the legislation soon to come before Congress, time was of the essence and efforts doubled in early 1972.

Steelman's political ambition placed him in opposition to the incumbent conservative Democrat from Dallas, Earle Cabell. Cabell, who was Dallas's mayor at the time of the Kennedy assassination, had won a seat in Congress in 1964, ending the conservative Republican Bruce Alger's career in elected political office. Cabell's 1972 primary campaign had been waged on the promise to bring the canal to Dallas, thereby improving its potential as an industrial trading hub. Hoping to find an issue upon which he could distance himself from Cabell, Steelman latched onto the Trinity River Canal Project, arguing that with the construction of a new international airport to be located between Dallas and Forth Worth (eventually called

DFW International Airport), canalization would be an outmoded duplication of shipping transit capacity, an unnecessary waste of federal tax dollars, and would bring only crime and pollution into the region. Steelman argued that Dallas citizens would be much better served if the money allocated to the canal project were refunded in tax breaks. Calling the project a "billion-dollar ditch," he managed to take the ideas of COST and translate them into practical concerns for Dallas citizens. Steelman won the GOP primary.[12]

Despite Steelman's success, grassroots opposition throughout the DFW metroplex remained embryonic until October 1972, when the canal project manager naively told a reporter that while the federal government was footing the bill for the project's construction, some start-up costs would have to be incurred by area citizens. For the first time, Dallasites were told that they would have to pay for the initial phase of the canal project through an additional $150 million property-tax hike. The result was a prioritization of the Canal Project as an issue in the general election. The established Dallas business community, for which the project was considered most important, began to organize their own operations in support of the canal. Unfortunately for them, it was too late. Thanks to COST and Steelman, a majority of Dallas citizens had already become convinced that the canal project was wasteful, particularly as national inflationary problems captured headlines and forced wage and price controls, when the space program—based in large part in Texas—had seen cuts in its funding, and when the good stewardship of tax dollars was becoming a far more salient concern. In November, with the canal project issue as a major backdrop, the Republican Steelman easily won a seat in Congress, upsetting the Democrat Cabell with an astonishing 56 percent of the vote.[13]

For the canal project's opponents, however, Steelman's election was only the beginning of the fight. Seeing that a bond election in Dallas would be a necessary first step on the path toward the canal's construction, COST shifted its focus away from Washington, DC, and back to more local avenues of influence. Sensing that momentum was on its side, COST closely aligned itself with environmental engineers in Dallas who began to leak reports to the press that the canal would result in deforestation and the pollution of several area lakes around which a number of DFW suburbs had been developed.

Although the Dallas business community tried to convince the area populace that "what is good for downtown is good for them," suburban residents balked. In early 1973, COST exposed a report showing that eight of the twenty-four River Authority directors owned land in the Trinity

River watershed, meaning that those business leaders most ardent in their support for canalization would also benefit most directly. The expanding suburban middle class in Dallas immediately objected. At this point, as middle-class animus against the city's business elite was growing in the context of a tax war, the Dallas business community began to respond. Hoping to reinvigorate support, members of the community's business elite poured more than $500,000 into a pro-canal public relations campaign, including a lavish gala celebration in support of the project. Every congressman from the area attended the gala except one—Alan Steelman.[14]

Established Republican leadership struggled along with conservative Democrats on how best to respond to the public backlash to the Trinity River Canal Project. Soon, COST organized its own public relations effort, in the weeks leading up to the March 13 bond election. With the slogan "Your money, their canal," COST rallied antitax conservatives and populists in both parties who had previously considered canalization a worthwhile and profitable endeavor. COST also welcomed the support of La Raza Unida, which rallied Hispanic voters against the canal through populist messages and antitax, antigovernment diatribes. In early March, John Tower, whose popularity among the most ideologically committed Texas conservatives had taken a hit just a year earlier when he had suddenly resigned from the advisory board of the Young Americans for Freedom—an action that sparked a letter of condemnation from Ronald Reagan and a significant backlash among young Texas Republicans—entered the fray on the side of business, trying to use his conservative credentials to rebuild credibility for the canal among suburban voters and Hispanics. Tower's decision to oppose COST was a mistake not only in that it cost him popularity among these constituencies, but also because it placed him on the losing side of an argument based on the principle that the federal government could not be trusted to do the right thing for local citizens.[15]

In the spring of 1973, just one year after COST organizers had been meeting in a living room with only a handful of participants, the Trinity River Canal Project went down to a staggering defeat. The story of the Trinity River Canal Project depicts a successful grassroots campaign operating with the support of a young Republican leader overcoming the economic power of Dallas big business on the basis of antigovernment, antitax, antielitist rhetoric. This conservative grassroots movement first attracted white suburbanites, but was eventually popular among Hispanics distrustful of a Democratic Party that it believed was all talk and no action when it came to helping their community. COST even attracted local environmentalist activists who, along with other Texas liberals, viewed the state Democratic Party—not the GOP—as their primary obstacle on the road to political inclusion. What transpired in Dallas because of this issue does not necessarily equate to a broader pattern of antiliberalism and Republican growth at the grassroots level, but it does indicate the variety of issues around which white suburban grassroots conservatives mobilized.[16]

McGovern's "Extremism"

Two years after losing to Alan Steelman, Earle Cabell was asked whether or not he believed George McGovern, the Democratic Party's presidential nominee in 1972, had helped or hurt his campaign that year. "Good God," Cabell replied. "He was poison in this area! I denounced him immediately. Sincerely, I thought he was a menace."[17]

Cabell, as did many other struggling Texas Democrats in 1972, refused to be seen with and even publicly denounced McGovern, not because of who McGovern was, but because of what McGovern allegedly stood for. During the early 1970s, as it became increasingly clear that the Democratic establishment was no longer the unchallenged representative of Texas's conservative grass roots, many conservative Texas Democrats were forced to choose between party loyalty and indirectly cooperating with Republican efforts to make state politics a war not of party, but of ideology.[18]

Primarily due to its impact on shaping public perceptions of liberalism, the 1972 presidential campaign was a monumental turning point in the history of modern American politics. Faced with a clear choice between a liberal Democrat and a Republican many, though certainly not all, viewed as conservative, Texans overwhelmingly rejected the party to which most had been at least nominally loyal since birth. Gareth Davies has understood this as a period in which liberalism came to be redefined as a philosophy of entitlement rather than of opportunity—a period when identity politics and civil rights seemed less extricable from Democratic liberalism and more connected with "handouts" than with equality. Representative of that perception and viewed by many as dangerous, weak, and extreme, George McGovern failed to replicate Hubert Humphrey's 1968 victory in Texas and, in the process, contributed to a widening divide between Texas conservatives and the national Democratic Party.[19]

Not only did Richard Nixon clearly benefit from this widening divide, but in fact, by prioritizing his own populist image while highlighting his opponent's liberalism, he helped to widen it further. Prior to 1972, Nixon's popularity in Texas had never quite manifested with enough votes to carry the state in an election. After narrow losses in 1960 and 1968, Nixon was desperate to win Texas in 1972.

One of Nixon's first and most famous opportunities as president to connect with his Texas audience came on December 6, 1969, when he made his way into the locker room of the University of Arkansas's football stadium following the top-ranked University of Texas football team's dramatic 15–14 win over the second-ranked Razorbacks. There, much to the dismay of Penn State fans, who were convinced that their undefeated Nittany Lions were the best team in America, Nixon presented the Longhorns with a plaque signifying his proclamation of Texas as college football's national champions for 1969. Nixon's actions in Fayetteville did not earn him any friends in Pennsylvania, but they certainly did in Texas—and Nixon desperately wanted to be liked deep in the heart of Texas.[20]

Despite his sometimes awkward best efforts, Nixon's popularity in Texas can more reasonably be viewed as a reflection of statewide displeasure over the perceived liberalization of the national Democratic Party. In fact, it was not so much that the Democratic Party was liberal, but that the Democratic Party seemed, to many Texans, to be radically and quickly moving to the far left. Critically important in this timeline was 1972. That year, Vietnam remained a tough issue for Nixon, even in hawkish Texas. Polls indicated that, in large part because of a perceived mishandling of Vietnam and the economy, many Texans actually preferred a new Republican nominee. Some Texas conservatives once again began preliminary efforts to organize a campaign operations base in Texas for Ronald Reagan, peppering the California governor with pleas to enter the race while gathering pockets of momentum in traditionally Republican strongholds like suburban Houston. Reagan rejected such pleas, but not without validating conservative concerns over Nixon by citing areas of disagreement between him and the president. Conservatives had largely distrusted Nixon since the so-called Compact of Fifth Avenue, a negotiation in 1960 between Nixon and Nelson Rockefeller, during which Nixon was perceived to have sold out to the party's eastern wing. Distrusted by many conservative Republicans, and hated by liberal Democrats, Nixon struggled to control his own image, while many Texans viewed Reagan as both a conservative hero and an image-management master.[21]

His own image problems an ever-present insecurity, Nixon believed that he had lost Texas in previous elections because he had been unable to convince voters that any significant ideological difference existed between Nixon and his liberal northern Democratic opponents. Vowing not to make the same mistake three times, Nixon purposed to distinguish himself from his Democratic opponent and used ideological labeling to do just that, though Nixon's opponent did much of the work for him. Just as Barry Goldwater had done for Lyndon Johnson in 1964, George McGovern in 1972 made Nixon's job in Texas easy.

Because he was perceived as a radically left-wing liberal, McGovern was never a serious threat to win Texas. As late as August, Nixon's lead in Texas polls reached as high as 30 percent.[22] This comfortably wide margin for the same man who had lost Texas just four years earlier cannot be explained as the result of any single issue, nor can it be explained as a collective change in Texans' hearts. Nixon's favorability ratings rose slightly in Texas during his first two years in office, with busing issues providing inroads into white suburban communities in places like Dallas and Houston, where school integration and suburban expansion seemed to be happening most rapidly. By mid-1972, however, despite the fact that busing remained a topic fresh on the minds of many Texans, Nixon's popularity began to dip. In the fall campaign, Nixon tried to stand on his diplomatic achievements—particularly his visits to China and the Soviet Union—but such efforts were only marginally effective in what was still a virulently anticommunist state. Nixon also championed economic issues like revenue sharing, a policy designed to send federal tax dollars into state coffers in order to subsidize state and local government. This was conceived as a way to curry favor with states' rights advocates, but actually angered many conservative Texans, who openly preferred federal tax breaks to revenue sharing. Nixon even tried to appeal to South Texas Mexican Americans, publicly thanking them for their contributions to national culture. Yet none of these efforts accomplished for Nixon what having McGovern as an opponent did.[23]

McGovern was unpopular in Texas for a variety of reasons. He was hardly a friend to the state's oil conservatives and was harshly criticized for his rather vague calls to "eliminate all tax loopholes," which were routinely then coupled with diatribes against the oil industry.[24] Aside from his stance on Vietnam, which openly appealed to the antiwar left wing of his party, McGovern's other stands on foreign policy also troubled Texas conservatives. McGovern could not, despite frequent pressure to do so, articulate a reasonable position on America's alliance with Israel or on Middle East policy in general. At the same time, his advocacy for a reduced nuclear arsenal and a stabilization of second-strike defense growth contributed to many Texans' growing association of liberalism (and simultaneously, the Democratic Party) with, if not weakness, then certainly with reductions in strength. His suggestion that newly appointed judges spend ten to fifteen days in jail in order to "see what it was like" was also not met with much enthusiasm. Neither was his defense of marijuana users, of whom he said jail time was inappropriate unless the user was also acting as a dealer.[25] Conservatives in Texas particularly disdained McGovern's open association with "long-haired hippies." In fact, frequently throughout the campaign, McGovern was derided as a friend to such constituents as a way to undermine his acceptability to traditional Democrats. Such images speak to the power of perception in shaping ideological associations made between voters and candidates as well as to gendered notions of strength and respectability.[26]

While virtually all conservative Texas Democrats abandoned the McGovern ticket during the fall campaign, McGovern's remaining supporters in Texas, including a pair of young campaign workers named Hillary Rodham and Bill Clinton, believed their candidate could offer the nation hope and optimism—things for which virtually every poll indicated Texans desperately yearned. Despite the fact that hope and optimism would indeed be powerful political forces in the coming years, they were not enough—however skillfully crafted—to outweigh the negative perception Texans had of McGovern's liberalism. Speaking at the unveiling of former president Bill Clinton's official White House portrait in 2004, President George W. Bush joked about Clinton's optimism, saying one would indeed have to be "optimistic to give six months of your life running the McGovern campaign in Texas!"[27]

Funny in hindsight, but far less so for Texas liberals at the time, McGovern's attempts to rally a Democratic base of support in Texas failed miserably in 1972. In 1968, the popular John Connally had organized all statewide campaign efforts for Humphrey, despite the fact that Connally disagreed with Humphrey on a number of issues—the war in Vietnam, most notably. Connally's support and loyalty in 1968 contributed to Humphrey's win in Texas. In 1972, Connally, following an appointment to Nixon's cabinet as secretary of the Treasury, chaired the Texas Democrats for Nixon organization. Connally's willingness to abandon the Democratic ship inspired many other conservative Texas Democrats to do the same and added respectability at a crucial moment for the state GOP.

Nixon's campaign strategy in Texas was based on efforts to connect McGovern to dangerous and irresponsible weakness, particularly with regard to Vietnam. Nixon often spoke in Texas of McGovern's willingness to "surrender" Southeast Asia to the communists. Nixon claimed that McGovern would roll back all of the current administration's foreign policy achievements and reduce the nation's arms holdings to a level "less than before Pearl Harbor." Sensing an opportunity, many Texas Republicans jumped on the bandwagon they hoped would fix an association among grassroots conservatives between weakness and the Democratic Party. Coordinated Republican campaign efforts across Texas routinely emphasized McGovern's liberalism ahead of local or state issues, even in local and state races. Texas Republicans constantly used the words *McGovern* and *surrender* in the same sentence, spoke often of Democratic weakness, and jumped at the chance to use the word *liberal* as the quickest and easiest descriptor of all such attitudes.[28]

While McGovern's liberalism became a major focus for conservative Texans, Texas was not a major focus for McGovern. This was particularly evident in August when McGovern scheduled a visit to the LBJ Ranch to confer with the former president and receive his endorsement. There, McGovern tried to find common cause with Johnson, citing Johnson's quest for peace in Southeast Asia, a strategy designed to shift the blame for American involvement in Vietnam from the Democrat Johnson to the Republican Nixon. McGovern also highlighted Johnson's insistence on larger roles for women in his campaigns, noting that LBJ was the first Texan to make such an insistence. Lastly, the Democratic nominee portrayed himself as sharing with Johnson a "deeply felt populist hostility to big business and to 'the interests.'"[29]

Although the event received considerable press coverage, McGovern's strategists were under no illusions that the meeting would boost their candidate's support in Texas. The discussion between the two public figures was scripted prior to the actual meeting and certain topics were deemed inappropriate and potentially dangerous. For instance, McGovern's staff members strongly discouraged their candidate from even mentioning Ralph Yarborough's name for fear that the association with such a liberal would permanently end any hopes they had for carrying Texas. McGovern was also told, for obvious reasons, not to mention John Connally, who was, again for obvious reasons, not on good terms with LBJ at the moment. "I see relatively little immediate value in trying to relate the meeting to the political situation in Texas," one frustrated McGovern strategist wrote of the press op with LBJ.[30]

Shortly after his meeting at the LBJ Ranch, McGovern was advised to pull all campaign monies allocated to television advertising in Texas. Strategists working in the McGovern campaign divided states into two categories: needed or not needed. Their analysis showed that 55 percent of McGovern's advertising expenditures was being wasted on states "not needed." Seeing no chance of carrying Texas, McGovern's campaign announced plans to funnel virtually all advertising expenditures into states he "needed," including California, New York, Pennsylvania, Illinois, Ohio, Michigan, New Jersey, and Massachusetts. Practically no effort was made by the McGovern campaign to change voters' minds in Texas or other parts of the South.[31]

What little media exposure McGovern was able to generate and control in Texas came through national channels, where his antiwar message, hostility to the oil industry, commitment to reducing the size of the military, and open appeals to civil rights and feminist activists contributed to an image of liberal entitlement rather than antielitist equality and opportunity. McGovern's style also caused problems. His speeches were often riddled with technicalities and he was regularly criticized for sounding like a professional economist, though his training was as an academic historian. He appeared passive and struggled to master the art of looking the camera or people in the eye. McGovern missed multiple opportunities to connect with middle-class whites in Texas, a failing that played perfectly into Nixon's strategy of characterizing the Democratic Party as the party of weakness, surrender, and northeastern establishment elitism.[32]

McGovern did appeal to the state's racial and ethnic minorities, even taking time to speak to the state's Native American population. McGovern appealed to black Texans and liberals by supporting "100 percent" the policy of busing—saying that he favored "busing children, busing teachers, and busing money." Whereas most Democratic candidates typically campaigned in East Texas hoping to earn white votes, McGovern campaigned in East Texas with the hope of earning the support of the region's African Americans. McGovern told crowds of East Texas blacks that the conservative wing of the Democratic Party stood directly between them and greater political freedom. He also told audiences in Texas that Nixon had failed to improve the nation's safety because he had failed to see that the root of criminal activity was white racism, drugs, and poverty. He told Texans that the solution to these issues was racial equality and gun control, even suggesting taxing toy guns and toy soldiers at a 50 percent clip as a way to discourage parents from conditioning their children to violence.[33]

McGovern often spoke about having a "constituency of the disaffected." Certainly, racial and ethnic minorities fit into this category, as did, in his estimation, America's youth. Having been trained in the academy, McGovern felt comfortable engaging students and faculty at colleges and universities, though his opponents used such instances as an opportunity to label the Democratic candidacy as one of "acid, amnesty, and abortion." In most cases, McGovern tried to sound like a populist when he spoke of the nation suffering from "Nixonism—which gives aid and comfort to the banks and big business at the expense of the little man," but rarely, if ever, did he target these messages to rural and working-class Texas Democrats. McGovern's attempts to appeal to Texans differed little from his attempted appeals to the antiwar left wing of his party. McGovern promised to end the war in Vietnam within the first ninety days of his administration. When given a chance to talk about local economic issues, he made comments such as, "Everybody is talking about high prices and boycotting the supermarkets. I say, the price of the war is too high and we should boycott the war!"[34]

McGovern's only effective strategy in Texas, and the one he had the best opportunity to use in order to connect with the populist leanings of both state conservatives and liberals, was to hammer the issue of corruption and government dishonesty. McGovern criticized Nixon for misleading the nation by failing to reveal his "secret plan to win the war" during the 1968 campaign, yet rarely managed to touch on issues of government corruption and dishonesty without doing so in the context of the Vietnam War. Thus, McGovern overshadowed a potentially fruitful campaign issue in Texas by indirectly emphasizing the very issues that Nixon had successfully used to paint the Democratic nominee as an agent of the Far Left—replete with images of surrender, weakness, and communist appeasement.[35]

In November, though voter apathy resulted in the lowest national turnout for a presidential election since 1948, Nixon trounced McGovern. Nationally, Nixon captured more than 60 percent of the vote, compared to McGovern's 37 percent. In Texas, the margin was even greater, with Nixon winning 66 percent of the vote, compared to McGovern's 33 percent. Nixon carried 246 of 254 Texas counties, became the first GOP candidate in history to win a majority of the state's Catholic vote, which he carried 56–33, and won 59 percent of Texas blue-collar workers. This success was even more apparent in the state's two largest cities. In Houston, Nixon won both of the city's Jewish precincts by more than 60 percent, won the blue-collar vote 68–31, and carried the youth vote 60–40. McGovern dominated among Houston blacks, 97–3, and won the Mexican American vote 68–32, but the small population and low turnout rendered these successes electorally insignificant. At the same time, Nixon's performance among Mexican Americans was impressive. In Dallas, Nixon carried an overall vote of 70 percent. He carried youth voters by as much as 84–16 in some precincts, blue-collar voters by an overall margin of 77–23, senior citizens—the most yellow of the yellow-dog Texans—78–22, and upper-class white voters by an astounding 89–11 percent.[36]

Nixon had finally won in Texas, carrying the state by a 2–1 margin. Nixon's landslide victory helped Texas Republicans gain seven seats in the state House of Representatives but only one additional seat in the state Senate. These gains were significant, but not overwhelming. In the weeks following the election, pundits in Texas assessed the fallout from the campaign and determined that Nixon's success was almost solely the result of McGovern's liberalism. Nixon was considered a moderate, still distrusted by most Texas conservatives, while those same voters viewed McGovern as a liberal "extremist." Conservative Democrats maintained control in most local and state races, while Nixon's attempt to be seen as nonpartisan—running as an almost independent and bipartisan "president of all Americans"—alienated many Texas Republican insiders. Virtually all political observers concluded that while the Texas GOP was making strides, Texas was not yet a two-party state; Nixon's support there was due to an utter rejection of what voters defined as McGovern liberalism.[37]

The Fluke, Take Three

Though most Texas Democrats managed to hold off their Republican challengers in 1972, McGovern's liberalism—coupled with the long shadow still cast by the Sharpstown scandal—proved fatal for some. Many Democrats, acutely aware of these problems, initially committed themselves not to a defense against such charges, but rather to an offense that actually tried to co-opt and employ the charges to their advantage. As had been tried six years earlier, conservative Democrats hopeful of unseating John Tower again tried to paint the Republican incumbent senator as a liberal connected to the traditionally distrusted and vilified GOP northeastern establishment.[38] The first and only fruits of these efforts came with the nomination of Harold "Barefoot" Sanders—a former state legislator from Dallas. Sanders's nomination caught the Tower camp off guard. Tower had spent much time and effort preparing for a race not against a moderate conservative but against a liberal, namely, Ralph Yarborough. Sanders upset that plan in the Democratic primary by, quite simply, lambasting Yarborough as a liberal. Turning conventional wisdom on its head, he hoped to do something similar to Tower in the general election. Sanders tried to market himself as a populist conservative—as a man of the people, open-collared and real—unlike the pinstripe-suited and "stuffy" Tower. Yet, by the end of the summer, it was apparent that, with McGovern at the head of the national ticket, winning with such a strategy would be difficult.[39]

Conversely, Tower based his campaign primarily on the push to make Texas a two-party state based on ideological polarization. Clearly a major part of that strategy would be to convince a majority of Texas voters that the Democratic Party was too liberal. Tower's efforts to associate Sanders with McGovern and Democratic liberalism were aided when, just days prior to the Democratic National Convention, Sanders made a critical mistake by telling a gaggle of reporters that he would faithfully support the presidential nominee of his party, no matter who that turned out to be. After McGovern's nomination, Sanders's favorability ratings across Texas dropped virtually overnight and in almost perfect correlation to the number of voters who perceived Sanders as liberal.[40]

Between June and November, with the stigma of McGovern liberalism overshadowing Sanders's entire campaign, the number of Texans characterizing the Democratic Senate nominee as "somewhat liberal" increased 10 percent while the number of Texans characterizing Sanders as "very conservative" decreased 10 percent. Even more important, the number of Texans characterizing Sanders as "middle of the road" declined by 6 percent. By the fall, Sanders knew that the source of his growing unpopularity was obviously McGovern. In response, he publicly announced that he would not make any public appearances with McGovern, despite repeated requests to do so from the national campaign. Nonetheless, despite these late efforts to create distance from McGovern, the association had been made in the public's mind and the damage had, therefore, been done.[41]

The proof that ideological associations with the liberal McGovern directly contributed to negative perceptions of Sanders and, consequently, contributed to Tower's victory in 1972 is in the proverbial pudding. Among voters who saw Sanders becoming more liberal, Tower won 57–33 percent. Among voters who saw Sanders staying conservative, Sanders won 50–40 percent. The problem for Sanders was that, according to statewide polling, there was a 20 percent swing in the number of voters identifying the Democratic Senate nominee as increasingly liberal versus those who saw him as remaining conservative. Tower carried self-identifying conservative Texans at a rate of 3–1, broke even with Sanders among moderates, and lost only among self-identifying liberals.[42]

Analyzing the campaign more broadly, it becomes apparent that Tower's 1972 strategy was rather predictable. As he had in 1966, Tower again peppered the pages of *Texas Football* magazine with lists of endorsements, ran television and radio advertisements emphasizing the importance of a "Two-Party Texas," lauded his reputation for bipartisanship in Congress, and highlighted his association with Nixon as a means of playing up the anti-McGovern angle. The campaign also had flair. Among Tower's chief campaign organizers was Nola Smith, who staged what she called "press the flesh" rallies at airports and civic halls across the state, always emphasizing the need to have "show-biz flavor"—something she routinely achieved by employing "Tower Girls"—attractive young women in sailor straws and matching skirts and blouses who theoretically added to the ambience of each rally.[43]

In other respects, however, Tower's campaign strategy was less predictable and, in fact, reflected the most well-organized and ambitious statewide Republican effort of the postwar era. Smith, along with John Knaggs and a host of other advisers, organized an efficient, well-informed, data-driven, target-marketing campaign designed to simultaneously retain the Republican base, undermine Democratic loyalties, and attract independent women, senior citizens, and business interests. The GOP established well-staffed canvassing operations in most counties and, to pundits, appeared to be a well-oiled machine. According to Smith, the campaign "probably utilized more modern, extensive survey research than any other campaign in Texas history." Tower's campaign also took advantage of the public's disdain for corruption. "This year above all years," Tower told party members in June, "is the chance to dispel the Democratic Party—the party with the barnacles on it—and to replace it with Republican government free from corruption."[44]

With enthusiasm, momentum, and a solid foundation, Tower's campaign also paved several significant and successful inroads beyond the traditional base of GOP support. Rather than relying solely on the urban vote, thereby leaving open the possibility of losing the rural vote by margins large enough to lose the election, Tower routinely made his presence felt in the Texas countryside as early as 1971. Employing what the campaign called a "rifle shot approach" to media information dissemination in rural counties, Tower's campaign sent press releases to the fifty most affected counties following any event of significance. If the event had to do with cattle, for example, Tower's campaign sent a press release to the fifty most affected cattle-ranching counties, highlighting Tower's awareness of the issue and the assistance he would provide to secure protection for cattle ranchers. If the event concerned cotton, a similar release went to the fifty most affected cotton-producing counties. In issues concerning wheat, grain sorghum, rice, peanuts, soybeans, sheep, goats, vegetables—whatever the commodity—Tower's voice was heard. Tower was a regular guest on radio stations like KGNC of Amarillo—stations with a heavily agricultural program offering and audience. The strategy clearly worked. Tower won 55.2 percent of the vote in the top 27 most populous counties, 55.2 percent of the vote in the next 53 most populous counties, and 54.1 percent of the vote in the 174 remaining rural counties. After the election, John Knaggs recalled that Tower's ability to win a majority of rural votes—something no Texas Re-

John and Lou Tower attend a 1972 campaign rally targeting Mexican American voters. (Courtesy of the John G. Tower Library and Archives, Georgetown, TX)

publican had ever done—was "the most significant achievement of the campaign."[45]

In 1972, Tower also became the first Texas Republican to win a plurality of Mexican American and Hispanic votes, outdoing even his own impressive 1966 performance in that regard. Tower had actively courted Mexican Americans and Hispanics in Texas since the early 1960s. He stepped up his efforts in the late 1960s and early 1970s and clearly benefited from these efforts in 1972. Tower marketed himself to Mexican American voters as a leader in the fight for education, employment, health care, and housing—despite mixed reviews on whether or not his credentials in these areas were as impressive as the Republican claimed. He also backed school lunch programs, vocational training, and community health centers for migrant workers. Most important, though, was his support for expanded congressional funding for bilingual education programs in Texas. Tower released statements and ran advertisements in Spanish-speaking communities advocating the teaching of both English and Spanish in public schools and allowing students to speak bilingually in class. Tower supported recruitment efforts for more Mexican American teachers and told audiences that "it is imperative that the Mexican-American be given the opportunity, which is rightfully his, to further his education." He called for a continued increase in Mexican American employment within the federal government and stressed the need to extend modern and industrial economic growth into Mexican American communities.[46]

Tower's efforts were generally received with enthusiasm by Mexican American and other Hispanic Texans, though initially that enthusiasm was not coupled with active participation. The most well-known grassroots organization established on behalf of Tower in these communities was called Tejanos por Tower. Tina Villanueva of Alice was among the Mexican Americans in South Texas willing to work on behalf of Tower through this organization, though even she told campaign workers that she would participate only in "low-key campaigning" so as to avoid the hostile backlash of local and loyal Democrats. Tradition told many Mexican Americans that to support a Republican was potentially hazardous to one's personal finances and economic stability. By October, however, Tejanos por Tower was gaining steam in South Texas and had established well-staffed offices in Houston, Austin, Dallas, El Paso, San Antonio, Edinburg, and Brownsville. Many prominent local Mexican American leaders rallied behind Tower after Yarborough's defeat in the Democratic primary and added credibility to the Republican's campaign.[47]

Leading all of these efforts on behalf of Tower was Humberto Aguirre, a former Democratic aide to Preston Smith. Aguirre played a central role in shaping Tower's evolving approach toward the Mexican American community and helped provide the Republican Party with a well-respected Mexican American voice. He introduced himself to the campaign in March by writing Tower that "the Democrats talked big to our people, and in the end did little for us. . . . When it comes to political parties, we know which side our tortilla is buttered on."[48]

Aguirre convinced the campaign that, despite the fact that it would take a significant financial investment, winning not just a fraction but a plurality of the Mexican American and Hispanic vote was not only possible, but with the right strategy would be probable and, in the end, well worth the cost. Aguirre also convinced the campaign to deploy some of its most highly qualified staffers to work polls and volunteer in rural Hispanic communities, rather than depend on local volunteers, whom he believed would not be reliable.[49] He called for extensive advertising on Spanish-speaking radio stations in these communities, pointing out that the average Mexican

American in rural South Texas did not own a television set nor did he or she read much. Aguirre also led efforts to undermine Mexican American loyalties to the Democratic Party by highlighting the corruption and abuse that community had endured at the hands of members of that party. He spoke before Mexican Americans across South Texas about what he called, "typical Democratic machine politics," reminding listeners of instances in which surplus food supplies were cut off two to three weeks prior to previous elections as a threat to those who considered casting a disloyal vote. He spoke of routine Democratic intimidation, harassment of potentially uncooperative voters, and of welfare recipients being told by Democratic operatives that they would have their checks recalled if they were seen at the opponent's camp. "The Democrats make it a point to indoctrinate the Mexican American into believing that the Democratic Party is the only party which can help him," Aguirre later wrote of his strategy. "Thousands of dollars are spent continuously to reaffirm the Mexican American's belief that the Republican Party is evil and does not care about the needs of the common people." Aguirre convinced many Mexican Americans not only that the Democratic Party—and specifically the Texas Democratic Party—was a false friend, but that Republicans like John Tower actually had a record of support for their community that warranted their enthusiasm and their vote.[50]

Aguirre's emphasis on using media and specifically radio to undermine Mexican American loyalties to the Texas Democratic Party—something he based on the perception of the party's corruption and tradition of abuse—was largely embraced by the Tower campaign but did not go unchallenged. Some Tower strategists argued that winning the rural Mexican American vote would be too costly and instead pushed a plan that would concentrate recruitment efforts on the seven heaviest urban concentrations, these being San Antonio, Corpus Christi, Dallas, Houston, El Paso, McAllen, and Austin. In this strategy, Tower would appeal to the Mexican American community on the basis of their sameness and common interest with the urban white community. Ultimately, the Tower campaign managed to do both—appealing to rural and urban Mexican Americans and Hispanics primarily through a coordinated media and advertising campaign featuring anti-Democratic and pro-Tower rhetoric that paralleled nicely with the overall conservative strategy of libertarian and free-market individualism, economic growth, and social tradition. The strategy worked; Tower became the first Republican running for statewide office in Texas to win a plurality of the Mexican American and Hispanic vote—taking a whopping 45 percent, 11 points higher than the level attained in 1966.[51]

Tower did not do as well among Texas's African Americans, something that did not come as a surprise considering the difficulty Republicans faced trying to organize grassroots operations in black communities similar to those organized for Mexican Americans. Sensing the futility of such efforts, Tower allocated virtually no money to winning the black vote in Texas, nor did black communities respond with any semblance of enthusiasm for his campaign. Black newspapers and radio stations contacted the campaign asking if it would like to advertise, but rarely did Tower respond in the affirmative. Under the leadership of Marci Sauls, the campaign's chief liaison to the black community, Tower eventually won a paltry 22,241 votes out of more than 513,459 blacks who had been targeted in eight "black counties"—as defined by population percentage and campaign decision. Though only 157,317 of those targeted actually voted, Tower's percentage in the black community was a respectable, though small and relatively inconsequential, 14.2 percent.[52]

Though John Tower had made inroads into parts of Texas that few if any statewide Republican candidates had ever achieved, in the end, his defeat of Harold Sanders was aided primarily by the national landslide against George McGovern. This was not Tower's first reelection; however, 1966 had not been a presidential election year and neither had 1961. Political observers then and later argued that Tower's success in those campaigns had been due in large part to low voter turnout. Winning reelection against a moderate Democrat in a year in which turnout was high, therefore, represents a significant achievement. It further reflects the degree to which Republican candidacies had grown viable since 1968.

In 1972, many Texans' growing displeasure with the social and political status quo manifested as opposition to national liberalism and an association of that liberalism with the Democratic Party. Nixon and Tower were among several to benefit as a result. Though unsuccessful, Republican Henry Grover—labeled as a maverick within his own party—ran a much stronger gubernatorial contest against Dolph Briscoe in the general election than had been anticipated, giving the state GOP hope that it might not be long before it would capture the ultimate prize in state politics—the governorship. Statewide, the GOP increased its number of representatives in the Texas House to seventeen. Though nowhere close to an elected majority, it was becoming far more common and respectable to vote GOP in local and national races than had been the case just years earlier.

Ultimately, the 1972 campaigns served as an acceleration point on the path toward burying the state's more than a century old "yellow-dog" loyalties. In 1973, in the wake of a Republican landslide unlike any other, one

Richard and Pat Nixon visit John and Nellie Connally at the Connally ranch in South Texas, 1972. (Courtesy of the Associated Press)

such yellow-dog showed conservative Texans that it was indeed possible to learn a few new tricks. In doing so, the floodgates of realignment began to open even more widely.[53]

The Connally Defection

In 1972, John Connally was the most influential of all conservative Texas Democrats. Connally's loyalties carried a great deal of weight among Texans. When he had fallen in line with the Humphrey campaign of 1968, most Texans had followed suit and supported the Democratic ticket. When he had refused to do so in 1972, most Texans had also refused and supported the Republican ticket. Connally's power was not unlike that wielded by Allan Shivers two decades earlier. However, the time was fast approaching when conservative dalliances with Republican presidential candidates would no longer be momentary or isolated cases of defection. Rather, the 1972 campaigns were creating momentum for a widespread realignment based on ideological persuasions.

Texans perceived Connally as a man of conservative conviction— someone unwilling to stand idly by as the Democratic Party drifted increasingly to the left. This perception intensified in May 1973 when Connally announced that he was officially leaving the Democratic Party to become a Republican. Connally's announcement shook the political world in Texas to the point that state newspaper editorials began to envision a scenario in which a Connally presidential campaign might be the necessary link connecting state conservatives with the Republican Party. Though Connally had served in Richard Nixon's administration as secretary of the Treasury and chaired the Democrats for Nixon operations in 1972, few Texas conservatives received the news of his switch as anything less than significant. Members of both parties characterized Connally as the quintessential rugged Texan—conservative and tough—and in possession of an important key to electoral success in Texas.[54]

Yet at the same time, Connally also appeared far more polished than did some of his conservative brethren. Connally biographer James Reston described the former Texas governor's presence in his home state as almost "regal." Throughout the 1960s and early 1970s, Connally masterfully utilized the media in Texas to communicate, as Reston put it, grace and charm, particularly as he refused to "spew race venom" as other southern governors were accustomed to doing. John Connally's Texas was the Texas of the space age—of skyscrapers, technology, and, beginning in May of 1973, Republicanism.[55]

Connally's decision to switch parties reflected what was becoming a much more common impulse among conservative Texans. After all, Connally's career had been marked by Democratic loyalties. Born in 1917 in a small town south of San Antonio, he had served as student body president at the University of Texas at Austin before joining the U.S. Navy during World War II, where he survived numerous close encounters with enemy combatants. Following the war, Connally worked closely with Lyndon Johnson's 1946 congressional campaign and was instrumental in securing Johnson's 87-vote win in the infamous Senate campaign of 1948. Taking a bullet from the same rifle that assassinated John Kennedy catapulted Connally into a position of national prominence, as did his subsequent gubernatorial elections in 1964 and 1966. Connally agreed to head Hubert Humphrey's Texas campaign after his good friend Lyndon decided not to seek the Democratic Party nomination again in 1968, but rivalries within the state party and liberalization at the national level, particularly on the issue of Vietnam, pushed Connally increasingly close to the Republican side of the aisle.[56]

Connally quickly became the new Texas Republican that all Republicans wanted their picture taken with. Though justifiably protective of his role as the state's preeminent GOP leader, John Tower immediately embraced Connally's party switch, praising the decision as a step on the path toward a legitimate two-party Texas and a majority conservative Republican Party.[57] Nobody, however, was more enthralled with the notion of rubbing elbows with Texas power than Nixon. Befriending John Connally was one way, Nixon believed, to bolster his own credentials in the Lone Star State. After appointing Connally as secretary of the Treasury in 1971, Nixon often consulted LBJ's former confidant on political decisions and told his staff to maintain close contact with Connally.[58] Nixon was fascinated by the aura Connally seemed to have in Texas. Connally's reputation as a man with deep political connections—someone who "knew where all the bodies were buried"—also drew Nixon to Connally as much as Connally was drawn to the Republican Party. Nixon admired Connally so much that, in early 1972, he seriously considered asking Agnew to step aside in order to make room for the former Texas governor on the national ticket. Only Connally's Democratic affiliation and personal reluctance to accept such a nomination prevented a post-Watergate Connally administration. In later years Nixon wrote that Connally was "the only man in either party who clearly had the potential to be a great president."[59]

The momentum gained by Connally's personal realignment suggested that real opportunity was on the immediate horizon for Texas Republicans. Enthusiasm in the party reached a fever pitch and proclamations of impending realignment peppered state GOP excitement. Unfortunately for the GOP, however, revived attention on scandal and corruption quickly quelled that momentum. Though in the long run the politics of scandal and corruption worked on behalf of a rising modern conservatism and a restructured Republican Party, in late 1973 and 1974 such politics threatened to destroy any and all such gains. The politics of scandal had grown potent in Texas through the Sharpstown Stock-Fraud Scandal that tore through Austin between 1971 and 1972, laying waste to many in the conservative Democratic establishment. The politics of scandal and corruption were revived in 1973 and 1974, though this time the focus was on a Republican White House.

Watergate and the Rise of Reagan

Though not the only scandal on the minds of Texas voters in the early 1970s, Watergate no doubt contributed heavily to the paranoia, distrust, and pervasive dissatisfaction citizens felt toward politics and government. Historians have debated the effect of Watergate in the context of modern conservatism's national growth in the last quarter of the twentieth century.

Some, like Jonathan Schoenwald, see Watergate as a stumbling block on the road to national Republican dominance. Others, like Bruce Schulman, see Watergate as enabling a GOP takeover by the most vocally antigovernment and populist conservatives within the party, like Ronald Reagan.[60] James T. Patterson has argued that Watergate simply brought to a head the growing animus against government that had been building for a decade. These antistatist attitudes helped tear down traditions and partisan loyalties both in Texas and nationally.[61]

By early 1975, with Gerald Ford's pardon of Nixon still fresh on people's minds, more than 60 percent of Americans believed that government leadership was worse than it had been a decade earlier. Polls in 1958 indicated that nearly 80 percent of the American public trusted the government to "do the right thing" when called to act. Those numbers began to decline in 1964 during Lyndon Johnson's administration and continued to weaken steadily until the Watergate scandal allowed for a flooding of antigovernment animosity and paranoia into the mainstream discourse of American politics. Though Watergate did not cause the decline in people's trust in government, it did lend credibility to and fuel antiestablishment personalities.[62]

In Texas, Watergate was a necessary step on the path toward a legitimate and competitive two-party political culture. As conservative Democrats had an increasingly difficult time distancing themselves from the perceived liberalization of the national party, established Texas Republicans like John Tower unsuccessfully tried to juggle their personal loyalties to Nixon with the public's disdain for corruption. In many ways, Watergate was a critical moment in the decline of Tower's viability as a spokesperson for Texas conservatives. Though Tower's antigovernment rhetoric became far more vitriolic in the aftermath of Watergate, his unflinching loyalty to Nixon during the scandal invited criticism.[63] Privately, Tower feared that Watergate would turn Texans away from the GOP, thus stalling or destroying gains he and other party leaders had made on the path toward two-party politics in the state.[64]

In reality, Tower's fears were only partially warranted. Many Texans did temporarily turn away from the GOP in the aftermath of Watergate. At the same time, however, conservative Texans were also still turning away from the Democratic Party. Independent registrations increased dramatically in the 1970s, particularly during the Watergate years. Meanwhile, state liberals eagerly embraced the vacancies left by defecting conservative Democrats and enhanced their presence and influence in Austin and in the state party.[65] The coincidence of Watergate and an already intensified antistatist culture contributed to the breaking apart of the established political status quo in Texas. The result was a tumultuous campaign culture in which more political organizations began to operate in and through the grass roots.[66]

The chief national beneficiary of this culture would eventually be Ronald Reagan. Although Reagan publicly supported both Nixon and the GOP throughout the Watergate scandal, his rhetoric promoted an agenda that was thoroughly anti-Washington, antigovernment, and that appealed to disaffected Texans angry over political corruption in both parties. In November 1973, Reagan visited Houston, billing himself as a "Crusader for the Disaffected," virtually the same phrase used by McGovern a year earlier, though within a much more conservative context. Reagan's speech lambasted corrupt politicians in both parties and demanded that the voice of the people be listened to and respected.[67] Reagan's team of political strategists began touting Texas as a place out of which a significant base of support might be established for a future presidential bid. The state, they argued, was "entering a period of rapid and possibly irreversible change about the way people feel toward institutions." Reagan's advisers added that "the public is currently angry, mean, and in a frustrated mood" and encouraged Reagan to take advantage of this mood by highlighting government's failures, misrepresentations, and incompetence, while at the same time using his skill and charm as a political communicator to bring a sense of hope and optimism to those who had neither.[68]

Reagan certainly capitalized on this collective anger and frustration, especially in Texas. During the spring of 1974, Reagan spoke at both Texas Republican fund-raisers—where the established leadership knew he was sure to draw a large turnout—and before local civic organizations unconnected to either major party. In February, he spoke to the Dallas Crime Commission about the need for stronger law enforcement, while at the same time linking criminal activity, disorder, and chaos to the incompetence and false promises of big government. Reagan made numerous other appearances in Texas between 1973 and 1975, prioritizing during each his hostility toward government, his anger at scandal and corruption, and his conviction that ideology was more important than party loyalty.[69]

As a result, many Texas conservatives, regardless of party, saw Reagan as a solution to the "corruption of the Washington establishment." Reagan attracted middle-class suburbanites and rural voters alike, and many of these individuals donated small sums to the Citizens for Reagan operation. Many, in donating to Citizens for Reagan, openly proclaimed that they preferred to give their money straight to Reagan rather than contribute it to the state Republican Party. For many conservative Texans, trust was offered first to Reagan, and only later to Reagan's party. Another direct outgrowth of Reagan's appeal in Texas was the adoption at the 1974 Texas GOP Convention of several resolutions highly critical of the Ford administration. Though mostly symbolic, these resolutions surprised some state party regulars who had pledged support for the administration in large part because of the significant roles that Texans like George Bush, Dick Cheney, and James Baker were playing in that administration.[70]

Watergate in and of itself was a major story in Texas, but was also— more importantly—another link in the chain that connected antistatist and populist conservatives with political credibility and power in the Texas Republican Party. The scandal undermined the established leadership of the GOP, encouraged new blood in the party through the rallying together of grassroots elements already being mobilized by social and economic issues, and thoroughly discredited liberalism because it was a philosophy dependent upon trusting the very government that evidence revealed could not be trusted.

The antiliberal backlash and simultaneous growth of antigovernment and antiestablishment hostility in the early 1970s accelerated realignment in Texas by prioritizing ideological loyalties ahead of partisan ones, and by altering the public's commonly held perceptions of which parties represented which philosophies. Among conservatives, the word *liberal* became much more synonymous with the word *Democrat*. Research reports conducted for the Republican National Committee prior to the start of the 1972 campaign season indicated that most Americans still associated liberalism with individualism, advocacy for the underprivileged, and a freethinking hostility toward special interests. With the expressed intent of undermining this definition, the RNC funneled strategy papers to state and local campaigns outlining a concerted effort to link liberalism with weakness, permissiveness, and relativistic amorality. By painting McGovern as a weak, bleeding-heart liberal, conservatives both nationally and in Texas managed to undermine the perceived ideological traditions of the Democratic Party.[71]

For state Democrats, intraparty divisions were exacerbated as conservatives found themselves increasingly at odds with the liberalizing national party. Though conservatives were still the dominant majority in Texas, the strength of national liberalism emboldened liberal Texans trying to operate within the Democratic Party. This emboldening intensified the animosity between ideological factions. McGovern's nomination in 1972 alienated large segments of the moderate and conservative population and forced many Texans to reexamine their political loyalties in light of the increasing estrangement between conservatism and the Democratic Party.[72]

Yet with success also came new concerns for the Texas Republican Party. Following the significant but short-term setbacks encountered as a result of Watergate, state Republicans quickly rebounded, though factions and disagreements also reemerged. These primarily focused on the future leadership and direction of the party. By 1976, those factions erupted into a small-scale intraparty civil war that culminated in the emergence of a new and reinvigorated base of grassroots conservatives rallied together behind the new national icon of populist conservatism—Ronald Reagan.

Chapter 6

Civil War

Populist Conservatism and the 1976 Campaigns

The rise of modern Texas conservatism experienced a critical turning point in 1976. That year, in the midst of a heated primary contest between Ronald Reagan and Gerald Ford, what can best be described as a political civil war broke out within the Texas GOP. The war was essentially a split between the established party leadership, still committed to making Texas a two-party state, and a populist conservative grass roots energized by surging antiliberalism, a nationally reinvigorated antistatism, and the emergence of several new and politically active conservative special interest groups. Though this brief but significant intraparty conflict was initially divisive, its ultimate outcome accelerated the process of partisan realignment based on ideological polarities, which, in the years following 1976, became increasingly connected with national issues and icons.

Yet, in the short run, the only thing the Texas GOP experienced was defeat. Reagan, the candidate most Texas conservatives supported, won the state's primary but eventually lost the party's nomination. Texans then rejected Gerald Ford in the general election, choosing instead to support a southern Democrat running as a Washington outsider, a born-again Christian, and a relative moderate. It is unlikely that many Texans realized in November 1976 that Jimmy Carter would be the last Democratic presidential candidate to carry Texas in the twentieth century. Why that happened cannot be understood without carefully examining the state's political culture and the state GOP's intraparty conflicts during the mid-1970s.

"God is very big in Dallas"

The state and national political culture that allowed for Ronald Reagan's 1976 bid for the presidency cannot be understood without recognizing the rapidly expanding influence of politically mobilized evangelical Christians. This was especially true in Dallas, where growing suburbs became hotbeds of activity for like-minded middle class and churchgoing conservatives.

155

The most significant shot fired in the early stages of the American culture wars landed, ironically, on January 22, 1973—the same day that Lyndon Johnson died. That day, though the event was not at the time deemed significant enough to steal LBJ's final headline, the U.S. Supreme Court handed down its decision in the landmark abortion case, *Roe v. Wade*. Though Johnson's death temporarily overshadowed the news of the court's decision, the long-term impact of *Roe*—a case originally filed in Dallas—contributed to the infusion of evangelicals into Texas politics and, more specifically, to the growing tide of grassroots activism that added to Reagan's momentum in 1976.

Interestingly, neither religion broadly nor religious issues specifically played a significant role in Texas politics prior to *Roe*. In 1971, for instance, Texas Republicans underscored the RNC's endorsement of the Equal Rights Amendment (ERA), an issue many evangelical religious groups would take up with great fervor in the coming years. The ERA passed the Texas legislature in 1972, without much debate and with the support of prominent Texas Republicans, including George Bush and John Tower.[1] Meanwhile, abortion played virtually no role in state or local campaigns in 1970 or 1972. For many young conservatives still evolving out of the Goldwater school, religion had no place in politics. Carol Reed of Dallas, for instance, who began her political education by joining a local Republican Women's Club in the 1960s before serving as vice president of the Texas Federation of Republican Women until 1975, when she became vice chairman of the Dallas County Republican Party, considered herself a committed libertarian—unwilling to promote government's involvement in most social issues, including abortion.[2] Republican state representative Betty Andujar of Fort Worth agreed, citing her fear that outlawing abortion would lead to the slippery slope of population growth and, eventually, a military dictatorship.[3] Even the Baptist General Convention of Texas remained libertarian on social issues. In 1971, responding to House Joint Resolution 191—also known as the "prayer amendment"—the Baptist General Convention of Texas voiced its support for the separation of church and state, saying that it was dangerous to allow government any say on what was or was not acceptable prayer. "The right to pray is safe now," wrote the convention. "The best thing that government can do for religion is to let it alone."[4]

Yet by 1976, both Stop-ERA and pro-life advocates had developed strong voices in state politics. *Roe* rallied those whose dissatisfaction with liberal Supreme Court rulings on issues like school prayer had been growing since the early 1960s, but whose dissatisfaction had not yet resulted in significant political mobilization. Within a year of the *Roe* decision, several grassroots organizations, such as Birthright and Texas Right to Life, were attracting support in both rural Catholic and suburban evangelical settings. Within one year of its founding, Texas Right to Life, under the leadership of Mary Jane Phelps, distributed at least one comprehensive packet describing the "sin of abortion" and its broader consequences to every pastor of a Southern Baptist church in Texas.[5] The politicization of the Southern Baptist Convention (SBC) in the late 1970s had its roots in organizations like Texas Right to Life, which communicated the need for churches to exercise a political voice—something the SBC had been reluctant to do in the 1960s and earlier in the 1970s.[6] By 1974, polls indicated that Texans' concern with social issues, declining morals, and the protection of traditional Christian values had significantly intensified.[7]

Busing also continued to mobilize the conservative grass roots, though in Dallas it was now coupled with religious overtones that had been largely absent from Houston's battle a few years earlier. Busing in Dallas became a bigger issue in the summer of 1975 when courts ruled that desegregation plans adopted by the Dallas Independent School District (DISD) in 1971 were inadequate. The Dallas busing controversy struck a chord with area suburbanites who viewed the issue as less about race than about another federal encroachment and the loss of property-tax payers' rights. While race no doubt informed the public's hostility, it did not singularly inspire resistance. Coupled with the growing fear that Texas youths were being subjected to a variety of federally encouraged immoralities, the busing issue evoked resistance. John Tower curried favor with Dallas's white citizens when he responded to the decision with a language of values and judgment, saying that if "the road to Hell is paved with good intentions, then speeding down that road is a fleet of yellow school buses. Forced busing is immoral, undemocratic, inherently racist, ineffective and counterproductive."[8]

In March 1976, one month prior to the Republican primary, the DISD announced plans to bus more than twenty thousand students during the following academic year. The cost was to be paid by an increase in property taxes, levied primarily on the very middle-class white conservatives who did not want their children to be bused. Dallas's white community had not previously been prone to massive resistance, the Mansfield High School incident of 1956 notwithstanding, but thanks in part to the recent mobilization of suburban evangelicals around issues of faith and family, new neighborhood organizations began to emerge and new political consciousnesses began to be pricked.[9] Even as the intensity of racial backlash cooled in the mid-1970s, issues of gender, sexuality, and morality captivated a growing segment of evangelical Texans who found entrée into the state's political arena through national issues made local.[10]

Evangelical Christianity did more than simply mobilize suburban conservatives. In Dallas, a city fast becoming an economic powerhouse (nine of the state's twenty largest corporations, with combined annual sales of $15.8 billion, were based in Dallas), religion was, as the *New York Times* described it, "big business." One anonymous poet even described the influence of religion in Dallas through verse:

> God is very big in Dallas,
> Just about everybody talks about God.
> I don't think you could ever amount to much in Dallas,
> If you went around bad-mouthing God.[11]

By 1975, religion had become a more common form of identification among Dallas's suburbanites. One's faith increasingly acted as a substitute for one's politics, particularly as many began to eschew traditional politics in the wake of national scandals and failures. For many, political traditions and loyalties were being replaced by faith. Evangelical Christianity became an identifier not simply of one's spiritual condition but of one's acceptability in the new social, economic, and political climate. Reinforcing this culture were dozens of new churches built in newly finished suburban subdivisions, allowing area residents greater convenience in their worship as well as fostering a spirit of communalism often inwardly focused on church growth and fellowship with other believers.[12]

By the mid-1970s, much about the Texas political culture had changed. Scandals undermined confidence in status quo government, social issues like abortion sparked the mobilization of grassroots conservatives, and growing suburbs reinforced that mobilization. These changes contributed to the public's impatience with philosophical factionalism within parties already struggling to maintain unity.[13]

Within this context, the Reagan insurgency of 1976 found its voice and its following. In Texas, traditional GOP politics, rooted in federal patronage and big business, meant that the state GOP was often little more than a tool of the RNC. As such, Democratic attacks against the GOP as the party of northeastern elitism were effective. By 1975, however, more Texans began to associate northeastern elitism with secular liberalism and amorality rather than country club conservatism or federal patronage. In cities like Dallas, where libertarian grassroots activism was already challenging partisan traditions, the emergence of mobilized evangelicals complicated the state's political climate and contributed to an atmosphere ripe for the Reagan Revolution.[14]

Reagan Country

With the possible exception of John Connally, Ronald Reagan was, by the mid-1970s, the most popular advocate of conservatism in Texas. There is little doubt that Reagan knew this and actively tried to benefit from it. Throughout 1975, Reagan crisscrossed Texas, making public appearances and speeches before a variety of businesses and politically active organizations and civic groups. Reagan's frequent visits fueled his popularity, which, in Texas, contributed to the construction of an iconography that made the former California governor appear larger than life.

Most of Reagan's invitations to speak in Texas came from organizations focused on economics, not social issues or religion. These organizations, however, understood the emerging language of the conservative crusade and incorporated that language into descriptions of their libertarian hero. On January 14, for instance, the Dallas chapter of the Texas Manufacturers Association billed Reagan, the keynote speaker at its annual banquet, as a "phenomenon."[15] The next day he was introduced to the San Antonio Chamber of Commerce as an "evangelist to spread the doctrine of the Free Enterprise System."[16] In June, Reagan spoke to the Texas Society of Certified Public Accountants (TSCPA), which promoted him as a man of law and order whose political ideology was drawing widespread support among Texas Republican "insurgents and American conservatives." The TSCPA succeeded in drawing a great deal more press coverage for its meeting in El Paso than was the norm, but Reagan was the real winner, as was often the case when other organizations in Texas undertook similar advertising campaigns. Between May and December of 1975, Reagan made appearances before sales and marketing executives in Houston, Veterans and Prisoners of War in San Antonio, GOP fund-raisers in Dallas and Beaumont, women's organizations in Dallas and Wichita Falls, and the Association of Builders and Contractors in Houston.[17]

During appearances not directly sponsored by the GOP, Reagan typically emphasized his affinity for speaking to apolitical audiences. Before businessmen in Houston he expressed relief at being able to speak before business leaders and not politicians. He told the National Soft Drink Association in Dallas that he had agreed to speak because he valued a chance to mingle with small-business owners—a core component, he proclaimed, of the American free enterprise system.[18] Reagan often constructed his speeches in such a way as to remove himself and his audience from the sense that they were there for political reasons at all. Reagan, who fancied himself a citizen-politician, managed to mobilize both social and economic conservatives in Texas without seeming political. His popularity as a speaker grew so rapidly that, by early 1976, Reagan was speaking to football banquets, Christian educators, real estate agents, fraternal lodges, journalists, university students, churches, advertising clubs, cable TV associations, and dozens of other groups and organizations across Texas.[19]

The use of newspapers and radio also advanced Reagan's popularity in Texas. In 1976, eleven major Texas newspapers and two dozen radio stations—more than in any other state except California—syndicated Reagan's political commentaries.[20] For common budgetary reasons that routinely plagued local radio, many stations frequently added, dropped, and readded programming, Reagan's commentaries included. These inconsistencies were frequently met with letter-writing campaigns initiated by grassroots conservatives demanding that stations continue to air Reagan's commentaries. Among a growing and increasingly unified following of disaffected conservatives, Reagan was becoming a statewide hero.[21]

Reagan also connected with Texas audiences because of his persona of rugged, cowboy individualism. The connection Texans made between Reagan and cowboys, the West, and the frontier indicates the extent to which iconography shaped the relationship that developed between Reagan and conservatives. Garry Wills has noted parallels between Reagan's appeal and that of one of Reagan's friends, John Wayne. Just as Wayne did on the silver screen, Reagan captured on the political speaking circuit an aura of the American West.[22] Reagan's oratory was often nostalgic, harkening back to "the wisdom of our founding fathers" who fought for "maximum freedom for the individual." Reagan also spoke to fears of America's "weakened military posture" and the "threat of Communist imperialism." Reagan managed to cast himself as a citizen-candidate, angry about government corruption and incompetence, nostalgic for frontier and free-market individualism, a champion of strength in the face of liberal weaknesses, and an advocate for traditional values.[23]

Not surprisingly, as Reagan worked to perfect his maverick persona during a variety of public appearances across the state, popular support for a Reagan White House bid intensified. Texas Citizens for Reagan, the primary campaign organization for Reagan in the state, received campaign contributions from Texans identifying themselves as self-employed workers in areas ranging from agriculture to medicine to education to middle management. Most gave only small amounts—$5 to $20, typically. Some went

Ronald Reagan waves his hat while riding in a horse-drawn wagon during a
Republican rally in Dallas. Reagan made frequent appearances in Texas throughout the 1970s. (Courtesy of the *Dallas Morning News*)

further, contributing advice along with money. In 1975, one Texan proclaimed that he was so disgusted with the "liberal decline" of America that
he was ready to leave the country, but not before he attempted to fight for
conservative causes through the donation of 10 percent of the earnings from
his small business, apparently his tithe to the growing church of Reagan.[24]

Reagan also attracted a substantial following among Texas hunters and
weapons enthusiasts. In September 1975, *Guns & Ammo Magazine* published an article lauding Reagan's record on Second Amendment rights and
reminding readers that "when dictators come to power the first thing they
do is take away people's weapons." Guns ensure, the article continues, "that
the people are the equal of their government whenever that government
forgets it is servant and not master of the governed."[25] Though edgy, such
language paralleled Reagan's rhetoric of individualism and smaller government. In the aftermath of the *Guns & Ammo* article, Reagan received a
wave of letters from Texans pledging their support. Many closed their letters with sentiments such as "You are in our prayers" and "We are praying
for you."[26]

With a packed speaking calendar, statewide radio exposure, and the
momentum of a grass roots increasingly mobilized by social issues, Ronald
Reagan, who seemed to speak to conservatives on the right side of every
issue, found that Texas was, by 1976, ripe for him. There was one problem
for Reagan in Texas, however; while the state leaders valued his contributions to Republican coffers and respectability, most did not value his potential candidacy for president. In Reagan's candidacy, state GOP leaders, ever
cognizant of the quest to earn legitimate second-party status, feared a repeat
of Goldwater's 1964 debacle. For these leaders, avoiding this fate meant
supporting the moderate and incumbent Gerald Ford rather than the maverick westerner with the brazen rhetoric and grassroots following. Clearly,
most state GOP leaders failed to understand something crucially important. Texans' partisan loyalties had been loosened since 1964, while persistent antipathy toward extremism made criticisms against liberals, who
increasingly seemed out of touch with mainstream America, a more powerful political weapon.

The Battle That Transformed Texas Politics

The 1976 Republican presidential primary was a watershed event in the
political history of Texas. For state Republican leaders loyal to the national
party, choosing between a popular maverick and a sitting president presented a delicate decision. Backing Ford was the expected play for Texas

party regulars, despite the fact that many of these leaders personally favored Reagan and treasured the voting power of Reagan's followers. Within this context, intraparty factionalism was personified in 1976 through the campaigns of easily recognizable and identifiable figures, an aspect of modern politics that, in the coming years, grew more important. As the emerging icon of populist conservatism, Reagan served as a catalyst for the eventual coalescence of conservative factions under a Texas Republican tent that unified social conservatives and libertarians under a banner of antiliberalism and modern anticommunism.[27]

Reagan operated as a catalyst in this process not only because he managed to exude a confidence and optimism that escaped many politicians during the dreary 1970s, but also because his image was crafted in such a way as to simultaneously appeal to these disparate conservative factions without contradiction. The growing importance of broadcast media, television in particular, added a dimension to the state and national political culture that was tailor-made for a former Hollywood actor.[28] Reagan's image as a citizen-candidate and frontier individualist was enhanced by campaign strategists, who labored to contrast that image with Ford's stiff and charmless demeanor, exploiting, as well, the perception that Ford was a moderate and untrustworthy tool of the corrupt Nixon and the liberal northeastern establishment. Ford struggled to deflect rumors that he had conspired with Nixon, negotiating his way to the vice presidency and ultimately the presidency in exchange for a pardon. Whereas cynicism, suspicion, and indifference typically characterized Texans' response to Ford, Reagan was consistently viewed as affable, positive, and honest. In fact, Reagan scored more points with Texas conservatives on the issue of honesty in government than he did with any other issue. Reagan even used this issue to revive the public's fear of communist subversion, arguing that under Ford's watch the Soviet Union had increased its use of spies in American intelligence agencies.[29] Reagan's ability to turn the public's suspicion and distrust of government into an advantage was an ironic twist on Watergate's immediate political ramifications.[30]

Two specific decisions in 1975 undermined Ford's image in Texas and contributed to the consolidation of Reagan's growing support. The first of these episodes involved a controversy between factions of the state GOP caused by Ford's appointment of W. J. Usery Jr. as national director of the Federal Mediation and Conciliation Service. Usery's appointment to this post was immediately met with disdain among key Texas conservatives, Ray Barnhart in particular. In August 1975, as chairman of the Harris County Republican Party, Barnhart demanded of both John Tower and

Ford that Usery be removed from his post. Barnhart's demand, which was initiated in cooperation with county Republican parties across the state, was based on the opinion that Usery's call to extend collective bargaining rights to government employees threatened the economic climate in Texas, which by 1975 was considered the most vibrant in the country. Barnhart believed that Ford's endorsement of Usery would be construed as an endorsement of "big labor" and would destroy the president's chances of carrying Texas in 1976.[31] Barnhart even threatened to ensure Ford's defeat in Texas during the general election unless the president removed Usery from the post. Usery, who had served in the Kennedy, Johnson, and Nixon administrations, was not removed, and Barnhart's displeasure with Ford and the Republican Party grew. The fractious exchange between Barnhart, Tower, and Ford was an early but clear warning that divisions between the administration and conservatives in Texas were unlikely to be resolved.[32]

The second decision that undermined Ford's support among Texas conservatives was his plan to close Webb Air Force Base in Big Spring, a small community in West Texas. Big Spring residents were extremely proud of Webb Air Force Base and feared the economic impact that closure would have on their community. Webb Air Force Base was in the midst of a $2 million renovation campaign, designed primarily to upgrade the dormitory and living conditions on base, when Ford's closure decision was announced. Although the base had enjoyed the highest number of clear weather days and boasted the greatest number of flying hours of all bases in the Air Training Command in 1975, Ford chose to close Webb on the basis of its outdated facilities and the fact that it had only two runways, whereas most other air force bases had three. In his decision, Ford also cited urban encroachment in the Big Spring area as contributing to logistical and economic problems that made continued operations at the base untenable. These rationales outraged Big Spring and other West Texas citizens who saw Ford as disingenuous and unfair. Big Spring residents also viewed Ford's decision as a reflection of the president's fundamental misunderstanding of the area's economy. In the coming months, grassroots volunteers working for Texas Citizens for Reagan portrayed Ford's decision as an indication that the president was out of touch with average Texans and could not be trusted to keep the state's economic interests in mind.[33]

Despite Ford's unpopularity in Texas due to these and other decisions, and despite Reagan's growing rock-star status during the same time, the early months of 1976 were not kind to Reagan's national campaign. In primary after primary, Ford used the power of the national party to discredit Reagan's challenge and take command of the race for the GOP nomination. The Texas Republican primary, scheduled for May 1, appeared headed for irrelevancy until Reagan finally won a dramatic victory in the North Carolina primary on March 23. Reagan could credit the win in North Carolina to Jesse Helms's influential political machine there. Of more specific benefit, however, was Helms's ability to raise issues like the proposed Panama Canal treaties, whereby the United States would eventually relinquish sovereignty over the vast Central American shipping waterway, as a channel for communicating Ford's weakness, moderation, and inability to directly meet the needs of America. Without Helms and the North Carolina primary, the Texas primary would not have mattered. With renewed momentum nationally, Reagan approached April with the Texas primary in view and Ford's image as a strong and capable leader severely undermined.

One of the first major battles fought between Ford and Reagan in Texas was for the endorsement of the man *Texas Monthly* referred to in April of 1976 as "THE man in Texas," John Connally.[34] Though he had only narrowly escaped the stain of scandal and corruption that so powerfully gripped a host of other Nixon administration officials, Connally was, in 1976, still a preeminent power broker in Texas. For Connally, the competitive courtship was a boost to his national credentials. As Ford and Reagan lobbied Connally for an endorsement, the former Texas governor coyly played hard to get, instead using his high profile to establish himself as a potential Republican presidential nominee for 1980.[35]

Throughout April, Connally refused to endorse either candidate. Press coverage afforded Connally opportunities to reestablish bipartisan credibility by criticizing establishment politics and declining ethics. He positioned himself as a noncandidate voice of reason, seeking to save the GOP nationally and popularize it in Texas.[36] Connally also tapped into the reservoir of antiliberal and antigovernment hostility, speaking often of the need to "clean up" the incompetence and corruption that plagued Washington. Offering no endorsement, nor any specifics on how to solve America's ills, Connally's message nonetheless resonated with those drawn to Reagan's criticisms of "big government."[37]

Evidence suggests that Ford coveted Connally's endorsement more than Reagan did, to the point that Ford often appeared desperate. Ford was even rumored to have offered Connally an appointment as secretary of State in exchange for an endorsement. Ford's infatuation was rooted in polls conducted less than a month prior to the election that indicated that a Connally endorsement would result in a 29 percent jump in the president's pledged support in Texas.[38] Though postelection analysis contradicted these earlier reports, revealing that Connally's endorsement would not have swayed voters to the extent that Ford thought, the courtship reveals much. For many conservative Texans, Connally represented the heritage and pride of Democrats and the principled conservatism that many in the state increasingly valued above partisan loyalty. As Connally stood at the forefront of partisan realignment in Texas, his role in the 1976 Republican primary reflected the significance of ideology and public perception not only in the minds of voters, but in the minds of candidates seeking to align themselves with certain individuals and images.[39]

While Ford tried to outduel Reagan for Connally's support, most Texas Republican leaders continued to back Ford, primarily out of loyalty to the national establishment and fear that Reagan could be a setback, as Goldwater had been twelve years earlier. Yet, state leaders' support of Ford gave credence to the perception of Reagan and his backers as antiestablishment, populist mavericks. Tensions between party regulars and Reagan's grass roots mounted that spring when twenty-seven members of the GOP's executive committee defiantly began to provide financial support to Reagan's chief grassroots operation in the state, the Texas Citizens for Reagan (TCR).[40]

TCR chapters were supervised by Ernest Angelo Jr. and Ray Barnhart, who vowed to make good on the threats he had issued Ford as a result of the Usery incident the previous year. Angelo and Barnhart took directives from Reagan's Texas campaign chairman Ron Dear, who understood that divisions between Texas GOP leaders were, by reinforcing Reagan's antiestablishment, maverick image, ironically fueling his candidate's support. By melding an organized grassroots organization with the leadership of a national campaign, Dear, Angelo, and Barnhart encouraged that maverick image and began describing their support for Reagan as part of a renegade political campaign that spoke to the souls of thousands of disaffected Texas conservatives who no longer wished to identify themselves with the establishment politics of either party.[41]

Thus in 1976, party elders who feared a repeat of 1964 and, as a result, supported Ford over Reagan under the banner of party unification, actually became the target of conservatives' antiestablishment ire. The division between the Texas Republican establishment and the Reagan grass roots can also be viewed through the lens of antiliberalism. Illustrating the power of connecting icons with philosophies, TCR undermined Ford's commitment to conservatism by invoking the names of moderate administration officials like Nelson Rockefeller, Elliott Richardson, Bill Scranton, and others whose reputations in Texas were as "liberal appeasers" and "conservative turncoats."[42]

Partially explained by his infatuation with receiving Connally's endorsement, Ford's struggles in Texas can also be blamed on inaccurate polling and research. As early as 1975, Ford's campaign became convinced that businessmen, particularly in the Texas oil industry, would stay loyal to the Democratic Party and not be a factor in the GOP primary. Ford, therefore, allowed Reagan to court the state's business community through a language of free-market capitalism and deregulation. Ford, on the other hand, overestimated his appeal to moderate Texans. Ford believed that most Texas Republicans were new arrivals, having migrated from the more moderate North in search of jobs in the thriving Sun Belt economy. Though this was partially true, Ford's belief that such Republicans would reject Reagan in Texas was flawed.[43] Ford's team further misinterpreted its candidate's approval ratings among Texas Republicans, which hovered in the low 70s, as a positive. Dismissing numbers that showed 30 percent of Texas Republicans disapproving of Ford's performance in the White House, Ford's team rested upon a belief that "New Texans" who had flocked to the Sun Belt during the oil boom would support the president, while businessmen would vote Democrat. Ford strategists were wrong on both counts.[44]

These same miscalculations nearly destroyed John Tower's career. By April 1976, Tower's signature, indicative of his leadership in Ford's Texas campaign, appeared at the bottom of virtually every piece of direct mail sent to Texas voters on behalf of the President Ford Committee. Tower's subservience to Ford in 1976 exemplifies the Texas GOP leadership's myopic view of party growth and the emerging conservative grass roots.[45]

Tower's decision seems odd, considering his recent political history. Before casting his lot with Ford, Tower, a committed conservative who as recently as 1966 had benefited from aligning his campaign with Reagan, advised John Sears, Reagan's national campaign manager, to create a vision for Reagan's campaign in Texas that quickly became a blueprint for conservative Texas politics. "Whatever the issue," Tower told Sears, "Governor Reagan should be portrayed as the courageous helmsman who can take command of a ship of state drifting aimlessly on stormy seas, cast overboard villains who cut the anchor cable, and, after consulting the moral compass prepared by our forefathers, sail the ship confidently forward to new and brighter horizons." Tower continued: "By making himself a proud and unapologetic spokesman for traditional middle class values, Governor Reagan

can win support from voters not wildly excited about Republican economics. He should make it clear he believes in God and that—Betty Ford to the
contrary notwithstanding—that the Ten Commandments have not yet
been repealed. He should praise honesty, thrift, and the work ethic, wax
rhapsodic about family life, condemn 'liberated' lifestyles, and object
strenuously to liberal affronts to Christian morality in textbooks, television,
etc." Tower added a concise capstone to his advice: "Governor Reagan
should direct his rhetorical fire at the Four Horsemen of the Liberal Apoca-
lypse . . . Big Government, Big Labor, Big Business and Big Media—who
have ridden roughshod over the political and economic liberties of the common man." Tower's advice speaks volumes to the senator's ability to tap into
the conservative mindset in Texas. Yet Tower was ultimately victimized by
this mindset because he endorsed Ford over Reagan when the choice seemed
to be between party respectability and steady growth versus the momentum
of a grassroots movement that seemed a replay of Goldwater's from 1964.
By endorsing Ford over Reagan in 1976, Tower unwittingly positioned
himself as a villain standing in the way of Texas conservatives' new hero.[46]

Tower's stature in Texas was further diminished when Reagan launched
an assault on both his and Ford's honesty. Throughout the Texas campaign,
Reagan, who privately belittled Tower's height during meetings and in
memos to staff (Tower stood approximately five feet five) and undermined
the senator's respect even among his own volunteers, hammered Tower as
often as he did Ford. Reagan labeled Tower a "flip-flopper" for his decisions
to reverse course on issues like immigration, a move motivated by the need
to align himself more accurately with Ford. Throughout April, TCR distributed brochures and ran advertisements citing numerous examples of
Ford's and Tower's dishonesty and inconsistency.[47]

Reagan's ability to connect conservative Republicanism with mainstream Texas values was a reflection of his political skill and charm as well
as his ability to contrast his agenda with both moderates and liberals, neither of whom, he argued, had the integrity or fortitude to lead the country
where it ought to be led. Reagan's popularity in 1976 forced many conservative Democrats to scramble as emerging GOP competition threatened
the status quo of state establishment politics. Democratic congressman
George Mahon, for instance, faced the toughest reelection campaign of his
life in 1976 when his Republican opponent, Jim Reese, staged a campaign
based almost exclusively on photographs of him and Reagan shaking hands,
accompanied by captions detailing his anti-Washington stand and promise
to cut government spending. Reese rarely mentioned Mahon in his campaign, though when he did he associated Mahon with the liberalism of the

national Democratic Party. Mahon, therefore, ran his entire reelection campaign not on the basis of his forty-two years of experience in Washington, but rather his experience as a Sunday school teacher at a Lubbock United Methodist Church, his advocacy of the death penalty, and calls for tougher crime laws and the elimination of federal welfare programs. Still, Reese took 45 percent of the vote against Mahon that November, the largest percentage ever won by any candidate opposing Mahon. Candidates across Texas used a similar combination of images and platform points to enhance their status with rural and urban conservatives of both traditionalist and libertarian persuasions.[48]

TCR also made great strides in attracting support in East Texas, traditionally the most Democratic of Democratic strongholds. In particular, TCR made concerted efforts to attract rural Texas Baptists who had long distrusted Republicans as the party of the northeastern establishment. National issues like abortion, homosexuality, and the Equal Rights Amendment emboldened the political activism of many Texas Baptists. Reagan's success in 1976 in using religion to his political advantage inspired many local conservatives, across the state and from both parties, to do the same.[49]

As local candidates began to employ Reaganesque qualities in their own campaigns, the image of "Reagan the Crusader" remained Republicans' most effective weapon in the fight to win conservative support in East Texas. In the only region of Texas ever to show George Wallace any significant support, Reagan slowly undermined some of the state's fiercest Democratic loyalties by bridging decades-old paranoia about moral decline with stereotypically patriotic exaltations of the free market. The East Texas economy, less diversified than other parts of the state, was still dominated by oil in 1976—as it had been for decades. More than 80 percent of the oil used by the Allied forces in World War II had been supplied by East Texas oil fields, a fact of which the citizens of the region were quite proud. Before Reagan made campaign stops in East Texas, during which his assault on Ford was based on crime and morality, Reagan campaign volunteers peppered the region with literature denouncing Ford as responsible for the "worst Energy Legislation in History" and the "total mess" of welfare, whereby the American principle of an "honest day's work for a day's pay" was being destroyed. This literature summarized Ford's leadership in the sarcastic charge that the commander in chief had been "infected with Potomac Water on the brain."[50]

Painting Ford as anathema to the East Texas economy made the portrayal of Ford as a social liberal more potent. During East Texas campaign stops, Reagan attacked Betty Ford for televised comments in which the

First Lady professed a belief that premarital sex was "okay." Reagan championed his wife, Nancy, as a better First Lady—a housewife, mother, and
strong supporter of her husband—womanly virtue personified. The facts
that Nancy was Reagan's second wife and that the couple's first child had
been born only seven months into their marriage were never used by Ford
as weapons to undermine Reagan's credibility on issues of tradition, morality, and social conservatism. Neither did Ford use Reagan's sporadic church
attendance against him. Rather, the battlefield of social values was forfeited
to Reagan without a fight.[51]

Ford was also placed on the defensive in Texas when he signed an ex-
tension of the Voting Rights Act that included sanctions against Texas that
did not apply to most other states. When Ford attempted to justify the
Texas provisions of the act, Reagan supporters in San Antonio organized a
protest in which the president was denounced for leading a "new wave of
carpetbaggers" to "look over the shoulder of your local officials," while trying to establish "Reconstruction, just as in 1865." For many Texas conservatives, regardless of partisan affiliation, Reagan captured a sense of both
rebellion and crusade, allowing many to reembrace an ideology of smaller
government, individual rights, Christian ethics, and a nostalgic American
past that no longer seemed extreme.[52]

Foreign policy further bolstered Reagan's reputation in Texas and, at
the same time, reinforced anticommunism and national security as major
tenets of modern conservatism. Reagan's handlers used a variety of foreign
policy issues to paint Ford as weak. Reagan couched Ford's policy toward
decolonization in Africa as well as his poor diplomatic relations with An-
gola and Cuba as weaknesses in the broader cold war. Reagan also stressed
that the United States had, in the age of détente, become a "second-rate
military power." Ford's credibility as a cold warrior was further undermined
on April 20 when reports were leaked from the Pentagon that indicated
Ford was waffling on a pledge to expand the navy by either five hundred or
six hundred ships, and that he had decided to wait until after the Texas
primary to make his decision. Reagan intimated that, for Ford, a loss in
Texas would mean a greater commitment to national defense, while a win
would mean that no such move was necessary. Ford appeared to be playing
politics with national security.[53]

Even Ford's response to these critiques worked to Reagan's advantage.
The more Ford cited complex statistical references of tonnage figures and
firepower comparisons, the more Reagan's emotional plea for unquestioned
military supremacy resonated in Texas. While campaigning in San Antonio, Ford equivocated, admitting that even if the United States did fall be-

hind the Soviets militarily, America's secure borders limited the need for increased military might.[54] Ford's muddled explanation contrasted to Reagan's more marketable call for increased military might and complemented criticisms of Henry Kissinger and the very concept of détente.[55] In 1964, Barry Goldwater's anticommunism was portrayed and subsequently seen in Texas as extreme and dangerous. In 1976, as Reagan warned Texans of an impending "World War III" with the Soviet Union and the potential that, under Ford, America's military would not be prepared, he was, thanks to a far more effective campaign—one that prioritized image—viewed as strong rather than extreme.[56]

As had been the case in North Carolina, the Panama Canal treaties provided Reagan with another perfect opportunity to win points as a hawkish defender of America's cold war interests. Negotiations for the transfer of sovereignty over the Panama Canal had been well under way prior to 1976, but Reagan's version of the issue made it appear that the president was backpedaling on his promise never to renegotiate sovereign American territory. Ford responded to Reagan's challenges by trying to use the issue to label Reagan as irresponsible and extreme. More often than not, however, he found himself, rather than Reagan, on the defensive for potentially destabilizing Latin America and opening the door for increased communist influence in the Western Hemisphere.[57]

On issues such as this, Ford's advisers badly miscalculated the importance of anticommunism and foreign policy to Texas conservatives. In fact, Ford's strategists purposely redirected their campaign away from foreign policy and national defense. This allowed Reagan to monopolize the issue and severely hampered Ford's chances in the state. Conversely, Reagan's campaign capitalized on the state's fervent anticommunism and used conservative demands for strong national defense and tougher foreign policy as a bridge connecting social conservatives and libertarians. These factions may not have agreed on everything, but they typically agreed that the United States was in a life-and-death struggle with communism and that failure in that struggle would almost certainly contribute to the already declining moral fiber of a nation riddled by liberal weakness since the 1960s.[58]

Viewed as a champion of small businesses, farmers, and traditional social values, Reagan had the ability to capture the populist mantra in Texas, and this was among his most impressive political feats in 1976. Ford mistakenly believed that the majority of Texans would consider "populist" only those candidates who attacked big business. Yet, as champion of "average Americans," Reagan brilliantly walked the fine line between his support for

big business—particularly the Texas oil industry—and his appeal to the
state's middle class. By using Ford's policies to his own advantage, Reagan
drew connections between the federal government's energy policy, the
wishes of big oil, and public demands for better economic conditions and
greater freedom from government. In the end, Ford's passive strategy
opened the door for Reagan to redefine populism as a much broader and
more conservative appellation.[59]

Part of Reagan's brilliance on this front was his ability to turn issues
that most affected corporate Texas into issues that affected average citizens.
On divesture, for instance, Reagan opposed the breakup of Texas oil companies, saying that such a move would decrease efficiency, productivity, and
result in higher gas prices for middle-class consumers.[60] Reagan also hammered Ford for his signing of the Energy Policy and Conservation Act
(EPCA), which established price controls on oil companies, a regulatory
measure that fueled the already tense relationship between Texas oil companies and the federal government. In fact, among many Texas oil barons,
particularly those who had become permanent fixtures at GOP fund-raisers,
Ford's signing of the EPCA was viewed as a stab in the back. Reagan attacked Ford's position on the EPCA, positioning himself as the only declared candidate in either party to say that he would have vetoed the legislation. Reagan also focused his objection to the EPCA on three principles
designed to connect the issue to middle-class consumers: (1) price controls
in the United States would increase dependence on foreign sources of oil;
(2) price controls were a disincentive for domestic producers and fundamentally un-American; and (3) price controls conflicted with conservation-
ist goals because fixed prices encouraged, rather than discouraged,
consumption.[61]

Though Ford's popularity in Texas plummeted after signing the EPCA,
his staff foolishly obsessed about the issue to the exclusion of others.[62]
While Ford's internal polls suggested that the EPCA had indeed cost Ford
support in Texas, the numbers clearly indicated that for many Texans,
Ford's signing of the EPCA contributed not solely to fears about divesture
and price control, but also significantly exacerbated broader fears about the
expansion of government into the private sector, the manipulation of economic forces by Washington, and a growing sense that rights were being
seized by the federal government. Ford's shortsightedness was costly.
Rather than understand the Texas political climate as broadly hostile to
government action, Ford mistook his unpopularity in the state as the direct
and sole result of the EPCA.[63]

On issue after issue and perception after perception, Reagan bested Ford in Texas. Reagan played the role of conservative hero in a state built upon the platitudes of independence, individualism, and freedom. Throughout April, Reagan's campaign appearances in Texas consistently outdrew Ford's. Reagan typically appeared before large gatherings of enthusiastic supporters and spoke about putting God back into public schools, eliminating wasteful research grants to higher education institutions, improving law enforcement, abolishing busing, and reversing Ford's inept energy policy. Into each topic, Reagan infused antigovernment animus and dire warnings of impending national insecurity. News coverage furthered this momentum, particularly as the media began to cast Reagan as a conservative who transcended partisanship. The public's awareness of this appeal acted as a self-fulfilling prophecy, drawing even larger numbers of undecided conservative Democrats into the Reagan tent.[64]

Reagan also effectively utilized both print and broadcast media to create free publicity through the construction of news events in which he blended a variety of issues and ideological strands into one cohesive conservative message. His radio spots in Texas meshed a broad conservative ethos with issues ranging from busing and property-tax payers' right to send their children to neighborhood schools to the potential industrial shutdown that would result in Texas should Ford's energy policies continue. Reagan also used radio to address farmers and effectively tapped into the state's reservoir of anticommunist fervor, particularly in spots on the evils of the Panama Canal treaties. In each of these spots, voters were reminded not only of why they should vote for Reagan, but how they could do so. "The *only* way to make Governor Reagan president is to vote in the *Republican* primary on Saturday, May 1. For Texas, the choice is clear. Ronald Reagan—the conservative who can *win*." These messages magnified the importance that fomenting a united and coalesced ideological front played in shaping modern conservatism, both nationally and in Texas, while also reinforcing the necessity of partisan realignment.[65]

Reagan's Texas campaign also demonstrated an effective use of targeted advertising among several other interest groups. He limited advertising spots directly focused on forced busing to Dallas, Houston, and San Antonio. He ran advertisements in Houston, Big Spring, San Antonio, and Corpus Christi that dealt exclusively with Ford's decision to close a series of air force bases in Texas, tied in with issues of national security. In San Antonio, Houston, Austin, and other parts of the Rio Grande Valley, the Reagan campaign purchased spots to discuss excessive utility rate increases.

Gulf Port cities were targeted with spots dealing with the renegotiations of the Panama Canal treaties, while Houston, Dallas, and San Antonio were targeted for messages on the impact of illegal Mexican immigrants on the local job market. Reagan's statewide spots dealt with the broader ideological conservatism being used to cast a wide net over all such issues. Each of these advertisements emphasized antibureaucracy, help for small business owners, what conservatives in Texas referred to as the difference between "Gun Criminal Control and Gun Control," and pornography's impact on family values and tradition.[66]

The efforts of both candidates' campaigns culminated on May 1, 1976, when Texas voters went to the polls in record numbers. Turnout was so high that several polling locations ran out of Republican ballots by midafternoon.[67] When the votes were tallied, Reagan had won an astounding 67 percent of the vote, swept every district, and claimed every delegate. Ford's strategists had calculated that they would need 140,000 votes to overcome Reagan's appeal among conservative Democrats. Ford received 152,022 votes—exceeding his goal by more than 12,000.[68] However, the Ford campaign grossly underestimated the potential Republican turnout in Texas, which gave Reagan over 310,000 votes. Notably, postelection analysis showed that Reagan would still have defeated Ford by more than 58,000 votes even without a single Democratic crossover vote. It was a massive and overwhelming rejection of Ford and a simultaneous embrace of Reagan.[69]

The Reagan Afterglow

For the next several months, Reagan and Ford continued to battle for the GOP nomination in primaries across the country. That August, Ford, after a long national struggle, narrowly captured the nomination at the Republican National Convention in Kansas City. Nonetheless, Reagan's decisive victory in Texas had a profound and lasting impact on the resolution of intraparty factionalism in that state—a shift driven by the influx of grassroots support for Reagan and conservative causes that seemed to question the authority of established political power. Among grassroots conservatives in Texas, Reagan personified what Jim Hightower would refer to in 1980 as the "disgruntled maverick"—an iconic figure of heroic frontierism that Texans could identify with and depend upon to stand up for the little guy in the fight against bureaucracy and big government. By encouraging initiative, self-reliance, individual freedom, and independence from government, Reagan tapped into the state's conservative impulse and then fueled its expansion.[70] The 1976 primary became the turning point for partisan and ideological realignment in Texas and forced state Republicans to ultimately embrace "Reagan Republicanism" as the means by which significant two-party realignment would occur.[71]

Reagan's support among the Texas grass roots, especially after his victory in the state, was also grounded in the visceral. One couple in Lewisville, a Dallas suburb, wrote to Reagan that they appreciated being treated as "intelligent" and as "winners"—not as "stupid losers," as "elitist liberals" tended to treat them.[72] Reagan's victory served as a justification for their conservative values—a legitimizing force that gave credence to the righteous indignation many felt toward Washington and establishment politics. Small-sum campaign contributions continued to pour into Reagan's coffers from Texans well after May. Many contributions were accompanied with exhortations to continue his "crusade for conservatism"—also frequently defined as "American values." One pastor in Galveston commented that he could not vote for Ford because Ford was a liberal. For this pastor, the "machinery" of partisan politics snuffed out his belief that change could be effected against the "Democratic Party and the overwhelming liberal Washington establishment."[73]

The sentiment expressed in this overflow of letters and contributions suggests much about the state of party politics in Texas and the ideological associations voters made between established leaders and parties. One Texan, comparing Reagan to Franklin Roosevelt, explained his support for Reagan this way: "Last May 1, I voted Republican for the first time in my life. The reason? I am sick and tired of 'party politics,' of which the Democratic Party has more than enough. Now that I have switched, I am beginning to see the same sort of thing from 'the fathers' of the GOP. Take a lesson from the Democrats, don't put political machinery ahead of what is best for the people. If the popular vote is behind a particular man, then put the party behind the man."[74] A Wichita Falls man wrote to Reagan that Texans like him were "sick, sick, sick and disenchanted with the whole picture in Washington. We want someone up there with the guts to buck the establishment, clean house and make a really honest effort to reinstate an old-fashioned honorable government for the people."[75] Other Texas conservatives likened Reagan's cause to the protection of America from the "gluttony, degradation, and pleasure-seeking that destroyed the Roman Empire."[76] These Texans frequently prioritized social issues like abortion over high taxes and government bureaucracy, but did not refrain from including those targets in their secondary attacks.[77]

Texas conservatives often spoke of liberalism and "the establishment" as synonymous—referring regularly to the "liberal establishment" or the "liberal Washington establishment." Many came to the GOP with a pre-conceived notion that the "establishment" of both parties—both state and federal—was inherently "liberal." Such views frequently reflected a belief that Reagan was the antithesis of establishment politics. This view was another crucial stepping-stone in the process toward partisan realignment in Texas. Conservatives were initially reluctant to embrace the GOP, but could do so with less guilt if the man they were placing their trust in appeared to be just as hostile to established party leadership as they were.[78]

Coinciding with antiestablishment animosity in Texas was a pervasive feeling that effective government and family traditions were inextricably connected. On July 6, Reagan gave a nationally televised speech in which he focused on the evils of "intrusive government." He used words like "domineering" and "dictatorial" to describe the culture of Washington and told his audience that he was "not a politician by profession." "I am a citizen," Reagan asserted, "who decided I had to be personally involved in order to stand up for my own values and beliefs." Reagan made direct appeals to Democrats, saying that he too had once been a Democrat, but the time came when he had to put his personal values ahead of party loyalty. "Vote not for a label," Reagan exhorted, "but for values you faithfully believe in."[79] One couple from San Antonio responded to the speech in a letter: "God bless you for your stand on moral issues. . . . Your talk on July 6, was inspirational, and gave the majority of the American people, (who we sincerely believe are honest and decent and believe in the fundamental values you spoke of) a ray of hope that at least they were being courageously and honestly represented by someone (the only candidate it seems) who sees and points out the extreme danger of the crumbling of the American family. Without this, our society can never endure."[80] Another supporter from Houston understood Reagan's appeal this way: "Mr. and Mrs. Public want straight talk from the shoulder and want somebody to call a spade, a spade. They understand and want tough talk from a contender and they want an 'Old Time Revival.'"[81] If nothing else, most Reagan supporters had one thing in common: they openly vowed to oppose Ford in November. Different conservatives reacted to the campaigns of 1976 in different ways, but significant partisan realignment in Texas first manifested as loyalty to Reagan, not to Republicans.[82]

At least three other conclusions can be drawn from Texans' response to Reagan's 1976 campaign. First, Reagan's persona bridged a gap between local politics and national issues. Many conservative Texans embraced Reagan because they believed he stood for their values. Though many of these values came to be defined by issues that transcended local issues, Reagan's rhetoric effectively showed how such issues threatened to affect individual neighborhoods, homes, and families. Second, Reagan's victory in Texas was so overwhelming that no conservative in the state could overlook it as an indicator of a changing political climate. In the coming years, Texas Republican leaders came to realize that "Reaganism" was the path toward a two-party state. Third, Reagan's supporters in Texas rejected Ford in 1976 as part of a liberal establishment that had controlling interests in both the Democratic and Republican parties. These populist conservatives charged Ford with ignoring their values from the moment Nixon resigned, and many cited the selection of Nelson Rockefeller to the vice presidency as evidence that Ford (and Ford's GOP) was a tool of the northeastern establishment. It was clear, in large part because of the transformative nature of the 1976 campaigns, that populist conservatism was on the rise and that the Republican Party had gained viability in large part because of Reagan. By the fall of 1976, with Reagan out of the picture, another populist emerged to effectively slay the dragon of the northeastern establishment.[83]

Texans for Jimmy

Though less divisive than the bitter rivalries that plagued the GOP, Democratic factionalism and image management still influenced Texas political culture in 1976. Despite the tumult raging in their rival's camp, Texas Democrats began to fracture that summer, when Jimmy Carter, by then the party's presumptive nominee, used his own campaign's letterhead to advocate the reelection of Calvin Guest as Texas Democratic Party chairman. Guest had been a loyal supporter of both Lloyd Bentsen and Dolph Briscoe, and was not popular among liberals within the state party. Many anti-Guest liberals were furious upon receiving the letter and many threatened to (and some did) revoke their support for Carter as a result.[84] Just days prior to the letter being mailed from Carter campaign headquarters, Texas land commissioner Bob Armstrong, whose leadership in the state party was paramount, publicly announced that he would not support the reelection of Guest to the chairmanship. Armstrong and his supporters were angry and embarrassed that the party's standard-bearer for that year had, without consultation of the Texas membership, endorsed the establishment's choice in opposition to a number of potential liberal options.[85]

The Guest affair was indicative of much underlying disunity. Liberal organizer Billie Carr was particularly angry over Carter's endorsement of Guest and, on behalf of Texas liberals, contacted the Carter campaign to demand an apology. Carr felt obliged to inform Carter that the fight for the state chairmanship had a long history and that the infusion of an "official" endorsement was a major setback on the path toward ideological reconciliation and unity. In August, Hamilton Jordan, overwhelmed with letters from Texas liberals voicing their displeasure over Carter's "butting in" to state issues, issued an apology to the Texas Democratic delegation. At the same time, he blamed the use of Carter-Mondale letterhead for the endorsement of Guest as a mistake made by campaign aide Frank Moore and announced Carter's neutrality in the election of a new Texas Democratic Party chairman.[86]

Despite Carter's unwelcome intrusion into state Democratic politics that summer, Texas still eventually cast its electoral lot with the peanut farmer from Georgia when the November election finally rolled around. The Democrats' ability to win in Texas in 1976 can be attributed to several things, not the least of which was that, both prior to and during the 1976 campaigns, Jimmy Carter defined himself in ways that resonated with Reagan backers. Carter marketed himself as a self-professed "born-again Christian," and as new political blood, capable of helping the nation start afresh after a demoralizing decade of scandal and war. Carter stressed patriotism, open and honest leadership, an end to lies and division, and reflected hostility toward the "Washington establishment."[87]

Carter's self-definition was not, however, constructed without difficulty. Carter decided prior to the close of primary season that, if his opponent was Ford, he would run against Washington—calling himself an outsider and Ford part of the "old guard" corrupt establishment. Carter feared, however, entering a popularity contest against Reagan, whose similar message had drawn thousands of supporters across the country, including the South and especially in Texas. Once Reagan was removed from the picture, Carter's strategy became clearer and much easier to implement.[88]

As Texas was a critical swing state, Ford's failures there significantly contributed to his doomed national campaign. Those failures were rooted in his loss to Reagan in the primary. During that campaign, Ford failed to convince Texas conservatives that he shared their animosity toward big government or that he shared their moral, religious, and social values. Part of this failure can be blamed on the reality that Ford did not, in fact, share that penchant for populist conservatism. In another sense, Ford's failure was tied to his ineffective advertising and public relations strategy—one that missed opportunities to capitalize on Carter's mistakes, much as it failed to capitalize on Reagan's. For example, Carter's famed interview with *Playboy* magazine, in which the Democratic nominee—quoting Christ's Sermon on the Mount—claimed that if the standard for adultery in God's eyes was mere lust, then he was an adulterer, infuriated conservative Democrats, including the influential pastor of the First Baptist Church of Dallas, W. A. Criswell. Christians' hostile response to Carter's interview had less to do with Carter's interpretation of scripture than with his judgment in granting an interview to what they considered a pornographic magazine. Criswell subsequently endorsed Ford. Also problematic for Carter was the reaction to the *Playboy* article among South Texas Hispanics. Less well known from the *Playboy* article was Carter's characterization of Lyndon Johnson as a "liar" on par with Nixon. For many Texas minorities, that characterization was disturbing and disagreeable. The fact that the Hispanic communities were also predominantly Catholic and openly disapproving of *Playboy* made the medium just as unsettling as the message.[89] Carter's relationship with Texas Hispanics was worsened by perceptions that the Democratic nominee was ignoring the community, though Ford once again failed to capitalize on that perception and made virtually no significant appeal to the state's Hispanic community. In fact, in both cases, Carter's weaknesses coming out of the *Playboy* interview, though initially detrimental, had no significant impact in Texas largely thanks to Ford's ignorance toward those issues.[90]

As critical to Carter's success as his ability to dodge such bullets was his ability to construct and stay on a populist message. Carter is well remembered for promising that he would "never lie," but was discouraged from making that his predominant message because, his strategy team argued, the focus would then be on his honesty rather than his opponents' dishonesty. Instead, his speeches deployed phrases like "Republican mess," or simply "Republican" in an effort to evoke deeply rooted animosities toward Ford, Nixon, and the GOP in general. His strategists further made it a point to include each of the following words or phrases in the vast majority of Carter's public speeches and Q&A sessions: "new," "fresh," "leadership," "unity," "hope and progress," "trust and confidence," and "mistakes of the Washington establishment." It was the final phrase that rang most true in Texas. Antigovernment sentiment worked to Carter's advantage during the 1976 general election.[91]

At the same time, Carter desperately tried to avoid being labeled. He did not want to make conservatism or liberalism an issue in the campaign in large part because he acknowledged it as a losing game. Carter's biggest obstacle in meeting this objective was his selection of a running mate. Walter Mondale's liberalism was not well received in Texas, and Carter struggled to redirect pointed questions regarding his running mate's political ideology.[92] Texas governor Dolph Briscoe, who had openly refused to even be seen with George McGovern in 1972, announced his endorsement of Carter in May, though his public enthusiasm was tempered when Mondale was selected as running mate.[93] When Mondale's voting record became an issue, as it did regularly on the issues of abortion and gun control, Carter stressed his own stand on the issues—quickly countering that he was personally opposed to both.[94]

Some issues, however, were simply too sensitive for Carter to redirect or manipulate. He chose to empathize with the antibusing crowd in East Texas, for instance, and often answered questions on the issue by recounting all the reasons why someone might oppose busing without resorting to racist motives. At the same time, however, Carter refused to dilute the importance of civil rights or his commitment to "breaking down all barriers."[95] Even more controversial than busing was Carter's support for an amendment to the 1964 Civil Rights Act that would extend civil rights to homosexuals. Carter also openly supported the pro-gay platform of the National Women's Agenda. Under fire in Texas and other parts of the "Bible Belt" for his receptivity to gay rights, Carter was routinely forced to come out against allowing gays in the military for what he justified as "national security reasons associated with potential blackmail."[96]

On November 2, 1976, Carter defeated Ford in Texas by a margin of 51–48 percent, part of a close but triumphant campaign that launched the Georgian into the White House. Running under a mantle of populist moderation, Carter attracted many Reagan conservatives who opposed Ford's establishment credentials and resented the intraparty conflicts that had prevented their candidate from winning the nomination. Those conservatives also embraced the idea of a southerner winning the presidency. Four years later, most of those same conservatives, given a choice between Reagan and Carter, would go in the other direction.

Six weeks prior to Carter's inauguration, pollster Patrick Caddell submitted a report on political strategy in which he made a number of prescient conclusions. "In the end, the decline [in Democratic popularity] in the South that took place in October because ideology was reversed only by regional pride," Caddell wrote. "This has some disturbing implications, however, for the future." Caddell continued, "Conservatives have become a larger and larger block of the electorate," and opined that the Democratic Party was on the brink of being forced to form a new coalition, because its current one was "fading fast." The essence of the report, written for Carter and his top advisers, was the debate surrounding which coalitions to approach and a concern that the party could not win an ideological battle for the public's hearts and minds. Democrats, Caddell asserted, "must transcend ideology" because, for liberals, ideology was a losing game.[97]

Less than two weeks later, Caddell issued a follow-up, at Carter's behest, in which he concluded that the "Democratic Party is in serious national trouble—with a shrinking and ill-defined coalition. We need a new and broader political coalition that can attract new support." The tenor of these reports no doubt seemed strange to many Democrats, still basking in the glow of their successful presidential campaign and the seeming demise of the GOP, which was still languishing in the wake of Watergate and Reagan-induced factionalism. Yet, in places like Texas, where partisan division and rancor could still powerfully manifest even over the issue of a campaign letterhead, the urgency of Caddell's assessment seemed quite relevant.[98]

Meanwhile, intraparty factionalism had destroyed the GOP's efforts to elect a president in 1976. As far as grassroots conservatives were concerned, that factionalism resulted in the party's nomination of the wrong candidate. Reagan's win in Texas exposed these divisions and suggested that partisan realignment might not simply coincide with ideological coalescence, but would actually depend on it. Yet, it was Jimmy Carter who seemed to benefit most directly from the state's political wrangling in 1976. Left without a clear choice between liberalism and conservatism, Texans supported the candidate most closely perceived as the maverick Washington outsider.

Ultimately, if the 1976 campaigns were a springboard for Texas conservatives, then the issues and events in the years leading up to America's next presidential election provided that same grass roots with momentum, direction, purpose, and drive. In the aftermath of 1976, as Texas changed politically, it also evolved demographically, economically, and socially. At play was a reciprocal dynamic whereby economics affected demographics and demographics affected economics, whereby social change motivated political activism and political change encouraged social activism, and whereby partisan realignment became less daunting to an older generation of loyal Democratic Texans, and no obstacle at all to younger Texans or recent migrants.

Chapter 7

The Gathering Storm

Republican Momentum and the Albatross of Jimmy Carter

As it turned out, Jimmy Carter was one of the best friends the Texas Republican Party could have ever asked for. Between 1977 and 1980, Carter, quite unintentionally of course, not only provided the Texas GOP with the context and ammunition it needed to finally achieve viable second-party status, but also helped lay the groundwork for the Lone Star State's future status as a bedrock of national conservative Republicanism. The viability of a Reagan presidency grew during these years, especially when sharply contrasted with the growing perceptions of Carter's weakness and inability to handle the mounting tally of foreign and domestic crises that seemed to threaten America's place in the global sun. This contrast also personified and magnified a related perception in Texas—that the Democratic Party had tied itself to the unattractive and failed visions of modern liberalism. These perceptions, fueled by a mix of national images and real policy debates—including debates over oil, energy, and foreign policy—formed a powerful catalyst for partisan realignment, at least so far as national and statewide campaigns were concerned. By the late 1970s, this storm of activity had brought with it the state's first Republican governor since Reconstruction and permanently altered most Texans' association between political ideology and partisanship.

Energy

Despite the 1978 debut of *Dallas,* CBS's hit television drama that popularly linked that city throughout the coming decade with Texas oil wealth, it was actually Houston that served as the capital of Texas's oil and gas industry in the late 1970s. Built largely on Houston's back, Texas became the nation's undisputed energy hub during the same time. It was a good time to be a Texas oil baron. Oil prices soared in 1978, thanks primarily to the international shock stemming from the shah's ousting in Iran. Subsequent price hikes arising from supply shortages contributed to a boom in the Texas economy, though the oil industry had been expanding for several years prior to 1978. Texas's business-friendly climate attracted industry giants like Exxon, Shell, and Gulf, each of which moved their headquarters to Texas during the 1970s, bringing with them employees from across the nation. At the same time, thousands of Texas companies found niche markets by producing drilling, piping, and mechanical production equipment, parts, and accessories. While oil shocks in 1973 and 1978 contributed to the nation's recession-riddled economy, in Texas oil was truly black gold.[1]

Texas's surging economy stood in stark contrast to the tremors felt in the national economy. After a year and a half of poor presidential relations with Congress and accelerating inflation, interest, and unemployment rates, Carter's national approval rating had fallen fast. Despite Texas's booming economic climate, Carter's popularity in that state slid just as it did in the rest of the nation. In the summer of 1978, with his approval rating in Texas below 40 percent, Carter chose Texas, and Houston specifically, as the launching pad for his renewed discussion on the national energy crisis.[2] It was a risky decision. Because the energy crisis contributed to the proliferation of Texas wealth, potential changes wrought by Carter on the industry worried most oil-vested Houstonians more than inflation or unemployment.[3]

Two specific measures were of particular concern. First, energy-conscious Texans adamantly opposed Carter's support for a Windfall Profits Tax. That tax would have coincided with welcomed price control deregulation, but also would have imposed heavy taxes on profits reaped by production companies above predetermined base prices. Texas oil leaders believed the answer to national energy woes lay not with such excise taxes, but with the increased domestic production they believed would result from deregulation. This had been the Republican position on the issue—and Reagan's position in 1976. Instead, however, Carter stressed conservation and increased importation.[4]

In a study commissioned by the Texas Energy and National Resources Advisory Council, the Interstate Oil Compact Commission concluded that, in Texas, the Windfall Profits Tax would cost state producers an estimated 69.16 million barrels of unproduced oil. The study further projected that the Windfall Profits Tax would cost the state upwards of $2.4 billion in crude oil revenue lost from the closure of a projected 3,385 marginal wells. The potency of this finding was widespread as marginal wells affected the vast majority of Texas oil businesses, not simply the larger and more well-known corporate producers. The study's doomsday scenario forecast the "premature abandonment" of more than 13,000 oil wells nationwide and ten-year losses of 175 million barrels of unproduced oil, with an accompanying monetary loss of $6.13 billion. Needless to say, these forecasts heightened the state's opposition to proposed changes in energy policy.[5]

The second concern to oil-vested Texans was Carter's Fuel Use Act of 1978. This act was designed to push power plants and other major consumers of oil and gas away from those energy sources and toward coal, with the ultimate intention that by 1990, no power plants in the United States would use natural gas. Included in the act was an allocation of $4 billion for a select group of power plants in the Northeast. Texas power plants estimated their cost in capital outlays for this conversion to be in excess of $30 billion. In 1978, the vast majority of the nation's power plants ran on some combination of gas and oil, with Texas being one of the major suppliers. Texans holding natural gas interests were especially concerned that the supplies they had been sitting on for years would go to waste. With half of the state's revenue coming from oil and gas companies, most state political leaders quickly joined the oil industry in denouncing Carter's proposals.[6]

In June 1978, Carter visited Houston, Beaumont, and Fort Worth, delivering speeches almost exclusively focused on energy during a two-day trip. His organizing theme was that America was losing the "energy battle" and that this had dangerous ramifications for the nation's economic and military security. Carter's political advisers were not enthusiastic about their boss's choice of theme. To contextualize a debate on energy as part of a larger battle was to create the image of winners and losers—a game in which Carter was already trailing in Texas, less than two years after barely eking out a win there.[7]

Carter ignored much of the advice he received from his staff on the Texas trip. Carter's staff encouraged him to find a nonpartisan voice on energy, inflation, and national defense and to keep his speeches brief. It further encouraged Carter to stress the cooperative nature of his plan—to link Texas's prosperity to the rest of the country's. Lastly, his staff strongly encouraged Carter to avoid telling Texans that it was time to move beyond oil as a primary energy source. Carter ignored the advice and his speeches in Texas were consequently not well received.[8] Instead, Carter bluntly told audiences of Texas oil barons that the time to move beyond oil and gas had arrived.[9] Not only did Texans with a vested interest in oil and energy production bristle at Carter's suggestions, but the style with which the administration's policies were presented contributed to Republicans' appeal.[10] Some in attendance during the Houston speech on June 23 recoiled at the didactic tone used by Carter, especially as he lectured Texans to "choose patriotism and the national interest over parochialism and self-interest."[11]

Predictably, Texas Republicans capitalized on Carter's failures on the energy issue. For instance, John Tower, whose popularity had dipped since 1976 due to his support for Ford over Reagan, jumped on the anti-Carter bandwagon and publicly committed himself to protecting Texas oil producers.[12] Tower's decision to rally to the side of big oil seemed wise, particularly in view of the mass coverage Reagan's radio diatribes on the subject were already receiving. In several of his syndicated radio commentaries, Reagan, like Carter, asserted that dependence on foreign oil was a national security risk. Unlike Carter, he strongly championed the acceleration of domestic exploration and production.[13] At the same time, by supporting the construction of nuclear power bases, including one in Dallas, Reagan managed to raise the appeal of alternative fuel sources without compromising his popularity. By carefully balancing support for alternative fuel sources and domestic oil drilling, production, and refinement, Republicans like Tower and Reagan seemed ahead of the curve in appealing to the mainstream. These varied responses, ranging from Carter's focus on moving beyond oil to the Republican focus on deregulation and domestic production, contributed to Carter's unpopularity and, in Texas, to the perception that Democratic liberalism was an enemy, not a friend.[14]

Fusing Economics and Social Conservatism

In addition to the popularity of the Republican position on energy, Texans also positively responded to Republicans on more general economic issues, largely because the party skillfully linked multiple economic problems back to Carter and the heavy-handed government that, in their estimation, was stunting the laws of free-market capitalism. For instance, Republicans across Texas adopted Reagan's viewpoint, highlighted in his radio programs, that inflation was a "covert government tax" most affecting those who could least afford it.[15] Conservatives blamed "big government" for hamstringing the market with excessive regulations and rarely missed an opportunity to link that government with incompetence, waste, liberalism, and the northeastern establishment. Those regulations, according to Republicans, were directly causing inflation, which reduced consumer purchasing power. Inflation was then linked to taxes and both were subsequently linked to unemployment.[16] The message had widespread appeal. Republicans even succeeded in attracting support among South Texas Hispanics by linking inflation and recession to welfare and women working outside the home, both sensitive cultural issues in proud and conservative Catholic communities.[17]

Republicans used economic issues to infuse morality and social conservatism into the state's white political culture as well. Connecting family values with the free market was easy in Texas. The megachurch growth of the 1970s, especially in places like suburban Dallas, reinforced a "health, wealth, and prosperity gospel" that justified the fusion for many affluent Texans. Many of those Texans expressed disdain for the secularism of northeastern communities, where, it was assumed, the only interaction between faith and finance stemmed from excessive wealth and guilt. Most of these Texans were confident in the future and in their own goodness and fairness. Their wealth was the result of honest and hard work and, they believed, a blessing from God.[18] Texas Republicans, including a young adviser named Karl Rove, seized upon these perceptions, highlighting the immorality of the liberal Northeast while connecting tangible policy issues, such as Carter's decision to cut guaranteed student loans to students whose parents were middle or upper class, with the image of a Democratic Party that wanted to steal from honest, hard-working Texans in order to subsidize "others."[19]

Political figures like Reagan, Tower, and Carter came to personify much of the state's political culture during the late 1970s, but politicians alone did not spark the growing intensity of evangelical activism that characterized state politics at the close of the decade. In fact, several dynamic religious personalities also put their stamp on the changing Texas political culture. Without question, Texas's most famous churchgoer was also one of the nation's most well-respected men. Though born a North Carolinian, Billy Graham had, in many ways, made Texas home. Since 1953, Graham had been a member of Texas's largest Southern Baptist church, the First Baptist Church of Dallas, whose pastor, W. A. Criswell, was the state's best-known preacher. Graham influenced Sun Belt political culture in a variety of ways, including a policy change regarding host cities for his crusades. Beginning in the mid-1970s, Graham began to select southern and western cities for his crusades more regularly than he had in the past and with greater frequency than he selected cities in other parts of the country. This gave medium-sized cities like Lubbock the opportunity to play host to a Graham Crusade and heightened the city's regional and national profile. The rationale for these decisions was that the Sun Belt offered low-cost production alternatives to the union-dominated labor supply and high production expenses of the Northeast. Nonetheless, Graham's presence in the state magnified the respectability and importance of social issues in Texas and made the state more fertile breeding ground for similar social and religious advances.[20]

Graham was certainly no friend of controversy and when charges broke in 1977 that his evangelistic association had improperly given funds to a Dallas lawyer rather than numerous Christian ministries for which the funds had ostensibly been raised, he repudiated the charges and blamed the media for attacking and misrepresenting the facts of the case. Unlike the most famous member of his congregation, however, W. A. Criswell rarely shied away from controversy. A respected conservative voice, Criswell drew himself into the partisan fray as an increasingly vocal proponent of Republican politics throughout the decade. Also unlike Graham, who had spent time in the 1960s touring with Martin Luther King Jr. advocating a peaceful acceptance of school integration, Criswell's firebrand style offered his affluent congregation a blending of traditional "southern values," economic self-affirmation, and evangelical social conservatism.[21]

Even more lasting in impact than Criswell's sermons was the proliferation of megachurches like Criswell's, which altered the state's traditionally social conservative dynamic. These churches, predominantly located in the growing Sun Belt, earned the description "mega" by their membership totals, which typically exceeded two thousand people during weekend services. However, megachurches were also defined as much by who was attending as by how many were attending. Almost exclusively Protestant, these churches provided suburban communities with a meeting place for expanding neighborhoods comprised of middle- to upper-class, college-educated whites. These churches served suburban enclaves by providing not only spiritual guidance but also intramural sports leagues, social mixers, and a host of other organized events, many of which allowed for the mobilization of like-minded and politically dissatisfied conservatives.[22]

With megachurches expanding just as rapidly as the suburban communities surrounding them, Dallas was becoming a new national hub for Christian ministry. High living costs forced many ministries out of Southern California and several relocated to Texas because of the friendly religious and economic climate. In 1972, Dallas attracted more than one hundred thousand high school and college students to Explo '72, a six-day evangelism training event sponsored by Campus Crusade for Christ and held in the Cotton Bowl. By the late 1970s, thriving Christian organizations like Keith Green's Last Days Ministries, which was, in many ways, a reflection of the relational wave known in the late 1970s as the "Jesus Movement," also came to call the Dallas area home. Building on that momentum, several other national organizations and leading figures, including multiple divisions of Campus Crusade for Christ, Pastor Chuck Swindoll, and the Trinity Broadcasting Network, all relocated to Dallas by the early 1990s.[23]

In addition to attracting national ministries, Dallas was also the base for many homegrown evangelists. Preachers like David Terrell of Fort Worth, for instance, managed to attract a statewide following thanks to widely broadcast radio sermons that warned of impending famine and doom. In 1974, Terrell even persuaded several hundred people to move to the tiny central Texas town of Bangs in an attempt to avoid the corruption of Texas's growing urbanity. The conservative Baptist James Robison also garnered a following during the 1970s. Operating out of suburban Dallas, the youthful and attractive Robison broadcast weekly sermons on fifty television stations nationwide and launched a tour of one-night rallies and stadium revivals, much like Graham's, throughout the state.[24]

Though Dallas dominated religion in much the same way that Houston dominated oil, Texas's largest city was not devoid of popular evangelical influence. Charles and Frances Hunter based their television ministry, *The Happy Hunters,* out of Houston and used that publicity to promote their fourteen books, resulting in a combined total of 4 million copies sold. The subject matter for the Hunters' books ranged from speaking in tongues to weight loss, and their television show was broadcast regularly in most Texas markets. Chris Panos, also of Houston, gained fame in the late 1970s as the "Christian James Bond"—a man who smuggled Bibles into communist countries and organized "spontaneous" crusades in places like India, where he, on more than one occasion, drew crowds of more than one hundred thousand. The success of Panos's ministry also inspired him to market a series of books and tapes on how average people could hold their own evangelistic crusades.[25]

Religious conservatism contributed to a growing dissatisfaction with the moral health of the nation. That dissatisfaction blended nicely with claims that the political process itself had become corrupt and that government was to blame not just for the poor economy but for social problems as well. For many social conservatives, however, issues of gender provided the most noticeable collision point between family values and declining morals. This collision did not go unnoticed by Texas's conservative hierarchy. The courting of feminist activists by the national Democratic Party had long worried many conservative Texas Democrats. In 1972, Texas ratified the Equal Rights Amendment. Each subsequent year between 1973 and 1977, members of the Texas legislature initiated proceedings designed to rescind that ratification, a move premised on the notion that radical feminism had infiltrated the party and threatened to extend the influence of the ERA beyond its originally stated intent.[26]

Texans' awareness of a gendered threat to the social order was heightened when Houston was chosen as host city for the 1977 National Women's Conference. During the four-day event, chaired by Bella Abzug, a prominent New York women's activist and future Carter appointee to the National Advisory Committee on Women, and attended by Rosalynn Carter, Lady Bird Johnson, Betty Ford, Jean Stapleton, Billie Jean King, and Margaret Mead, delegates passed an agenda that included planks on abortion, the ERA, and gay rights. Among many feminists, the simple evocation of "Houston" would connote a spirit of cooperation and progress for years to come.[27]

Regardless of feminists' popular memory, however, the conference was hardly a united front. In fact, between 15 and 20 percent of the delegates in attendance voted against one or more of the planks mentioned above.[28] Conservative antifeminists gained their most powerful recognition not by dissenting within the convention halls but by staging protests outside of them and claiming exclusion. Asserting that only women who blindly assented to the feminist platform were genuinely welcome to attend, rogue "Pro-Family conventions" that acted as protest gatherings gained steam in and around Houston.[29] Led by Phyllis Schlafly, these protest movements, eleven thousand strong at one point, garnered as much press coverage as did the main event.[30] Schlafly proclaimed: "Houston will finish off the women's movement. It will show them off for the radical, anti-family, pro-lesbian people they are."[31] Incapable of ignoring the protests or the distraction, leaders inside the convention dismissed these conservative factions as "clones" of the John Birch Society and even the Ku Klux Klan. Adding fuel to the fire, these appellations only incited greater protest and frequent press coverage of the event, particularly in Texas.[32]

From a historical perspective, the legacy of the "Spirit of Houston" seems mixed. It also appeared that way to contemporaries in the Texas press. Editorials proclaimed the event as evidence that "real power in America lies in coalition building." Both conservative and liberal factions were recognized as important political blocs. Attracting these blocs was seen as a gateway for a shift in the balance of power at the state and national level. However, the agenda voted on and approved by conservative women opposed to "Houston" was not simply a statement of diametric opposition. During its rogue convention to counter "Houston," the Pro-Family Coalition passed planks on the following: limited and lower taxes, reductions in government spending and waste, security and national defense, local government control, opposition to the ERA, and a pro-life statement. Schlafly made sure that Texans knew these planks were voted on and passed in this order as an indication of what issues conservative women prioritized and believed were most important.[33]

Thus, whereas the goal of the feminist agenda was to gain entrée into the national political discourse by way of introducing a feminist agenda, conservative women chose an opposite strategy. Rather than prioritize gay rights, abortion, or the ERA, conservative women doffed their collective hats to and unified under the rhetoric of populist conservatism. These conservative women strengthened the growing power of the Republican Party, both nationally and in Texas, by connecting the social conservative agenda with that of a populism that emphasized strength, efficiency, and the liberation of Americans from the yoke of big government. This amalgam of special interests helped conservatism coalesce in Texas, contributed to redefinitions of liberalism, and even helped win the loyalties of Hispanic women in places like San Antonio, where the local GOP used family, abortion, and the ERA to undermine Democratic appeals to Catholics.[34]

Ultimately, as the momentum of social issues blended with economic recession and an energy crisis, conservative factions with seemingly little in common united under a worldview that simultaneously appealed to multiple constituencies on the basis of discontent, fear, and antiliberalism. From affluent urbanites to rural Baptists and from insurgent antifeminists to middle-class suburban evangelicals, a rather eclectic set of constituents came to share a belief that the nation was in decline, that Texas was threatened, and that an immoral and liberal big government was to blame.

Giveaway

Texans also came to believe that Jimmy Carter's government had signed away sovereign American territory to a Soviet-friendly government in Panama. Having been introduced in 1976 as a significant political issue and a conservative rallying point, the Panama Canal treaties continued to spark debate through 1977 and into 1978, coinciding with criticisms against Carter's energy policy and the growing association of liberalism with radical feminism and national decline. In Texas, the treaties also touched other economic nerves. On March 15, 1978, Texas congressional representatives received a report entitled "Economic Impacts of the Proposed Panama Canal Treaties on Texas." Among other claims, the report stated that Texas, "perhaps more than any other state, stands to be impacted" by the treaties. As the third-largest state in the value of its agricultural exports, Texas would be adversely affected by the trade restrictions the report claimed would result from the treaties. Relating the entire Texas economy to agriculture, and agricultural production to free trade, the report concluded that the Panama Canal treaties jeopardized fifty thousand Texas jobs, $670 million in annual personal income, and $318 million in federal, state, and local taxes.[35]

Needless to say, many Texans believed they had good reason to oppose the treaties. Yet most public outcries were premised on a fusion of these economic concerns with a fear of "handing the country over to communism," as one West Texan put it in 1978. Though the economic ramifications of the treaties were significant, Texans were equally concerned with the perception that to abandon the Panama Canal was to abandon Central America to communism. To a significant degree, many Texans viewed the Panama Canal treaties as a giveaway to communism in the Western Hemisphere, an invitation for a "second Castro," and another cold war defeat.[36]

A variety of individuals used this fusion to foment fear and promote partisan realignment in Texas. Richard Viguerie was one such individual. Though he no longer lived in Texas, Viguerie was among those Lone Star natives with a passion to lift the GOP to new national prominence on the back of the reinvigorated "New Right." Viguerie was long an observer of conservative Texas politics whose early career included stints working with the anticommunist radio preacher Billy James Hargis and Young Americans for Freedom. In 1975, Viguerie founded a new political magazine, *Conservative Digest*. Two years later, following the National Women's Conference in Houston, he saw an opportunity to take a giant leap forward in the mobilization of a "New Right." Sensing the influence wielded by the more than eleven thousand protesters who had unified as part of the "Pro-Family" coalition and rally, Viguerie committed to unite those protesters—and millions of others—through a direct mail campaign designed to sustain frustrations and mobilize the grass roots. Building on this vision, Viguerie mailed 75 million fund-raising letters for conservative causes in 1977 and 1978. The "father of direct mail," Viguerie showed a political genius not simply in his use of mass mailings to mobilize conservatives but in his ability to use those mailings to organize diverse groups with diverse complaints against a single source: big government. Soon, his fund-raising skills, conservative activism, and ability to mobilize the grass roots drew national media attention. In January 1978, the *Washington Post* somewhat prophetically reported that Viguerie was helping the GOP "steal Jimmy Carter's 1976 anti-government campaign issue and turn it against him and his Democratic allies in Washington."[37]

In early 1978, Viguerie organized a new incarnation of the "Truth Squad" that had aided Reagan's Texas campaign two years earlier. This Truth Squad was essentially a tour of conservative politicians barnstorming across the nation and drawing significant amounts of free airtime on local and national news programs by "exposing the lies" that undergirded the Carter administration's relinquishment of the Panama Canal. Though Carter had signed the treaties in 1977, bipartisan conservatives still fought against congressional ratification, while Republicans used the issue to bolster their support in Texas among anticommunists, social conservatives, and antiliberals who saw the treaties as an irresponsible "giveaway."[38]

Viguerie may not have been the first to initiate debate on the Panama Canal treaties, but his direct mail operation encouraged conservatives' already hostile and reactionary posture. Rarely one to miss an opportunity, John Tower adopted the issue as a prelude to his reelection bid in 1978. In 1977, Tower, whose personal opposition to the canal "giveaway" stretched back to 1966, claimed to be receiving as many as four thousand letters a week from Texas citizens voicing disapproval.[39] One particular flood of letters poured into Tower's office in October 1977, shortly after Carter gave an interview to a Denver radio station during which he rejected comparisons between the Panama Canal Zone and other territories "like Texas," which Carter argued the United States had "bought and paid for." A great many Texans were outraged to hear their state described in such a way. Tower, responding to the overflow of mail, personally scolded Carter, didactically saying that "the independence of the Republic of Texas was purchased with the red blood of patriots, as I'm sure you are now aware, and not with U.S. dollars. Texas existed as an independent nation from 1836 to 1845 when she voluntarily surrendered her sovereignty to become one of the United States." Tower added sarcastically that Carter was "certainly correct in rejecting any analogy between Texas and other situations. Texas is unique and will forever remain thus." Even on an issue as complicatedly international as the Panama Canal treaties, Texans managed to make the fight a personal one.[40]

By February 1978, polls indicated that 79 percent of Texans were opposed to the treaties, while only 11 percent supported them. Not surprisingly, 86 percent of Texas Republicans opposed the treaties, whereas only 5 percent supported them. Just as significant, however, was the fact that at a rate of 80–12, Democrats in Texas also opposed the treaties. Consequently, conservative Democrats in Texas who felt strongly that the Panama Canal issue was a national priority were given little choice but to publicly oppose Carter and side with the GOP.[41]

The organization of a mobilized conservative grass roots was further evidence of the power that the canal debate had in Texas. For instance, the National Society of the Sons of the American Revolution initiated operations across Texas in the late 1970s, with a noticeably large base in Houston. This organization opposed the treaties on grounds that the canal had been paid for and was therefore owned by the American taxpayer. The federal government, then, had no right to "give it away."[42] Another grassroots organization, the Emergency Committee to Save the US Canal Zone, based its operations upon the precedent of Texas annexation, arguing that the Canal Zone should be admitted to the Union as a new state in order to give the more than forty thousand U.S. citizens inhabiting that zone full representation in Congress, and requiring "the President to defend their territory in accordance with the supreme law of the land." This organization, of which Phyllis Schlafly was a member, strongly objected to the relinquishing of the canal to "the Marxist Revolutionary Government of Panama" and couched its objections firmly in the context of anticommunism.[43] Opposition also came from individual agitators. For instance, George S. Petley of Houston, billing himself in the late 1970s as a "researcher, lecturer, and former Canal Zone resident," undertook a series of speaking tours throughout the state. During these lectures, Petley frequently compared the Canal Zone to Fort Knox, saying that the comparison was valid not just because both were property of American taxpayers, but also because giving away the canal would be just as destructive to American interests as would a hypothetical giving away of Fort Knox. The Panama Canal was "economically and strategically . . . our greatest territorial possession," Petley wrote in his promotional literature. "We cannot afford to—and must not—lose it!" Petley also drew laughs from his audiences by routinely quipping that America should not "give Panama our Canal. . . . Give them Kissinger instead!"—further indication that grassroots conservatives were distancing themselves from the moderation and internationalism of previous GOP administrations.[44]

As national icons and citizen agitators fomented antiliberalism in Texas on the grounds that the canal treaties represented a foreign "giveaway," the association of Democratic policies with liberalism grew stronger, while the association of liberalism with weakness slowly paralyzed the Texas Democratic Party. In early 1978, twice as many Texans still identified themselves as Democrat than Republican. Yet, twice as many Texans also identified themselves as conservative rather than liberal. Texas conservatives from both parties increasingly identified Carter with liberalism and saw America's problems as the failure of liberalism. The less popular Jimmy Carter was in Texas, the clearer it became to Texas Republicans that partisan realignment was finally on the horizon.[45]

Sensing momentum on national issues, the Texas GOP distributed brochures in the summer of 1978 that listed examples of Carter's liberalism run amok. These brochures were easily identified by large-print headlines that read, "Carter is NO Conservative," "Carter's Liberal Policies," and "Carter's Liberal Appointments."[46] The image of Carter and liberalism as failed only encouraged the ideological commitments of several smaller Texas cities, including Midland, where city officials rejected federal development funds, citing their desire to maintain "the spirit of independence" and their "freedom from federal government."[47] The "widespread perception" that Carter's administration was "too liberal on a number of major issues nationally" discredited most Democratic efforts to elicit Texans' support for federal programs.[48]

Also potent as a coalition-building force among the grass roots was Carter's policy toward the Soviet Union. Conservatives in Texas were dismayed by Carter's proposed reductions in military spending, which Republicans portrayed as acquiescence, appeasement, and defeatism in the global war on communism. For instance, Carter's decision to discontinue the B-1 bomber was particularly unpopular both as an act of weakness and as a blow to the Texas economy, especially in Dallas, Fort Worth, and San Antonio, where defense and aviation manufacturing was economically vital. Nearly 60 percent of Texans polled in 1978 favored an increase in military spending, while only 17 percent favored reductions. Most Texans were also opposed to SALT-II negotiations, for which Carter unsuccessfully attempted to rally support by soliciting the backing of Texas clergy, even going so far as to suggest sermon topics on peace and the Christian perspective of war.[49]

By early 1978, it was evident that the Democratic Party was as weak in Texas as it had ever been. Despite the best efforts of state and local conservative Democrats to distance themselves from the Carter administration in 1977 and 1978, the nationalization of state political culture created a new and challenging context. Within that context, icons like Reagan represented conservatism and the local interest, while Carter's image as a weak failure almost single-handedly unraveled the tradition of one-party dominance long enjoyed by state Democrats. With midterms approaching, Texas Republican eyes focused ravenously on the upcoming midterms.

The 1978 Midterms

With all due respect to John Tower's senate victory in 1961, the most groundbreaking electoral achievement by a Texas Republican during the twentieth century occurred in November 1978, when William P. Clements became the first Republican governor of Texas since Reconstruction. Clements's victory, coming in the wake of the events of 1976, reflected an emerging bridge between conservative factions while also highlighting the influence of Reagan's still-growing popularity. Clements's victory was the capstone of a 1978 midterm season that reinforced several old rules of Texas politics, including the reality that, for a Republican to win election, voters needed to see distinct ideological contrast. Reagan's persistent presence on the Texas GOP campaign trail helped make that distinction clearer, as did the perception that Jimmy Carter, the Democratic Party's obvious standard-bearer, was the embodiment of liberalism gone awry.[50]

Texas Republicans tapped Clements as a possible nominee for governor in early 1978. Attracted to Clements's record as deputy secretary of Defense under both Nixon and Ford, as well as his respectability within the state's oil and gas establishment, state Republicans launched the most expensive Republican candidacy in state history. Spending over $1.8 million in television and radio advertising during the primary alone, state Republicans aggressively targeted Reagan voters from 1976 with the hope of uniting previously divided conservative factions behind a candidate whose image as a populist conservative was quickly being constructed for the general campaign.[51]

Funding aside, Clements's biggest asset was Carter's intense unpopularity. Carter's unpopularity also exacerbated continuing divisions within the state Democratic Party and contributed to John Hill's surprising primary victory over the incumbent governor, Dolph Briscoe. Hill, the state's attorney general, handily defeated the establishment Briscoe by capitalizing on the perception that Briscoe was a do-nothing governor. Conservatives, apathetic in their support for Briscoe, failed to turn out for the primary, while motivated liberals took full advantage. Yet Hill's divisive campaign proved to be a long-term negative as far as Democratic dominance was concerned. Conservatives were dismayed over Hill's aggressive attacks and feared that liberal activism was threatening to strangle the party's position of dominance. Many began to talk more openly of jumping the party ship.[52]

Elected on the atypical strength of liberal turnout and elated in victory, Hill was shortsighted in his understanding of the immediate Texas political culture. His first significant move in the general campaign was to ask Jimmy Carter for an endorsement during a mid-May trip to Washington in which he and several other Texas liberals sat down with the president to discuss the upcoming campaigns. By so clearly connecting himself to Carter, Hill made Clements's strategy of making the contest a referendum on Carter much easier.[53]

Clements was not shy in his efforts to use Carter's endorsement against Hill. Texas polls released shortly after Hill received Carter's endorsement

Bill Clements in his Southeastern Drilling Company office prior to winning the governorship in 1978. Notice the western décor. (Courtesy of the *Dallas Morning News*)

indicated that 80 percent of Texans wanted new leadership in both Austin and Washington.[54] These same polls indicated that Carter himself was listed among the "things" Texas voters saw as "most problematic" with the state—not just the nation. Though displeased with Carter, Texans still identified with the broad ideological doctrines championed by both Reagan and Carter in 1976, and surveys consistently showed that Texans saw the solutions to their woes not in federal activism but in winning the "fight [against] the federal government." Clements was determined to make Carter the focal point of his campaign, while tying Hill to Carter.[55]

At the same time, Hill was overconfident and ran a relatively passive general campaign. He failed to unify his party and many conservative Democrats, alienated by the divisive primary campaign against Briscoe, joined Republicans in making Hill's association with Carter a chief issue.[56] Hill was also consistently lambasted in the press, which reported conservatives' criticism of the Democratic nominee's support for the ERA and the pro-choice abortion lobby.[57] On more local issues, Hill fared little better. When a Briscoe-sponsored tax-cut package stalled and eventually died in the Texas legislature, conservatives on both sides of the aisle blamed Hill. Hill, they argued, indirectly defeated the tax-cut plan by organizing a coalition of moderate and liberal Democrats in the Texas House of Representatives. Voters and Briscoe insiders alike blamed Hill for "playing governor," indirectly raising taxes, and began to publicly support the Clements campaign.[58]

Taking advantage of the Democratic factionalism, Texas Republicans effectively coupled national issues with the intense anti-Carter sentiment to broaden the tent underneath which conservative Texans could align. Clements's platform did not initially include discussion of national issues such as defense spending, détente, or the Panama Canal. By the time of the general election, it did. Clements also regularly included diatribes in his campaign speeches against the deregulation of oil and gas (which many Texans believed Carter had promised them in 1976), as well as hot-button issues like local control for education, tougher crime laws that included similar sentences for similar crimes, and support for the death penalty. In addition, Clements touted a $314.8 million tax reduction plan, certainly attractive to fiscal conservatives.[59]

Clements established credibility on these issues not simply by promoting his own résumé, but also by aligning himself with the heavyweights of Texas conservatism and national Republicanism. John Connally offered his ringing endorsement in August, which was broadcast statewide via radio and television.[60] Clements also earned endorsements from Briscoe and George Bush.[61] Clements additionally accepted the endorsement of New York congressman Jack Kemp, who rallied with Clements in Texas to support a taxpayer's bill of rights.[62]

Clements also aggressively courted Reagan supporters. Infusing his campaign with issues such as busing, school prayer, abortion, gun control, and communism, Clements asked Reagan to campaign with him across the state that fall. Reagan was initially asked to focus his speeches on national security and direct attacks on Carter. Reagan, no doubt, enjoyed the opportunity, though when an increasing number of evangelicals began to pressure the Clements campaign to take a stronger stand on social issues, Clements responded by loosening Reagan's speech topic restrictions. Subsequently, Reagan's impact on the campaign began to increase. Reagan made campaign appearances with Clements on September 1 (in Austin) and again on October 19 as keynote speaker at the Fort Worth luncheon to kick off the Convoy for Clements organization. He was also asked to lead campaign efforts in San Antonio and Lubbock, two of the top six vote-producing counties for Reagan in his 1976 presidential primary campaign.[63] Largely thanks to Reagan, Clements had, by October, established campaign centers in every urban and suburban county across the state and in more than 130 rural counties, each of which was chaired by a registered and conservative Democrat.[64]

In a narrow race, Clements used Carter's unpopularity, Reagan's appeal, and a rhetoric that fused multiple strands of conservative thought under a unified banner of antiliberalism to defeat Hill and give the governor's mansion a Republican resident. The victory was a watershed for Republican acceptability in Texas. Fueled largely by the momentum of Reagan's 1976 bid and Texans' dissatisfaction with Carter, Clements hastened the reconciliation of divisions that had left the Texas GOP temporarily fractured after 1976. He helped recast the party as a new and stronger coalition of fiscal and social conservatives, united by a common interest in anticommunism and anti-Carter liberalism. In doing so, Clements attracted, as Reagan also could, disaffected conservative Democrats—one more step along the road that led toward large-scale partisan realignment in the state.

Clements's victory in 1978 also likely saved John Tower's career. Tower's 1978 reelection bid was his toughest to date, and the obstacles he faced were predominantly of his own making. Tower fell into disfavor with the growing conservative grass roots because of his opposition to Reagan in 1976, though many also began to dig into Tower's past, where they found further ammunition in Tower's support for Nixon over Reagan in 1968. These shortcomings seemed to reflect Tower's growing inability to relate to the changing nature of Texas conservatism. In 1978, for instance, despite making some gains by opposing the Panama Canal treaties, Tower lost more favor among social conservatives by supporting proposed legislation that would have permitted federal funds to be used for abortions, without restriction, while Texas's junior senator, Democrat Lloyd Bentsen, opposed the measure. Tower's libertarianism seemed outdated on such social issues,

Ronald Reagan and Gerald Ford campaign with Bill Clements during the 1978 gover-nor's race. (Courtesy of the *Dallas Morning News*)

at least by Texas standards. When he argued that morality could not be legislated, some began to call Tower a social liberal.[65]

Tower's image problem manifested in several other ways as well. In the late 1970s, Tower appeared noticeably less rugged, western, or Texan than did Connally, Reagan, or even Clements. Once an ardent Goldwater sup-porter, Tower was, in 1978, more often remembered for his fondness for wool suits bought from Savile Row in London than for his conservative image or résumé. If populist conservatism seemed rooted in western wear, then Tower's image simply did not fit the bill. Even Tower's education at the London School of Economics, once used by conservative Democrats as a way to undermine the then prospective senator's conservatism, was now being used by conservatives in his own party as evidence that he could not be trusted and had been influenced by "foreign" elements.[66]

Tower responded to these attacks by trying to shift voters' focus off him and onto the national Democratic Party. In speeches across the state, he criticized Carter's foreign policy and raised the specter of a renewed So-viet threat. He also increasingly defined himself as an enemy of the "north-eastern liberal establishment"—something he had been much less inclined to publicly say of himself in recent years.[67] At the same time, Tower, after privately mending fences between himself and Reagan, took every opportunity he could to publicly affirm his fondness for Reagan and reveled in the opportunity to appear with Reagan at GOP fund-raisers in Texas.[68]

The benefit of adding Reagan's endorsement went beyond the scope of mere association with a popular conservative. Reagan could credibly say things to Texas voters that Tower, because of his opposition to Reagan in previous years, no longer could. For as much as Tower attempted to rail against Carter and liberalism, none of his efforts were as effective as having Reagan do the talking for him. "Together we can stop Jimmy Carter and his band of fumbling advisors," Reagan wrote on behalf of Tower in a direct mailing to Texas voters, "by seeing that conservatives like John Tower are not replaced by liberals."[69] George Bush and former Texas governor Allan Shivers joined Reagan in putting their names on direct mailings that endorsed Tower and denounced the liberal alliance between "big labor, big government, and the liberal elements of the Senate and House of Representatives." Shivers's endorsement was particularly effective in attracting older conservative Democrats. Clearly, image management shaped Tower's 1978 campaign.[70]

Public image was also crucial for Tower's opponent, Congressman Bob Krueger. Krueger was a former Duke University English professor who was partial to quoting Shakespeare on the campaign trail. Krueger was widely regarded as a liberal, though his campaign advertisements and brochures were emblazoned with the word "CONSERVATIVE"—in all capital letters—followed in much more subdued print by the word "Democrat."[71] Krueger, whose claim to fame in Texas was that he had almost succeeded in getting the House to approve a natural gas deregulation bill, joined Tower in what was one of the nastiest campaigns in Texas history. When Krueger attempted to use Tower's divorces as a wedge between the incumbent and social conservatives, going so far as to charge Tower with rampant womanizing, Tower's campaign responded by circulating rumors that the bachelor Krueger was actually a closet homosexual. Krueger responded by inserting a photograph of himself with two unidentified adult women, three young girls, and a dog—vaguely referred to in the photo's caption as "family"—into new campaign circulars.[72]

The campaign was littered with a variety of other steps and missteps. Krueger campaigned as a "good ole boy"—the antithesis of the upper-crust elitism many ascribed to Tower. Tower used the "good ole boy" appellation to associate Krueger with the establishment. While Tower attacked Carter on foreign policy, Krueger made some headway by charging that his opponent cared little for the daily affairs of ordinary Texans. Krueger lost ground among conservative businessmen, though, when he unwisely introduced himself to the Downtown Kiwanis Club of Houston by saying, "If you're looking for someone who is just a spokesman for business, you're not looking for me."[73] Krueger tried to undercut Tower's popularity among Mexican Americans by reminding them of the incumbent Republican's opposition to civil rights legislation in the 1960s and also took advantage of a 1978 Justice Department decision to use the Voting Rights Act as a means to command authority of Texas election laws in response to allegations of voter discrimination. Tower adamantly opposed this action as federal usurpation of state power and garnered some support among white Texans as a result. However, among minorities, Tower's popularity slid.[74]

Krueger's biggest mistake, however, was his decision to bring in national celebrities like Rosalynn Carter and Walter Mondale to campaign on his behalf. Rather than attract minority voters, as had been his hope, Krueger's decision, like John Hill's, was far more effective in sending conservative white Texans back into the Republican camp. After a long and tough campaign, Tower barely won reelection, defeating Krueger by only 1 percent of the vote.[75]

Clements's victory in the governor's race probably saved Tower's reelection, but not every Republican had the same good fortune. James Baker, for instance, fell 12 points short in his bid for attorney general, eventually losing to the state's incumbent secretary of State, Mark White. Baker entered the race with great enthusiasm. He had run Gerald Ford's 1976 general campaign in Texas and believed he understood the evolving Texas political culture. He intended to anchor his campaign in antiliberal and anti-Carter appeals. However, unblessed with the good fortune of Clements and Tower, Baker faced many of the same obstacles that George Bush had in his senate campaign against Lloyd Bentsen in 1970. In the end, it was clear that Republican success in Texas was still heavily dependent upon defining one's conservatism against another's liberalism and that, without a liberal to run against, the default vote was still Democratic.[76]

Baker entered the race assuming he would square off against Price Daniel Jr., the liberal son of the former Texas governor of the same name. That assumption was shattered, as was Baker's well-planned campaign strategy, when White did to Daniel what Baker had hoped to do—defined him as a liberal and captured the growing conservative antiliberal backlash. Throughout the primary, the moderate White attacked Daniel as a "liberal" with ties to Carter. The Texas press did not help Daniel; many metropolitan newspapers ran editorials critiquing the extent of Daniel's leftward leanings.[77] White further infused a sense of state pride and populist provincialism into the race when he associated Daniel's campaign with "foreign influence"—which he defined as federal encroachment and the influence of northern "outsiders" migrating into Texas.[78]

In positioning himself to Daniel's right, White also neutralized the "liberal" issue for the general campaign against Baker. Thus, a major difference between the campaigns of Tower and Clements and that of Baker was the perceived conservatism of their Democratic opponents. Baker's strategy for the general election was supposed to center on magnifying his opponent's liberalism. Campaign staff repeatedly assured Baker that Daniel's liberalism was "potentially the most damaging" part of his record. Against White, however, the same charges were ineffective, not simply because they were less true about White, but also because White had already used the same strategy to defeat Daniel in the primary.[79] Left scrambling to devise a new approach, Baker's strategists emphasized the need to get to the right of White on three issues: crime, energy, and federal encroachment. Baker also accused White of ignoring the problem of illegal immigration from Mexico, yet courted the Hispanic vote by charging that White was "dragging his feet" on "minority concerns."[80]

The only specific issue Baker consistently used to any degree of effect was White's public support of the Equal Rights Amendment, which Baker believed would be a benefit with social conservatives. However, Baker's consistent argument against the ERA was less about moral decline and radical feminism than it was a simple declaration that everything the ERA was intended to do was already provided for by the Fourteenth Amendment and was, therefore, nothing more than constitutional tampering and federal encroachment. Baker's strategy on the ERA was effective to the degree that he maintained the support of ardent libertarians, but his approach alienated social conservatives, who wanted to hear a stronger denunciation of "radical feminism" and abortion.[81]

Failing to rally evangelicals on social issues, Baker struggled to find other ways to label White a liberal. In part because he feared alienating socially conservative blue-collar families, Baker even failed to associate White's endorsement from the ACLU and the United Auto Workers with liberalism. Baker ultimately chose to emphasize the theme of "independence"—defined broadly in order to incorporate an agenda that gave greater freedom and protection to police officers without having to fight bureaucratic red tape while also connecting his own "independence" as beyond the influence of "political power structures which still dominate Texas politics"—meaning the established Democratic leadership in Austin. Still, nothing seemed to work. Baker's inability to outconservative White was particularly frustrating to Republicans who understood the importance of shaping antiliberalism in the public mind. The strategy likely would have succeeded against Daniel, but against White, Baker was swimming upstream in his efforts to be Texans' lone conservative option.[82]

Baker's campaign was also noted for Reagan's absence from it, and it was only when discussing his "independence" that Baker managed with any success to convey a Reaganesque vision of antigovernment conservatism. It was also usually (and only) within the context of a discussion on independence that Baker was able to use Carter against his Democratic opponent. Baker did this by highlighting areas of incompetence in Washington and by linking Texans' frustrations with Carter to existing and/or potential problems in Texas. In the end, however, Baker flopped where Clements had flourished. Baker failed to outconservative White and lost his bid for attorney general.[83]

A similar and noteworthy political race also unfolded on the dusty plains of West Texas, in the fight to replace forty-three-year incumbent Democrat George Mahon. The seventy-six-year-old Mahon announced his retirement from the U.S. Congress in 1977, and Kent Hance soon became the frontrunner to win the vacant seat. Hance, like Mahon, was a conservative Democrat. He was also a resident of Lubbock, a graduate of Texas Tech University, and a friend to the farming constituency that dominated the South Plains—all important factors to the constituents of the nineteenth congressional district. Hance also shared much in common with his Republican opponent. Both had been publicly critical of the Carter administration's oil policies and each recognized the importance of connecting with the agricultural constituents who dominated the Lubbock region of the district. On the issues, there seemed to be little distinction between the candidates, but this campaign, as was so often true in Texas, was ultimately more concerned with image than issues.[84]

Unlike Hance, the Republican nominee in the nineteenth district had a significant image problem. He was not a native West Texan. He had no affiliation with Texas Tech University, as did both Hance and Mahon, but was instead an Ivy Leaguer, with degrees from both Harvard and Yale. His family had moved to Midland during the oil boom of the 1950s and was forced to fight the labels of "carpetbagger" and "Yankee." Simply put, Hance's opponent, the thirty-two-year-old George W. Bush, lacked West Texas credibility—and the Hance campaign knew it. Throughout the race, Bush was attacked in Lubbock as an outsider, ignorant of the needs of area farmers, and incapable of representing West Texas in the U.S. House of Representatives. In one particularly effective and memorable radio advertisement run by the Hance campaign, Bush's lack of Texas credibility was

George W. Bush announcing his bid
for Congress in Lubbock, July 19,
1977. (Courtesy of the Associated
Press)

bluntly characterized: "In 1961, when Kent Hance graduated from Dim-
mitt High School in the 19th congressional district, his opponent George
W. Bush was attending Andover Academy in Massachusetts. In 1965, when
Kent Hance graduated from Texas Tech, his opponent was at Yale University. And while Kent Hance graduated from the University of Texas Law
School, his opponent—get this folks—was attending Harvard. We don't
need someone from the Northeast telling us what our problems are."[85]

Bush faced additional challenges beyond his roots—challenges that
had also plagued his father's campaign efforts in the 1960s and 1970s. The
nineteenth congressional district encompassed much of West Texas, with
Lubbock as the largest city in the northern region of the district, and Midland the largest in the south. While the Permian Basin oil boom of the
1970s fueled a growth in wealth and prestige in Midland, it did not give the
city the population expansion necessary to compete with its sister city in the
north. Lubbock, therefore, continued to serve as the de facto seat of congressional power and did, for all intents and purposes, decide who the next
congressman from that district would be.[86] Lubbock was one of the state's
most traditionally Republican urban centers, but because of the popularity

and strength of conservative Democrats like Mahon, Lubbock routinely split its vote between Republicans at the national level and Democrats locally.[87] Additionally, Lubbock was home to one of Reagan's strongest support centers, and any support for the son of George H. W. Bush was seen by some as aid to a potential Reagan presidential rival.[88]

An inexperienced campaigner, Bush failed to impress during speaking engagements in Lubbock. Before a political science class at Texas Tech University, Bush, in answering questions about the U.S. grain embargo against Russia, promised to work toward the elimination of the embargo, but then launched into a tirade against Cuba and the evils of communism. When quizzed about the apparent contradiction in his support for the continued embargo of Cuba, Bush appeared befuddled. Later that day, as he and some campaign workers walked past a fraternity lodge less than a mile from campus, Bush had to be restrained from physically confronting a student from the class who called the GOP candidate an "idiot" and pelted him with snowballs. Bush's cause was further damaged when a series of alcohol-saturated parties promoted as "Bush Bashes" attracted Texas Tech students to venues where few if any of the students attending were asked for proper identification to prove they were of drinking age.[89] Shortly after the last of these parties, less than a week prior to the election, local conservatives distributed a letter to pastors throughout the district explaining that such behavior was "un-Christian" and should be soundly repudiated via the ballot box.[90]

Regardless of why Bush lost—and despite his problems, he still managed 47 percent of the vote—this small campaign in West Texas demonstrates the broad power, malleable nature, and multiple applications of antiliberalism in Texas. In this case, Bush was a victim of his own party's strategy of defining outside influences as foreign and dangerous—whether they originated in Moscow or Andover, Massachusetts. In a race between two conservatives, the people of West Texas defaulted to a tradition of independence, local control, and Christian family values.[91]

In other races across the state, 1978 proved to be a relatively big year for the GOP. Though some races, such as the one in the nineteenth district, enabled conservative Democrats to remain in power, elsewhere Republicans not only won the governorship and retained Tower's Senate seat, but also won several local races and forced many to choose between ideological conviction and partisan loyalty.

The Texas GOP's biggest congressional success story was Ron Paul, who unseated the liberal Bob Gammage in the twenty-second district, representing the south side of Houston down the coastal plain to Brazosport on the Gulf of Mexico. Two years earlier, Gammage had defeated Paul by only 236 votes in the closest congressional race in the nation. Gammage's record, including his voting history on labor issues, was more liberal than he advertised—particularly to the affluent constituents in his district.[92] Paul took advantage of this and also gained national notoriety when Reagan stumped on his behalf in September. No GOP candidate in Texas could find a better friend than Reagan, who told an audience of legislators in Houston that Paul's opponent should be "quarantined" so that the liberal "contagion doesn't spread." Whether Reagan was campaigning for Paul or for any one of several other Republican candidates, his attacks deftly combined disarming humor and quick wit with an empowering conservative rhetoric, tinged with a populist ethos and laced with antiliberal and anti-Carter critiques. His campaigning for Paul, for instance, had far less to do with Gammage than with the leftward slide of the national Democratic Party.[93]

As he campaigned in Texas, Reagan earned credibility by reminding his audiences that he too had once been a Democrat. Once a rapport with his audience had been established, Reagan launched into his standard diatribe—one that the 1978 midterms allowed him to perfect on the road to 1980. Reagan typically opened his speeches by saying, "I'm not going to present you with a long list of what is wrong with the current administration or the Democrat-controlled Congress. We'd be here all night." Reagan then usually mentioned Jimmy Carter, Tip O'Neill, or Ted Kennedy as a way to undermine emotional connections many Texans still had to the Democratic Party. By linking the Democratic Party to personalities like Carter, O'Neill, and Kennedy, Reagan created an association between these Democratic leaders and all Democrats—a strategy particularly effective in a state hostile to both Carter and northeastern liberalism.[94]

Reagan then typically shifted to, depending on the location, any number of hot-button conservative topics. While campaigning for Paul, Reagan stressed pocketbook issues. He criticized Carter for contributing to the nation's "welfare mess" and also linked busing and affirmative action to government incompetence and irresponsible wastefulness. He accused Democrats of waging "devastating attacks against the people" and assured those in south Houston that he and the GOP were "on their side." He spoke of Democrats waging "economic warfare against American families" and charged liberal congressmen with "ineptitude." In a city struggling to reconcile issues like busing, Reagan's speech to this audience of affluent suburban Houston families was tailor-made. Regardless of location, though, Reagan's language was always plain, conversational, and emotional.[95]

Reagan, more than any other political figure in the state, tore down the barriers of loyalty and tradition that had kept many Texans voting Democrat for so long. "Family, work, neighborhood, freedom, peace," Reagan told several Texas audiences in 1978. "We should not repeat those words until they become second nature. We should meditate on their meaning and how our policies can be applied to them. They should be on our lips. But, they must also be in our hearts, just as they are in the hearts of Americans all across this country."[96] He referred to Democrats as "elitists" and quoted Thomas Jefferson as if the two had been good friends growing up. Reagan rarely shied away from the populist tag, but more typically associated his brand of conservatism with the integrity and wisdom of the "common man"—the property-owning, independent individualist whose prestige and importance Jefferson had championed. Reagan's intentional association with Jefferson not only contributed to his being perceived as an advocate for "the people" but meshed nicely with the nostalgic aura that surrounded his call for patriotism, family, and the recapturing of the greatness that he and most Texans believed defined America's past.[97] He eloquently spoke of freedom and hope and contrasted the American Dream with the Soviet threat—a threat, he said, that was not being dealt with appropriately by the Democratic leadership in Washington. He appealed to fiscal conservatives, hawks, and evangelicals—all at the same time and seemingly without contradiction. Reagan's rhetoric and skill were especially effective in uniting urban, suburban, and rural conservatives, each of whom came to the political table with a different appetite, but all of whom left Reagan's banquets fully satisfied.[98]

The significance of Reagan's presence in Texas throughout the 1978 midterms cannot be overemphasized. Without Reagan, the Republican Party would not have been as successful, and without that success, the stage would not have been so neatly set for Reagan's next bid for the White House in 1980. In a state proud of its own independent heritage, Reagan was a natural fit. A feeling permeated Texas in the late 1970s, expressed through the sentiments of longtime volunteers, campaign organizers, and other grassroots activists, that Reagan, with his unshakable commitment to defense and his grandfatherly appeals to patriotism and family, had almost single-handedly removed the fear and guilt many middle-class whites historically endured for voting Republican. This newfound respectability for Republicanism in Texas manifested most visibly through grassroots mobilization in cities and small towns. The Texas Federation of Republican Women (TFRW) was one such organization. By 1978, the TFRW had organized 130 clubs statewide, with more than six thousand volunteers. These women had been contributing to conservative mobilization for years, but it was not until the late 1970s, when rallied behind the national candidacy of Reagan in 1976 and the anti-Carter candidacies of 1978, that they became a force to be reckoned with. The TFRW alone supplied more than thirty-eight thousand hours of volunteer support for GOP candidates in 1978, and most of those call centers and campaign headquarters were established because of Reagan's primary campaign in the state two years earlier. Including all other conservative organizations operating in Texas, more than thirty-seven thousand grassroots workers mobilized in support of Republican campaigns and conservative causes in 1978. Texas Republicans were not just gaining respectability; they were on their way to overtaking the Democratic Party as the top party in the state.[99]

As 1980 approached, the Texas sky braced for a Republican storm. The state's political climate was affected by race, economics, energy policy, social debates, rising evangelicalism, and the iconography of two national figures who became inextricably associated with political philosophy in Texas. Grassroots conservatives mobilized around many issues, but the one commonality these factions shared that contributed more than anything else to their impact in Texas during the late 1970s was the iconic popularity of Ronald Reagan and unpopularity of Jimmy Carter. The study of how Texas supported Carter in 1976 and then came to reject him so vehemently and so quickly four years later is also the study of why Texas's tradition of Democratic dominance finally fell by the wayside during the late 1970s.

Chapter 8

Revolution
Reagan and Texas in 1980

Ronald Reagan's election in 1980, highlighted by his overwhelming win in Texas, was a culmination of more than two decades of political change, hastened by a host of economic, social, and demographic forces. It also established Texas as a legitimate two-party state and, eventually, as the preeminent bedrock of modern conservatism. For years, the state GOP had fought and failed to establish itself as a viable second party. When not presented with a clear dichotomy between conservatism and liberalism, Texas voters usually defaulted to Democratic tradition and loyalty. Yet after 1976, and particularly by 1978, intraparty factionalism within the GOP was replaced by a growing coalescence of conservatism united under a banner of antiliberalism and anti-Carter animus.

Reagan's popularity, especially when contrasted to Carter's unpopularity, served as the primary catalyst advancing partisan realignment in Texas. Without Reagan, Republican conservatism seemed, to many, aimless. With Reagan, the state GOP finally achieved a needed image of respectability, simultaneously establishing itself as the new voice of mainstream populist conservatism.

The Setting

As the 1980 campaigns approached, it seemed that Jimmy Carter could not catch a break. In addition to his well-chronicled struggles with inflation, energy, and Iran, Carter's image in Texas took another unfortunate hit when Mother Nature decided to unleash her wrath and further highlight several of the administration's perceived failings. Seventy-eight Texans died as a result of a record-breaking heat wave during the summer of 1980. In Houston, where 92 percent of buildings were air-conditioned, energy demands reached all-time highs. In Dallas, one woman approached a parked truck loaded with bags of ice and, without a word to the driver, climbed into the back of the vehicle and lay down on the cargo. In West Texas, the

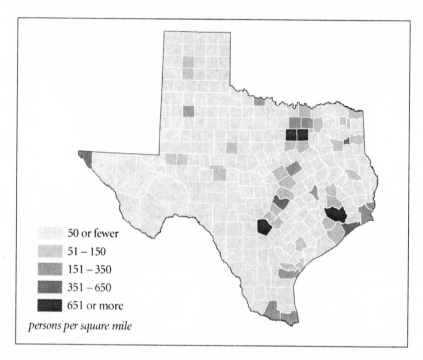

The state's population density in 1980.

heat scorched the state's cotton crop, inciting small-scale panic among farmers.[1] Then, in August, Hurricane Allen, a category 5 storm (though it was only a category 3 storm when it made landfall) tore through South and Central Texas with winds in excess of 115 miles per hour, causing hundreds of millions of dollars in damage and leaving seven dead. In the aftermath of Hurricane Allen, Carter allocated federal disaster aid to much of the state but chose to exclude two counties in South Texas where the damage had been less severe. The residents of these counties, most of whom were Mexican American, were outraged and threatened to withdraw their support. Across Texas, Carter was blamed for policies seen as having contributed to high energy costs and agricultural struggles—shortcomings that were intensified as the winds blew and the mercury rose on thermometers across the state.[2]

As the weather left most Texans agitated, conservative Texas Democrats felt increasingly disconnected from their national party and held out little hope of reconciliation. Liberals, on the other hand, joined Republicans in believing that realignment might have finally arrived. Texas liberals had longed for the day when they would control their own party, free from the shackles of the conservative establishment. Yet, many Texas liberals also understood that the party they were inheriting control over had a serious image problem.[3]

Jim Hightower was one such liberal. In 1980, Hightower, a former editor of the *Texas Observer* and among the state's most prominent liberals, described the state's evolving political culture as one dominated by "disgruntled mavericks" and acknowledged that these mavericks, though certainly no friends to the financial establishment, were increasingly attracted to the Republican brand of populist conservatism. Hightower was correct in that most Texans no longer saw the Democratic Party as the voice of "disgruntled mavericks." Rather, most mainstream conservatives viewed the national Democratic Party as a voice for special interests and other racial, ethnic, and radical minorities.[4]

These perceptions were driven by the national political culture. Non-Texans like Reagan, Carter, and even Ted Kennedy came to symbolize what many Texans viewed as either right or wrong with the country, but also came to embody the values they wanted to either embrace or reject at the local level. These icons attracted and unified "disgruntled mavericks" around core issues and made finding the right image imperative for political success. In this context, Reagan was even more popular because he was perceived not only as an agent of change, but as "one of us"—a "disgruntled maverick"—a western cowboy fed up with the mess in Washington and determined to do something about it. Reagan supporters in Texas identified with the former California governor on many issues, but it was his image more than the specifics of his platform and policies—especially when contrasted to the image of national liberal Democrats—that won admiration.[5]

Cries coming from the grass roots reflected this shift. One anonymous disgruntled maverick from Brownwood described Texans' political attitudes this way: "Hell, most everybody around here calls themselves a Democrat, but that don't mean they're a bunch of crazy liberals." Identified in his local paper only as an "old Cowboy," this citizen did more than simply reflect the idea that the Democratic Party had become increasingly synonymous with radical liberalism. This "old Cowboy" also reflected an emotional hostility toward the incumbent president: "Carter's ruined our defense position. He's let some dinky little country push us around and kidnap our people. He's sacrificed our farmers with his wheat embargo and ruined our economy while he runs giveaway programs. . . . Maybe Reagan can turn things around."[6]

The conservative unification that resulted from iconographic personalities and mass political culture does much to explain Texas's behavior as a whole. However, it would be a mistake to argue that mass culture made local distinctions unimportant. Each small town and city in Texas brought unique characteristics to the political table. One such city was San Antonio. No city in Texas enjoyed as strong a heritage of independence as did the Alamo City. Additionally, San Antonio boasted one of the heaviest military concentrations in the nation, with two major air force bases (Lackland and Randolph), an army medical center, and United Services Automobile Association (USAA)—the predominant financial hub for veterans and families of the U.S. armed services. San Antonio also had the largest Hispanic population (60 percent) of any major city in the United States and was the congressional home of Henry B. Gonzalez, the liberal regarded by many in San Antonio as the city's "patron saint."[7]

In early 1980, Jimmy Carter chose San Antonio as the location for a major policy speech on immigration. It was the first of many efforts by Carter to elicit support from the city's ethnic community. Carter's identification of San Antonio as a central gauge for Mexican American and Hispanic issues was not surprising. By 1980, San Antonio had emerged as the most popular locale for national politicians wishing to say anything of substance on the issue. The city became a hotbed for both conservatives and liberals, vying for the loyalties of a community traditionally wedded to the Democratic Party but increasingly wooed by values-focused social conservatives, themselves wedded to Reagan. As Democrats fought to maintain support in San Antonio, the Texas GOP initiated a voter registration drive targeting the city's Hispanics. The result was a remarkable increase in the number of GOP voters in the area. By that spring, new Republican voters outnumbered new Democratic voters in Bexar County four to one. Significant gains were made with Hispanics, though the GOP also used a pro-life, pro-family, traditionalist appeal to register new white voters as well.[8]

As Republicans made gains with Hispanics, Democrats feuded about how best to counter. While many wanted to focus on issues of discrimination and economics, others, sensing that the political mood was being shaped by perceptions, chose to emphasize heritage and ideology. For instance, several Carter administration officials, including Special Assistant Esteban E. Torres, a native Texan, addressed Texas Hispanics not by proposing new policy or discussing discrimination, economics, or the nuances of other issues, but by reminding his audiences of the evils of Republican elitism and the Democratic "common man" tradition of Thomas Jefferson, Andrew Jackson, Franklin Roosevelt, John Kennedy, Lyndon Johnson and, in 1980, Jimmy Carter. Though legacy and tradition were keys to the state's political climate, some Hispanic civic leaders, including several businessmen representing the League of United Latin American Citizens, nationally headquartered in Corpus Christi, found the strategy condescending and dismissive.[9]

While San Antonio emerged as a national focal point for debate on Hispanic issues, several other cities and geographically distinct areas in Texas reflected a variety of other complexities, out of which coalesced a much wider swathe of new conservative converts. Austin, for instance, emerged as a national leader in electronics manufacturing and technology. Motorola moved its headquarters to Austin in 1975, bringing with it an initial twenty-five hundred new jobs.[10] Texas's fastest-growing city during the 1960s and a growing beacon for white-collar jobs in the electronics industry, Austin was also the state's intellectual hub. In addition to hosting the state's two most influential periodicals, the *Texas Observer* and *Texas Monthly,* Austin was home to the University of Texas, among the nation's largest universities. UT's nearly forty thousand students had traditionally acted as a loyal voting bloc for liberal interests. By the close of the 1970s, however, UT students were increasingly preoccupied with their job prospects in a nationally deflated economy. Though UT's student body was still considered an important liberal bloc, political candidates viewed it as "more conservative than most."[11] With the local economy booming and uncertainties surrounding the national economy, an increasing number of graduating UT students moved into jobs in the local sector, contributing both to greater partisan equilibrium and population growth.[12]

Austin also experienced tumult over busing, just in time for the fall elections. In August, the city initiated a busing program to address concerns over persistent segregation in local schools. Arguing that property-tax payers' rights were being violated, numerous white-collar and suburban neighborhood organizations formed to resist busing. Some organizations even sought the resignations of school board members they believed had betrayed their neighbors by buckling under social pressures. After several years, these organizations succeeded. Busing laws in Austin were rescinded in 1987. In the fall of 1980, however, the controversy heightened the salience of conservatives' antitax, antigovernment, and populist rhetoric.[13]

Other smaller cities in Texas arrived at the anti-Carter meeting from different directions. Longview, located in far East Texas, fumed over oil. Longview produced more independent oil than any other city in the United States. Area voters reviled Carter's energy policies, the Windfall Profits Tax in particular, and believed that Carter had reneged on promises he made in 1976 to deregulate the industry. The city's ire with national Democratic leadership had a long history. Longview had provided Barry Goldwater with his largest majority vote in the nation in 1964 and virtually its entire chamber of commerce was actively backing Ronald Reagan in 1980.[14]

Demographics also greatly affected the political culture of the region. Tyler, located between Dallas and Longview, acted as a demographic hinge between the Deep South and the Southwest. Roughly 15 percent of its residents were African American, while only 3 percent were Hispanic. To the west, Tyler's neighboring thirteenth congressional district was barely 5 percent black. That district had been originally settled by people from northwest Oklahoma and western Kansas; these parts of the district were traditionally Republican. To Tyler's east was the first congressional district, which was 22 percent black and traditionally Democratic. At the same time, Tyler's district—the fourth—was one of the most staunchly Democratic by registration, but was carried by Nixon in 1972 at a 72–28 clip. Carter recaptured the district in 1976, but by only 2 percentage points and only as a protest against Ford. The district was one of Reagan's strongest in 1976. In 1978, the fourth district overwhelmingly supported both Bill Clements and John Tower. Tyler was at the fulcrum of social, economic, and traditional political forces in East Texas. While Tyler slowly urbanized, the surrounding area was still predominantly comprised of farmers with an antielitist populist heritage. Little suburban sprawl marked the territory, yet Reagan's free-market Republicanism seemed much friendlier when mixed with fear that the nation's social travails threatened to invade East Texas if something was not done to stop their advance.[15]

To the south, in Central Texas, the old breed of state politics was still firmly reflected in local attitudes. Central Texas's eleventh district, for example, offered few white-collar jobs and maintained a farming tradition that was accompanied by generationally consistent Democratic loyalty. Carter earned a solid 57 percent of the vote in the eleventh district in 1976 while Tower and Clements came up far short in their bids to win Republican converts from the area in 1978.[16]

By 1980, however, the GOP's budding friendship with social conservatism finally seemed to be threatening those generational loyalties. In the spring of 1980, a controversy involving Baylor University coeds and *Playboy* magazine erupted into a highly visible reflection of how morality and family values could quickly trump other issues and offer a gateway to greater Republican respectability. When Dr. Abner McCall—president of the conservative Southern Baptist university and himself a prominent Reagan supporter—threatened to expel any coeds who posed nude for the magazine, the school newspaper wrote an editorial highly critical of what it called the administration's "censorship." Controversy raged across the campus and the

A volunteer sorts and packages newspapers produced and distributed by the Reagan campaign in Texas, 1980. (Courtesy of the *Dallas Morning News*)

city. Shortly after the editorial was published, McCall shut down the news-paper for three weeks. When the paper finally began publishing again, the three editors responsible for the diatribes against McCall's policies had been fired and replaced. For students, the incident brought to light far more than just a debate on sexual morality; it had also created a divide on the campus over whether or not the university had a right to mandate behavior and re-strict free speech. Not surprisingly, considering that Baylor had sent more student delegates to the 1976 GOP convention than had any other college in the country, most students seemed to back the administration.[17]

Off campus across Waco and the surrounding region, McCall's stance was also overwhelmingly applauded. Waco operated as a hub of grassroots religious conservatism both before and after the *Playboy* controversy. Churches in the area actively assisted "independent" organizations like the Moral Majority in distributing letters, fliers, brochures, and other forms of communication—each promoting vilified images of liberalism resulting in a decline in American prestige across the globe, military weakness, moral laxity, and communist "appeasement." Efforts like these were aided by a pervasive fear at the grass roots that liberal proposals like the Equal Rights

Amendment would ultimately lead to things like the legalization of gay marriage. Such fears became hot topics in Waco throughout the summer and fall of 1980.[18]

In Dallas, the political climate was more complex. In 1980, Dallas boasted 650 companies whose net worth exceeded $1 million, the fourth most of any city in the United States. The abundance of million-dollar companies fueled development and expansion in the city by essentially acquiescing to higher than market property taxes, thus easing the burden on city residents. However, when the Supreme Court disallowed this practice, home owners—long accustomed to shouldering among the nation's lowest overall tax burdens—found property taxes accelerating. A renewal of anti-tax rhetoric ensued.[19]

Dallas also shared San Antonio's reliance on the military as a major component of its economic base. The fighter plane manufacturer Ling-Temco-Vought Corporation based its operations in Dallas, as did General Dynamics. The military's industrial presence in Dallas heightened the city's awareness of national security issues and made national defense budget debates, including Carter's proposal to eliminate the B-1 bomber, a great concern. The conservative philosophy that emphasized strong national defense paralleled the city's economic participation in the military-industrial complex.[20]

Dallas also had social problems that affected its political climate in 1980. A report earlier that year revealed that the city had led the nation in total number of sexual assaults during the previous year. The city was embarrassed by this national attention and initiated a renewed campaign for increased security and crime prevention. The renewed attention given to crime benefited the state GOP, as did the growing pains that accompanied suburban sprawl. As late as the mid-1970s, Interstate 635, known in the area as the Lyndon B. Johnson Freeway, unofficially served as the city's northern boundary. By 1980, tens of thousands of area residents had flocked to the new suburbs north of I-635, partly in response to the decay of the inner city and perceptions that the Dallas Independent School District could not maintain a high standard of education. The largest such suburb to spring up north of I-635 was Plano. Plano became one of the metroplex's largest suburbs and, by 1980, established its own independent school district. Thus, in addition to being a cog in the nation's military-industrial complex, an epicenter of religious conservatism, and an area with a renewed focus on crime, the metroplex was also emblematic of larger patterns of white migration into more homogenous communities, complete with their own school districts, zoning commissions, tax policies, and city managers.[21]

At the same time, it was clear that the DFW metroplex was at the forefront of the state's economic boom. Economists ranked Dallas's economy the second best in the nation, while Fort Worth's, with its mix of military and agricultural industry, ranked ninth. San Antonio ranked fourth and Houston ranked first. The fact that Texas had the most vibrant economy in the nation should have been good news for incumbents. Instead, the vibrant Texas economy moved more residents into the middle class, which resulted in new construction, extended suburban boundaries, encouraged sprawl, and hastened ideological polarization. The thriving economy attracted businesses and labor from across the nation, many of which relocated to Texas without the baggage of political loyalty dogmatically tying them down to a single party.[22]

"The Real Base"

For all of these reasons, Texas was at the epicenter of the GOP's growing national strength. Not only did presidential contenders George Bush and John Connally hail from Texas, but Reagan's organization was so well established in the state that political observers like Tom Wicker of the *New York Times* declared it to be the "real base of the Reagan campaign."

Yet, it was not solely for these reasons that Texas became the locus of campaign attention in 1980. Of all the southern states Carter carried in 1976, none was as crucial to the incumbent president's reelection prospects as Texas. In the aftermath of the 1978 midterms, animosity toward Carter intensified. Beyond national issues of stagflation and global embarrassment, Carter was unpopular for many reasons. He was widely viewed as having reneged on a campaign promise to deregulate natural gas. His energy policy was unpopular among the state's oil power. The vast majority of the state had opposed ratification of the Panama Canal treaties. Carter's popularity was slipping among Hispanics, while grassroots conservatives were mobilizing in both suburban and rural communities.[23] Meanwhile, thanks largely to his campaign team, Texas quickly warmed to Reagan. Texans like Ernest Angelo Jr., Chester Upham, Ray Barnhart, Ron Dear, and Bill Clements each influenced the campaign nationally and in Texas.[24] Between 1978 and 1980, Reagan maintained an active speaking schedule before civic and business organizations across the state. At the top of Reagan's priorities for Texas was the enlistment of grassroots Democrats and independents to his conservative cause. Reagan believed that grassroots Texas Democrats and independents largely shared his philosophy on taxes and government waste. The path to Democratic hearts in rural Texas, however, also necessitated communicating that Reagan, more than his GOP rivals and more than the born-again Southern Baptist Carter, was a true friend to ethics, morality, and family values.[25]

Reagan accomplished this through carefully crafted speeches that appealed to both economics and tradition. Reagan's oratorical skills were the perfect complement to a team of speechwriters who knew how to frame big ideas with emotion and passion. Reagan spoke as a populist, a conservative, a Christian, an anticommunist, and a commoner. He presented himself as the embodiment of hope in contrast to Carter's malaise. He magnified problems, simplified solutions, and romanticized an American past that may never have actually existed. In several speeches, Reagan attacked big government and lionized localism, calling for a return "of the local fraternal lodge, the church congregation, the book club, the farm bureau."[26] On God, Reagan was no less passionate, arguing that Americans must "turn back to God" and warning, "Without such a joining of forces, the materialistic quantity of life in our country may increase for a time, but the quality of life will continue to decrease. Our country is in need of and ready for a spiritual renewal. Such a renewal is based on scriptural reconciliation."[27]

When appropriate, Reagan masterfully tailored his rhetoric for conservative Democrats in rural Texas. His language served the symbolic purpose of appealing to rural and agrarian values, even though the state was clearly headed in an urbanizing direction. The invocation of such neo-Jeffersonian agrarian virtue contributed to a nostalgia for small-town values in Texas by using "farmers" as shorthand for the forgotten American whose idyllic conservative political climate had been plowed under by liberal expansionism and invasion.[28] Yet, Reagan also knew how to blend issues into a web of dissatisfaction and discontent with the status quo of Democratic leadership in Washington, always identified in tandem with liberalism, big government, and threats to the American "way of life."[29] This blending allowed Reagan to maintain consistency with his message regardless of the audience. Whether he was speaking to businessmen or farmers, Reagan sought to capitalize on the nation's desire for hope.[30]

Reagan's most skillful accomplishment was his ability to simultaneously champion conservatism, malign liberalism, and claim with credibility that he was not an ideologue. This was not accomplished by accident. Reagan attacked liberalism directly only when he knew he had a sympathetic audience—such as most of those he encountered in Texas. "We all know how liberals win," Reagan proclaimed in several newsletters mailed to his Texas supporters. "They buy votes with big promises and bigger spending programs. They appeal to those who are willing to trade freedom and pay outrageous taxes in exchange for the mirage of cradle to grave security of the bottom line profit that comes from big government contracts."[31]

Reagan rarely referred to "liberals" without referring to "Liberal Democrats" or the "liberal establishment." He linked his Democratic opponents to elitism and ideology—both characteristics historically applied to Republicans with much greater frequency and negative impact, particularly in Texas. In doing this, Reagan indirectly promoted his own brand of conservatism, created a belief that Republicans were the true party of the common man, and appeared above the ideological fray by condemning Democrats for a dogmatic adherence to leftist political philosophies. Accordingly, his more specific attacks on Carter resonated all the more. Reagan accused Carter of changing "voting laws to make it possible for liberal Democrats and big labor to stack and steal elections." He claimed that Carter had weakened America's "defense by dropping the B-1 bomber and cutting back our Navy, making special deals with the Soviet Union, and otherwise appeasing communism." In these cases, Reagan's rhetoric was not subtle. Words like "freedom," "steal," "weaken," and "appeasement" evoked visceral responses and created urgency in conservative and nonpartisan minds alike, most of whom came to believe that liberals were as extreme and dangerous as Goldwater had seemed in 1964.[32]

Thanks largely to Reagan's charismatic expression and personification of the conservative philosophy, contextualized within a timely and beneficial set of demographic and socioeconomic forces, the Republican Party gained much-needed respectability in Texas. This respectability meshed with perceptions that the Democratic Party had been overtaken by national liberalism. Many began to jump the Democratic ship and strengthen a growing conservative coalition of "disgruntled mavericks," religious conservatives, and free-market libertarians, all of whom could agree on at least one thing—that Jimmy Carter was not one of them.

Contenders, Pretenders, and Unification

Reagan may have been the most popular Republican in Texas, but he was not the only one hanging his hopes for national office there. Long one of the most popular ex-governors in the state, John Connally also wanted the presidency. His bid to establish himself as a nationally viable candidate, however, got off to a rocky start. In February 1978, Connally organized a fund-raiser celebrating the Eisenhower-era Republican Party. Rather than pour his every effort into the occasion, Connally procrastinated. The event was plagued by last-minute logistical problems and raised only $400,000 of a publicized $1.5 million goal. The shortfall was only part of his problem. On the night of the event, rather than organize a series of tributes to the Eisenhower era—the purported theme of the fund-raiser—Connally dominated the evening, delivering a speech that most in attendance found far too long and political. Though the speech focused on the problems of the Carter White House, it was the right speech given at the wrong time and in the wrong place.[33]

Off to a bad start, Connally next purchased the earliest presidential campaign TV advertisement in history, broadcast in October 1979, and set about building his own campaign war chest.[34] Though several of the nation's largest corporations contributed, Connally's ideas about the presidency and the importance of personality drew more attention than his relationship with big business or his economic plans. In 1979, Connally told *Texas Monthly* magazine that "personality is the one essential issue in presidential politics. We are too often mesmerized by matters of policy, looking for the smallest difference that will distinguish candidates, when the big difference—those of personality—are out there for all to see." These statements unintentionally opened the door for criticisms of Connally's personality. Connally had long been viewed nationally as a bit of a "wheeler dealer"—an image helpful in the early 1960s, but harmful in a post-Watergate era that largely distrusted typical politicians.[35]

Nonetheless, as 1980 approached, Democratic insiders quietly feared that Connally was, potentially, their most formidable opponent. A former Democrat from a southern state, Connally, they feared, posed a greater threat to Carter's reelection than did Reagan.[36] Democrats' fears were largely allayed after they conducted a study of Connally's appeal in critical swing states, Texas included. Though now a Republican, Connally was not perceived by the mass public as a true conservative. However, neither was Connally "establishment" or "New Right." If image was everything, as Connally had declared to *Texas Monthly*, then his image lacked, as one Democratic analyst put it, "coloration." Carter's staff began to argue that Connally was the easiest prospective opponent to define because no definition yet existed. Despite this confidence, Carter's advisers became foolishly distracted by Connally and, to a significant degree, dismissed Reagan as a viable national candidate.[37]

Connally, whose campaign may have started in 1976 when Ford and Reagan bickered over his endorsement, a contest that led to the abbreviated introduction of Connally's name as a potential compromise candidate that year, largely based his campaign on a belief that he could steal Reagan's supporters, especially those in Texas. Connally's "ace in the hole" was the perception of his electability. As Carter had, to a more limited extent, successfully done in 1976, Connally chose to align himself with Reagan's rhetoric while dismissing the former Hollywood actor as an extremist. Like Carter, however, Connally also underestimated Reagan's skill in deflecting the charge.

Connally's campaign suffered from a dearth of originality. Borrowing rhetoric from Reagan at every turn—almost to the point of plagiarism— Connally spoke openly against ratification of the Equal Rights Amendment, was adamantly pro-life, and outdid even the Gipper's passion on the issue of illegal immigration.[38] Even more curiously, and reflecting the growing realization that increased minority voting was both an existing threat and a potential new ally, Connally appealed to Texas minorities by actually praising Reagan. He frequently cited the statistic that 20 percent of Reagan's appointees during his first year as governor were minorities as evidence of Republican progressivism on race. In theory, Connally hoped to attract Reagan supporters who were fearful that perceptions of Republican extremism would result in Carter's reelection. He chose to do this by associating himself closely with Reagan, even praising his opponent, in the hopes that minority backers would be softened to the new conservative agenda. It was a curious strategy and one that benefited Reagan far more than it did Connally.[39]

Connally was also hurt by the actions of loyal conservative Democrats in the state legislature. In 1979, in what Connally biographer James Reston called a "decidedly Wild West" event, a handful of Connally supporters in the state legislature began to push a bill to move the Texas presidential primary election up from May to March 11. The goal was to provide Connally with an early and important win, thus giving momentum to his national campaign. The bill won backing from Governor Clements, but when it officially appeared before the legislature, no vote could be had because no quorum existed; twelve liberal legislators, who collectively came to be known as the "Killer Bees," went missing in action in order to prevent a quorum and kill the bill. The situation gained national attention, but not in a good way. The zany antics of the "Killer Bees" made Connally's home state look like a circus. Political observers across the country called the legislature a "laughing stock" and Connally's reputation as a backroom political "wheeler-dealer" once again came to the forefront, though this time, he looked like a failure.[40]

Connally also failed to win the critical support of social conservatives.

Though he had tried to appeal to evangelicals on abortion and the ERA, he also suggested that he would reconsider the U.S. support of Israel if American oil interests were ever threatened. He also supported the establishment of a Palestinian state within Jordan. Evangelicals were not alone in charging anti-Semitism, but they were the most important.[41]

Ultimately, Connally's campaign fatally stumbled even before it got out of the starting gate. Despite his southern appeal, his Texas popularity, his relative moderation, and an impressive war chest donated by some of the nation's most powerful corporations, Connally never even made it to the Texas primary. He withdrew after defeats in Florida and Iowa, leaving Reagan with only one other legitimate challenger for Texans' hearts and minds—another Houstonian, George H. W. Bush.[42]

Bush challenged Reagan with a different strategy than had Connally; he aggressively campaigned against both Reagan and his populist conservative philosophy. Bush's strategy was equally doomed. Loyalty alone should have given Bush a thriving home state advantage, but Reagan appealed to Texas conservatives far more than did Bush. Failing to recognize the success of the new conservative agenda and particularly the antiliberal backlash that accompanied it, Bush derided Reagan's antigovernment populism, forging instead a broadly defined "human rights" theme, similar in tone to Carter's.[43] Characterized as a "Republican for all factions," Bush seemed everywhere and nowhere—all at the same time.[44] He believed that Republicans were desperate to defeat Carter and would make electability a top priority. Therefore, in order to appear electable nationally, Bush embraced his moderation. Famously critiquing Reagan's economic policy as "voodoo economics," Bush found that his opposition to Reagan's proposed tax cuts was particularly harmful to his cause in Texas.[45]

Bush also consistently stayed to Reagan's left on social issues. He openly supported the ERA and opposed a constitutional ban on abortion.[46] Setting himself up in opposition to Reagan on specific issues like taxes and "values" did not make Bush seem more electable to Texans, but more liberal, particularly in contrast to Reagan. The larger issue at stake, therefore, was image. Reagan's appeal as a ranch owner from the West overshadowed Bush in Texas, who had difficulty shaping his public persona because of the perception that he had moved to the state only for political reasons and was, in reality, a carpetbagging New Englander—the same strategy Kent Hance had used to defeat Bush's son, George W., in the nineteenth district's congressional race two years earlier.[47]

Unlike in 1976, when Reagan defeated Ford by a shockingly wide margin, there was much less drama leading up to the 1980 Texas Republican primary. Reagan consistently outpolled Bush by no fewer than 25 points in surveys taken throughout the campaign. In some parts of the state, Reagan's lead over Bush exceeded 60 percent.[48] Yet when voters actually went to the polls, Reagan defeated Bush as expected, but by a slimmer margin than predicted—only 4 points. Bush cut into Reagan's lead during the final week of the campaign for three main reasons. First, the expectation of a Reagan landslide depressed voter turnout, giving Bush an opportunity to narrow the gap simply by getting his supporters out to the polls. Second, Bush shifted gears late in the campaign and decided to join Reagan in making Carter the chief issue of the election.[49] When Bush shifted his attacks away from Reagan, he seemed less divisive, less moderate, more conservative, and more Texan. Lastly, Bush began to match Reagan's rhetoric on national defense. This strategy was particularly effective in Houston, where Bush made small inroads by adopting Reagan's stance on numerous foreign policy issues.[50]

Bush's rightward shift failed to win him the primary, but it solidified which direction the Texas GOP was to take. As more conservatives united under the GOP tent, motivated to do so in the wake of rejecting established Republican moderation, lamenting Carter's failures, and reembracing Reagan, it was clear that Bush, though a Texan, represented the last hope of the old breed of party loyalists willing to sacrifice their conservatism for palatability with the old national GOP establishment. It was not until Bush adopted most of Reagan's platform that his support in Texas increased. The battle over whether the Texas GOP would embrace a moderate past or a populist conservative future was over, and Reagan had won. The grand irony for those like Bush was that what finally pushed the Texas (and national) GOP over the edge was its willingness to embrace what they had long perceived as too great a risk.[51]

Bush's conservative shift in Texas contributed to his nomination for the vice presidency. The combination of Reagan and Bush helped unify the Texas GOP, whereas it had remained fatally divided in 1976.[52] Yet, the unification was the result of far more than a convenient political partnership. The state GOP entered the 1980 presidential campaign as a force to be reckoned with. Its agenda mirrored the national party's, communicated the tenets of populist conservatism, and took advantage of internal divisions within the Democratic Party. Within this newly constructed political culture, Texas voters were left with the same question that had traditionally defined state politics; it was a clear choice between conservatism and liberalism.[53]

Revolution

In 1979, Phil Gramm, a young conservative Democrat in Texas's sixth congressional district and future convert to the Republican Party, canvassed churches, restaurants, and neighborhoods to investigate the level of support in his district for Jimmy Carter. Gramm's findings did not encourage him to offer Carter his endorsement. Gramm's district, which covered rural and small towns stretching from South Dallas to Bryan, was typically Texan— traditionally Democratic though vociferously antiliberal and willing to break party ranks in presidential elections. The district, which had overwhelmingly rejected McGovern liberalism in 1972, returned to the fold in 1976 and supported Carter. Yet by 1980, Carter's populism and moral authority were being questioned. Rather than rally behind tradition and partisan loyalty, Gramm gained favor in his district by opposing much of Carter's legislative agenda and encouraging other conservative Texas Democrats to do the same.[54]

Whereas Carter fell out of favor with conservative Democrats like Phil Gramm, Reagan had no such problem. Masterfully using television and radio to broadcast his conservative qualifications to the entire state, Reagan publicized endorsements from several prominent Texas political leaders. Former governors Allan Shivers, John Connally, and Preston Smith joined current governor Bill Clements in not just endorsing Reagan but also appearing together in front of cameras as a show of conservative unity on behalf of the Republican nominee.[55] John Tower also lent his support, not so much by enthusiastically endorsing Reagan, but rather by simply hammering Carter. Tower spoke to civic groups across Texas about "trimming the bureaucratic fat" from Washington, called Carter "weak on defense," and labeled Democratic tax policies as "punitive" and "overbearing." On the issue of Carter's promises from 1976 to deregulate the oil and gas industry, Tower practically called the president a liar.[56]

With Texas grassroots enthusiasm for Republican conservatism at an all-time high, and Carter's unpopularity crushing Democratic credibility at the national level, the state's political loyalties and traditions quickly began to change. For the first time since Reconstruction, Republican candidates in Texas enjoyed a widespread optimism that they could be not only collectively competitive but individually successful—even at the local level.[57] Reagan himself was the source of that optimism and unity. GOP candidates for every office imaginable contacted the Reagan campaign asking, not for a joint appearance—though Reagan's willingness to do that was always welcome—but simply for Reagan to mention, by name, particular candidates in his speeches across Texas.[58] Reagan's support was so important that even conservative Democrats like Gramm and Kent Hance began to identify their campaigns with the Republican presidential nominee.[59]

Reagan skillfully blended his national rhetoric with local issues to elicit a visceral connection between conservatives and the Republican Party. Whether he was campaigning to businessmen in Dallas, oil barons in Houston, Mexican Americans in San Antonio or El Paso, defense contractors in Fort Worth, or farmers at local and county fairs in West Texas, conservatives of almost every ilk felt that Reagan supported them personally.[60] Part of this was simply public relations skill, but much more of Reagan's success could be attributed to the thematic approach to his rhetoric. Reagan's speeches were tailored in only small ways depending on his audience, while Carter and national Democrats seemed much less capable of offering a single message to multiple constituencies.[61]

Reagan's appeal was further reflected by the success of his fund-raising efforts. Texas provided Reagan with a unique opportunity to build his campaign coffers without having to do much to appeal to state or local issues. There were two main reasons for this. First, older, wealthier Republican conservatives inclined to donate large sums to the Reagan campaign were used to a system in which state and local politics, long dominated by the Democratic Party, were largely off limits to the GOP. As such, by 1980 the tradition that Texas Republicans invest their resources in national success was a well-established practice. At the same time, Reagan's appeal to socially conservative and more rural Democratic Texans reflected a branding of conservatism that was appealing regardless of region. Though the Texas GOP did well with its more affluent constituents, Reagan also received more small donations from rural Texans in 1980 than did Carter.[62] Also important was the dramatic infusion of out-of-state dollars. For instance, an independent organization known as Americans for Effective Presidency (AEP) raised more than half a million dollars and spent it on anti-Carter advertising in Texas, Illinois, and Ohio. Anti-Carter funds flowed into Texas from all parts of the country.[63]

One of Reagan's greatest allies in Texas was Bill Clements, who had made Carter's defeat a personal goal. Clements also served as the campaign chairman for Reagan-Bush in Texas.[64] Though he had been elected largely because he was a friend to Dallas and Houston big business, with some social conservative crossover, Clements invested his political capital in 1980 into the mobilization of grassroots Texas conservatives. Clements raised more than $2.5 million in funds for the Reagan-Bush campaign in Texas, which embarked on the most successful grassroots Republican operation in

Volunteers staff a Reagan-Bush phone bank in Dallas, 1980.
(Courtesy of the *Dallas Morning News*)

state history. By the end of September, the Reagan-Bush campaign had more than thirty thousand volunteers staffing fifty phone centers in thirty-nine cities across the state, each operating sixty-six hours per week. By election day, these call centers alone had reached more than 3 million Texans on behalf of the Reagan campaign.[65] The success of the call centers inspired the Carter campaign to attempt a similar grassroots mobilization in Texas, though with only $400,000 raised and public animus against Carter running high, their efforts fell flat.[66]

Clements also spearheaded an organization known as the Texas Victory

Committee. He and his wife, Rita, served on the board of this committee along with numerous other influential Texas Republicans, including Ernest Angelo Jr. and former Goldwater and 1960s Republican guru Peter O'Donnell. In addition to overseeing operations at all fifty of the state's volunteer call centers, the Texas Victory Committee organized phone bank systems in 177 of Texas's 254 counties. The massive reach achieved by these centers combined with the mobilization of grassroots conservatives under the control of the state GOP to foster a sense of party loyalty among middle-class, working-class, and rural conservatives. Such participation shifted the emotional connection of the grass roots away from one of a temporary cross-voting protest to one of manifest partisan realignment. In early October, the Dallas County Reagan phone bank, because its call center had already reached its capacity of five thousand volunteer workers, turned away literally hundreds of supporters looking to donate their time on Reagan's behalf.[67]

The telephone, however, was not the state's only weapon in the public relations battle for Texans' hearts and minds. The Texas Victory Committee also sent more than five hundred thousand letters to undecided voters in the state, eighty-four thousand letters to conservative voter groups active in various parts of the state, and eight hundred thousand letters to rural voters.[68] Throughout 1980, phone banks and direct mail helped reach hundreds of thousands of Texans. The campaign also organized dozens of special interest voter groups, many of which found their driving force in Texas. For instance, Roger Staubach served as the national chairman for one of the most prominent of these voter groups, Athletes for Reagan-Bush. Staubach, a former naval officer, Heisman Trophy winner, and Super Bowl–winning quarterback for the Dallas Cowboys, also enlisted the services of Houston Astros pitcher Nolan Ryan, Dallas Cowboys head coach Tom Landry, Cowboys defensive coordinator Ernie Stautner, and former Cowboy defensive standouts Bob Lilly and LeRoy Jordan. Four years earlier, NFL Films had dubbed the Cowboys "America's Team"; in 1980, America's Team, whose very mascot recognized the heroic nature of the cowboy in American history, was more or less on Reagan's team.[69] Staubach's support for Reagan was particularly effective in Texas. Admired and trusted far more than most politicians, Staubach used his stature in Texas to promote Reagan as a necessity for America's future. In direct mailings, Staubach told Texans that he was not yet a registered Republican but was voting for Reagan because he was "scared about what has happened to the United States under Jimmy Carter." "To me," Staubach continued, "a vote for Ronald Reagan in 1980 is a vote for the future of my children."[70]

Ronald Reagan receives a jersey from Dallas Cowboys legends Roger Staubach and Tom Landry, 1980. (Courtesy of the *Dallas Morning News*)

Texas was also the operating hub for Hispanics for Reagan-Bush. This organization was partly developed in response to the Texas Victory Committee's assessment that its one weakness was in the need for advertisements reaching Mexican Americans and other Hispanics. With headquarters in Texas and a major branch of operations in California, Hispanics for Reagan-Bush helped organize Republican efforts and extend the party's reach into these communities across the state.[71]

Voter groups for Reagan-Bush reached almost every imaginable constituency. Sportsmen and Conservationists for Reagan-Bush operated in Texas, Pennsylvania, Florida, Illinois, and Ohio. National Small Business for Reagan-Bush operated in Texas, Oklahoma, Illinois, Michigan, New York, Pennsylvania, New Jersey, and California. Other voter groups actively supporting the Reagan campaign effort in Texas through direct mail, local meetings, and a general fostering of identification with Republican activities included Lawyers for Reagan-Bush, Realtors for Reagan-Bush, Seniors for Reagan-Bush, Veterans for Reagan-Bush, and Youth for Reagan-Bush.[72] The Reagan campaign in Texas did a particularly effective job of mobilizing support among college students in state universities. This was accomplished through cooperative efforts with student groups like College Republicans and Young Republicans, who provided entrées for the Reagan campaign into fraternity and sorority houses, agriculture clubs, and campus ROTCs.[73]

That Reagan's campaign went out of its way to identify so many different voter groups, yet maintained a relatively consistent and simple message with each of them, reflects an important Republican strategy—and one that was essential to political transformations in Texas. Conservative Republicans made small interest groups and voting blocs feel recognized and valued. This contributed to Reagan's persona as a populist with an interest in the lives of ordinary Americans.[74]

The marketing of political ideology developed into one of the most powerful strategic political weapons in the conservative arsenal of 1980. Despite the fact that much of his career had been built by opposing liberals in his own party, Jimmy Carter became a symbol of liberalism, much in the same way that Reagan became a conservative icon. The potency of negatively associating Carter with liberalism was further highlighted by the visibility of economic and foreign policy failures. The more Carter was associated with failure, the more failure was associated with liberalism, and liberalism was circularly associated with the Democratic Party. At every campaign stop in Texas, Carter desperately and noticeably tried to avoid the term *liberal*, which ironically made the appellation that much more potent a weapon.[75]

On the other hand, Carter feebly tried to embrace a Democratic tradition that seemed somewhat old-fashioned to most Texans. Carter always reminded voters of their Democratic heritage at his campaign stops in Texas, routinely employing antiquated—at least in view of the 1980 political culture—attacks against Republicans. Carter threw the word *Republican* around as if he were speaking of evil itself, and routinely associated Republicans with "antipopulism."[76] At a rally in Beaumont, Carter accepted a pair of cowboy boots and told his audience that he was going to use them to "stomp Republicans" and "step around all their horse manure."[77]

Undermining Reagan's popularity in Texas was a daunting task. Initially, while hoping to recast the word *Republican* into the evil moniker it had once been, Carter also pinned his hopes on defining Reagan as an extremist. Yet when Reagan showed righteous indignation in response to such attacks, he appeared to be the victim of dirty politics.[78] Carter then began to suggest that Reagan lacked both the intelligence and the temperament necessary to avoid international confrontations.[79] Nothing seemed to work. Ironically, by late October, Carter was exerting far more energy trying to buttress his own hawkish credentials against attacks that his liberal weaknesses had invited the Iran hostage crisis and subsequent embarrassments, not to mention the Soviet Union's invasion of Afghanistan and the relatively unpopular response of an Olympic boycott.[80]

Reagan's Texas campaign also publicly identified Carter's failures and broken campaign promises with a lack of honesty.[81] Reagan's ability to turn Carter's greatest assets in 1976—his honesty and ethics—against him in 1980 was a particular coup.[82] Carter was accused of corruptions and abuses including leaking classified information, fudging statistics, and misusing federal employees.[83] Attacking Carter's honesty successfully reminded Texans that corruption in Washington, DC, was bipartisan. Adding to the perception that political corruption knew no partisan boundaries was the fact that Texas House Speaker and Democrat Billy Clayton had been on trial in Houston for the better part of the year, defending himself against allegations that he had illegally awarded insurance contracts to state employees. The Clayton scandal was widely reported throughout the state and made attacks against other Democrats, particularly Carter, seem more credible.[84]

Texas Republicans painted Carter as weak and incompetent, while Reagan blasted the incumbent president for being "missing in action"—a reference with military connotations to Carter's lack of leadership in Washington. When Carter's ideology and moral integrity were not being called into question, his energy policy was. Conservative campaigns in Dallas and Houston typically focused on Carter's hostility toward the oil industry. When Reagan used the energy issue, he rarely failed to mention America's dependency on foreign sources of oil or connect that dependency to the administration's problems in Iran. Reagan's ability to transform the perception of conservatism and negatively redefine liberalism as a failed philosophy was the result of Republican strategists' ability to mesh issues into one mammoth problem of incompetence, corruption, big government, and lack of moral leadership.[85]

Unlike Reagan's well-oiled campaign machine, Carter's advisers never managed to structure a message consistent enough to unify a cross-section of Texas voters. Failing to make "Republican" synonymous with evil, and failing to connect Reagan to extremism, Carter chose to go after Texas liberals. In speeches across Texas, Carter stressed his support for big labor, health care reform, equal rights for women and minorities, mass transit, and energy conservation. In Brownsville, Carter campaigned on bilingual education, his doubling of funds for student-aid programs, his expansion of Head Start programs to include migrant workers' children, and he promised to extend health care benefits to larger numbers of impoverished Mexican Americans. Carter's appeals worked for him in South Texas, but against him when they were broadcast to the rest of the state so that Republican conservatives could decry further expansions of federal bureaucracy and inattention to white middle-class issues. Carter's campaign strategy in Texas appeared bifurcated and convoluted, which only enhanced the attractiveness of Reagan's simple, cohesive, and ideological message.[86]

Texas Republicans also promoted their budding friendship with the state's evangelicals. In July, at a Christian booksellers' convention in Dallas attended by more than fifteen thousand evangelicals, the Reagan campaign spent $1,000 to set up a "Reagan Info Booth" containing $20,000 worth of "Reagan vs. Carter Issues Tracts"—about 500,000 such tracts—for distribution at the convention and thence at five thousand bookstores across Texas. The success of this endeavor prompted the spending of an additional $35,000 to mail 225,000 more of the tracts to Protestant and Catholic clergy nationwide. Social conservatives appreciated the Republican courtship of evangelicals, which inclined them toward conservatives like Reagan who appeared to be sincerely interested in attracting Christian support.[87]

Though Carter's spirituality was more well known than Reagan's, the Republican's relationship with the Texas religious establishment was far healthier. On August 22, Reagan spoke before the Religious Roundtable's National Affairs Briefing in Dallas. Leading up to the event, Reagan was frustrated and uncertain over how he should approach his speech to this audience and even told one adviser that he would just "wing it."[88] Ultimately, Reagan's speechwriters managed to craft a speech that was, in their words, "denominationally clean." The speech was also written to include what Reagan's handlers called "code words"—meaning religious allusions that only evangelicals would pick up on, but that would illustrate a deep awareness of and commitment to fundamentalist Christianity.[89]

Despite the initial difficulties of Reagan and his speechwriters, when Reagan arrived at the podium to address an audience of evangelicals in Dallas, the result was a smashing success. As adeptly as a pastor, Reagan preached the authority of scripture, calling it "God-breathed." He articulated the need for America to revive its ethical code based on biblical standards.[90] He lamented America's "moral decline" and related that decline to increased "peril [faced] from atheist tyranny abroad." Reagan's speech even drew the praise of national Jewish leaders, not just for its reassertion of support for Israel, but also because of Reagan's general stand on morality and ethics.[91]

Reagan did something else with this speech—something that was tactically brilliant in light of Texas's Democratic heritage and his awareness that Carter would be using that heritage as his chief strategy in Texas. Reagan evoked sympathy and camaraderie from the evangelical crowd by linking Carter's attacks against him and other Republicans to Christ's warnings

that Christians would endure persecution. In doing this, Reagan established that he and his audience had a common enemy. We are "all perse-
cuted together by Democrats and liberals," Reagan said.[92] Reagan's
appearance in Dallas solidified his support among evangelicals in Texas by
successfully demonstrating a credible awareness of biblical teachings and
then linking those teachings to modern America's problems. Reagan's appearance at the Religious Roundtable's National Affairs Briefing in Dallas
was such a brilliant political success that the campaign included the text of
the speech in new brochures distributed to churches throughout the state.[93]

Following the success in Dallas, Reagan made numerous personal appearances at churches across the state during the campaign, including one
memorable stop at the First Baptist Church of Dallas, where he was welcomed by the famed pastor, W. A. Criswell.[94] Reagan also enjoyed the support of Abner McCall, the Baylor University president who had famously
taken a stand against *Playboy's* recruitment of Baylor coeds earlier that year.
McCall led the McClennan County Reagan-Bush campaign and drew the
support of numerous other rural Baptists in the county, most of whom had
supported Carter in 1976.[95] Reagan's relationship with Texas religious organizations was so tight that by October, Robert Strauss, himself a Dallasite
and the chairman of the Carter-Mondale Committee, publicly charged that
multiple churches and religious organizations had merged illegally with
political action committees to raise money for Reagan.[96]

These efforts resulted in an overflow of correspondence from evangelicals, each expressing concern over a multiplicity of issues, but all sharing a
single-minded and committed support for Reagan's campaign against liberalism. Some Texans detailed their own conversion to Reagan Republicanism. Many of these Republican converts shared that they had long been
hesitant to embrace the GOP. For many, the GOP had never been trustwor-
thy and had always been seen as a friend "only of the rich." However, the
confluence of recent events, liberal failures, Democratic shifts to the left,
and Reagan's campaign had convinced them otherwise. As pastors, lay
leaders, and average churchgoers wrote the Reagan campaign of their support for the Republican fight against the ERA, humanism, socialism, communism, abortion, the acceptance of the theory of evolution, high taxes,
and a host of other evils, the relationship between social conservatives in
Texas and the Republican Party grew much more secure.[97]

The possibility of increased defense spending under a Reagan presidency, combined with a generally hawkish conservative climate, further
contributed to Reagan's popularity. The military-industrial complex had
contributed to the economic growth of communities like Dallas, Fort

Worth, and San Antonio since the 1960s.[98] While many Texans were encouraged by the potential economic benefit of a Reagan-led military, far more were attracted to the emotional elements of a patriotic renewal of American prestige and power across the globe. Such an attraction almost thoroughly scuttled Carter's plan to label Reagan as dangerous. In San Antonio, for instance, Henry Cisneros, then a pro-Carter city councilman, remarked to one reporter that "Carter's hole card was that Reagan would be seen as a horrible alternative. But so far, he doesn't look that horrible. He goes out and talks to the working people in language they can understand." Lyndon Johnson's former press secretary and longtime Texas political insider, George Christian, began privately telling Carter campaign officials as early as September that the national defense issue would be as strongly anti-Democratic as it had been in 1972, when George McGovern's failed campaign helped redefine and imbue notions of liberalism with inherent military weakness. With Reagan promising to restore American pride and prestige to pre-Vietnam levels, a promise that came with hope for increased financial benefits to much of the state, Carter's foreign policy failures were magnified.[99]

Reagan also enjoyed a relatively prosperous courtship of Mexican American and other Hispanic voters in Texas. In 1976, Gerald Ford carried only 13 percent of Hispanic voters in the state. In 1980, Reagan's Texas campaign team hoped to capitalize on several legitimate opportunities to garner as much as 25 percent of the state's Hispanic vote.[100] Reagan's efforts to attract Texas Hispanic voters were successful for four reasons. First, Reagan made numerous personal appearances before Hispanic crowds in Texas. On September 16—Diez y Seis de Septiembre or Mexican Independence Day, most commonly celebrated in Texas and Southwest border states—Reagan appealed to a Mexican American crowd in Harlingen on the basis of community, tradition, freedom, independence, and the value of work. Observers noted Reagan's ability to connect with Hispanics' sense of hope for a better future, but were also impressed by the Republican Party's acknowledgement of political neglect in these communities.[101] Even Carlos Puente, a former La Raza organizer turned born-again Christian in 1977, was attracted to the Reagan campaign. By the mid-1980s, Puente—along with many other Hispanic political activists—began donating their time to the Republican National Hispanic Assembly.[102] Thus, the second reason Reagan was able to earn the support of many Texas Hispanics was his ability to capitalize on a pervasive distrust and dislike of Carter. Reagan accused Democrats of failing to deliver on their promises to Texas Hispanics. He then promised to do better.[103] The third main reason for Reagan's success among Hispanics in 1980 was that Bill Clements went out of his way to soften the GOP's image among that minority and largely succeeded. Clements appointed numerous Hispanics to positions within his administration and successfully used the Texas press to publicize those appointments.[104] The fourth reason explaining Reagan's support among Texas Hispanics was a related point—advertising and public relations. The Reagan campaign saturated Spanish-speaking television stations with advertisements lauding the virtues of the GOP and disparaging the Democratic Party and its presidential ticket.[105] In October, Reagan strategists in Texas mailed more than 250,000 letters to Texans with Spanish surnames. The mailing included a brochure outlining the differences between the Republican and Democratic parties in Texas on various social issues of particular importance in Catholic communities.[106]

Reagan was also careful not to insult or patronize Mexican American and other Hispanic voters. Prior to speaking engagements, Reagan carefully digested tips on how to interact in these settings. He was told to refer often to the culture, tradition, and pride of these communities. He was told always to emphasize family, neighborhood, dignity, and self-respect. When listing ethnic minority groups in Texas whose problems had not been adequately addressed by the Democratic Party, Reagan was told to mention Hispanics first. Reagan was also given a list of "don'ts." He was told not to refer to "Chicanos" or "Latinos." He was also told never to wear "Mexican-style" clothing, speak Spanish, or refer to the Alamo or "Illegals." Reagan's efforts were successful; he received more than twice as many votes from Texas Hispanics than Ford had received from that community four years earlier.[107]

All told, Reagan and his Texas Republican allies were simply better at public relations than were Democrats in 1980. Direct mailings, press releases, public appearances, television commercials, and a simplified yet effectively constructed message broke down barriers that stood in the way of a conservative realignment of the state's Republican Party. Though an adopted rather than native son, Reagan, acting as the state party's most recognizable figurehead, gifted Texas Republicans with widespread social acceptability among conservatives, moderates, and even increasing numbers of state Hispanics. Virtually every Reagan-Bush campaign center across Texas struggled to keep in stock enough brochures, buttons, bumper stickers, and yard signs to meet public demand. Walk-in traffic to these headquarters was heavy, the consumption of Reagan-Bush advertising seemed insatiable, and word of such activity became a hot topic in local restaurants, grocery stores, and neighborhoods across Texas.[108]

Conversely, Carter's efforts in Texas floundered, especially toward the end of his campaign. His appearances were usually scheduled in the heat of the day, which noticeably annoyed the press team following him. Additionally, the press corps hammered Carter for not establishing a clearer theme in his campaign and belittled the retreads of anti-Republican and Democratic-loyalty messages to which Carter routinely reverted. Furthermore, the cloud of the Iran hostage crisis typically followed Carter to each campaign stop, where local reporters emphasized that the president's performance in Texas was critically important to his reelection prospects.[109]

Carter's national gaffes also affected his standing in Texas. The day following the final nationally televised presidential debate, during which Carter responded to a question about which issue he believed was most important by telling the audience which issue his thirteen-year-old daughter, Amy, thought was most important, Reagan stumped across Texas, mockingly asking rhetorical questions of the crowd, which responded in unison, "Ask Amy! Ask Amy!"[110]

Ultimately, Carter lost his image war with Reagan not simply because he was on the wrong side of popular opinion on a host of issues, or because a revitalized GOP attracted so many traditionally Democratic voters, but because in the battle for public opinion, conservatism seemed patriotic and practical while liberalism appeared outdated, extreme, and failed. On the night before the election, Reagan spoke to a national audience on this very theme. His speech captured the essence of his popularity in states like Texas: "Not so long ago, we emerged from a world war. Turning homeward at last, we built a grand prosperity and hoped—from our own success and plenty—to help others less fortunate. Our peace was a tense and bitter one, but in those days the center seemed to hold. Then came the hard years: riots and assassinations, domestic strife over the Vietnam War and in the last four years, drift and disaster in Washington."

Reagan then invoked the name of an old friend: John Wayne. Wayne's death in 1979 was treated in the press with headlines like "The LAST American Hero" and "Mr. America Dies." "Well," Reagan said, "I knew John Wayne well, and no one would have been angrier at being called the LAST American hero. Just before his death, he said in his own blunt way, 'Just give the American people a good cause, and there's nothing they can't lick.'" Reagan continued: "I find no national malaise, I find nothing wrong with the American people. Oh, they are frustrated, even angry at what has been done to this blessed land. But more than anything they are sturdy and robust as they have always been." Reagan ended his speech with a story about tourism in Washington, DC, saying, "These visitors to that city on the Potomac do not come as white or black, red or yellow; they are not Jews or Christians; conservatives or liberals; or Democrats or Republicans. They are Americans awed by what has gone before, proud of what for them is still . . . a shining city on a hill."[111]

Jimmy Carter and the Democratic Party could not overcome the collision of forces working against them in Texas in 1980. The state's economy was thriving, though no credit was given to Carter. Instead, Carter and the Democratic Party seemed to threaten the basis for that economic surge, specifically on issues of energy and defense. The Texas economy attracted Americans from across the nation who helped diffuse the anti-Republican tradition that had previously dominated state politics. These factors contributed to the rise of thriving suburbs in areas like Dallas, where the social activism of evangelical Christians was among the most pronounced and influential in the nation. The rise of suburbia and the growing respectability of Republicanism were not unrelated or unforeseen phenomena in other parts of the nation. Yet, the way in which Texas's economy was structured, the state's diverse racial demography, and the overall size and importance of Texas to national realignment gave the state a unique importance and regional identity. Whereas Reagan carried southern states like Alabama, Arkansas, Mississippi, North Carolina, South Carolina, and Tennessee each by less than 2 percent in 1980, his margin of victory in Texas was a comfortable 14 points.

On November 4, 1980, the Texas Republican Party's decades-old drive for legitimate second-party status finally meshed with the momentum of modern American conservatism to usher in the Reagan Revolution. Reagan's victory was different than either of Eisenhower's, or even Nixon's in 1972. The *Texas Observer* editorialized that the elections of 1980 had served as a "neutron bomb" on the state Democratic Party.[112] *Texas Monthly* declared the 1980 elections to be the death knell of what was left of modern American liberalism.[113] Texans would not give their electoral votes to a Democratic presidential candidate again in the twentieth century.

Conclusion

Among the notable casualties of Reagan's revolution in 1980 was Houston's famously liberal congressman Bob Eckhardt. Eckhardt had represented Houston's eighth congressional district since 1966, when he carried an astonishing 93 percent of the general election vote. Between 1968 and 1976, Eckhardt ran for reelection every two years, his percentage of the general election vote never falling below 60, or below 77 in the primary. In 1978, Joe Archer became the first to legitimately challenge Eckhardt in the Democratic primary by suggesting that the incumbent was more liberal than Democrat, at least by Texas standards. Calling out Eckhardt on issues of gun control and energy policy, Archer won 47 percent of the vote. A young local attorney from the area, Archer set the stage for another young attorney, Republican Jack Fields, to finally unseat Eckhardt in 1980 in one of the more memorable local races of the year.[1]

The shifting political winds of the late 1970s staggered an unprepared Eckhardt, who had also faced, but repelled, similar struggles over busing a decade earlier. Between 1979 and 1980, locals challenged Eckhardt's support for Carter, specifically on abortion, the Panama Canal, tax exemptions for private Christian schools, and the hostage crisis in Iran.[2]

Fields was primed to take advantage of these winds and ran a classically antiliberal campaign against the incumbent. He de-emphasized party while emphasizing ideology, and made conservatism on national issues the centerpiece of his campaign. His radio, newspaper, and television ads emphasized the conservative perspective on "forced busing," school prayer, "Tax Dollars for Homosexual legal representation," congressional pay raises, "Foreign Aid to Communist Countries," the proposed "bailout" of New York City, balancing budgets, lower taxes, strong national defense, and opposition to the Department of Education. Fields also portrayed himself as "an avid hunter . . . opposed to all forms of gun control" and highlighted Eckhardt's "D"—the grade the NRA had given the incumbent on gun rights. Fields even benefited from the support of controversial oil magnate and part-time radio commentator Eddie Chiles, whose famous catch phrase, "I'm Eddie Chiles and I'm mad as hell!" had spawned a local fad of bumper stickers proclaiming, "I'm Mad Too, Eddie!" Fields, whose campaign slogan emphasized that a vote for him was a vote "for change," successfully tapped every antiliberal and populist-conservative impulse of the late 1970s—and he also outspent his opponent, thanks to significant backing from the district's corporate and oil interests. In October, an editorial in the *Houston Post* called Fields a "slick media creation" but acknowledged that the appeal of the conservative message might be more than Eckhardt could overcome.[3]

Fields, however, left nothing to chance. On October 16, Bryan Wirwicz, the news secretary for the Fields campaign, mailed Eckhardt a copy of a letter that he claimed had been received and opened by the Fields campaign by mistake. The letter, which came with a $5 contribution to the Eckhardt campaign, was purportedly written by a Mark Florio of Virginia. In the letter, Florio, addressing Eckhardt, wrote that the $5 contribution was a reflection of his annual effort to support "liberal Democrats" like "Ted Kennedy." "I for one am glad you support school busing and gun control," Florio's letter explained. "I'm proud that you have stood up and worked against all those new weapons systems in Congress. Most of all I am glad you have fought to keep prayers out of the schools." The letter clearly appeared to be evidence that Eckhardt's liberalism had attracted the support of East Coast liberals. Before returning the wrongfully opened letter to Eckhardt, Wirwicz sent a copy to local newspapers.[4]

As it turned out, Florio was actually a committed conservative who worked indirectly for the National Conservative Political Action Committee (NCPAC). The letter had been intentionally designed for the purpose it achieved. Intentionally mailed to Fields, intentionally opened despite the fact that the envelope was addressed to Eckhardt, and intentionally leaked to local media, the letter achieved the desired effect. In Republican campaign material and in the press, Eckhardt drew increasingly strident and unflattering comparisons to "ultra-liberals" like Ted Kennedy, Jimmy Carter, and even George McGovern.[5]

Efforts to make Eckhardt seem like an outsider in his own district did not dissuade Fields from holding his own fund-raisers in Dallas, Washington, and Chicago. Yet Fields also enjoyed the support of more than two thousand volunteer "blockworkers" who canvassed over fifteen thousand homes in the eighth district, door-to-door. In November, despite winning more votes in 1980 than he had in 1968, when he carried 71 percent of the

Ronald Reagan and George Bush campaign together in Austin, 1984.
(Courtesy of the Ronald Reagan Presidential Library, Simi Valley, CA)

vote, Eckhardt lost his reelection bid to Fields, 52–48. The antiliberal campaign meshed with the district's rapid population growth, almost all of it in suburbs—where Fields took 73 percent of the vote—to doom the Democratic incumbent. Certainly, Eckhardt was not the first liberal to lose an election in Texas under similar circumstances, nor would he be the last. Yet in the context of Reagan, Carter, and the revolutions of 1980, the defeat of a formerly popular seven-term congressman was obviously reflective of the onrushing partisan realignment clearly strangling the loyalties and traditions of Texas politics.[6]

The Reagan Revolution of 1980 established Texas at the forefront of modern American conservatism. Four years later, Dallas was selected as the host city for the Republican National Convention. Twenty years earlier, Ronald Reagan had been the lone bright spot in Barry Goldwater's futile campaign against the Texan and incumbent president, Lyndon Johnson. In 1984, just twenty-one years since the very mention of Dallas conjured images of motorcades, assassinations, and shame, Ronald Reagan—the standard-bearer for a new generation of Republican conservatives—accepted his renomination for the presidency less than one mile from Dealey Plaza. To be sure, times had changed. The Dallas of 1984 was the Dallas of fictional oil baron and ruthless businessman J. R. Ewing. It was the Dallas of "America's Team," led by their evangelical head coach, Tom Landry. And it was home for a thriving base of conservative Reagan Republicans. The 1984 Republican National Convention became both Texas's and Dallas's opportunity to showcase themselves afresh to the nation.[7]

In the less than three decades prior to the 1984 Republican National Convention, Texans' loyalties were challenged, traditions retired, and politics changed. This transformation did not occur overnight, nor was it shaped by any single issue or cause. Certainly, economics was a key. In the aftermath of World War II, new industries descended upon the state, diversifying the economic climate and contributing to what became the nation's strongest state economy for much of the 1960s and 1970s. Race also played a major role. As African American enfranchisement heightened the importance of minority voting in Texas, diversity and liberalism came to dominate the Democratic Party, pushing many white conservatives, initially against their will, to the GOP. Yet the active presence of Mexican Americans and other Hispanics in Texas complicated the state's racial climate and created a dynamic unique in the South. Religion was another major factor. A revival in politically active evangelicals suddenly and forcefully began to alter the state's political agenda in the early 1970s. At the same time, government itself seemed less and less capable of solving the problems of crime, chaos, and disorder that so many Americans had, in the past, turned to government to solve.

Yet, even the combination of these impulses does not fully explain the transformations occurring in Texas during this time. If these impulses formed a basis for political change, then image, perception, and iconography gave that basis its personality and momentum. Throughout the 1980s, Texas Republicans continued to embrace the support of their traditional base—affluent elites—but also welcomed the support of, as Jim Hightower once called them, "disgruntled mavericks." These mavericks, not to be confused with Dallas's relatively new NBA franchise, were comprised of working-class populists, evangelical Christians, suburban middle-class traditionalists and aspiring business leaders, college-aged fraternity and sorority members, and older citizens who blamed the decadence of the 1960s and selfishness of the 1970s on the failures of liberalism and the national Democratic Party, which came to be vilified across much of Texas as weak and amoral.

In Reagan's Texas, it was Republicans who best voiced patriotism, tradition, and faith. It was Republicans who sought to eliminate race from the political discourse, publicly conceiving of all citizens as color-blind, nonhyphenated Americans. It was Republicans who wanted to lower taxes, not raise them. It was Republicans who defended faith and religion. And it was Thomas Jefferson, long embraced as the father of the Democratic Party, whom Reagan grew so fond of quoting—for Jefferson represented the Founding Fathers, the revolution against tyranny, the demand for power to the people, and a respect—at least rhetorically—for the central place that faith played in shaping America's ideals.[8]

In 1996, Joseph Ellis wrote of Jefferson's political genius in the context of his timelessness as an American icon. "A crucial component of Jefferson's genius," Ellis wrote, "was his ability to project his vision of American politics at a level of generalization that defied specificity and in a language that seemed to occupy an altitude where one felt obliged to look up and admire without being absolutely certain about the details."[9] Much the same can be said of Reagan, who, at the 1992 Republican National Convention in Houston, amusingly stole a page from the Democratic playbook of just four years earlier by saying that he had known and was a friend of Jefferson's and that the Democratic presidential nominee of that year, Bill Clinton, was no Thomas Jefferson.

Texas has continued to play a pivotal role in shaping national politics since the 1980s. Houston's George Bush ran for and won the presidency in 1988, earning a measure of revenge against the man who had defeated him in the 1970 Senate race—Lloyd Bentsen. Bentsen ran in 1988 as the Democratic Party's vice presidential nominee alongside former Massachusetts governor Michael Dukakis. Despite a 17-point lead following the Democratic National Convention that summer, the Democratic ticket was soundly defeated that November, thanks largely to image warfare fought primarily with some of the era's most vicious campaign commercials. Those advertisements positioned the campaign as what a majority of Texans saw as a battle between patriotic conservatism and malaise-ridden and failed liberalism. Bill Clinton won two terms to the White House in the 1990s, but failed to carry Texas in either of his campaigns. The polarizing Clinton presidency pushed still more Texans into the Republican Party and, in 2000, the GOP gave its presidential nomination to Texas governor George W. Bush and his running mate, Dick Cheney, who—despite an official Wyoming residency—had deep ties to both the Reagan and Bush administrations as well as to the Houston oil industry of the 1990s. In two tightly fought national campaigns, the junior Bush won eight years in the White House, carrying his home state of Texas with ease on both occasions.[10]

The roots of national conservative Republican growth between 1980 and 2004 were located deep in the heart of Texas. By 2002, those roots were finally and fully evident at the state and local levels. Traditions and loyalties died harder at these levels than they did at the national level, where images were more easily and effectively employed as a barometer of ideological loyalties. Yet the early years of the new millennium found Republicans in control of every statewide office in Texas, both houses of the state legislature, and both of the state's U.S. Senate seats. For decades, Republicans and liberal Democrats had worked toward the same goal in Texas—a two-party state. Liberals, in cooperation with moderate Democrats, eventually succeeded in ousting the conservatives from control of the Texas Democratic Party. Eventually, Republicans also succeeded, emerging not simply as a viable second party but as the dominant party—in what some liberal Democrats have lamented is, once again, ironically, a one-party state.

In 2008, Leigh Clemons, commenting on what she called a "performing culture," had this to say about the Lone Star State: "What we learn from the Texan is the importance of performance in creating and maintaining a cultural identity that, both powerful and fragile, constantly repeats and changes our understanding of history, myth, and memory—and of identity itself."[11] Almost without question, Texas politics has conformed to this pattern. The rise of modern Texas conservatism not only coincided with a similar ascendancy nationwide, but also gave the movement shape and momentum. With its unique regional identity and boundless expanse of political bravado, Texas has become the heart of modern conservative Republicanism.

Notes

Abbreviations

AGAP   Annelise Graebner Anderson Papers, Hoover Institution on War, Revolution, and Peace, Stanford University, Stanford, CA

BAP   Bruce Alger Papers, Texas/Dallas History & Archives Division, Dallas Public Library, Dallas, TX

CAH   Center for American History, University of Texas, Austin, TX

CRP   Citizens for Reagan Papers, Hoover Institution on War, Revolution, and Peace, Stanford University, Stanford, CA

DHP   Deaver & Hannaford, Inc. Papers, Hoover Institution on War, Revolution, and Peace, Stanford University, Stanford, CA

DMN   *Dallas Morning News*

GC   General Correspondence

GFL   Gerald R. Ford Presidential Library, Ann Arbor, MI

GMcGP   George S. McGovern Papers, Seeley G. Mudd Manuscript Library, Princeton University, Princeton, NJ

GMP   George Mahon Papers, Southwest Collection, Texas Tech University, Lubbock, TX

HGP   Henry B. Gonzalez Papers, Center for American History, University of Texas, Austin, TX

HI   Hoover Institution on War, Revolution, and Peace, Stanford University, Stanford, CA

JBP   James A. Baker III Papers, Seeley G. Mudd Manuscript Library, Princeton University, Princeton, NJ

JCF   Political Operations (Jerry Carmen) Files, Ronald Reagan Presidential Library, Simi Valley, CA

JCL   Jimmy Carter Presidential Library, Atlanta, GA

JCP   Jimmy Carter Papers (Pre-presidential), 1976 Campaign Files, Jimmy Carter Presidential Library, Atlanta, GA

JTP   John G. Tower Papers, John Tower Library, Southwestern University, Georgetown, TX

LBJL   Lyndon B. Johnson Presidential Library, Austin, TX

OHC   Oral History Collection, University of North Texas, Denton, TX

PHP   Peter Hannaford Papers, Hoover Institution on War, Revolution, and Peace, Stanford University, Stanford, CA

PRP   Papers of the Republican Party [microform], George Smathers Libraries, University of Florida, Gainesville, FL

PSP   Preston Smith Papers, Southwest Collection, Texas Tech University, Lubbock, TX

REP   Robert C. Eckhardt Papers, Center for American History, University of Texas, Austin, TX

RRCF   Pre-presidential Papers of Ronald Reagan, 1980 Campaign Files, Ronald Reagan Presidential Library, Simi Valley, CA

RRL   Ronald Reagan Presidential Library, Simi Valley, CA

SEF   Staff Office Files, Domestic Policy Staff, Stu Eizenstat, Jimmy Carter Presidential Papers, 1977–81, Jimmy Carter Presidential Library, Atlanta, GA

SGML   Seeley G. Mudd Manuscript Library, Princeton University, Princeton, NJ

SWC   Southwest Collection, Texas Tech University, Lubbock, TX

TO   *Texas Observer*

WCP   Waggoner Carr Papers, Southwest Collection, Texas Tech University, Lubbock, TX

WPCP   William P. Clements Papers, Cushing Library, Texas A&M University, College Station, TX

Introduction

1. George Reedy to Ernest Goldstein, memorandum, "Forces at Work in Texas," May 23, 1968, box 70, White House Central Files: Political Affairs, LBJL; Key, *Southern Politics in State and Nation*, 254–76.

2. Phillips, *American Theocracy*, 233, 249.

3. Reagan carried Texas in 1980 and 1984; George H. W. Bush carried Texas in 1988 and 1992; Dole carried Texas in 1996; George W. Bush carried Texas in 2000 and 2004.

4. Campbell, *Gone to Texas;* Jackson, *Crabgrass Frontier.*

5. Goldberg, *Barry Goldwater;* Perlstein, *Before the Storm.*

6. Barr, *Reconstruction to Reform;* Brown, *Hood, Bonnet, and Little Brown Jug;* Carleton, *Red Scare;* Bass and De Vries, *Transformation of Southern Politics;* Black and Black, *Rise of Southern Republicans.*

7. Robinson, "Public Affairs Television"; Flamm, *Law and Order.*

8. Zaretsky, *No Direction Home.*

9. Phillips, *The Emerging Republican Majority.*

10. Campbell, *Gone to Texas;* Jackson, *Crabgrass Frontier;* Bass and De Vries, *Transformation of Southern Politics.*

11. Foley, *White Scourge.*

12. For more on South Texas social and political culture, see Carroll, *Felix Longoria's Wake.*

13. George Reedy to Ernest Goldstein, memorandum, May 23, 1968, box 70, White House Central Files: Political Affairs, LBJL. See also Campbell, *Gone to Texas;* Key, *Southern Politics in State and Nation;* Green, *Establishment in Texas Politics.*

14. George Reedy to Ernest Goldstein, memorandum, May 23, 1968, box 70, White House Central Files: Political Affairs, LBJL; Campbell, *Gone to Texas,* 225–29; Key, *Southern Politics in State and Nation;* Green, *Establishment in Texas Politics.*

15. White, *"It's Your Misfortune."*

16. Critchlow, *Phyllis Schlafly.*

17. Black and Black, *Rise of Southern Republicans;* White, *"It's Your Misfortune,"* 370.

18. Carter, *The Politics of Rage;* Crespino, *In Search of Another Country;* Critchlow, *Phyllis Schlafly;* Dallek, *Right Moment;* Flamm, *Law and Order;* Kruse, *White Flight;* Lassiter, *Silent Majority;* Link, *Righteous Warrior;* McGirr, *Suburban Warriors;* Schoenwald, *Time for Choosing.*

1. The Eyes of Texas

1. Key, *Southern Politics in State and Nation,* 254–55.

2. Campbell, *Gone to Texas.*

3. Bridges, *Twilight of the Texas Democrats,* 1–22; Campbell, *Gone to Texas,* 242–46.

4. Blight, *Race and Reunion;* Bridges, *Twilight of the Texas Democrats,* 1–22; Campbell, *Gone to Texas,* 287–89.

5. Barr, *Reconstruction to Reform;* Foley, *White Scourge.*

6. Barr, *Reconstruction to Reform;* Foley, *White Scourge;* Campbell, *Gone to Texas.*

7. Barr, *Reconstruction to Reform;* Foley, *White Scourge;* Campbell, *Gone to Texas.*

8. Green, *Establishment in Texas Politics.*

9. Barr, *Reconstruction to Reform;* Campbell, *Gone to Texas.*

10. Barr, *Reconstruction to Reform;* Campbell, *Gone to Texas.*

11. Brown, *Hood, Bonnet, and Little Brown Jug;* Campbell, *Gone to Texas,* 344–45.

12. Brown, *Hood, Bonnet, and Little Brown Jug;* Campbell, *Gone to Texas,* 344–45; Key, *Southern Politics in State and Nation,* 254.

13. Brown, *Hood, Bonnet, and Little Brown Jug;* Campbell, *Gone to Texas,* 350–52, 374–76; Key, *Southern Politics in State and Nation,* 264–65.

14. Brown, *Hood, Bonnet, and Little Brown Jug;* Campbell, *Gone to Texas,* 350–52, 374–76; Key, *Southern Politics in State and Nation,* 264–65.

15. Campbell, *Gone to Texas,* 361–64; Foley, *White Scourge,* 118–40.

16. Campbell, *Gone to Texas,* 361–64; Foley, *White Scourge,* 118–40.

17. Bridges, *Twilight of the Texas Democrats,* 1–22.

18. Green, *Establishment in Texas Politics;* Key, *Southern Politics in State and Nation,* 254–55.

19. Campbell, *Gone to Texas,* 396–410; White, *"It's Your Misfortune."*

20. Campbell, *Gone to Texas,* 396–410; White, *"It's Your Misfortune."*

21. Campbell, *Gone to Texas,* 396–410; White, *"It's Your Misfortune."*

22. Campbell, *Gone to Texas,* 396–410; White, *"It's Your Misfortune";* Jackson, *Crabgrass Frontier.*

23. Campbell, *Gone to Texas,* 396–410; White, *"It's Your Misfortune."*

24. Bridges, *Twilight of the Texas Democrats,* 1–22; Green, *Establishment in Texas Politics,* 58–100; Key, *Southern Politics in State and Nation,* 254–56.

25. Bridges, *Twilight of the Texas Democrats,* 1–22; Green, *Establishment in Texas Politics,* 58–100; Key, *Southern Politics in State and Nation,* 254–56.

26. Bridges, *Twilight of the Texas Democrats,* 1–22; Green, *Establishment in Texas Politics,* 58–100; Key, *Southern Politics in State and Nation,* 254–56.

27. Bridges, *Twilight of the Texas Democrats,* 1–22; Green, *Establishment in Texas Politics,* 58–100; Key, *Southern Politics in State and Nation,* 254–56.

28. Campbell, *Gone to Texas,* 406.

29. Green, *Establishment in Texas Politics,* 77–120.

30. Green, *Establishment in Texas Politics*, 111–12; Campbell, *Gone to Texas*, 414–15.

31. Green, *Establishment in Texas Politics*, 111–12; Campbell, *Gone to Texas*, 414–15.

32. Green, *Establishment in Texas Politics*, 121–34.

33. Dallek, *Lone Star Rising*, 185–224; Campbell, *Gone to Texas*, 414–15; Green, *Establishment in Texas Politics*, 55, 69–76.

34. Campbell, *Gone to Texas*, 410–11; Green, *Establishment in Texas Politics*, 77–100.

35. Carleton, *Red Scare!* Green, *Establishment in Texas Politics*, 120–34.

36. Carleton, *Red Scare!* Green, *Establishment in Texas Politics*, 120–34.

37. Campbell, *Gone to Texas*, 415–16; Dobbs, *Yellow Dogs and Republicans*.

38. Campbell, *Gone to Texas*, 415–16; Dobbs, *Yellow Dogs and Republicans*.

39. Green, *Establishment in Texas Politics*, 171–92.

40. Campbell, *Gone to Texas*, 415–16; Dobbs, *Yellow Dogs and Republicans*.

41. Green, *Establishment in Texas Politics*, 135–50; Olien, *From Token to Triumph*.

42. Green, *Establishment in Texas Politics*, 135–50; Olien, *From Token to Triumph*.

43. Dobbs, *Yellow Dogs and Republicans;* Green, *Establishment in Texas Politics;* Olien, *From Token to Triumph.*

44. Weeks, *Texas in the 1960 Presidential Election*, 48; *DMN*, July 21, 1960, 12A.

45. Olien, *From Token to Triumph*, 172–74.

46. Ibid.

47. Campbell, *Gone to Texas*, 433.

48. Ibid.

49. John Tower, "The Value of the Two-Party System," speech, Brownwood, TX, 1961, box 19, JTP.

50. James A. Bertron to George O. Fowler, letter, *Human Events*, February 27, 1961, box 437, JTP; Mrs. R. G. Freeman to Tower, letter, May 19, 1961, GC, box 437, JTP.

51. Betty Andujar, oral history, September 12, 1993, Fort Worth, TX, interview by Kristi Strickland, OHC. For more on the role of women in building the GOP, see Rymph, *Republican Women*.

52. "Conservative Democrats" to "Democratic Voters," form letter, May 15, 1961, box 437, JTP.

53. Tower to "Fellow Conservatives," form letter, March 22, 1961, box 438, JTP.

54. "Tower on the Issues: Houston, March 13, 1961"; "Platform-Answers to Questions Asked John Tower, October 1960–March 1961," both in box 438, JTP.

55. 1961 campaign files, box 439, JTP.

56. George Christopher to Tower, "Committee for Texas: Composed of Citizens of Texas Whose Primary Political Interest Is the Welfare of Texas," letter, April 26, 1961, box 437, JTP.

57. Press release, February 15, 1961, box 438, JTP; GC, box 437, box 439, box 706, JTP; Bridges, *Twilight of the Texas Democrats*, 1–22; Campbell, *Gone to Texas*, 433.

2. Growing Pains

1. "Outlawing the Communist Party in Texas," box 882, folder 3, ACLU Papers, SGML.

2. Unidentified newspaper clipping, box 1, BAP.

3. Dallas County GOP newsletter, October 28, 1954, box 1, BAP.

4. 1954 campaign literature, box 1, BAP.

5. "Free Enterprise vs. the Something-for-Nothing Philosophy," speech, April 26, 1955, SMU, Dallas, box 2, BAP.

6. Alger, September 24, 1956, box 2, BAP.

7. "Coffee with Your Congressman, Bruce Alger," transcript, October 26, 1956, box 2, BAP.

8. Precinct #114 GOP, "Six Reasons to Vote for Bruce Alger," undated, box 2, BAP.

9. Olien, *From Token to Triumph,* 139–41, 151.

10. Alger to Eichner, Eisenhower-Nixon Texas Headquarters, letter, October 18, 1956, Speech Proposal; press release, October 24, 1956, box 2, BAP.

11. Alger, "The Mainstream of Freedom," speech, September 18, 1959, box 5, BAP.

12. Washington Report, by Congressman Bruce Alger, 5th District, Texas, March 5, 1960, box 7, BAP.

13. General Edwin A. Walker Correspondence-Literature, 1961–62, box 10, folder 23, BAP.

14. Alger to AG Hill, letter, February 12, 1962, box 10, BAP.

15. Green, *Establishment in Texas Politics,* 165.

16. Alger, form letter, April 13, 1961, box 10, BAP.

17. Alger, "God in Our Government: August 30, 1962," commentary, box 13, BAP.

18. "Do You Want a Public Housing Project in Your Neighborhood?" Brochure from Dallas Voters against Public Housing, undated, box 13, BAP.

19. Republican—State of Texas—Correspondence, 1963, box 23, BAP.

20. Campaign material, 1962, box 13, BAP.

21. Peter O'Donnell, press release, December 21, 1962, box 23, BAP.

22. Bill Jones, 1962 campaign speech, transcript, undated, box 13, BAP.

23. Washington Report by Congressman Bruce Alger, 5th District, Texas, November 30, 1963, box 23, BAP.

24. Ibid.

25. "Alger Campaign, May 6, 1964," meeting notes, box 29, BAP.

26. Ibid.

27. Earle Cabell, oral history, October 2, 9, 16, 1974, Dallas, TX, interview by Ronald E. Marcello, OHC.

28. 1964 campaign correspondence, miscellaneous letters, box 29, BAP.

29. Republican—State of Texas—Correspondence, 1963, box 23, BAP.

30. Micklethwait and Wooldridge, *Right Nation.*

31. *Houston Chronicle,* June 26, 1964, box 4C512, Harris County Democratic Party Records, CAH.

32. Ibid.

33. Tower, "Conservatism Unashamed," January 1963, box 17, folder 1, Press Office, JTP.

34. Transcript, John Tower Oral History Interview II, 9/22/71, by Joe B. Frantz, Internet Copy, LBJL.

35. *Texas Monthly,* April 1976, 111, box 9, David Stoll Collection, HI.

36. *New York Daily News,* October 21, 1964, box 337, series 1, Records of the Democratic National Committee, LBJL; Lassiter, *Silent Majority,* 231.

37. Transcript, John Tower Oral History Interview I, 8/8/71, by Joe B. Frantz, Internet Copy, LBJL; Olien, *From Token to Triumph,* 188.

38. Kitchel, "Extremism in the Defense of Liberty," draft copy, undated, box 5, Denison Kitchel Papers, HI.

39. Perlstein, *Before the Storm;* White, *Making of the President, 1964,* 98–129; Nash, *Conservative Intellectual Movement.*

40. Neal Allen, Randall County chairman, to Goldwater, letter, April 14, 1961, GC on Tower Campaign, 1961, box 437, JTP.

41. Telephone Canvass and Results & Summary Report, February to March 1961, box 439, JTP.

42. "The Public Image of Senator Barry Goldwater: A Pilot Study," conducted for Peter O'Donnell Jr., Opinion Research Corporation, Research Park, Princeton, NJ, October 1963, box 443, folder 14, Tower Senate Club, 1964 Goldwater Presidential Campaign, JTP.

43. "Texas Attitudes toward Kennedy and Johnson," August 1964, "Confidential Report of Results of a Statewide Survey of Voters," Louis, Bowles and Grace Research Consultants, box 9, Office Files of George Reedy, LBJL.

44. Press release, January 27, 1964, box 3H516, Stephen Shadegg Papers/Barry Goldwater Collection, CAH; McGirr, *Suburban Warriors;* Perlstein, *Before the Storm;* White, *Making of the President, 1964,* 98–129.

45. *Texas Monthly,* April 1976, 111.

46. Ibid.; Piereson, *Camelot and the Cultural Revolution;* Hofstadter, *Paranoid Style.*

47. *Texas Monthly,* April 1976, 111.

48. "A Declaration of Republican Principle and Policy," undated, box 442, folder 2, Tower Senate Club, 1964 Goldwater Presidential Campaign, JTP.

49. Seconding speech to the Goldwater nomination, box 442, folder 12, Tower Senate Club, 1964 Goldwater Presidential Campaign, JTP.

50. Ibid.

51. John Bainbridge, "The Super-Americans," 1962, box 9, David Stoll Collection, HI.

52. "The Goldwater Candidacy and the Christian Conscience: The Response of Protestant Theologians," pre-election material, September 1964, box 6, Office Files of Bill Moyers, Presidential Papers of Lyndon B. Johnson, LBJL.

53. "Citizens for Goldwater-Miller: Victory Manual," September 7, 1964, box 3H513, Stephen Shadegg Papers/Barry Goldwater Collection, CAH.

54. "Secret: For a Free People," National Republican Convention: Platform Committee, July 1964, box 442, folder 13, Tower Senate Club, 1964 Goldwater Presidential Campaign, JTP.

55. Barry Goldwater, "Liberalism Has Failed," in *The Conservative Tide: A Student Journal of Fact and Opinion,* November 1963, box 17, folder 7, Press Office, JTP.

56. Perlstein, *Before the Storm.*

57. "Barry Goldwater Speaks Out on the Issues," box 3H514, Stephen Shadegg Papers/Barry Goldwater Collection, CAH; "Speaker's Handbook," box 3H513, Stephen Shadegg Papers/Barry Goldwater Collection, CAH.

58. 1964 Texas Republican Precinct Plan—Confidential, box 625, Preston Smith Papers, SWC; William F. Erwin, letter, October 28, 1964, box 4C512, Harris County Democratic Party Records, CAH; O'Donnell to "Texas Editors," letter, October 23, 1964, box 3H516, Stephen Shadegg Papers/Barry Goldwater Collection, CAH.

59. Democratic National Committee, "A Goldwater Primer in Five Parts," undated, Barry Goldwater Files, box 406, GMP.

60. White, *Making of the President, 1964,* 190–220.

61. AFL-CIO Committee on Public Education, "The Extremists," undated, box 52, series 2, Records of the Democratic National Committee, LBJL.

62. *Austin American Statesman,* July 18, 1964, 1A.

63. Goldwater, campaign speech at Colt Stadium, Houston, October 15, 1964, Office Files of Bill Moyers, LBJL; Jody Baldwin to Pam Rymer, memorandum, subject: Summary of "trend" reports for the week of Sept. 27–Oct. 3, Polls, box 3H516, Stephen Shadegg Papers/Barry Goldwater Collection, CAH.

64. Bass and De Vries, *Transformation of Southern Politics,* 306.

65. Hart, *Sound of Leadership,* 164.

66. *Austin American Statesman,* July 19, 1964–July 28, 1964, 1A.

67. Personal—For the President: Points on Campaign Strategy, 1964, box 71 (1 of 2), Confidential File: Political Affairs, Presidential Papers of Lyndon B. Johnson, LBJL.

68. Pamphlets, stickers, records of the Texas State Democratic Committee, LBJL.

69. Transcript, John Tower Oral History Interview III, 11/1/71, by Joe B. Frantz, Internet Copy, LBJL.

70. *Austin American Statesman,* November 2, 1964, 1A.

71. Ibid.

72. Reagan, "A Time for Choosing," speech transcript, October 27, 1964, Office Files of Bill Moyers, LBJL.

73. Bass and De Vries, *Transformation of Southern Politics,* 312; *DMN,* October 28, 1964, 5A; James A. Leonard to Bush, letter, June 2, 1965, box 5, George Bush Senate Campaign File, WCP.

74. *DMN,* November 4, 1964, 1A.

3. Reconstructing Conservatism

1. Address by Ben H. Carpenter, president, Texas and Southwestern Cattle Raisers Association at its Annual Membership Convention, March 26, 1968, "Speeches," box 613, Dolph Briscoe Papers, CAH.

2. Robinson, "Public Affairs Television."

3. Flamm, *Law and Order.*

4. Robinson, "Public Affairs Television."

5. Memorandum to the president, September 23, 1964, through Walter Jenkins, from: Bill Moyers, Subject: Release of the FBI Report on Riots, box 4, Office Files of Bill Moyers, Presidential Papers of Lyndon B. Johnson, LBJL; "An Indictment of the Democratic Party, 1961–1968," reel 7, frames 37–44, PRP; "Political Profiles of the States, 1968: March 1, 1968," part 2, reel 5, frame 457, PRP; Crime and Delinquency, June 1968, part 2, reel 6, frame 451, PRP.

6. Flamm, *Law and Order;* "Political Profiles of the States, 1968: March 1, 1968," part 2, reel 5, frame 457. PRP; Crime and Delinquency, June 1968, part 2, reel 6, frame 451, PRP.

7. U.S. Department of Justice, Office of Justice Programs, Bureau of Justice Statistics, Crime, State Level, State-by-State and National Trends, 1960–1980 (see the Justice Department's Web site).

8. Flamm, *Law and Order;* "Political Profiles of the States, 1968: March 1, 1968," part 2, reel 5, frame 457, PRP; Crime and Delinquency, June 1968, part 2, reel 6, frame 451, PRP.

9. Memorandum for W. Marvin Watson, August 1, 1966, box 368, White House Central Files: Public Relations, LBJL.

10. *Austin American Statesman,* August 2, 1966, A1; Lavergne, *Sniper in the Tower.*

11. "The Tower Massacre," *Daily Texan,* August 5, 1966.

12. "The State of the Republican Party as of February 1965: Report by RNC Chairman Dean Burch," part 1, series B, reel 4, frame 733, PRP.

13. Ibid.

14. Ibid.

15. Ibid.; *Houston Chronicle,* May 6, 1965, box 4C514, Harris County Democratic Party Records, CAH.

16. *Lubbock Avalanche-Journal,* September 8, 1966, 1A.

17. *Fort Worth Star-Telegram,* October 23, 1966, box 63, JTP.

18. *TO,* October 28, 1966, 7; *TO,* December 9, 1966, 24, box 63, folder 11, Press Office, JTP; unidentified 1966 newspaper article, box 63, folder 7, Press Office, JTP.

19. El Paso County GOP, "How to Canvass and Win the Latin-American Voter of Low Income," box 2, Citizens for Reagan Papers, HI; James Leonard to Tower, memorandum, April 25, 1966, box 711, folder 1, Austin Offices, JTP.

20. M. P. Maldonado, chairman, Amigocrats for Tower Committee, form letter, 1966, box 725, JTP.

21. Radio address transcription, April 20, 1966, box 28, WCP.

22. Garcia, *Viva Kennedy,* 166, 179–80.

23. Olien, *From Token to Triumph,* 208.

24. Marvin Collins to O'Donnell, letter, October 10, 1966, Austin Office, box 711, folder 11, JTP; Olien, *From Token to Triumph,* 210–11; Reston, *Lone Star,* 301–2, 314.

25. *Houston Chronicle,* October 18, 1965; *Amarillo Daily News,* October 20, 1965.

26. Louis Harris and Associates, Inc., report prepared for Walter Cronkite, *CBS News,* box 2M750, Walter Cronkite Papers, CAH; *Tyler Courier-Times Telegraph,* October 23, 1966.

27. "A Look at John G. Tower: Candidate for the United States Senate," box 814, folder 4, Campaign/Political: Washington Office, JTP.

28. Lance Tarrance to Jim Leonard, letter, October 19, 1966, box 710, folder 9, Austin Office, JTP.

29. Jerry Kamprath to Tower chairmen, memorandum, July 27, 1966, box 711, folder 21, Austin Office, JTP; Tower Topics, October 8, 1966, box 711, folder 20, Austin Office, JTP.

30. W. N. Dorsett to Carr, letter, November 28, 1966, box 2, 1966 Senate Campaign Correspondence File, WCP; John W. Key Jr. to Carr, letter, November 29, 1966, box 2, 1966 Senate Campaign Correspondence File, WCP; *DMN,* November 8, 1966.

31. Office of the Governor, press memorandum, March 8, 1966, box 41, WCP; Radio spot text, 1968 Gubernatorial Campaign Files, box 5, WCP.

32. "Support Governor Reagan for President," brochure, Campaign '68, box G0152, Governor Ronald Reagan Papers, 1967–75, RRL; Opinion Research Corporation: Issues and Forces in 1968 Presidential Election, box 2M752, Walter Cronkite Papers, CAH; "The New Conservatism," *Atlas World Press,* March 1978, box 85, DHP.

33. Memorandum for Mr. Bundy, Subject: President Johnson's Foreign Policy Positions as developed in the 1964 Election Campaign, October 29, 1964, box 41, National Security File: Subject File, Presidential Papers of Lyndon B. Johnson, LBJL.

34. Media appearances, transcripts, 1967, GC, box 435, GMP; Reagan to Goldwater, letter, May 27, 1971, box 2, Denison Kitchel Papers, HI.

35. McGirr, *Suburban Warriors.*

36. *TO,* March 3, 1967, 8; Davidson, *Race and Class;* Bass and De Vries, *Transformation of Southern Politics,* 502.

37. *TO,* May 12, 1967, 10.

38. Ibid.

39. *TO,* May 26, 1967, 8.

40. *TO,* November 10, 1967, 11.

41. Jerry Hursh to Doug Bennet, memorandum, October 15, 1968, box 178, Office Files of Frederick Panzer, LBJL.

42. Opinion ballots, 1968, box 374, GMP.

43. Ben Carpenter, form letter, September 6, 1968, box 613, Dolph Briscoe Papers, CAH; "Texas Party Faithful Aren't," *Evening Star,* September 10, 1968, box 407, GMP.

44. "Politics on the 'King's Ranch,'" *New York Times Magazine,* June 5, 1966, box 661, ACLU Papers, SGML.

45. Address by Ben H. Carpenter, president, Texas and Southwestern Cattle Raisers Association at its Annual Membership Convention, March 26, 1968, "Speeches," box 613, Dolph Briscoe Papers, CAH; *DMN,* March 3, 2006.

46. Texas State Democratic Convention, program, September 20, 1966, Austin, box 615, PSP.

47. "Politics on the 'King's Ranch.'"

48. Reston, *The Lone Star,* 344, 370–71.

49. Ibid., 342–43.

50. Ibid.; Bass and De Vries, *Transformation of Southern Politics,* 41–56.

51. Reston, *The Lone Star,* 366–71.

52. Ibid.

53. Ibid.

54. Bartley, *The New South,* 396; *Public Papers of the Presidents:* Lyndon B. Johnson (1968), 963.

55. Opinion Research Corporation: Issues and Forces in 1968 Presidential Election, box 2M752, Walter Cronkite Papers, CAH; The Humphrey Handbook for the 1968 Presidential Campaign, part 2, reel 5, frames 589–642, PRP.

56. Reston, *The Lone Star,* 372–74; Remarks of Hubert H. Humphrey to the Houston Area Labor Leaders, September 11, 1968, box 281, series 1, Records of the Democratic National Committee, LBJL.

57. *Houston Chronicle,* September 10, 1968.

58. MLS to Harold, "The Candidate's Guide to Radio," memorandum, February 16, 1968; Television spot, general text, undated; press release, May 23, 1968; Preston Smith, form letter, undated; advertisement copy, May 24, 1968, all in box 435, GMP; GC, box 615; F. Clifton White to Preston Smith, letter, October 12, 1970, box 625, PSP; Mike McKinnon to Mahon, letter, May 18, 1971, box 435, GMP.

59. *Houston Chronicle,* November 27, 1966, November 10, 1968.

60. Hawkins Menefee, "The Two-Party Democrats, The Study of a Texas Political Faction," MA thesis, University of Texas, Austin, January 1970, box 1, John Knaggs Papers, John Tower Library, Southwestern University, Georgetown, TX.

61. Candidate Strategy for 1968: Confidential (First Draft), March 6, 1967, box 639, folder 3, Tower Senate Club, JTP; *TO*, October 18, 1968, 1–4; "Republican Research Report: Is the Democratic Party Fit to Govern? May 15, 1968," part 2, reel 6, frame 328, PRP.

62. *DMN*, November 9, 1966, 12A–13A.

63. Note to editors, July 26, 1968, Congressional Quarterly Service, box 2M752, Walter Cronkite Papers, CAH; Fred Panzer to president, memorandum, September 8, 1967, White House Name File: Ronald Reagan, LBJL; Belden poll, September 1967, box 178, Office Files of Frederick Panzer, LBJL; statewide poll, September 29, 1967, box 70, White House Central Files: Political Affairs, LBJL.

64. Speech, Rice Hotel, Houston, October 26, 1967, tape 296, Ronald Reagan Gubernatorial Audiotape collection: 1965–74, RRL.

65. *Dallas Times Herald*, October 27, 1967; *TO*, December 22, 1967, 2; press conference, Rice Hotel, Houston, October 26, 1967, tape 296, Ronald Reagan Gubernatorial Audiotape collection: 1965–74, RRL.

66. Speech, Rice Hotel, Houston, October 26, 1967, tape 296, Ronald Reagan Gubernatorial Audiotape collection: 1965–74, RRL.

67. Press release, November 13, 1967, box G0152, Governor Ronald Reagan Papers, 1967–75, RRL.

68. Note to editors, July 26, 1968, Congressional Quarterly Service, box 2M752, Walter Cronkite Papers, CAH; Fred Panzer to president, memorandum, September 8, 1967, White House Name File: Ronald Reagan, LBJL; Belden poll, September 1967, box 178, Office Files of Frederick Panzer, LBJL; statewide poll, September 29, 1967, box 70, White House Central Files: Political Affairs, LBJL; GC, Box 4, Kathryn R. Davis Papers, HI.

69. *DMN*, August 7, 1968, 5A, August 6, 1968, 1A.

70. *DMN*, August 5, 1968–August 9, 1968.

71. Ibid.

72. "Meeting of the Republican National Committee, August 9, 1968: Remarks by Richard M. Nixon," part 1, series B, reel 7, frames 52–66, PRP; Reston, *The Lone Star*, 372–76.

73. Governor Wallace on the *Joey Bishop Show*, transcript, box 281, series 1, Records of the Democratic National Committee, LBJL; Cannon, *Governor Reagan*, 263–65; Isserman and Kazin, *America Divided*.

74. "Meeting of the Republican National Committee, August 9, 1968: Remarks by Richard M. Nixon," part 1, series B, reel 7, frames 589–642, PRP; memorandum for Nixon and Agnew, September 20, 1968, box 15, AGAP.

75. Memorandum for Nixon and Agnew, September 20, 1968, box 15, AGAP.

76. William Loeb, publisher, Manchester Union League, to Tower, telegram, June 18, 1968, box 250, JTP.

77. Nixon for President Committee, letter, White House Name File: Richard Nixon, LBJL.

78. Texas poll, October 13, 1968, box 178, Office Files of Frederick Panzer, LBJL.

79. Republican Research Report: The Crisis in Credibility, June 9, 1966, part 2, reel 4, frames 606–26, PRP.

4. "I am a Sick American"

1. *Lubbock Avalanche-Journal,* April 15, 1971.
2. Carter, *Politics of Rage;* Robinson, "Public Affairs Television."
3. John Bainbridge, "The Super-Americans," 1962, box 9, David Stoll Collection, HI.
4. Texas Issues, undated, box 52, series 2, Records of the Democratic National Committee, LBJL.
5. Green, *Establishment in Texas Politics,* 186–90; Tygiel, *Baseball's Great Experiment,* 269–79; GC-1954, box 3R417, Sam Rayburn Papers, CAH.
6. Green, *Establishment in Texas Politics,* 186–90.
7. Ibid.
8. Ibid.; Transcript, Billy Graham Oral History Interview, Special Interview, 10/12/83, by Monroe Billington, Internet Copy, LBJL.
9. Mahon, form letter, August 1959, GC, Local Reactions, Civil Rights, box 337, GMP.
10. GC, Civil Rights Act, Local Reactions, 1963–64, box 337, GMP.
11. Ibid.; GC, box 71, White House Central Files: Political Affairs, LBJL; "Texas Attitudes toward Kennedy and Johnson, August 1963, Confidential Report of Results of a Statewide Survey of Voters," Louis, Bowles and Grace Research Consultants, box 9, Office Files of George Reedy, LBJL.
12. John Tower, "A Statement Relative to the Civil Rights Bill," *Life* magazine, box 17, folder 10, Press Office, JTP; Reston, *The Lone Star,* 294–317.
13. Reston, *The Lone Star,* 294–317.
14. Kruse, *White Flight;* Lassiter, *Silent Majority.*
15. GC, Civil Rights Reactions, box 386, GMP.
16. *DMN,* July 3, 1964, August 7–11, 1965; Davidson, *Race and Class;* "An Indictment of the Democratic Party, 1961–1968," part 2, reel 7, frames 209–10, PRP; *New York Journal-American,* February 12, 1964; Support for and Opposition against Civil Rights Bill, 1964, box 6, series 1, Records of the Democratic National Committee, LBJL.
17. Mahon to Bill Billingsly, letter, April 10, 1968, box 334, GMP; GC, Civil Rights, 1966, 1967, box 336, GMP.
18. "Statement in Opposition to the Housing Provisions of the Administration's Proposed 'Civil Rights Act of 1966'—Prepared at the Request of John Tower, by Robert L. Thornton, American Law Division, July 19, 1966"; draft remarks of Senator Tower, undated, box 250, JTP.
19. The 1968 Elections: A Summary Report with Supporting Tables, part 2, reel 8, frames 187, 189, PRP.
20. The 1964 Texas Republican Precinct Plan—Confidential, box 625, PSP.
21. The 1968 Elections: A Summary Report with Supporting Tables, part 2, reel 8, frame 186, PRP; Olien, *From Token to Triumph,* 214–18.
22. *DMN,* August 9, 1968, 1A; Fred Panzer to the president, memorandum, September 17, 1968, box 27, White House Central Files: Political Affairs, LBJL; Texas poll, September 29, 1968, box 178, Office Files of Frederick Panzer, LBJL.

23. *DMN,* August 9, 1968, 1A; memorandum for Nixon and Agnew, September 20, 1968, box 15, AGAP.

24. George Wallace—Southern Liberal: A Profile in Political Description, box 16, AGAP; memorandum for Nixon and Agnew, September 20, 1968, box 15, AGAP; Olien, *From Token to Triumph,* 214–18.

25. George Wallace—Southern Liberal: A Profile in Political Description, box 16, AGAP; memorandum for Nixon and Agnew, September 20, 1968, box 15, AGAP; Olien, *From Token to Triumph,* 214–18.

26. O'Donnell to Tower, letter, September 12, 1968, box 250, JTP.

27. Schoenwald, *Time for Choosing,* 252.

28. Lynda L. Kaid, interview with author, November 7, 2006, Gainesville, FL. Kaid served as a campaign worker for Paul Eggers's gubernatorial campaign in 1970 and John Tower's senate campaign in 1972.

29. Campaign research files, 1968, box 618–20, PSP.

30. Johnny Morales, director of advertising and PR, Cen-Tro Advertising and Public Relations, Austin, "Suggested Campaign Plan," box 615, PSP; Arthur Ellis to Howard Dudley, letter, April 12, 1968, miscellaneous campaign material, folder 15—Mexican Americans, box 615, PSP.

31. Preston Smith, statement, undated, Lubbock, 1968 campaign speeches, box 615, PSP.

32. Gonzalez to Carr, letter, October 11, 1965; "Texas Migrant Labor: The 1965 Migration," report, July 17, 1966, HGP; miscellaneous clippings, box 2004-127/58, 2004-127/355, HGP.

33. Assorted speeches, 1965–67, box 2004-127/321, HGP.

34. Newspaper clippings, 1969–70, box 2004-127/64, HGP.

35. La Raza Unida Party, box 17, New Left Collection, HI.

36. Assorted speeches and public statements, box 2004-127/321, HGP.

37. "Arriba Humphrey," October 1968, box 2004-127/51, HGP.

38. Lynda L. Kaid, interview by author, November 7, 2006, Gainesville, FL.

39. Gloria Villanueva-Anderson, oral history, April 19, 2004, Denton, TX, interview by Dulce Ivette Ray, OHC.

40. Garcia, *Viva Kennedy;* Tyler et al., *Handbook of Texas.*

41. Nola Smith to Betty Andujar, letter, July 2, 1971, box 451, JTP; Republican Party of Texas, State Convention, program, June 13, 1972, box 450, JTP.

42. Marci Sauls to Nola Smith and Jim Tosch, memorandum, undated, Subject: Black Texans for Tower: Campaign Strategy, box 451, JTP; Nola Smith to William Clements, letter, August 17, 1972, box 446, JTP.

43. Tyler et al., *Handbook of Texas.*

44. Ibid.

45. *San Antonio Express,* February 16, 1972; Tower, speech to State Convention, September 19, 1972, box 450, JTP.

46. Lassiter, *Silent Majority,* 225.

47. Robert Eckels to Bob Eckhardt, letter, February 25, 1969, box 95-147/83, REP.

48. Ibid.

49. GC—Busing, 1969–70, box 95-147/83, REP.

50. Ibid.

51. Ibid.

52. Ibid.

53. "Election Results since 1966: Eight District, Texas," box 95-147/87, REP.

54. GC—Busing, 1971–72, box 95-147/83, REP.

55. Ibid.

56. GC—Gun Control, 1970–72, box 95-147/134, REP.

57. GC—Law & Order Policy, 1970, box 386, GMP.

58. Ibid.

59. Ibid.

60. *San Antonio Express and News,* May 3, 1970; Bass and De Vries, *Transformation of Southern Politics;* Olien, *From Token to Triumph,* 222–26; Reston, *The Lone Star,* 378.

61. Campaign Files, 1970, box 4zd552, Ralph Yarborough Papers, CAH.

62. Jimmy Wisch, to James A. Turman, letter, March 17, 1970, box 4zd552, Ralph Yarborough Papers, CAH; press release, April 1, 1970, GC, "Here is what Ralph Yarborough has done to help [your] county," box 4zd552, Ralph Yarborough Papers, CAH.

63. Reston, *The Lone Star,* 378.

64. *Houston Chronicle,* September 13, 1970; *Houston Post,* November 6, 1970; Lloyd Bentsen—Texas, November 19, 1970, part 2, reel 9, frames 356–57, 376, PRP; Five Reasons to Vote for Bush for United States Senator, August 6, 1970, George Bush's Answers to Some of the Questions People Ask, August 1970, From: Bush for Senator Headquarters, direct mailing, all in Bush 1970 Campaign Files, box 11, John Knaggs Papers, John Tower Library, Southwestern University, Georgetown, TX.

65. Clemons, *Branding Texas.*

5. Poisons

1. *DMN,* October 29, 1972, January 23–24, 1973, 1A.

2. *DMN,* March 25, 1972; Sharpstown Stock Fraud Scandal—Clippings, box 758, folder 11, Austin Files, JTP; Sharpstown Stock Fraud Clippings, box 4C518, Harris County Democratic Party Records, CAH.

3. William F. Buckley, *Firing Line,* transcript, February 25, 1973, telecast on PBS, Audiovisual Collection, HI.

4. Sharpstown Stock Fraud Scandal—Clippings, box 758, folder 11, Austin Files, JTP.

5. "Crime in the Streets," Law and Order File, box 613, Dolph Briscoe Papers, CAH; *Texas Monthly,* April 1976, 112, box 9, David Stoll Collection, HI.

6. Press release, September 24, 1971, box 659, Dolph Briscoe Papers, CAH.

7. Speech, July 9, 1971, Ben Kaplan Associates; announcement, undated; speech, July 21, 1971, Elgin, TX; speech, August 26, 1971, Jacksonville, TX, all in box 659, Dolph Briscoe Papers, CAH.

8. Press release, April 5, 1972, box 589, PSP; KRAN Country Music Radio, April 11, 1972, box 589, PSP.

9. Fred Agnich, oral history, January 6, 1972, Dallas, TX, interview by Jim W. Riddlesperger, OHC.

10. Betty Andujar, oral history, September 6, 1979, Fort Worth, TX, interview by Ronald E. Marcello, OHC.

11. Bass and De Vries, *Transformation of Southern Politics,* 313; *DMN,* July 15, 1972, 1A.

12. "The Unholy Trinity Incident," *Texas Monthly,* June 1973.

13. Ibid.

14. Ibid.

15. Tower to Reagan, letter, June 23, 1971; BW to Nola Smith, memorandum, undated; Gary Bruner to Nola Smith, memorandum, undated, re: YAF, all in box 451, JTP.

16. "The Unholy Trinity Incident."

17. Earle Cabell, oral history, October 2, 9, 16, 1974, Dallas, TX, interview by Ronald E. Marcello, OHC.

18. Ibid.

19. Davies, *Opportunity to Entitlement.*

20. Miscellaneous newspaper clippings, box 117, folder 6: Clippings, JBP.

21. Republican National Committee, July 22, 1971, Denver, CO, part 1, series B, reel 8, frames 552–69, PRP; "GOP Credibility Problem," *New York Post,* July 5, 1972, box 779, GMcGP; Reagan, form letter, January 1972, Political File, 1967–72, box 17, DHP.

22. *DMN,* August 20, 1972.

23. Charls E. Walker, remarks, November 29, 1972, Dallas, box 16, Charls E. Walker Papers, HI; 1972 Campaign Factbook, part 2, reel 11, frame 391, PRP; *Public Papers of the Presidents:* Richard M. Nixon (1972), 888–93; Davies, *Opportunity to Entitlement.*

24. "Economy File," box 784, GMcGP.

25. Campaign files, box 782, 784, GMcGP; "Face to Face on the Issues," *Life,* undated, box 779, GMcGP.

26. Lawrence A. Carpenter to McGovern, letter, June 15, 1972, box 631, GC, GMcGP.

27. "Judy Woodruff's Inside Politics," CNN, November 18, 2004, transcript, GC, box 600, GMcGP; *Washington Post,* May 15, 1972; *DMN,* February 3, 1972; Media Strategy, March 9, 1972, part 2, reel 11, frames 890–99, PRP.

28. Frederic Malex to staffers, memorandum, October 20, 1972, box 117, folder 13: Committee for the Re-Election of the President, JBP; McGovern Manual, part 2, reel 10, frames 653–778, PRP.

29. Memorandum for Milt Gwertzman, August 17, 1972, box 329, GMcGP.

30. Ibid.

31. McGovern to Elizabeth Doremus, letter, August 26, 1971, box 600; Lawrence A. Carpenter to McGovern, letter, June 15, 1972, box 631; Charles Guggenheim to McGovern, "TV Advisors, Inc," letter, August 22, 1972; letter from TV Advisors, Inc., September 7, 1972, box 874, all in GMcGP.

32. Davies, *Opportunity to Entitlement;* Campaign files, box 784, GMcGP; Don O'Brien to McGovern, memorandum, June 9, 1972, box 329, GMcGP.

33. Hal Goodman, "Material for Senator McGovern," March 31, 1972, box 329; Incomplete FCC Correspondence, May 31, 1972, box 329; McGovern, to Juanita Ahtone, letter, August 26, 1971, box 600; GC, "Report on the Conference of American Associates of Political Consultants," March 11–13, 1972, box 631; Jesse Jackson, address, March 18, 1972, box 777, "Blacks," "Untitled Speech on Crime," box 779, all in GMcGP.

34. Brands, *Strange Death;* Incomplete FCC Correspondence, May 31, 1972, box 329, GMcGP.

35. GC with "Professors from Texas," box 600, Hal Goodman, "Material for Senator McGovern," March 31, 1972, box 329; "Corruption File," box 779; "Vietnam, misc. File," box 800, all in GMcGP.

36. 1972 Election Report, part 2, reel 12, frames 171, 182, 206, PRP.

37. *Austin American Statesman,* June 13, 1972; *Lubbock Avalanche-Journal,* November 9, 1972; *TO,* December 1, 1972, 4–6; "Texas Still Not a Two-Party State," *Houston Chronicle,* November 19, 1972; 1972 Election Report: Editorial Reaction, December 6, 1972, part 2, reel 12, frame 226, PRP.

38. 1972 Election Report: The Cities—Dallas, December 11, 1972, part 2, reel 13, frames 860–955, PRP.

39. "A Research Proposal Presented to the Honorable John Tower, for the 1978 Senatorial Campaign," June 1977, box 542, folder 19, Tower Senate Club, JTP.

40. "There Is a Difference," box 639, folder 5, Tower Senate Club, JTP.

41. Ibid.; Bass and De Vries, *Transformation of Southern Politics,* 313; *DMN,* July 15, 1972, 1A.

42. "A Research Proposal Presented to the Honorable John Tower, for the 1978 Senatorial Campaign," June 1977, box 542, folder 19, Tower Senate Club, JTP; Decision Making Information Polls, September 1974, box 638, folder 16, JTP.

43. Knaggs to Nola Smith, letter, June 1, 1972, box 450, JTP; Culberson, Heller & Norton to Nola Smith, letter, Texans for Tower, July 24, 1972, box 446, JTP.

44. Republican Party of Texas, State Convention, program, June 13, 1972, Galveston, box 450, JTP.

45. Report on Campaign in Rural Texas: Texans for Tower—1972, box 454, JTP.

46. Statement to Mexican-Americans, by Tower, May 5, 1972, box 450, JTP.

47. Nola F. Smith to William Clements, letter, August 17, 1972, box 446, JTP.

48. Humberto Aguirre to Tower, letter, March 28, 1972, box 451, JTP.

49. Humberto Aguirre to Nola Smith, memorandum, Weekly Progress Report, October 12, 1972, box 450, JTP.

50. The Mexican-American Vote in Texas: February 7, 1973, by Aguirre, box 454, JTP.

51. Strategy memorandum, undated, box 451, JTP.

52. Marci Sauls to Nola Smith, memorandum, Weekly Progress Report, October 2, 10, 1972, box 450, JTP; Marci Sauls to Nola Smith, memorandum, Target Percentage for State, box 458, JTP.

53. Patterson, *Grand Expectations.*

54. "Democrats for Nixon," press release, October 31, 1972, box 782, GMcGP; *Dallas Morning News,* August 21, 1972; *Public Papers of the Presidents:* Richard M. Nixon (1972), 893–901; Reston, *The Lone Star,* 443–44.

55. "Farewell to LBJ: A Hill Country Valediction," *Texas Monthly,* May 1973; "John Connally Between the Acts," *Texas Monthly,* September 1973; Reston, *The Lone Star,* 321–22.

56. Reston, *The Lone Star.*

57. Tower, Watergate Speech (Draft), 1974, box 20, folder 1, Press Office, JTP.

58. Handwritten notes, February 15, 1971, box 2, John Ehrlichman Papers, HI.

59. Memorandum, August 22, 1972, Committee for the Re-Election of the President, box 117, folder 13, JBP; Reston, *The Lone Star,* 378–80, 443–44.

60. Schoenwald, *Time for Choosing*, 220; Schulman, *The Seventies*, 43–48, 51; Shirley, *Reagan's Revolution*, chap. 2.

61. Patterson, *Restless Giant*.

62. Peter Hannaford to Reagan, memorandum, July 3, 1974, box 1, PHP; Poll Reports, part 2, reel 12, frame 986, PRP.

63. Tower, "The Hidden Tax of Government Regulation," September 1975, box 17, folder 53, Press Office, JTP; Tower, draft letter, August 8, 1975, box 17, folder 51, Press Office, JTP.

64. Tower, draft of op-ed for *Dallas Times Herald*, December 1973, box 17; folder 40, Tower, draft of op-ed, 1974, box 17, folder 41; Tower, Watergate speech (draft), 1974, box 20, folder 1, all in Press Office, JTP.

65. "Bob and George Go to Washington; or, The Post-Watergate Scramble," *Texas Monthly*, April 1974.

66. Brands, *Strange Death*, 132; Cannon, *Governor Reagan*, 386.

67. Ibid.; *Chicago Tribune*, November 19, 1973, 1, box 92, Issues Office, Noel Sterrett Files, JCP.

68. Hannaford to Reagan, memorandum, July 3, 1974, box 1, PHP.

69. *Dallas Times Herald*, February 12, 1974; *Washington Post*, October 21, 1973; press conference and speech, Houston, April 28, 1974, tapes 547, 548, Ronald Reagan Gubernatorial Audiotape collection: 1965–74, RRL.

70. GC, 1974–75, Texas, box 45, CRP; Olien, *From Token to Triumph*, 236–38.

71. McGovern Manual, part 2, reel 10, frames 653–778, PRP; Davies, *Opportunity to Entitlement*.

72. *DMN*, February 3, 1972; Schoenwald, *Time for Choosing*, 251–65; Schulman, *The Seventies*, 113–14.

6. Civil War

1. *DMN*, March 23–25, 1972; Republican National Committee, July 22, 1971, Denver, CO, part 1, series B, reel 8, frame 570, PRP; Equal Opportunity for Women, April 27, 1973, part 2, reel 12, frame 436, PRP; GC, box 400, GMP.

2. Carol Reed, oral history, July 27, 1993, Dallas, TX, interview by Kristi Strickland, OHC.

3. Betty Andujar, oral history, September 6, 1979, Fort Worth, TX, interview by Ronald E. Marcello, OHC.

4. House Judiciary Committee Files, 1971, HJR 191, box 334, GMP; GC—Abortion, box 373, GMP.

5. "Abortion in Texas," *Texas Monthly*, March 1974.

6. Questionnaire on Church and State, box 376, GMP; "Abortion File," box 659, Dolph Briscoe Papers, CAH.

7. Decision Making Information: A Study of National Attitudes, Prepared for Reagan, July 1974, box 57, DHP; "The Book of Dallas," *New York Times*, 1976 op-ed, box 9, David Stoll Collection, HI; Schoenwald, *Time for Choosing*, 252; Schulman, *The Seventies*, chap. 4, 164.

8. Draft op-ed, *Dallas Times Herald*, September 21, 1975, box 17, folder 55, Press Office, JTP.

9. *Public Papers of the Presidents: Gerald Ford* (1976–77), 1262; *DMN*, March

13–14, 1976, A; Texas Issues Outline, April 3, 1976, box 19, Presidential Briefing Book, GFL.

10. "The Book of Dallas"; Lassiter, *Silent Majority.*

11. *Texas Monthly,* April 1976, 74.

12. "The Book of Dallas."

13. *Texas Monthly,* April 1976, 107, box 9, David Stoll Collection, HI.

14. Davidson, *Race and Class,* 17–18.

15. Texas Manufacturing Association, Dallas, January 14, 1975, box 92, CRP.

16. Telegram to Reagan, Western Union, November 25, 1974; speech, Chamber of Commerce, San Antonio, January 15, 1975, both in box 92, CRP.

17. Texas GOP Fundraiser, Dallas, June 20, 1975; Sales and Marketing Executives of Houston, May 28, 1975; Texas GOP Fundraiser, Dallas, June 20, 1975; Texas GOP, Beaumont, June 21, 1975; P.O.W. Reunion, San Antonio, June 28, 1975; National Federation of Republican Women, Dallas, September 12, 1975, box 94; Assn., Builders & Contractors, Houston, November 14, 1975; Woman's Forum, Wichita Falls, November 18, 1975; National Soft Drink Assn., Dallas, November 19, 1975; Southern Rep. Conference, Houston, December 13, 1975, box 96, all in CRP.

18. National Soft Drink Assn., Dallas, November 19, 1975, box 96, CRP.

19. Sales and Marketing Executives of Houston, May 28, 1975, box 93, CRP; speech invitations, Texas, box 19, CRP.

20. Newspaper Clients of Reagan, November 30, 1976, Radio Stations with RR Broadcasts, box 106, CRP.

21. Support letters, July 1975, box 84, CRP.

22. Wills, *John Wayne's America.*

23. Reagan for President: Citizen for Reagan, draft letter, box 1, CRP; Shirley, *Reagan's Revolution,* 92.

24. Campaign Contributions to Texas Citizens for Reagan, April 1976, box 3, CRP; Merritt D. Orr to Joseph Coors, letter, November 28, 1975, box 5, CRP.

25. *Guns & Ammo,* September 1975, box 38, CRP.

26. GC, 1975, box 20, CRP; support letters, box 84, CRP.

27. Olien, *From Token to Triumph.*

28. *DMN,* March 24, 1976; *Washington Post,* March 26, 1976, box 63, DHP.

29. How They Stand / Presidential Candidates' Positions—Edition III / May 1976, box 6, CRP; *Public Papers of the Presidents:* Gerald Ford (1976–77), 1066, 1262–69.

30. "Possible Carter Campaign Strategy: Attack Ronald Reagan," box 92, Issues Office, Noel Sterrett Files, JCP.

31. Ray Barnhart to Ford, letter, August 1, 1975, box 1258, folder 53, Bill Keener Files, JTP.

32. Ray A. Barnhart to Nofziger, letter, August 29, 1975, box 5, CRP.

33. Hannaford to Reagan, memorandum, April 13, 1976, box 6, PHP.

34. *Texas Monthly,* April 1976, 108, box 9, David Stoll Collection, HI.

35. *New York Times Magazine,* August 8, 1976, box 2M449, Phillip Scheffler Papers, CAH.

36. *DMN,* March 11, 1976.

37. *DMN,* March 12, March 13–14, March 18, March 20–21, 1976.

38. *DMN*, April 16–17, 1976.

39. Market Opinion Research: Texas Statewide Study, box H6, President Ford Committee Records, 1975–76, GFL.

40. "Reasons for Reagan: Texas Citizens for Reagan Primary News," box 6, PHP.

41. Jeff Bell to Hannaford, memorandum, April 12, 1976, box 6, PHP; undated press release, box 31, CRP.

42. *DMN*, April 25, 1976; "Reasons for Reagan: Texas Citizens for Reagan Primary News," box 6, PHP.

43. Market Opinion Research: Texas Statewide Study, box H6, President Ford Committee Records, 1975–76, GFL; Texas Issues Outline, April 3, 1976, box 19, Presidential Briefing Book, GFL.

44. *DMN*, April 25, 1976, 1A–13A; Market Opinion Research: Texas Statewide Study, box H6, President Ford Committee Records, 1975–76, GFL.

45. Pro-forma letter from President Ford Committee—Texas, April 3, 1976, box 6, PHP.

46. Mike Kelly, on behalf of Tower, to John Sears, letter, August 22, 1975, box 5, CRP; Sears Correspondence, May 1976, box 71, CRP.

47. Hannaford to Reagan, memorandum, April 13, 1976, miscellaneous campaign files, box 6, PHP.

48. GC; Mahon to Dan Hanna, member, Board of Christian Men, letter September 2, 1976, box 376; rough notes on "Views of George Mahon," prepared for 1976 campaign, all in GMP.

49. Olien, *From Token to Triumph,* 246; *DMN*, May 4, 1976, 5A; May 5, 1976, 14A; A Study of Political Attitudes in the State of Texas, Prepared for Tower, March 1977, Campaign Records, 1978, box 10, file 18, WPCP; Reagan dinner, June 20, 1975, box 1258, folder 55, Bill Keener Files, JTP.

50. For Governor Reagan: East Texas Economy, Issues Pertinent to East Texas, April 7, 1976, box 6, PHP.

51. Ibid.; "Reasons for Reagan: Texas Citizens for Reagan Primary News," box 6, PHP; "Ronald Reagan on Equal Rights for Women," April 27, 1976, box 38, CRP.

52. Earl Lively, memorandum, undated, box 6, PHP.

53. *Corpus Christi Caller,* April 20, 1976; press release by Reagan state cochairmen Ray Barnhart and Barbara Staff, box 6, PHP.

54. "Possible Texas Speech," April 26, 1976, David Gergen Files, Texas Speeches, GFL.

55. Texas Issues Outline, April 3, 1976, box 19, Presidential Briefing Book, GFL; speech excerpts and press releases, April 1976, box 29, CRP.

56. Speech excerpts and press releases, April 1976, box 29, CRP.

57. *DMN*, March 18, 1976, 8A, March 20–21, 1976, 11A, 36A; Texas Correspondents Interview, April 21, 1976, box 53, Ron Nesson Papers, 1974–77, GFL.

58. William J. Casey to Ford, letter, July 29, 1976, box 37, Presidential Handwriting File, GFL.

59. Robert Teeter to Bo Calloway, memorandum, December 5, 1975, box B2, Marik File—Market Opinion Research, President Ford Committee Records, 1975–76, GFL; Texas Issues Outline, April 3, 1976, box 19, Presidential Briefing Book, GFL.

60. "Ronald Reagan on Oil Company Divesture." May 13, 1976, box 39, CRP;

Robert Teeter to Bo Calloway, memorandum, December 5, 1975, box B2, Marik File—Market Opinion Research, President Ford Committee Records, 1975–76, GFL.

61. Robert Teeter to Bo Calloway, memorandum, December 5, 1975, box B2, Marik File—Market Opinion Research, President Ford Committee Records, 1975–76, GFL; Texas Issues Outline, April 3, 1976, box 19, Presidential Briefing Book, GFL.

62. Jerry Jones to Dick Cheney, memorandum, November 20, 1975, box 19, Richard Cheney Files, 1974–77: Campaign Subject File, GFL; Robert Teeter to Bo Calloway, memorandum, December 5, 1975, box B2, Marik File—Market Opinion Research, President Ford Committee Records, 1975–76, GFL.

63. Texas Issues Outline, April 3, 1976, box 19, Presidential Briefing Book, GFL.

64. *DMN,* April 14, April 15, 1976.

65. Texas radio ad transcripts, box 6, PHP.

66. *DMN,* May 1, 1976, 25A; Chamberlain-Frandolig Inc., "Capturing Texas: The Most Critical State," March 15, 1976, box 31, CRP.

67. Market Opinion Research: Texas Primary Survey, April 15, 1976, box C11, MOR Texas Primary Survey Files, President Ford Committee Records, 1975–76, GFL.

68. *New York Times Magazine,* June 6, 1976, box 33, CRP.

69. Certified Results of May 1 Texas Primary, May 18, 1976, box C11, MOR Texas Primary Survey Files, President Ford Committee Records, 1975–76, GFL.

70. John Tower, op-ed draft, *New York Times,* October 28, 1976, box 17, folder 68, Press Office, JTP; *Washington Monthly,* October 1980, 57, box 3, Bill Boyarsky Papers, HI.

71. News release, March 16, 1978, San Antonio, Campaign Records, 1978, box 9, File 15, WPCP.

72. GC, Bill and Mary Chaillot, letter, July 7, 1976, box 75, CRP.

73. Sears Correspondence, May 1976, box 71, CRP; GC, Bill and Mary Chaillot, letter, July 7, 1976, box 75, CRP; Robert Berry to Reagan, letter, July 15, 1976, box 75, CRP; *DMN,* March 24, 1976, 22A.

74. Durwood Foote to Reagan, Citizens for Reagan Hq, letter, May 13, 1976, Sears Correspondence, May 1976, box 71, CRP.

75. Sears Correspondence, May 1976, box 71, CRP.

76. GC, Bert and Lorraine Clayton to Reagan, letter, July 6, 1976, box 75, CRP.

77. Davidson, *Race and Class,* 196.

78. GC, Robert Berry to Reagan, letter, July 15, 1976, box 75, CRP; Sears Correspondence, May 1976, box 71, CRP.

79. Text of Reagan's nationwide television address, ABC, July 6, 1976, box 121, folder 6: Press Releases, 1976, JBP.

80. Michael and Sara Walsh to Reagan, letter, July 6, 1976, box 75, CRP.

81. Sears Correspondence, May 1976, box 71, CRP; W. J. Martin Jr. to Citizens for Reagan Committee, letter, July 30, 1976, box 75, CRP.

82. "Reasons for Reagan: Texas Citizens for Reagan Primary News," box 6, PHP.

83. Draft press release, Television News Inc., undated, "Reagan reveals he was not consulted by Ford on VP; California Governor Issues Warning not to Ignore '72 Mandate," box 13, CRP.

84. Miscellaneous files, box 11, Records of the Office of Congressional Liaison, Frank Moore Files, JCL.

85. Billie Carr to Hamilton Jordan, letter, September 7, 1976, "Texas Folder," box 219, Issues Office, Rick Hutcheson Files, JCP.

86. Ibid.; "Revised Letter, August 1976," "Texas Folder," box 219, Issues Office, Rick Hutcheson Files, JCP.

87. Ezra Wintz to Jerry Rafshoon, letter, December 19, 1974; "Themes and Issues—April 1976," box 2, Issues Office, SEF: 1976 Presidential Campaign Files, JCL.

88. *Wall Street Journal,* July 14, 1976.

89. Miscellaneous files, box 316, Minority Affairs Coordinator, Raymone Bain Files, JCP.

90. Leonel Castillo to Chuck Parrish, letter, September 15, 1976, box 316, Minority Affairs Coordinator, Raymone Bain Files, JCP.

91. "9/8 Campaign Themes," box 2, Issues Office, SEF: 1976 Presidential Campaign Files, JCL.

92. Debates—Briefing Material for Third Debate, box 9, Issues Office, SEF: 1976 Presidential Campaign Files, JCL; *New York Times,* July 17, 1976.

93. *DMN,* May 6, May 16, 1976.

94. Briefing—Tough Issues, Debates—Briefing Material for Third Debate, box 9, Issues Office, SEF: 1976 Presidential Campaign Files, JCL.

95. "On Busing," box 31, Issues Office, Sam Bleicher Files, JCP.

96. "Gay Rights"; NBC *Tomorrow Show,* transcript, March 19, 1976, both in box 34, Issues Office, Sam Bleicher Files, JCP.

97. Pat Caddell, "Initial Working Paper on Political Strategy," December 10, 1976, box 4, Press Office, Jody Powell Files, Jimmy Carter Presidential Papers, JCL.

98. Patrick Cadell to Carter, memorandum, December 21, 1976, box 4, Press Office, Jody Powell Files, Jimmy Carter Presidential Papers, JCL.

7. The Gathering Storm

1. Political Brief: Texas, box 406, JCF.

2. V. Lance Tarrance and Associates, A Preliminary Report to the Clements for Governor Committee, January 1, 1978, box 28, folder 4, JBP; "Texas Trip 6/78," box 291, SEF.

3. "Texas Overview," "3/24/79–3/25/79 Trip to Oklahoma and Texas," box 124, Staff Office Files: Office of Staff Secretary, JCL; V. Lance Tarrance and Associates, A Preliminary Report to the Clements for Governor Committee, January 1, 1978, box 28, folder 4, JBP.

4. V. Lance Tarrance and Associates, A Preliminary Report to the Clements for Governor Committee, January 1, 1978, box 28, folder 4, JBP.

5. Texas Briefing: Office of Policy Coordination, box 24, AGAP.

6. Ibid.

7. Rafshoon to Carter, memorandum, June 7, 1978, box 8, Staff Office, Assistant to the President for Communications, Rafshoon Files, Jimmy Carter Presidential Papers, JCL.

8. George Bristol to Carter, memorandum, June 7, 1978, Caryl Conner to Rafshoon, memorandum, June 21, 1978, box 8, Staff Office, Assistant to the President for Communications, Rafshoon Files, Jimmy Carter Presidential Papers, JCL.

9. "Houston Speech Text—Third Draft," box 8, Staff Office, Assistant to the President for Communications, Rafshoon Files, Jimmy Carter Presidential Papers, JCL.

10. "Texas Speeches—6/23–24/78," box 6, Hendrik Hertzberg Papers, JCL.

11. "Texas Trip 6/78," box 291, SEF.

12. John Tower, op-ed draft, box 17, folder 68, Press Office, JTP.

13. *Viewpoint* with Ronald Reagan, "Oil and the Shah of Iran," box 39, CRP.

14. Texas Briefing: Office of Policy Coordination, box 24, AGAP.

15. *Viewpoint* with Ronald Reagan, "Reagan on Unemployment," box 39, CRP.

16. *Viewpoint* with Ronald Reagan, "Ronald Reagan on Spiritual Commitment," box 39, CRP.

17. V. Lance Tarrance and Associates, A Preliminary Report to the Clements for Governor Committee, Campaign Records, box 10, file 21, WPCP; "Hispanic Issues," box 414, JCF.

18. Political Brief: Texas, Box 406, JCF.

19. Questionnaire on Church and State, box 376,GMP; Texas Political Brief, October 26, 1980: Office of Policy Coordination, box 25, AGAP.

20. "The Power and the Glory of Billy Graham," *Texas Monthly,* March 1978; "The Baptist Pope," *Christianity Today,* March 11, 2002.

21. "The Power and the Glory of Billy Graham"; "The Baptist Pope."

22. Patterson, *Restless Giant.*

23. "The Power and the Glory of Billy Graham."

24. Ibid.

25. Ibid.

26. "Texas Overview" "3/24/79–3/25/79 Trip to Oklahoma and Texas," box 124, Staff Office Files: Office of Staff Secretary, JCL.

27. Schulman, *The Seventies,* 186.

28. Miscellaneous Files, box 6, Office of Public Liaison: Margaret Costanza Files, JCL.

29. *Houston Post,* November 23, 1977, A17, Staff Office Files: First Lady's Staff—Press Office, JCL.

30. *Wall Street Journal,* January 3, 1978.

31. Critchlow, *Phyllis Schlafly,* 187.

32. Miscellaneous Files, box 6, Office of Public Liaison: Margaret Costanza Files, JCL.

33. *Houston Post,* November 23, 1977, Staff Office Files: First Lady's Staff—Press Office, JCL.

34. RNC executive meeting, March 12, 1977, Washington, DC, part 1, series B, reel 15, frame 003, PRP.

35. "Economic Impacts of the Proposed Panama Canal Treaties on Texas," March 15, 1978, box 316, GMP.

36. GC, Panama Canal, box 316, GMP.

37. Richard Viguerie, phone interview with author, December 7, 2006; *Wall Street Journal,* January 3, 1978; Texas Briefing: Office of Policy Coordination, box 24, AGAP; Briggs Initiative, 1978, box 4, PHP; *Atlas World Press,* March 1978, "The New Conservatism," box 85, DHP; *Washington Post,* January 19, 1978.

38. *Washington Post,* January 19, 1978.

39. "Panama Canal: 1977–1978," box 1339, folder 38, Houston Office, JTP; Tower to Donald Dozer, letter, August 11, 1966, box 78, Donald M. Dozer Papers, HI.

40. Tower to Carter, letter, October 26, 1977, John Tower Name File, White House Central Files, Jimmy Carter Presidential Papers, JCL.

41. Opinion Research Corp., Princeton, NJ, "Statewide Survey in Texas on Attitudes toward the Panama Canal Treaty," February 1978, box 11, George D. Moffett Files, JCL.

42. Citizens Groups, Panama Canal File, box 66, Donald M. Dozer Papers, HI.

43. Emergency Committee to Save the US Canal Zone, 1977, box 68, Donald M. Dozer Papers, HI.

44. George Petley to Dozer, letter and attached advertisement, March 2, 1976, box 68, Donald M. Dozer Papers, HI.

45. Opinion Research Corp., Princeton, NJ, "Statewide Survey in Texas on Attitudes toward the Panama Canal Treaty," February 1978, box 11, George D. Moffett Files, JCL.

46. *Texas Advocate,* June 1978, box 542, folder 22, Tower Senate Club, JTP.

47. Briefing for Campaign Appearances: Midland, TX, April 30, 1980, box 55, Hannaford / California Headquarters Files, RRCF.

48. "Texas Trip 6/78," box 291, SEF.

49. Ibid.; "Strategy," box 12, Office of Public Liaison: Bob Maddox (Religious Liaison) Files, JCL.

50. For an overview, see Bridges, *Twilight of the Texas Democrats,* 1–22.

51. *TO,* April 28, 1978, 7; *Texas Monthly,* October 1978, 188; V. Lance Tarrance and Associates, Clements for Governor, Primary Campaign Plan, Final Draft, March 11, 1978, Campaign Records, 1978, box 14, file 5, WPCP.

52. *Public Papers of the Presidents:* Jimmy Carter (1978), 934, 1168.

53. Ibid.

54. V. Lance Tarrance and Associates, A Preliminary Report to the Clements for Governor Committee, Campaign Records, box 10, file 21, WPCP.

55. V. Lance Tarrance and Associates, Clements for Governor, Primary Campaign Plan, Final Draft, March 11, 1978, Campaign Records, 1978, box 14, file 5, WPCP.

56. *Lubbock Avalanche-Journal,* October 19, 1978, box 9; *DMN,* October 1, 1978, box 17, *Midland Reporter Telegram,* October 17, 1978, box 17, all in Campaign Records, 1978, WPCP.

57. *Lubbock Avalanche-Journal,* October 19, 1978, box 9; *DMN,* October 1, 1978, box 9, *Midland Reporter Telegram,* October 17, 1978, box 17, all in Campaign Records, 1978, WPCP.

58. Olien, *From Token to Triumph,* 257.

59. Bill Clements Position Papers, Campaign Records, 1978, box 15, file 1, WPCP.

60. Olien, *From Token to Triumph,* 256–57.

61. *Austin American-Statesman,* September 14, 1978.

62. News release, September 9, 1978, Campaign Records, 1978, box 9, file 16, WPCP.

63. GC, Tom C. Reed to Mike Deaver, letter, June 13, 1978, Campaign Records, 1978, box 14, file 6, WPCP.

64. Olien, *From Token to Triumph,* 255–56.

65. *Houston Post,* July 3, 1977.

66. Olien, *From Token to Triumph,* 247.

67. Remarks by Tower upon Being Presented the Annual President's Award of the American Defense Preparedness Association in Washington, DC on April 27, 1978, box 20, Press Office, JTP; "Why John Tower Will Go Down to Defeat," undated poll analysis, box 542, folder 10, Tower Senate Club, JTP.

68. Nofziger to Tower, letter, April 26, 1977, box 873, folder 7, Washington Office, JTP; letter from Nancy Palm, September 1977, box 542, folder 7, Tower Senate Club, JTP.

69. Reagan, direct mailing, June 1978, box 572, folder 14, Tower Senate Club, JTP.

70. Bush, direct mailing, December 1977, box 572, folder 7, Tower Senate Club, JTP; Shivers, direct mailing, undated, box 560, folder 23, Tower Senate Club, JTP.

71. Mark Pinsky, "The Texas Chameleon," *New Times Magazine,* November 1, 1974, box 560, folder 25, Tower Senate Club, JTP.

72. Political Brief: Texas, box 406, JCF.

73. Olien, *From Token to Triumph,* 249.

74. "Voting Rights Act," Comparison Papers, box 561, folder 7, Tower Senate Club, JTP.

75. Olien, *From Token to Triumph,* 252.

76. Ibid., 262.

77. Miscellaneous Files, box 37, folder 1: General 73–78, JBP.

78. Baker News Digest and Analysis, no. 2, April 18, 1978, box 37, JBP.

79. Jim Cicconi to James Baker, memorandum, December 22, 1977, box 37, folder 1: General 73–78, JBP.

80. "Opposition and Issues Report," box 37, folder 2: General 1978, JBP.

81. Ibid.

82. Press release, May 5, 1978, box 37, folder 10: Strategy, 1978; "Baker Clips," box 37, folder 2: General 1978, JBP.

83. Letter from Frank J. Donatelli, August 10, 1978, box 28, folder 5; Miscellaneous Files, box 37, folder 1: General 73–78, JBP.

84. "Biographical Profiles on Congressmen Elected in 1978—Democrats, 1978," "Democratic Study Group," box 204, folders 4–5, Kent Hance Papers, SWC; "A Shrub Grows in Midland: W's 1978 West Texas Campaign for Congress," *TO,* June 25, 1999, Political Brief: Nineteenth District, box 406, JCF.

85. "A Shrub Grows in Midland."

86. "Surveys," box 25, Kent Hance Papers, SWC.

87. Political Brief: Nineteenth District, box 406, JCF.

88. "A Shrub Grows in Midland."

89. Leaders of the Republican Party in Lubbock accused the Hance campaign of planting the ad and funding the event. Hance advisers indirectly denied the charge simply by stating that no such advertisement had been approved in their particular office. The actual source of the parties remains in question, though it is highly likely that the ads were placed by someone sympathetic to the Hance campaign.

90. "A Shrub Grows in Midland."

91. Political Brief: Nineteenth District, box 406, JCF.

92. Political Brief: Twenty-Second District, box 406, JCF.

93. *Houston Post,* September 12, 1978.

94. Remarks by Reagan, September 11, 1978, box 24, Hannaford / California Headquarters Files, RRCF.

95. Ibid.

96. Remarks by Reagan, September 12, 1978, box 24, Hannaford / California Headquarters Files, RRCF.

97. John McClaughry to Hannaford, memorandum, April 2, 1980, box 1, PHP.

98. Speech by Reagan, September 12, 1978, Dallas, box 104, CRP; "Texas Trip 6/78," box 291, SEF.

99. *DMN,* November 1, 1980; Olien, *From Token to Triumph,* 242–43.

8. Revolution

1. *Time,* July 14, 1980, 21, box 1, Bill Boyarsky Papers, HI.

2. Texas Briefing: Office of Policy Coordination, box 24, AGAP.

3. DMI, "A Statewide Survey of Voters in Texas," June 1980, box 201, Richard Wirthlin—Political Strategy Files, RRCF.

4. *Washington Monthly,* October 1980, 57, box 3, Bill Boyarsky Papers, HI.

5. Ibid.

6. *Middletown Journal,* October 12, 1980, box 483, Research & Policy Files, RRCF. The "dinky little country" referred to was Iran.

7. Texas Political Brief, October 26, 1980: Office of Policy Coordination, box 25, AGAP.

8. Speech, February 15, 1980, San Antonio, box 9, "San Antonio Trip—6/12/80," "San Antonio Trip—9/8/80," box 10, Staff Offices, Special Assistant to the President—Esteban Torres, Records of the Office of Hispanic Affairs, Jimmy Carter Presidential Papers, JCL.

9. "Suggested Talking Points for Ambassador Esteban E. Torres for Tejanos for Carter, April 12–13, 1980," box 9, Staff Offices, Special Assistant to the President—Esteban Torres, Records of the Office of Hispanic Affairs, Jimmy Carter Presidential Papers, JCL.

10. Population Growth during the 1960s, Texas Cities over 100,000, box 541, PreBriefing Materials Files, RRCF; "States-Texas-Austin," (3/3), box 525, Briefing Materials Files, RRCF.

11. "Local Issues—Austin, TX," box 414, JCF.

12. Political Brief: Tenth District, box 406, JCF.

13. "Local Issues—Austin, TX," box 414, JCF.

14. Briefing for campaign appearances: Longview, March 25, 1980, box 54, Hannaford / California Headquarters Files, RRCF.

15. Political Brief: Thirteenth District, box 406, JCF.

16. Political Brief: Eleventh District, box 406, JCF.

17. Briefing for campaign appearances: Waco, April 23, 1980, box 55, Hannaford / California Headquarters Files, RRCF; Miscellaneous Files, box 525, Briefing Materials Files, RRCF.

18. GC, box 253, Political Operations—William Timmons Files, RRCF; "Ronald Reagan File," box 13, Press Office, Jody Powell Files, Jimmy Carter Presidential Papers, JCL.

19. Texas Political Brief, October 26, 1980: Office of Policy Coordination, box 25, AGAP.

20. Texas Briefing: Office of Policy Coordination, box 24, AGAP.

21. Political Brief: Ft. Worth, August 8, 1980, box 406, JCF; Plano Political Brief, October 6, 1980, box 415, JCF.

22. Houston Chamber of Commerce Information Packet, box 541, Briefing Materials Files, RRCF.

23. Tom Wicker, *New York Times,* April 22, 1979.

24. "Thoughts on Campaign Strategy," undated research report prepared for John Sears, box 5, PHP; press release, May 11, 1979, box 112, Ed Meese Files, RRCF; Ron Dar to Charlie Black and Andy Carter, memorandum, May 23, 1979, box 112, Ed Meese Files, RRCF; anonymous memorandum to Omar Harvey, February 1, 1978, Campaign Records, 1978, box 14, file 5, WPCP.

25. Reagan, "The Year of the Elephant," transcript, September 26, 1978, box 3, PHP.

26. Speech excerpts, undated, box 29, CRP.

27. *Viewpoint* with Ronald Reagan, "Ronald Reagan on Spiritual Commitment," box 39, CRP.

28. Drew, *Portrait of an Election,* 209, 213.

29. Wills, *Reagan's America,* 406–16.

30. C. T. Clyne Company, The Reagan Candidacy: Advertising Strategy for 1980, October 25, 1979, box 6, DHP.

31. Citizens for the Republic newsletters, 1979, box 110, CRP.

32. Letter, Reagan and the Citizens for the Republic, March 5, 1978, box 873, folder 7, Washington Files, JTP.

33. *Los Angeles Herald Examiner,* February 6, 1978, box 85, DHP.

34. *New York Times,* October 31, 1979.

35. "The Truth about John Connally," *Texas Monthly,* November 1979.

36. "Texas Overview" "3/24/79–3/25/79 Trip to Oklahoma and Texas," box 124, Staff Office Files: Office of Staff Secretary, JCL.

37. Eddie Mahe Jr., "Analysis: 1980 Presidential Campaign," December 5, 1978, box 4Ad34, George Christian Papers, CAH; Hannaford to Deaver, memorandum, July 6, 1979, box 8, DHP; *Reagan Country Update,* newsletter, September 1979, box 50, Ronald Reagan Subject Collection, HI; Austin poll, Summer 1979, box 461, Research & Policy Files, RRCF.

38. GC, Political, April 5, 1976–November 22, 1976, box 553–52A, 52B, 72, 202, 232C; Campaign '80 Briefing Book, box 1209-192, F-2, John Connally Papers, LBJL.

39. Campaign '80 Briefing Book, box 1209-192, F-2, John Connally Papers, LBJL.

40. Reston, *The Lone Star,* 563–64.

41. Ibid.

42. Ibid., 575.

43. Box 128, folder 3, Issues Papers, 1979, JBP.

44. *New York Magazine,* January 21, 1980, box 86-107/11, Allan Shivers Papers, CAH.

45. *DMN,* April 24, 1980, 14A.

46. "George Bush on Abortion—Draft," November 14, 1979, box 128, folder 3, Issues Papers, 1979, JBP.

47. *DMN,* April 4–5, 1980.

48. DMI, "A Statewide Telephone Survey of Republican Voters in Texas," April 24, 30, May 2, 1980, box 200, Richard Wirthlin—Political Strategy Files, RRCF.

49. *DMN,* April 4, 1980, 16A; press release, April 30, 1980, box 8, DHP.

50. *Dallas Times Herald,* April 10, 1980, box 13, Ronald Reagan File, Press Office, Jody Powell Files, Jimmy Carter Presidential Papers, JCL; DMI, "A Statewide Telephone Survey of Republican Voters in Texas," April 24, 30, May 2, 1980, box 200, Richard Wirthlin—Political Strategy Files, RRCF.

51. White, *America in Search of Itself,* 284–311.

52. Rick Shelby to Jerry Carmen, memorandum, September 16, 1980, box 406, JCF.

53. Drew, *Portrait of an Election,* 209, 213.

54. Campaign '80 Briefing Book, box 1209-192, F-2, John Connally Papers, LBJL; "Rep. Phil Gramm (D-TX-6)," box 124, Staff Office Files: Office of Staff Secretary, JCL.

55. *DMN,* November 1, 1980.

56. *Abilene Reporter-News,* November 1, 1980, 1980 Campaign Final Week [2], box 21, Hendrik Hertzberg Papers, JCL.

57. Fall Campaign Trips—Texas, box 145, Ed Meese Files, RRCF.

58. Mrs. St. John Garmond to Reagan, letter, August 12, 1980, box 387, Regional Political Files, RRCF.

59. Briefing for Campaign Appearances: Lubbock, April 9, 1980, box 54, Hannaford / California Headquarters Files, RRCF.

60. Doug McSwane to Charlie Black, Andy Carter, and Ernie Angelo, memorandum, September 16, 1979, box 112, Ed Meese Files, RRCF; Fall Campaign Trips—Texas, box 145, Ed Meese Files, RRCF.

61. Olien, *From Token to Triumph.*

62. Ibid.; White, *America in Search of Itself.*

63. Patrick H. Caddell, Memorandum II: Debate Strategy, October 21, 1980, in Drew, *Portrait of an Election,* 417.

64. Memorandum for Reagan-Bush Committee, October 14, 1980, box 25, AGAP.

65. Ibid.

66. *US News & World Report,* October 13, 1980; *New York Times,* October 5, 1980.

67. *US News & World Report,* October 13, 1980; *New York Times,* October 5, 1980; Bill Clements, Ernest Angelo, Rick Shelby, Peter O'Donnell, and Chet Upham to Bill Timmons, letter, September 29, 1980, box 253, Political Operations—William Timmons Files, RRCF. The grassroots mobilization through these call centers is even more impressive when compared to similar activities in other states. In Florida only nineteen call centers operated on behalf of the Reagan campaign, and of those, ten were professional and only nine were staffed by volunteers. West Virginia had ten volunteer phone banks working for Reagan, while Arkansas had only eight, Kentucky had two, Missouri three, Oklahoma five, North Carolina three, South Carolina seven, and Mississippi four. Georgia, Tennessee, and Virginia had none.

68. Phone Bank and Direct Mail Operations by State, box 253, Political Operations—William Timmons Files, RRCF. As with their phone bank operations, Texas Republicans easily outpaced their comrades in other states in the area of direct mail. By late October, Alabama Republicans had mailed only ten thousand letters to undecided voters. Kentucky and Oklahoma reported similar figures, while no Reagan-

sponsored direct mail campaigns to undecided voters existed in Arkansas, Georgia, Mississippi, North Carolina, or West Virginia.

69. Press release, October 30, 1980, box 248, Campaign Operations—Mike Deaver Files, RRCF.

70. Roger Staubach, letter, October 25, 1980, box 317, Director of Citizens' Operations—Max Hugel Files, RRCF.

71. Bill Clements, Ernest Angelo, Rick Shelby, Peter O'Donnell, and Chet Upham to Bill Timmons, letter, September 29, 1980, box 253, Political Operations—William Timmons Files, RRCF.

72. General Files, Reagan-Bush Campaign, box 379, Regional Political Files, RRCF.

73. Chet Upham to "Wayne," memorandum, May 14, 1980, box 412, JCF.

74. Voter Group Files, box 316, Director of Citizens' Operations—Max Hugel Files, RRCF.

75. Patrick H. Caddell, Memorandum II: Debate Strategy, October 21, 1980, in Drew, *Portrait of an Election,* 417; "The Next Four Years—Abilene, TX Sat. 11/1/80," 1980 Campaign Final Week [2], box 21, Hendrik Hertzberg Papers, JCL.

76. Patrick H. Caddell, Memorandum II: Debate Strategy, October 21, 1980, in Drew, *Portrait of an Election,* 417; "The Next Four Years—Abilene, TX Sat. 11/1/80," 1980 Campaign Final Week [2], box 21, Hendrik Hertzberg Papers, JCL.

77. Operations Center to Reagan-Bush Campaign, memorandum, October 23, 1980, box 23, AGAP.

78. James Baker and Myles Martel to Reagan, memorandum, box 134, folder 6: Strategy Team, 1980, JBP.

79. Martin Franks to Carter, memorandum, June 26, 1980, box 79, Staff Office Files, Chief of Staff, Hamilton Jordan, Jimmy Carter Presidential Papers, JCL.

80. Operations Center to Reagan-Bush Campaign, memorandum, October 23, 1980, box 23, AGAP; White, *America in Search of Itself,* 399–401.

81. James Baker and Myles Martel to Reagan, memorandum, box 134, folder 6: Strategy Team, 1980, JBP.

82. Paul Russo to All Republican Members, memorandum, September 5, 1980, box 873, folder 10, JTP.

83. White Paper on Incumbency Abuses by the Carter Administration, October 23, 1980, box 20, AGAP.

84. Texas Political Brief, September 12, 1980, box 253, Political Operations—William Timmons Files, RRCF.

85. *DMN,* April 3, April 18, 1980; Operations Center to Reagan-Bush Campaign, memorandum, October 24, 1980, box 23, AGAP; Baker to Reagan, memorandum, Debate Strategy—Robert Teeter, box 134, JBP.

86. "10/30/80—Speeches for 11/1/80," Houston Rally, 1980 Campaign Final Week [2], box 21, Hendrik Hertzberg Papers, JCL; remarks of George Bush at Republican BBQ, Midland, October 7, 1980, box 21, AGAP.

87. Detailing of US Pro-Life Organizations—Single Issue Groups, box 301, Director of Citizens' Operations—Max Hugel Files, RRCF.

88. "Friends" lead-in to Reagan speech, August 22, 1980, typescript, box 12, DHP.

89. Bill Gribbin to Ed Meese, Bill Gavin, and Mike Deaver, memorandum, box 437, Speech Files, RRCF.

90. "Friends" lead-in to Reagan speech, August 22, 1980, typescript, box 12, DHP.

91. Bill Gribbin to Ed Meese, Bill Gavin, and Mike Deaver, memorandum, box 437, Speech Files, RRCF.

92. "Roundtable Speech in Dallas: Religious Values and Public Policy in the 1980s," box 437, Speech Files, RRCF.

93. Address by Reagan, the Roundtable National Affairs Briefing, Dallas, August 22, 1980, box 10, Fred Charles Iklé Papers, HI.

94. Smith, *The Rise of Baptist Republicanism,* 62.

95. Texas Political Brief, September 12, 1980, box 253, Political Operations—William Timmons Files, RRCF.

96. *DMN,* October 2, 1980, 37A.

97. Sandra Martin to Reagan, letter, August 29, 1980, Marjorie Gunnerson to Reagan, letter, October 24, 1980, Religious Correspondence, box 342, Director of Citizens' Operations—Max Hugel Files, RRCF; Religious Correspondence, box 343, Director of Citizens' Operations—Max Hugel Files, RRCF.

98. *DMN,* April 3, 1980.

99. Interview transcripts, ABC affiliate in Houston, broadcast in Tyler, September 24, 1980, box 10, Fred Charles Iklé Papers, HI; *Washington Post,* September 14, 1980.

100. Texas Political Brief, October 26, 1980: Office of Policy Coordination, box 25, AGAP; Voter Groups—Hispanics and American Indians, box 256, Political Operations—William Timmons Files, RRCF.

101. Fall Campaign Trips—Texas, box 145, Ed Meese Files, RRCF.

102. Carlos Puente, oral history March 11, 2003, Fort Worth, TX, interview by Dulce Ivette Ray, OHC.

103. Fall Campaign Trips—Texas, box 145, Ed Meese Files, RRCF.

104. Operations Center to Reagan-Bush Campaign, memorandum, October 5, 1980, box 23, AGAP.

105. Memorandum to Reagan-Bush Committee, October 14, 1980, box 25, AGAP.

106. Alex Armendaris to Bill Timmons, memorandum, October 5, 1980, box 387, Regional Political Files, RRCF.

107. "Suggested Do's and Don't's for TX Trip," box 439, Speech Files, RRCF.

108. General Files, Reagan-Bush Campaign, box 377, Regional Political Files, RRCF.

109. *CBS Evening News* with Walter Cronkite, October 20–23, 1980, transcript, box 2M758, Walter Cronkite Papers, CAH.

110. White, *America in Search of Itself,* 404–7.

111. News release, Television Address by Governor Ronald Reagan: A Vision for America, November 3, 1980, box 1, PHP.

112. *TO,* November 28, 1980, 3–4.

113. *Texas Monthly,* December 1980, 5.

Conclusion

1. Election Results since 1966: Eight District, Box 95-147/87, REP.

2. GC, 1979–1980, box 95-147/303, REP.

3. Campaign advertisements; *Houston Post,* October 25, 1980, box 3M20, REP.

4. "Republican Dirty Tricks," box 3M21, REP.

5. Ibid.

6. "Texas Eighth Congressional District Campaign Update: September 1980"; election results, box 3M21, REP.

7. "Protester Campsite Brief," August 9, 1984, box 19, folder 1, RNC Archives, City of Dallas, 1983–84, Dallas Public Library.

8. Wills, *Reagan's America*.

9. Ellis, *American Sphinx*, 217.

10. Jamieson, *Packaging the Presidency*, 459–84.

11. Clemons, *Branding Texas*, 123.

Bibliography

Archival and Manuscript Sources

Center for American History, University of Texas, Austin, TX

Dolph Briscoe Papers
George Christian Papers
Walter Cronkite Papers
Robert C. Eckhardt Papers
Henry B. Gonzalez Papers
Harris County Democratic Party Records, 1952–77
Sam Rayburn Papers
Phillip Scheffler Papers
Stephen Shadegg Papers / Barry Goldwater Collection
Alan Shivers Papers
Ralph W. Yarborough Papers

Cushing Library, Texas A&M University, College Station, TX

William P. Clements Papers

George Smathers Libraries, University of Florida, Gainesville, FL

Papers of the Republican Party [microform]

Gerald R. Ford Presidential Library, Ann Arbor, MI

Gerald R. Ford Presidential Papers, 1974–77
  Ron Nessen Papers, 1974–77
  President Ford Committee Records, 1975–76
  Presidential Briefing Book
  Presidential Handwriting Files
  White House Operations, Richard Cheney Files, 1974–77
  White House Press Secretary's Office
    David Gergen Files
    Ron Nessen Files, 1974–77

Hoover Institution on War, Revolution, and Peace, Stanford University, Stanford, CA

Bill Boyarsky Papers
Citizens for Reagan Papers

Kathryn R. Davis Papers
Deaver & Hannaford, Inc. Papers
Donald M. Dozer Papers
John Ehrlichman Papers
Annelise Graebner Anderson Papers
Peter Hannaford Papers
Fred Charles Iklé Papers
Denison Kitchel Papers
John McLaughry Papers
New Left Collection
Ronald Reagan Subject Collection
David Stoll Collection
Charls E. Walker Papers

Jimmy Carter Presidential Library, Atlanta, GA

Jimmy Carter Papers (Pre-presidential), 1976 Campaign Files
Jimmy Carter Presidential Papers, 1977–81
   Office of the Assistant to the President for Communications
   Office of the Assistant for Public Outreach: Robert Lee Maddox's Subject Files
   Office of Public Liaison
      Margaret Costanza Files
      Bob Maddox (Religious Liaison) Files
   Records of the Office of the Assistant to the President for Women's Affairs
   Records of the Office of Congressional Liaison, Frank Moore Files
   Records of the Office of Hispanic Affairs, 1979–81
   Records of the Speechwriter's Office, 1977–81
   Staff Office Files
      Cabinet Secretary and Assistant for Intergovernmental Affairs
      Chief of Staff, Hamilton Jordan
      Domestic Policy Staff, Stu Eizenstat
      First Lady's Staff
      Press Office, Jody Powell
      Office of the Staff Secretary
   White House Central Files Subject File, 1977–81: Texas
   White House Central Name File: John Tower
Hendrik Hertzberg Papers, 1977–81
George D. Moffett Files, 1977–85
Carlton Neville Collection, 1976–77

John G. Tower Library and Archives, Southwestern University, Georgetown, TX

John Knaggs Papers
John G. Tower Papers

Lyndon B. Johnson Presidential Library, Austin, TX

George Christian Papers

John Connally Papers
Democratic National Committee Papers
Lyndon B. Johnson Presidential Papers, 1963–69
   National Security File, 1963–69, Subject Files
   Office Files of the White House Aides
      George Christian Files
      Richard N. Goodwin Files
      Harry C. McPherson Files
      Bill Moyers Files
      Frederick Panzer Files
      George E. Reedy Files
   White House Central Files, Subject Files
      Political Affairs
      Public Relations
      States—Territories
   White House Name Files
      Richard Nixon
      Ronald Reagan
Reference File: 1968 Campaign
Texas State Democratic Committee Papers

Ronald Reagan Presidential Library, Simi Valley, CA

Governor Ronald Reagan Papers, 1967–75
   Research Files
Pre-presidential Papers of Ronald Reagan
   1980 Campaign Files
      Briefing Material Files
      Campaign Operations—Mike Deaver Files
      Director of Citizens' Operations—Max Hugel Files
      Director of Political Operations—William Timmons Files
      Hannaford / California Headquarters Files
      Ed Meese Files, 1976–80
      Political Operations (Jerry Carmen) Files
      Regional Political Files
      Research and Policy Files
      Speech Files (Robert Garrick and Bill Gavin)
      Richard Wirthlin—Political Strategy Files

Seeley G. Mudd Manuscript Library, Princeton University, Princeton, NJ

American Civil Liberties Union Papers
James A. Baker III Papers
George S. McGovern Papers

Southwest Collection, Texas Tech University, Lubbock, TX

Waggoner Carr Papers

Kent Hance Papers
George Mahon Papers
Preston Smith Papers

Texas / Dallas History & Archives Division, Dallas Public Library, Dallas, TX

Bruce Alger Papers
Republican National Convention Archives, City of Dallas, 1983–1984

Oral Histories

Lyndon B. Johnson Presidential Library, Austin, TX

Billy Graham
John G. Tower

Oral History Collection, University of North Texas, Denton, TX

Fred Agnich
Betty Andujar
Alma Box
Earle Cabell
Carlos Puente
Carol Reed
Florence Shapiro
Vivian T. Sparks
Gloria Villanueva-Anderson

Interviews Conducted by the Author

Lynda L. Kaid (November 7, 2006)
Richard Viguerie (December 7, 2006)

Published Primary Sources

The Public Papers of the Presidents of the United States: James E. Carter, 1977–1981.
    Washington, DC: U.S. Government Printing Office, 1977–81.
The Public Papers of the Presidents of the United States: Gerald R. Ford, 1974–1977.
    Washington, DC: U.S. Government Printing Office, 1974–77.
The Public Papers of the Presidents of the United States: Lyndon B. Johnson, 1963–1969.
    Washington, DC: U.S. Government Printing Office, 1965–70.
The Public Papers of the Presidents of the United States: Richard M. Nixon, 1969–1974.
    Washington, DC: U.S. Government Printing Office, 1969–74.

Newspapers, Magazines, and Periodicals

Austin American-Statesman
Daily Texan
Dallas Morning News
Houston Chronicle

Houston Post
Lubbock Avalanche-Journal
Nation
National Review
New York Times
San Antonio Express-News
Texas Monthly
Texas Observer
Washington Post

Audiovisual Material

Firing Line. Hosted by William F. Buckley, Audiovisual material, 1966–99. Hoover Institution Archives, the Hoover Institute, Stanford University, Stanford, CA.

Ronald Reagan Gubernatorial Audiotape Collection: 1965–74. Ronald Reagan Presidential Library, Simi Valley, CA.

Town Meeting of the World: The Image of America and the Youth of the World, with Senator Robert F. Kennedy and Governor Ronald Reagan. Hosted by Charles Collingwood. CBS Television Network and CBS Radio Network. May 15, 1967. Ronald Reagan Presidential Library, Simi Valley, CA.

Secondary Sources

Alexander, Gerard. "The Myth of the Racist Republicans." *Claremont Institute for the Study of Statesmanship and Political Philosophy: Claremont Review of Books* (Spring 2004).

Anderson, Patrick. *Electing Jimmy Carter: The Campaign of 1976.* Baton Rouge: Louisiana State University Press, 1994.

Andrew, John A., III. *The Other Side of the Sixties: Young Americans for Freedom and the Rise of Conservative Politics.* New Brunswick, NJ: Rutgers University Press, 1997.

Baer, Kenneth S. *Reinventing Democrats: The Politics of Liberalism from Reagan to Clinton.* Lawrence: University of Kansas Press, 2000.

Barr, Alwyn. *Reconstruction to Reform: Texas Politics, 1876–1906.* Dallas: SMU Press, 1971.

Bartley, Numan V. *The New South: 1945–1980.* Baton Rouge: Louisiana State University Press, 1995.

Bass, Jack, and Walter De Vries. *The Transformation of Southern Politics: Social Change and Political Consequence since 1945.* Athens: University of Georgia Press, 1995.

Bell, Daniel, ed. *The Radical Right: The New American Right.* Rev. ed. New York: Anchor, 1963.

Berman, William. *America's Right Turn: From Nixon to Bush.* Baltimore, MD: Johns Hopkins University Press, 1994.

Black, Earl, and Merle Black. *The Rise of Southern Republicans.* Cambridge, MA: Belknap Press of Harvard University Press, 2002.

Blight, David W. *Race and Reunion: The Civil War in American Memory.* Cambridge, MA: Belknap Press of Harvard University Press, 2001.

Blum, John Morton. *Years of Discord: American Politics and Society, 1961–1974.* New York: Norton, 1991.

Brands, H. W. *The Strange Death of American Liberalism*. New Haven, CT: Yale University Press, 2001.

Brennan, Mary C. *Turning Right in the Sixties: The Conservative Capture of the GOP*. Chapel Hill: University of North Carolina Press, 1995.

Bridges, Kenneth. *Twilight of the Texas Democrats: The 1978 Governor's Race*. College Station: Texas A&M University Press, 2008.

Brinkley, Alan. "The Problem of American Conservatism." *American Historical Review* 99 (April 1994): 409–29.

Brown, Norman D. *Hood, Bonnet, and Little Brown Jug: Texas Politics, 1921–1928*. College Station: Texas A&M University Press, 1984.

Campbell, Randolph B. *Gone to Texas: A History of the Lone Star State*. New York: Oxford University Press, 2003.

Cannon, Lou. *Governor Reagan: His Rise to Power*. New York: Public Affairs, 2003.

Carleton, Don E. *Red Scare! Right-Wing Hysteria, Fifties Fanaticism, and Their Legacy in Texas*. Austin: Texas Monthly Press, 1985.

Carroll, Patrick J. *Felix Longoria's Wake: Bereavement, Racism, and the Rise of Mexican American Activism*. Austin: University of Texas Press, 2003.

Carter, Dan T. *The Politics of Rage: George Wallace, the Origins of the New Conservatism, and the Transformation of American Politics*. New York: Simon & Schuster, 1995.

Clemons, Leigh. *Branding Texas: Performing Culture in the Lone Star State*. Austin: University of Texas Press, 2008.

Cohen, Lizabeth. *A Consumer's Republic: The Politics of Mass Consumption in Postwar America*. New York: Knopf, 2003.

Cox, Patrick. *Ralph W. Yarborough: The People's Senator*. Austin: University of Texas Press, 2001.

Crespino, Joseph. *In Search of Another Country: Mississippi and the Conservative Counterrevolution*. Princeton, NJ: Princeton University Press, 2007.

Critchlow, Donald T. *The Conservative Ascendancy: How the GOP Right Made Political History*. Cambridge, MA: Harvard University Press, 2007.

———. *Phyllis Schlafly and Grassroots Conservatism: A Woman's Crusade*. Princeton, NJ: Princeton University Press, 2005.

Dallek, Matthew. *The Right Moment: Ronald Reagan's First Victory and the Decisive Turning Point in American Politics*. New York: Free Press, 2000.

Dallek, Robert. *Flawed Giant: Lyndon Johnson and His Times, 1961–1973*. New York: Oxford University Press, 1998.

———. *Lone Star Rising: Lyndon Johnson and His Times, 1908–1960*. New York: Oxford University Press, 1991.

———. *Ronald Reagan: The Politics of Symbolism*. Cambridge, MA: Harvard University Press, 1984.

Davidson, Chandler. *Race and Class in Texas Politics*. Princeton, NJ: Princeton University Press, 1990.

Davies, Gareth. *From Opportunity to Entitlement: The Transformation and Decline of Great Society Liberalism*. Lawrence: University Press of Kansas, 1996.

Diamond, Edwin, and Stephen Bates. *The Spot: The Rise of Political Advertising on Television*. Cambridge, MA: MIT Press, 1992.

Dobbs, Ricky F. *Yellow Dogs and Republicans: Allan Shivers and Texas Two-Party Politics*. College Station: Texas A&M University Press, 2005.

Drew, Elizabeth. *Portrait of an Election: The 1980 Presidential Campaign*. New York: Simon & Schuster, 1981.

Edsall, Thomas, and Mary Edsall. *Chain Reaction: The Impact of Race, Rights and Taxes on American Politics*. New York: Norton, 1991.

Ellis, Joseph J. *American Sphinx: The Character of Thomas Jefferson*. New York: Vintage, 1998.

Flamm, Michael W. *Law and Order: Street Crime, Civil Unrest, and the Crisis of Liberalism in the 1960s*. New York: Columbia University Press, 2005.

Foley, Neil. *The White Scourge: Mexicans, Blacks, and Poor Whites in Texas Cotton Culture*. Berkeley: University of California Press, 1997.

Frank, Thomas. *What's the Matter with Kansas? How Conservatives Won the Heart of America*. New York: Owl, 2004.

Fried, Richard M. *The Russians Are Coming! The Russians Are Coming! Pageantry and Patriotism in Cold-War America*. New York: Oxford University Press, 1998.

Garcia, Ignacio M. *Viva Kennedy: Mexican Americans in Search of Camelot*. College Station: Texas A&M University Press, 2000.

Goldberg, Robert A. *Barry Goldwater*. New Haven, CT: Yale University Press, 1995.

Goldwater, Barry. *Conscience of a Conservative*. Shepherdsville, KY: Victory, 1960.

Green, George Norris. *The Establishment in Texas Politics: The Primitive Years, 1938–1957*. Norman: University of Oklahoma Press, 1979.

Greenberg, David. *Nixon's Shadow: The History of an Image*. New York: Norton, 2003.

Greenshaw, Wayne. *Elephants in the Cottonfields: Ronald Reagan and the New Republican South*. New York: Macmillan, 1982.

Hart, Roderick P. *The Sound of Leadership: Presidential Communication in the Modern Age*. Chicago: University of Chicago Press, 1987.

Hayward, Steven F. *The Age of Reagan: The Fall of the Old Liberal Order, 1964–1980*. New York: Prima, 2001.

Heale, M. J. *McCarthy's Americans: Red Scare Politics in State and Nation, 1935–1965*. Athens: University of Georgia Press, 1998.

Heineman, Kenneth J. *God Is a Conservative: Religion, Politics, and Morality in Contemporary America*. New York: New York University Press, 1998.

Hofstadter, Richard. *The Paranoid Style in American Politics and Other Essays*. Cambridge, MA: Harvard University Press, 1996.

Isserman, Maurice, and Michael Kazin. *America Divided: The Civil War of the 1960s*. New York: Oxford University Press, 2000.

Jackson, Kenneth T. *Crabgrass Frontier: The Suburbanization of the United States*. New York: Oxford University Press, 1985.

Jamieson, Kathleen H. *Packaging the Presidency: A History and Criticism of Presidential Campaign Advertising*. New York: Oxford University Press, 1984.

Kazin, Michael. "The Grass-Roots Right: New Histories of U.S. Conservatism in the Twentieth Century." *American Historical Review* 97 (February 1992): 136–55.

———. *The Populist Persuasion: An American History*. New York: Basic, 1996.

Key, V. O. *Southern Politics in State and Nation*. Knoxville: University of Tennessee Press, 1949.

Klarman, Michael J. "How Brown Changed Race Relations: The Backlash Thesis." *Journal of American History* 81 (June 1994): 81–118.

Knaggs, John R. *Two Party Texas: The John Tower Era, 1961–1984*. Austin: Eakin, 1986.

Kruse, Kevin M. *White Flight: Atlanta and the Making of Modern Conservatism*. Princeton, NJ: Princeton University Press, 2005.

Lamis, Alexander. *The Two Party South?* New York: Oxford University Press, 1984.

Lassiter, Matthew D. *The Silent Majority: Suburban Politics in the Sunbelt South*. Princeton, NJ: Princeton University Press, 2005.

Lavergne, Gary M. *A Sniper in the Tower: The Charles Whitman Murders*. Denton: University of North Texas Press, 1997.

Lawson, Steven F. *In Pursuit of Power: Southern Blacks and Electoral Politics, 1965–1982*. New York: Columbia University Press, 1985.

Link, William A. *Righteous Warrior: Jesse Helms and the Rise of Modern Conservatism*. New York: St. Martin's, 2008.

Matusow, Allen J. *The Unraveling of America: A History of Liberalism in the 1960s*. New York: Harper & Row, 1984.

McCombs, Maxwell, and Donald Shaw. "The Agenda-Setting Function of the Mass Media." *Public Opinion Quarterly* 36 (1972): 176–87.

McGinnis, Joe. *The Selling of the President: 1968*. New York: New York University Press, 1988.

McGirr, Lisa. *Suburban Warriors: The Origins of the New American Right*. Princeton, NJ: Princeton University Press, 2001.

Micklethwait, John, and Adrian Wooldridge. *The Right Nation: Conservative Power in America*. New York: Penguin, 2004.

Moorehead, Richard. *50 Years in Texas Politics: From Roosevelt to Reagan, from the Fergusons to Clements*. Burnet, TX: Eakin, 1982.

Nash, George H. *The Conservative Intellectual Movement in America since 1945*. Wilmington, DE: ISI, 1996.

Olien, Roger M. *From Token to Triumph: The Texas Republicans since 1920*. Dallas: Southern Methodist University Press, 1982.

Patterson, James T. *Grand Expectations: The United States, 1945–1974*. New York: Oxford University Press, 1996.

———. *Restless Giant: The United States from Watergate to Bush v. Gore*. New York: Oxford University Press, 2005.

Patterson, T. E., and Robert D. McClure. *The Unseeing Eye: The Myth of Television Power in National Politics*. New York: Putnam, 1976.

Perlstein, Rick. *Before the Storm: Barry Goldwater and the Unmaking of the American Consensus*. New York: Hill & Wang, 2001.

———. *Nixonland: The Rise of a President and the Fracturing of America*. New York: Scribner, 2008.

Phillips, Kevin P. *American Theocracy: The Perils and Politics of Radical Religion, Oil, and Borrowed Money in the 21st Century*. New York: Viking, 2006.

———. *The Emerging Republican Majority*. New Rochelle, NY: Arlington House, 1969.

Piereson, James. *Camelot and the Cultural Revolution: How the Assassination of John F. Kennedy Shattered American Liberalism*. New York: Encounter, 2007.

Powers, Richard G. *Not without Honor: The History of American Anticommunism*. New York: Free Press, 1995.

Reston, James. *The Lone Star: The Life of John Connally.* New York: Harper & Row, 1989.

Robinson, Michael J. "Public Affairs Television and the Growth of Political Malaise: The Case of the 'Selling of the Pentagon.'" *American Political Science Review* 70 (1976): 409–32.

Rymph, Catherine E. *Republican Women: Feminism and Conservatism from Suffrage through the Rise of the New Right.* Chapel Hill: University of North Carolina Press, 2006.

Schlafly, Phyllis. *A Choice, Not an Echo.* Alton, IL: Pere Marquette, 1964.

Schneider, Gregory. *Cadres for Conservatism: Young Americans for Freedom and the Rise of the Contemporary Right.* New York: New York University Press, 1999.

Schoenwald, Jonathan. *A Time for Choosing: The Rise of Modern American Conservatism.* New York: Oxford University Press, 2002.

Schulman, Bruce. *From the Cotton Belt to Sunbelt: Federal Policy, Economic Development, and the Transformation of the South, 1938–1980.* New York: Oxford University Press, 1991.

———. *The Seventies: The Great Shift in American Culture, Society, and Politics.* New York: Free Press, 2001.

Schulman, Bruce, and Julian E. Zelizer, eds. *Rightward Bound: Making America Conservative in the 1970s.* Cambridge, MA: Harvard University Press, 2008.

Schwartz, Tony. *The Responsive Chord.* Garden City, NJ: Anchor, 1973.

Shirley, Craig. *Reagan's Revolution: The Untold Story of the Campaign That Started It All.* Nashville, TN: Nelson Current, 2005.

Slotkin, Richard. *Gunfighter Nation: The Myth of the Frontier in Twentieth-Century America.* Norman: University of Oklahoma Press, 1998.

Smith, Oran. *The Rise of Baptist Republicanism.* New York: New York University Press, 1997.

Sugrue, Thomas J. *The Origins of the Urban Crisis: Race and Inequality in Postwar Detroit.* Princeton, NJ: Princeton University Press, 1996.

Tygiel, Jules. *Baseball's Great Experiment: Jackie Robinson and His Legacy.* New York: Oxford University Press, 1997.

Tyler, Ronald, Douglas E. Barnett, and Roy R. Barkley, eds. *The New Handbook of Texas.* Austin: Texas State Historical Association, 1996.

Ward, Brian. *Just My Soul Responding: Rhythm and Blues, Black Consciousness, and Race Relations.* Berkeley: University of California Press, 1998.

Weeks, Oliver Douglas. *Texas in the 1960 Presidential Election.* Austin: University of Texas Press, 1961.

———. *Texas One-Party Politics in 1956.* Austin: University of Texas Press, 1957.

———. *Texas Presidential Politics in 1952.* Austin: University of Texas Press, 1953.

White, Richard. *"It's Your Misfortune and None of My Own": A New History of the American West.* Norman: University of Oklahoma Press, 1991.

White, Theodore H. *America in Search of Itself: The Making of the President, 1956–1980.* New York: Harper & Row, 1982.

———. *The Making of the President: 1964.* New York: Atheneum, 1965.

———. *The Making of the President: 1968.* New York: Atheneum, 1969.

———. *The Making of the President: 1972.* New York: Atheneum, 1973.

Whitfield, Stephen J. *The Culture of the Cold War.* Baltimore, MD: Johns Hopkins University Press, 1991.

Wilentz, Sean. *The Age of Reagan: A History, 1974–2008*. New York: HarperCollins, 2008.

Williams, Daniel K. "From the Pews to the Polls: The Formation of a Southern Christian Right." Ph.D. diss., Brown University, 2005.

Wills, Garry. *John Wayne's America*. New York: Simon & Schuster, 1997.

———. *Reagan's America*. New York: Penguin, 1988.

Woods, Jeff. *Black Struggle, Red Scare: Segregation and Anticommunism in the South, 1948–1968*. Baton Rouge: Louisiana State University Press, 2004.

Zaretsky, Natasha. *No Direction Home: The American Family and the Fear of National Decline, 1968–1980*. Chapel Hill: University of North Carolina Press, 2007.

Index

Italic page numbers refer to illustrations

CPSIA information can be obtained at www.ICGtesting.com
Printed in the USA
LVOW11*0907300716

498046LV00003BA/7/P

9 780813 125763